GO PREACH!

The Bible & Liberation

An Orbis Series in Biblical Studies

Norman K. Gottwald and Richard A. Horsley,
General Editors

The Bible & Liberation Series focuses on the emerging range of political, social, and contextual hermeneutics that are changing the face of biblical interpretation today. It brings to light the social struggles behind the biblical texts. At the same time it explores the ways that a "liberated Bible" may offer resources in the contemporary struggle for a more human world.

Already published:

The Bible & Liberation Series

GO PREACH!

Mark's Kingdom Message and the Black Church Today

Brian K. Blount

ORBIS BOOKS

Maryknoll, New York 10545

The Catholic Foreign Mission Society of America (Maryknoll) recruits and trains people for overseas missionary service. Through Orbis Books, Maryknoll aims to foster the international dialogue that is essential to mission. The books published, however, reflect the opinions of their authors and are not meant to represent the official position of the society.

Library of Congress Cataloging-in-Publication Data

Blount, Brian K., 1955-
    Go preach! : Mark's kingdom message and the Black church today /
Brian K. Blount.
        p.   cm. – (The Bible & liberation series)
    Includes bibliographical references and index.
    ISBN 1-57075-171-4 (pbk.)
    1. Jesus Christ – Teachings. 2. Bible. N.T. Mark – Criticism,
interpretation, etc. 3. Kingdom of God – Biblical teaching. 4. Afro-
Americans – Religion. I. Title. II. Series.
BS2417.K5B55 1998
231.7′2–dc21   97-48668
                                                                      CIP

For Sharon

"We will have to repent in this generation not merely for the hateful words and actions of the bad people, but for the appalling silence of the good people. Human progress never rolled in on the wheels of inevitability, but on the tireless efforts of men and women willing to be co-workers with God."

—Martin Luther King, Jr.,
The Trumpet of Conscience

Contents

Part IV
THE MEANING OF MARK'S KINGDOM MESSAGE
FOR TODAY'S BLACK CHURCH

Preface

I have long been interested in the social and political nature of the Synoptic Gospels. This fascination is clearly a critical part of the preunderstanding I have brought to my study of the kingdom of God language in the Gospel of Mark. The traditional question has always been somewhat muted: does Mark's narrative present a Jesus whose spiritual message has social and political implications? The more intriguing inquiry begins with a bolder interrogative: does Mark's narrative present a Jesus whose kingdom message is as social and political as it is spiritual? This latter question has been primary in both the research and writing phases of this project. I believe that it has been answered affirmatively. Mark, I will argue, has offered us the narrative presentation of a Jesus whose apocalyptic revelation of God's kingdom shatters the institutions, laws, and codes that structure religious and political society in first-century Palestine.

In Jesus, the mythological and the historical intersect. His narrative entrance represents the in-breaking of God into the human circumstance. His battles with the chaotic forces of nature, with human illness, and with demonic possession re-present on earth the cosmic battle God has engaged with the forces of Satan. Jesus wins his encounters because he has the authority to wield the power of God's future kingdom in the midst of the human historical present. He wields that power through the tactic of preaching. In each manifestation of Jesus' kingdom preaching, his teaching with supernatural authority, his miracles, and his exorcisms, the power of God's kingdom intervenes in the human circumstance to destroy the satanic boundaries of ignorance, illness, and possession that separate humans from God and from one another. Additionally, in each of those preaching moments the natural boundaries of sabbath, purity, and cultic code are broken down. Because these codes were so integrally connected with the way in which Israelite society was socially and politically structured, these preaching challenges wreaked as much political havoc as they threatened cultic transformation.

The result was predictable; the religio-political leaders of Jesus' own people found his efforts intolerable. They, therefore, as early as 3:6, just after a series of particularly portentous preaching manifestations, sought to destroy him. It is little wonder that, some twelve chapters later, the cross stands as the inevitable end of his preaching ministry.

That same cross is also narratively presented as the inevitable end of a discipleship ministry that preaches the kingdom with Jesus' transformative and boundary-breaking intent. And yet this is precisely the call that Mark's Jesus issues to his followers. God's son authorizes his disciples to wield God's kingdom power so that they will be, as he once was, catalysts for the in-breaking of God's future, transformative power in the midst of the human, historical present.

This study is a narrative one. The conclusions I reach therefore have to do with Mark's narrative Jesus, not the historical figure upon whom there is so much current speculative focus. I have engaged the narrative of Mark from a particular sociolinguistic perspective that considers the language of the story against the contextual back- and foregrounds that give it life. In an examination of key Markan kingdom statements throughout the text, I have attended first to the narrative's context of situation. That is, I have tried to recreate, examine, and value the symbolic world created by the text. I have then tried to read the text in light of that world. I have done so with the understanding that the text's unique universe stamps meaning indelibly upon its characters and images. One can therefore only obtain that meaning by way of that universe.

At the same time, I also considered the narrative in light of its broader context of culture, the socio-historical setting in which Mark most likely wrote, and his readers most likely read. This, too, is a symbolic world out of which readers process and give comprehension to narrative language. It is my contention that in the cultural world of 70 C.E. Judaism Mark's narrative would have been processed with as much socio-political as redemptive-religious emphasis.

Finally, I approached the text through the lens of my own sociolinguistic context, my life-relationship to the text as an African-American Christian, and the preunderstanding of an African-American church that has historically been as socio-politically as spiritually engaged in the world. I recognize that this perspective influences the way I read the data. I am convinced, however, that the influence is, in the first place, not unlike the kind of influence present in *every* text reading, and that, secondly, it enables me to see aspects of the text's potential for meaning that readers from other perspectives might miss.

Still, I do not believe that the part of the text's potential for meaning that I have encountered is *the* meaning of the text. Other readers with other life relationships and preunderstandings might value, and indeed have valued, other segments of that potential for meaning. I therefore offer this reading of Mark's kingdom of God language as neither a corrective for other present readings, nor as a final answer that pretends to negate any need for a future reading. I offer it instead as an addendum to, rather than a substitute for, every other, similarly positioned (if not as similarly admitted) sociolinguistic reading of Mark's story.

Finally, just as, and perhaps because, I write from the perspective of the black church in the United States, it is also to that church that I turn when I consider the application of Mark's language to the contemporary discipleship community. This reading has not been done with an exclusive eye toward uncovering a narrative meaning; it has also been my objective to apply that meaning to the life and predisposition of a twentieth/twenty-first century church whose own preaching ministry could benefit tremendously from an apocalyptic message originally addressed to a mythological, first-century church.

There are many persons to whom I am indebted for the successful completion of this study. I am particularly grateful to Thomas W. Gillespie, President of

Princeton Theological Seminary, and to James F. Armstrong, Academic Dean, for an extended year's study leave. It was during that time that I completed the primary research and much of the writing. I am convinced that without such support the work would yet remain in its earliest stages. I am also very appreciative of the support I have received from the Biblical Studies Department at Princeton Seminary. My colleagues, particularly Patrick D. Miller, former department chair, and Beverly Roberts Gaventa, present chair, have been supportive and encouraging throughout the writing process. There have been some significantly difficult moments; I would not have so successfully overcome them without their deeply appreciated help. I am also thankful for the assistance of Professors Don Juel and Robert MacGlennan, who read earlier versions of the manuscript and offered commentary, critique, and support. My assistant, Paul R. Heins, deserves special mention for all the research and editing work he has put into this project, and an earlier one in which his efforts went unmentioned. His tremendous indexing and bibliographic skills allowed me to concentrate on the final presentation of the text, and his meticulous and patient research in the library provided me with an exemplary reservoir of raw data from which I could develop my thesis. I mention finally my family. My wife, Sharon, was a constant source of encouragement throughout the cycle of emotions I endured while working on this project. And my children, Joshua and Kaylin, have been a valued source of calm and perspective just when I needed them the most. It is for them and countless other young men and women like them, constituents, and perhaps leaders of the future African-American church, that I hope this study will have the most meaning.

Part I

Making the Case

An Introduction

1

The Kingdom of God
as Boundary Crossing

A REMINDER FROM THE PAST: HIGH JOHN DE CONQUER

In the Gospel of Mark the kingdom of God is like the American slave myth of High John de Conquer. High John was a human creation that represented divine intention. High John was the realization of a future hope in the midst of present travail. High John was a promise from the end time that provoked perseverance and championed change in the here and now time. High John was a fragile, floating, rainbow-streaked bubble whose collapsing, micro-thin skin was resurrected somewhere else tomorrow just after it had been crushed in its place today. High John was a pocket of resistance.

High John was a man, a black-messiah man, a deliverer, who, despite the horrors of present reality, conjured up trust for a better tomorrow. From 1619 to 1865 in the United States of America, racial difference provided the rationale for the human enslavement of black African peoples.[1] High John was a pocket of faith who helped those enslaved peoples survive.

> High John de Conquer came to be a man, and a mighty man at that. But he was not a natural man in the beginning. First off, he was a whisper, a will to hope, a wish to find something worthy of laughter and song. Then the whisper put on flesh. His footsteps sounded across the world in a low but musical rhythm as if the world he walked on was a singing drum. The black folks had an irresistible impulse to laugh. High John de Conquer was a man in full, and had come to live and work on the plantations, and all the slave folks knew him in the flesh.

---

1. While the "Emancipation Proclamation," which declared all slaves residing in confederate territory free, was signed by President Abraham Lincoln on January 1, 1863, it actually freed relatively few slaves. It did not apply to slaves in border states fighting for the Union, nor did it affect slaves in southern areas already controlled by the Union. Of course, confederate states not under Union jurisdiction did not obey the order. Slavery was not effectively ended in America until the passage of the thirteenth amendment to the Constitution on December 18, 1865.

3

The sign of this man was a laugh, and his singing symbol was a drum beat. No parading drum shout like soldiers out for show. It did not call to the feet of those who were fixed to hear it. It was an inside thing to live by. It was sure to be heard when and where the work was the hardest, and the lot most cruel. It helped the slaves endure. They knew that something better was coming. So they laughed in the face of things and sang, "I'm so glad! Trouble don't last always."

Old Massa couldn't know, of course, but High John de Conquer was there walking his plantation like a natural man. He was treading the sweat-flavored clods of the plantation, crushing out his drum tunes, and giving out secret laughter. He walked on the winds and moved fast. Maybe he was in Texas when the lash fell on a slave in Alabama, but before the blood was dry on the back he was there.

Old John, High John could beat the unbeatable. He was top-superior to the whole mess of sorrow. He could beat it all, and what made it so cool, finish it off with a laugh. Distance and the impossible had no power over High John de Conquer.

Way over there, where the sun rises a day ahead of time, they say that Heaven arms with love and laughter those it does not wish to see destroyed. He who carries his heart in his sword must perish. So says the ultimate law. High John de Conquer knew a lot of things like that. He who wins from within is in the "Be" class. *Be* here when the ruthless man comes, and *be* here when he is gone.[2]

High John is a projection of power, an objective "story" manifestation of a subjective belief, a force of thought that intervened in the spiritual reality of human life and represented a future possibility of freedom and respect that did not exist in the present. As such High John was *like* the kingdom of God. He was not a preview of the future reality of freedom, he was a piece of that freedom in the present instant when a slave believed in his existence and the power that existence represented and fostered. When his story was told, in those moments when slaves could see the possibilities of what he stood for, what his reality interjected into their reality, then, *for that particular instant in time*, the actual future was in their grasp. At the precise flash, no matter how fleeting, when the vision encouraged by this myth encouraged a slave to endure the hopeless situation of a family separated by an auction block, when it prompted a slave to chance escape despite the threat of severe beating or even capital punishment, when it convinced an individual slave or an entire plantation filled with slaves that freedom would come despite the grip their masters held on their lives, the future intervened into the present.

But High John's power is established in the foundation of faith. A slave who did not *believe* in the future reality he represented drew no inspiration from the telling of his tale. Indeed, hearing such a story may well have made a nonbe-

---

2. Zora Neale Hurston, "Sometimes in the Mind," in *The Book of Negro Folklore,* Langston Hughes and Arna Bontemps, editors (New York: Dodd, Mead and Company, 1958) 93–94, 95.

liever cynical. No doubt such a slave would have seen High John as a harmful diversion from reality, a "pie-in-the-sky" kind of wish unfulfilled, a spiritual narcotic that numbed fellow slaves to the manifest horror of their lot. For such a slave High John would not have deserved trust because he did not inspire the kind of action needed to instigate change. He made black folk think that some supernatural force like himself would bring the change for them. For such a slave High John would have seemed more like an aimless ship drifting with the tide of the times than a firmly directed pocket of resistance. But for one who believed in the story and what its telling represented, High John de Conquer was the face of the future peering powerfully and transformatively into the present.

> Sho John de Conquer means power. That's bound to be so. He come to teach and tell us. God don't leave nobody ignorant, you child. Don't care where He drops you down, He puts you on a notice. He don't want folks taken advantage of because they don't know. Now, back there in slavery time, us didn't have no power of protection, and God knowed it, and put us under watch-care. Rattlesnakes never bit no colored folks until four years after freedom was declared. That was to give us time to learn and to know. 'Course, I don't know nothing about slavery personal like. I wasn't born till two years after the Big Surrender. Then I wasn't nothing but a infant baby when I was born, so I couldn't know nothing but what they told me. My mama told me, and I know that she wouldn't mislead me, how High John de Conquer helped us out. He had done teached the black folks so they knowed a hundred years ahead of time that freedom was coming. Long before the white folks knowed anything about it at all.[3]

In that moment when black folks "knowed" about freedom and were convinced it was coming to shatter the boundaries that held them shackled in slavery, the power, the force of hope for the future that High John de Conquer represented in the horrific present was *like* the kingdom of God in the narration of Mark's Gospel of Jesus the Christ.

MARK'S KINGDOM MESSAGE: A THESIS

Mark's cultural environment was saturated with mythological imagery and story. The evangelist learned well from the Jewish writers who preceded him. The apocalyptic premise that God's strategic objective was to do battle with the forces of chaos and destruction in order to bring humankind into relationship with God, and thereby to save it, could not be explained by theoretical propositions or encyclopedic statistics; it had to be narrated. Therefore, Mark, like the Jewish writers upon whom he depended, appealed to mythological storytelling in order to depict apocalyptic symbols of supernatural salvation like the kingdom of God.

---

3. Ibid., 96.

In Israel's case, it was a story of supernatural intervention. It was pre-understood that the God of the Exodus event had shattered the boundaries that separated the divine and human realms. God's strategic purpose was to fashion a people from the family of Hebrew slaves incarcerated in Egypt. God's strategic method was the miracle. Ten times the Egyptians were plagued by an otherworldly power that demanded a this-worldly transformation from slavery to freedom. Ten times the recalcitrant Egyptians defied the supernatural demand. Even after they finally let the Hebrews go they were insufficiently convinced; Pharaoh's army pursued the people whom God had chosen and set free. God, therefore, entered the human realm once more, this time with a pillar of fire and a divided sea. Those intervening actions altered the Egyptian landscape and the socio-political circumstance of the Hebrew slaves. The Hebrew people became a free people.

God's interventions and the electing intention behind them transformed this newly freed Hebrew people into the people of Israel, the people of God. God had intervened in human history in order to make a supernatural point and execute a divine choice. God chose Israel. And then God intervened on Israel's behalf in order to consecrate them and give them a land. An interventionist orientation had been skillfully encoded into the story that narrated the genesis of the people.

The interventionist perspective did not end with this historical recollection. Apocalyptically minded Jewish writers of the first century c.e. believed that this same God would intervene in the future to prosecute a new strategic agenda, the redemption and vindication of the people Israel who had fallen upon difficult historical and political times. The land their God had promised them was no longer theirs. By the time Mark wrote it belonged to Gentiles, specifically the Romans and those who represented Roman interests. The fervent belief among what was left of the people Israel was that the God who had fashioned the Exodus would once again invade their tragic human circumstance. In this new case God would establish a supernatural province in the midst of what was presently an occupied human domain. God would save and vindicate Israel as God's chosen people. Mark also believed. He encoded this strategic premise of salvation and vindication into the language of his narrative by way of a well known symbolic image: the kingdom of God.[4]

---

4. John Shea, *Stories of God: An Unauthorized Biography* (Chicago: The Thomas More Press, 1978) 77–116. Shea is so persuaded by the Gospel writers' determination to convince their audiences that God's kingdom intervention was on the imminent horizon, and that it had been proleptically realized in the ministry of Jesus, that he talks in terms of an interventionist model. This model is based upon the interpretative realization *that* God has acted in human history. The focus is on *how* God has acted, which is to say, how God has *intervened* into human affairs. The biblical record from creation forward is a chronicle of this intervening activity. It is on the basis of such salvific intervention in the past, both spiritual and political, that "apocalyptic" kingdom intervention can be expected in the present and future.

Though Shea acknowledges that Mark's own writing operated from this interventionist perspective, he counsels that contemporary interpreters should employ an intentional model when reading the Markan text. While the intentional model recognizes the validity of "apocalyptic intervention" for the cultural reality of biblical times, it counsels advancement beyond the mythological naiveté of the ancients. By its reckoning, modern interpreters should concentrate on the more science-friendly "values and intentions" of God. The "fact" of an intervening God has, in the face of historical observation and scientific reality, become less tenable. "The key to the story is not the

In Mark's time many, like the evangelist himself, presumed that the moment of this kingdom intervention was imminent, and that it would be ushered into place through the efforts of a divinely appointed Messiah acting in God's stead. Many came claiming to be that appointee. Mark's story charged that anyone who made such a claim, other than the Jesus around whom his narrative was centered, was a false messiah and a counterfeit prophet.

Mark understood the stakes; Messiah figures claimed a loyal discipleship corps. Those who believed in a man's claim to represent the kingdom power and plan of God would follow the mission plan he laid out as *the* tactical way to participate in God's strategic kingdom design. Most Messiah figures offered a tactical plan of violent revolution. Rome stood in the way of God's kingdom strategy just as Egypt once had. God would overthrow Caesar the way God had overthrown Pharaoh. God would intervene directly and militarily. The Messiah figure would be God's general leading the ground assault. Those who wanted to participate in the invasion of the kingdom power into the human arena had but to join ranks with the Messiah figure and follow him in his campaign against the Gentiles. In so doing they would actually be participating in the extension of the kingdom power into the human realm. They would become part of the transformative kingdom effort. They would lay the present foundation for the apocalyptic reality God would ultimately and imminently build. The time for revolt had come; God was ready to usher in a new era of independence for Israel. God needed revolutionary soldiers to launch it.

According to Mark, though, this revolutionary story misrepresented God's strategic kingdom intent. God did not want simply to reconstitute Israel as it had been, an independent, Davidic-like kingdom that was constantly chastised by prophetic messengers for its failure to represent God's kingdom interests in its corporate life. God was determined to remake Israel into the kind of community God had always intended, a light whose inner focus on justice would be a transforming and inviting beacon for all the world. In Mark's opinion, Israel

---

fact of divine activity but the reason behind it, not *that* God acted in history but *why* he acted" (Shea, 101). In this model the fact of God's past intervention, the assurance of God's future intervention, and the sense of urgency that accompanied its imminent expectation are downplayed, and, in the case of the future components, even dismissed.

Modern (and post-modern) interpreters of Hebrew and New Testament narrative should therefore perceive that while the mythological stories of intervention reveal the concerns which obsess God, they do not divulge God's *modus operandi*. By way of example, one takes from these stories assurances that, because God acted mythologically to save God's people from oppression, God dislikes oppression and values justice. Because God is mythologically revealed as a faithful covenant partner, God values loyalty and righteousness. It is on this basis that contemporary humans who read and treasure these apocalyptic stories should seek righteousness and justice against oppression, not because God has intervened in the past and will do so again in the future on behalf of the oppressed, but because the divine reality values these qualities as the benchmarks of appropriate living (Shea, 8).

While Shea's comments are extremely valuable for my own work, they carefully disguise the fact that interpreting Mark through an intentional lens will guarantee that his narrative language is understood from a contemporary sociolinguistic perspective, and not from the sociolinguistic perspective that he assumed formed the social and narrative context in which he wrote and his readers read. It would be likely, then, that meaning accessed in the contemporary moment would be quite dissimilar from the meaning accessed in Mark's dramatically different, interventionist, socio-historical moment.

had become a land of divisive and oppressive boundaries. Economic boundaries separated the poor from the aristocracy. Cultic boundaries separated the ritually pure from the majority of Israelites who worked on and lived from the land. Political boundaries separated leaders from those whom they were given the responsibility to serve. Legal boundaries separated the broken and infirm from the wholeness and healing they sought. Ethnic boundaries separated Jew from Gentile. Mark's Jesus proclaimed a messiahship whose tactical objective was the shattering of those boundaries. For it was only in this way that God's strategic kingdom intent to save, which is to say, redesign and remake Israel, could be tactically achieved.

Mark's primary narrative theme is that in Jesus God has once again invaded human history. His preaching way represented God's kingdom way. And his way, as so powerfully depicted in Mark's narrative story, was the way of intervention. In Jesus' preaching the power and the reality of the future kingdom of God was realized in the human, socio-historical present. In the various manifestations of that preaching, e.g., the healings, the exorcisms, and the teachings, God's future power invaded and transformed the human present. Jesus' preaching shattered economic, political, cultic, legal, and ethnic boundaries. It was as though in his preaching Jesus opened up a present pocket of future power that resisted and overwhelmed the boundaries separating Jews from each other and Jews from Gentiles. In Mark's narrative story, then, Jesus' preaching was the future kingdom exploding transformatively into the present moment.

In other words, the kingdom of God is, to borrow a modern military phrase, an apocalyptic "pocket of resistance." In a strategic sense this pocket comes from the future; it remains the actuality and substance of the future. Though it is partially realized in a present human circumstance, it is initiated, sustained, and controlled by divine prerogative from its consummate future location. However, in the tactical arena where strategic theory comes alive in practical application, this pocket operates from and depends upon human conduct. Human performance, in this regard, never *becomes* the consummate kingdom of God. Instead, it tactically *re-presents* the strategic reality of that kingdom, particularly as it is portrayed in Jesus' life and ministry.

Mark used Jesus' preaching, then, as the tactical representation of God's future kingdom. In his narrative presentation, the present manifestation of the future kingdom equalled Jesus' preaching. But Jesus' preaching, as we shall see, also equalled socio-political crossings of cultic, ethnic, and legal boundaries. The narrative conclusion, therefore, must be that the present representation of the future kingdom of God took place in Jesus' shattering of oppressive and divisive human boundaries. In other words, Mark encoded the apocalyptic preunderstanding that God intervenes transformatively in human history into his Jesus story. He did it by presenting Jesus as a boundary-breaker who preaches, that is to say, who acts in the name of the coming kingdom of God. The correct messiahship path to follow, therefore, was not the old one of violent and militaristic revolution against the occupying Gentile presence. The correct path was the transformative preaching one that followed Jesus into the hope for a new Israel whose leadership would be more concerned about justice than tradition, service than lordship, and whose kingdom kinship would be as open to Gentiles as it was to Jews.

These two warring stories and the storytellers who backed them clashed head-on in the tense times of the Jewish-Roman war. The more popular story was the one that fanned the revolutionary flames of patriotic independence. Supporters of this story could count on the wrath of the Romans. More importantly, however, they could also bask in the loyalty and zealous support of their fellow kingdom believers. Mark's counter-story guaranteed anger and hostility from all sides. For its followers there would be no place of sanctuary; the Romans saw every Jew as another potential revolutionary. And certainly those Jews who supported the militaristic messiahs would see these Jesus supporters as troublemakers. At best, the latter challenged the cherished, traditional institutions and power structures of Israel; but, to their discredit, they also championed a traitorous call for including Gentiles within God's kingdom design.

Supporters of Jesus' kingdom story who followed Jesus' boundary-breaking preaching tactics were therefore bound to suffer in the harshest of ways. Mark narrated this threat with the image of the cross. Given Jesus' determined efforts to shatter the socio-political boundaries of traditional Israel, the cross, a socio-politically directed punishment, was bound to be his inevitable end. It would also be the inevitable end of anyone who stubbornly, or perhaps one might say faithfully, chose to follow him. Mark's conclusion: Jesus' boundary-breaking kingdom way led directly to the cross.

And yet, Mark's Jesus and Mark's narrative story about him continued to call people to follow Jesus' kingdom way. This was because Jesus' way was the right way. Despite the fact that it was a way that all but guaranteed suffering and even death, it was God's way. The evidence lay in God's vindication of Jesus. Jesus was the one upon whom the divine voice and favor landed at his baptism. Jesus was the one who was transfigured with Moses and Elijah. And Jesus was the one who, after meeting his inevitable end, was raised from the dead by God. When God acted in human history, it was to vindicate Jesus and his messiahship way. That vindication was an assurance for Mark's readers; though the suffering would come, so too would come God's transformative kingdom power and salvation.

Mark wants this kingdom preaching story to do something in the lives of his readers. He narrates the disciples as Jesus-followers who are able to manipulate the transformative power of the future kingdom into the present through their healing and exorcism preaching manifestations. Because the readers of this story are encouraged to sympathize with Jesus, but identify with Jesus' disciples, it seems all but certain that the evangelist wants them to take up the boundary-breaking charge to preach the kingdom that the disciples were trained for, but in the end were either too dull to understand or too timid to accept. They, the readers, must, therefore, *Go preach!* the boundary-breaking kingdom power that Jesus' ministry initiated. They are to finish the story Mark's narration about Jesus began. They are to become the kingdom preachers whose interventionist message challenges and then transforms the human socio-political landscape. They are to become the present pockets of transformative resistance that represent the future reality of the consummate kingdom of God. Their transformative, boundary-breaking preaching, then, is to represent tactically what God is doing strategically. That is, they are to invade the human circumstance of oppressive and divisive boundaries with the saving kingdom reality of justice and universal inclusion.

HOPE FOR THE FUTURE:
A BOUNDARY-BREAKING BLACK CHURCH

This Markan message has a particular meaning for the African-American Christian: We, too, can kingdom-build. It is at this imperative point that I think Mark's interventionist narrative has corresponding meaning for the contemporary black church. The message is, Go preach! That is not to say, Go talk from a lofty pulpit in a well-attended and even better-funded megachurch. It is to say, instead, Go break down the boundaries that oppress African-Americans and divide African-Americans from each other and African-Americans from other Americans. It is in such a way that, like Jesus — like the disciples who followed him, and like the first-century Markan readers who read about both of them — contemporary African-American Christians can participate in the tactical invasion that is the rule of God's future kingdom breaking into the socio-political present. It is how African-Americans build and become present pockets of future kingdom resistance.

Mark's strategic mandate demands a tactical response. Such a response begins with the identification of the boundaries that warrant a kingdom trespass. I believe that we determine the present boundaries in the same way that we determine the boundaries that preoccupied Mark; we initiate a careful study of the African-American context of culture. We could, for example, focus on the ever-widening boundary that separates the black middle and upper classes from the burgeoning black underclass. This is a regrettable part of the contemporary African-American context of culture that cries out for intervention. Here is one such point in the socio-political present where the future power of God's kingdom must be brought to bear. Here is a place where those who follow the transformative kingdom way of Jesus are sorely needed. Here is one such place for the person who hears the mandate to Go preach!

Having identified the boundaries, the next step is to begin the process of transformatively attacking them with manifestations of kingdom preaching. The manifestations Mark mentioned in his narrative were healing, exorcism and teaching. We will see how these first-century, sometimes mythological manifestations correspond with the preaching mandate for the twentieth- and twenty-first-century African-American Jesus disciple.

I would argue, however, that the push to act transformatively in the face of the oppressive and divisive boundaries that afflict the African-American cultural context will not develop simply because those boundaries have been identified. History has demonstrated that even when oppressive situations are recognized as such, transformative behavior does not necessarily follow. The Negro Church of the segregationist period in the United States provides one such example. Faced with a recognition of the discrimination and racism that daily destroyed the lives of African-Americans, the Negro Church counseled an accommodationist tactical response that was based upon a spirituality more concerned about personal salvation than communal transformation.[5] What is needed for transformative, boundary-breaking kingdom behavior is an interventionist orientation of the type that fueled Mark's narrative presentation of Jesus as God's kingdom agent.

African-Americans, then, are called to do more than understand their cultural context. We are also called upon, in the face of the oppressive and divisive cultural context in which we live, to rekindle the indicative belief that provoked intense, imperative behavior in the lives of those who followed Jesus, the belief that the God who intervened in the past will intervene in the imminent future. In the preparatory meantime it must be preunderstood that the tactical, boundary-breaking invasion of that future kingdom intervention will come through us, through our interventionist, kingdom preaching. It is why Mark summons us with the same imperative call that he issued in the first century: Finish the Story! Go Preach! The black church, ignited by such an interventionist agenda, can tactically re-present the future kingdom in the present socio-historical moment in the same way that Mark believed his readers could. The black church can become a present pocket consumed with the force and presence of future kingdom resistance.

To be sure, the strategic kingdom goal remains salvation, life lived in the presence of God. The question I will consider throughout my analysis of Mark's kingdom language is, how can this strategic goal be tactically accomplished in the socio-historical as well as the spiritual human circumstance? William Pannell reflects the annoyance of many oppressed Christians who hear sanctimonious words of spiritual solace in the midst of very painful physical need, when he writes,

> My friend kept asking me, "Don't you think that all that those people need is Jesus?" and I would say, "Well, you need more than Jesus. Why do you think we need less than you do?" Not even Jesus said that he was all that people needed. He fed the hungry, provided medical care for the lame, the halt, and the blind, and chided the ultra-conservatives in the religious establishment for their slavish devotion to tradition even as they ignored the claims of mercy and justice upon their resources.[6]

---

5. E. Franklin Frazier, *The Negro Church in America* (New York: Schocken Books, 1974) 51. "The Negro church with its own forms of religious worship was a world which the white man did not invade but only regarded with an attitude of condescending amusement. The Negro church could enjoy this freedom so long as it offered no threat to the white man's dominance in both economic and social relations. And, on the whole, the Negro's church was not a threat to white domination and aided the Negro to become accommodated to an inferior status. The religion of the Negro continued to be other-worldly in its outlook, dismissing the privations and sufferings and injustices of this world as temporary and transient."

6. William Pannell, *The Coming Race Wars? A Cry for Reconciliation* (Grand Rapids: Zondervan Publishing House, 1993) 29.

Jesus, in other words, trespassed oppressive and divisive socio-historical boundaries. Boundary trespass is the kingdom mandate that gives imperative content to Mark's preaching call. In fact, I would maintain that in Mark's case, given what I will argue is his very selective use of "save" language, it is through boundary trespass that the tactical realization of salvation occurs. This is so because boundary trespass equals the kingdom. As the kingdom draws near in tactical pockets of resistance, so, too, does the presence of God draw near. And salvation, by definition, is life lived in the divine presence. In this way, then, salvation obtains a socio-political content. It is redefined from an interventionist perspective.

Mark's call to the African-American church, then, is to bring the kingdom near in pockets of boundary-trespassing resistance. The inevitable short-term result of such activity will be suffering. The call to the black church, however, is not that it go forth and suffer, but that it go forth and preach, recognizing that because of the kind of preaching it will do, suffering will follow. Boundary transformers will be no more warmly received in the latter twentieth century than Jesus was in the first. And yet, if Mark is to be trusted, this way that leads to suffering is the way that will be vindicated as God's kingdom way. Michael Eric Dyson's depiction of the efforts of Martin Luther King, Jr., is illustrative.

> Martin understood that, often, the only reward for speaking the truth unadorned, for voicing the uncomfortable reality and painting the plain picture, is a bullet. But he also understood that his death could be redemptive only if it forced our nation to comprehend the idiocy of racial hatred, and only if it brought the liberation of Americans, black and white, one day nearer.[7]

Redemption, salvation, in such a perspective, comes by way of an interventionist conviction that fuels boundary-breaking kingdom activity. Redemption exists in that moment where future power throbs so powerfully that it radically transforms present reality. In such a pocket moment the present becomes the future, and tactical human behavior re-presents the transformative reality that is the kingdom of God.

---

7. Michael Eric Dyson, *Reflecting Black: African-American Cultural Criticism* (Minneapolis and London: University of Minnesota Press, 1993) 248–49.

2

Defining the Kingdom

A Review

We are indebted to Albrecht Ritschl for kindling modern scholarly interest in the kingdom of God. As Gösta Lundström acknowledges, Ritschl's theological interest during the second half of the nineteenth century reversed the lack of attention paid to the kingdom in the first half of that century. Indeed, so great was his fascination that he earned the moniker "theologian of the Kingdom of God."[1]

Ritschl defined the kingdom as the dominion of God which is made effective through the will of the covenanted people of God, "in accordance with our conviction that the Dominion of God through Christ has established a community which allows itself to be ruled by God."[2] In other words, the power of God's kingdom is realizable in the contemporary human circumstance as a Christ community directed by God's rule.

According to Ritschl, Jesus initiated this contemporary kingdom possibility. Knowing himself to be Messiah, he fashioned a community of subjects who recognized him as the bearer of God's dominion. By being obedient to God's sovereignty as expressed through Jesus' life and ministry this community of believers participated with Jesus in the establishment of the kingdom reality here on earth. Though future in its final form, the kingdom had the contemporary look of a this-worldly, ethical reality. "Thus Ritschl could say that, through the exercise of righteousness, the kingdom of God would come into being within a short space in the community of the followers of Christ, in a manner that is exemplified by the growth of the seed and the working of leaven on dough."[3] The kingdom of God, then, was not simply the eschatological vitality of a future world, it was the socio-historical transformation of the present world.

---

1. Gösta Lundström, *The Kingdom of God in the Teaching of Jesus: A History of Interpretation from the Last Decade of the Nineteenth Century to the Present Day*, Joan Bulman, translator (Richmond: John Knox Press, 1963) 3.

2. Ibid., 3–4. Quoted from Ritschl, *Unterricht in der christlichen Religion*, 3d ed., Bonn, 1886, 3.

3. Ibid., Lundström, 4.

Ritschl's theological argument helped ignite the turn-of-the-century social gospel movement. For Walter Rauschenbusch, the movement's most well-known U.S. proponent, the kingdom was clearly this-worldly in its orientation and transformative in its purpose. As Norman Perrin observes, for Rauschenbusch the kingdom is a symbol which represents the myth of God actively intervening in the history of human living.[4] Rauschenbusch believed the myth to be as real for modern humanity as it had been for the ancient Hebrews. Particularly, it was real in the struggle for social justice; God intervened on behalf of the oppressed. And when God moved, human as well as divine tools were put to effective use. "Christian people were 'to use the prophetic insight and moral determination which their Christian discipleship ought to give them in order to speed and direct' the transformation of society."[5]

As for Ritschl, so for Rauschenbusch, everything began with Jesus. His life and ministry represented the clear content of God's divine kingdom. "He came to found a new society on earth, and he laid down the principles of conduct which were to govern men in this new society."[6] Like the prophets whom he succeeded, Jesus promulgated a religion of revolution. The prophets looked for a this-worldly transformation that would overturn the oppressions of their present age. The messianic hope which realized itself in Jesus was just such a revolutionary, socio-political ambition.[7]

> The change he was inaugurating was so radical, that after its consummation it would be found that the first had become last and the last first.... Such a reversal of values presupposes sweeping changes in the general conceptions and judgments prevalent in human society, and necessarily also in the social and political institutions in which these conceptions and judgments find their embodiment.[8]

For Jesus, the aim of this socio-political, this-worldly revolution was the future kingdom of God. Indeed, his ministry had already inaugurated it in the present.

Like Ritschl, Rauschenbusch also argued that Jesus' human disciples could continue the transformative kingdom effort through ethical obedience to God. "Christ initiated his kingdom on earth by establishing a community of spiritual men, in inward communion with God and in outward *obedience* to him. This was the living germ of the kingdom."[9] Thus, though Christ does seek the redemption of the individual, that concern is subsidiary to the theocratic hope for a transformed human politic. "It is not enough to christianize individuals; we

---

4. Norman Perrin, *Jesus and the Language of the Kingdom* (Philadelphia: Fortress Press, 1976) 70.

5. Mark Chapman, "Walter Rauschenbusch and the Coming of God's Kingdom," in *The Kingdom of God and Human Society*, Robin Barbour, editor (Edinburgh: T & T Clark, 1993) 186–87.

6. Walter Rauschenbusch, *The Righteousness of the Kingdom*, Max L. Stackhouse, editor (Nashville: Abingdon Press, 1968) 63.

7. Ibid., 72.

8. Ibid., 75.

9. Ibid., 87.

must christianize societies, organizations, nations, for they too have a life of their own which may be made better or worse."[10]

For Rauschenbusch, then, the kingdom appeared to be a pocket manifestation. Though it is itself not of the present, it transforms the present. "Apocalypticism had set up the theory of the two eras, 'this age' and 'the coming age,' and separated them by a chasm. At least in some of his sayings we can see Jesus working away from that view to the thought that the old era was even then passing into the new."[11]

And yet, Rauschenbusch's conclusion is radically different from the pocket model I espouse. For him, when the future breaks into the present, it is not distinct from it; it is absorbed by it. The future kingdom becomes the present kingdom so that the times and the realities particular to each appear to merge in a contemporary, believing community. "All these acts and sayings [of Jesus] receive their real meaning when we think of them in connection with the kingdom of God, the ideal human society to be established."[12] Instead of a qualitatively distinct, transient, though effectively transformative, pocket moment, the kingdom becomes a presently stable, humanly enacted, social reality.

Ritschl's and Rauschenbusch's contemporaries offered other, equally damaging critiques. Ritschl's pupil, Johannes Weiss, charged correctly that his teacher's kingdom conclusions were more a product of his liberal, nineteenth-century, theological-ethical orientation than they were derivative from the gospel narratives. Rauschenbusch, too, was interested in presenting a kingdom theory that reflected the theological and ideological positions of nineteenth and early twentieth-century liberalism. It was an evaluation that, while fitting his social theory, missed the future oriented and divinely distinctive disclosure of the kingdom that was so critical to the synoptic presentation of Jesus.

> The "Social Gospel" modernises Jesus and reads into the Gospel ideas which properly belong to optimistic American philosophy and anthropology. With evolutionary ideas abroad in the world, Rauschenbusch was even capable of declaring that the idea of the Kingdom of God was the result of expressing the theory of evolution in religious terms. At the root of the "Social Gospel" we find a moral, humanistic, and immanent conception of God, as is always the case with liberal theology not only in America but everywhere else.[13]

For his part, Johannes Weiss promoted an historical-textual reading of the kingdom of God language.[14] In his seminal 1892 work, *Die Predigt Jesus vom*

---

10. Ibid., 112.

11. Walter Rauschenbusch, *Christianizing the Social Order* (New York: The Macmillan Company, 1914) 65.

12. Walter Rauschenbusch, *Christianity and the Social Crisis* (Louisville: Westminster/John Knox Press, 1991) 70.

13. Lundström, 26.

14. "In this regard, it might not be superfluous if we attempt once more to identify the original historical meaning which Jesus connected with the words 'kingdom of God,' and if we do it with special care lest we import modern, or at any rate alien, ideas into Jesus' thought world."

Reiche Gottes (*Jesus' Proclamation of the Kingdom of God*), he recognized a parallel between Jesus' future oriented presentation of the gospel narratives and similar themes in Jewish apocalyptic. Weiss therefore concluded that the kingdom of God was, for Jesus, an apocalyptic concept. Humans maintained a participative role; a primary plank of the Lord's Prayer was that they pray for the kingdom's arrival (cf. Matthew 6:10a; Luke 11:2b). They did not, however, have the power to establish it. Though imminently anticipated, it was wholly future and totally divine, radically transcendent and completely otherworldly. "Either the βασιλεία [kingdom] is here, or it is not yet here. For the disciples and for the early church it is not yet here."[15] When Jesus speaks of a present sense of the kingdom, he does so only paradoxically. Therefore, the ethics Jesus taught were an ethics of repentance designed to prepare believers for the coming of a cataclysmic, future moment of judgment, not an ethics of kingdom construction.

In fact, even Jesus was incapable of constructing the future kingdom in his contemporary historical circumstance. As Mark 13:32 and 14:25 indicate, he also waited without any foreknowledge for God to establish it. Jesus was therefore less a messianic initiator of the kingdom than he was a prophetic witness. Enrapt in spiritual enthusiasm, he foresaw, and even anticipated in his miracles and exorcisms, the ultimate kingdom reality. He was, however, powerless to bring it about. Even his grandest tactical act, his death on the cross, did not force God's strategic hand. The kingdom breaks in of its own sudden accord like a divine storm of judgment poised both to destroy and renew.[16] "Thus, since Jesus is now a rabbi, a prophet, he has nothing in common with the Son of Man, except the claim that he will *become* the Son of Man. Thus even he cannot intervene in the development of the kingdom of God. He has to wait, just as the people have to wait, until God once again definitively takes up the rule."[17]

Weiss's work lays the groundwork for my pocket of resistance model in two ways. Because he sees the kingdom as radically future, the only way it can have a present effect, even in the work of Jesus, is in the sense of a foreign pocket erupting into the territory of human present time. "Rather, Jesus does so [speaks of the presence of the kingdom of God] because by his own activity the power of Satan, who above all others is the source of evil, is being broken."[18] In other words, the future kingdom of God intervenes through the present miracle and exorcism work of Jesus in a way that is beyond human control and understanding. But Weiss cannot obtain the full yield of such a realization because he argues that in the first-century mind there existed two parallel, mythological realities, the heavenly and the earthly. Even though Jesus' activities obtain a tangible present transformation, Weiss maintains that they are merely phantasms, pointers to what has occurred in the heavenly world, not real achievements in the human

Johannes Weiss, *Jesus' Proclamation of the Kingdom of God*, Richard Hyde Hiers and David Larrimore Holland, translators and editors (Philadelphia: Fortress Press, 1971) 60.

15. Weiss, 73–74.

16. Wendell Willis, "The Discovery of the Eschatological Kingdom: Johannes Weiss and Albert Schweitzer," in *The Kingdom of God in 20th-Century Interpretation* (Peabody, MA: Hendrickson Publishers, 1987) 4.

17. Weiss, 82–83.

18. Ibid., 78.

one. "But these are moments of sublime prophetic enthusiasm, when an aware-ness of victory comes over him [Jesus]."[19] He can admit the uniqueness of these Jesus events, but he need not acknowledge their transformative significance in human history; such significance is restricted to the heavenly plane.

Weiss also prefigures a key component of the pocket of resistance model when he argues for a this-worldly kingdom realization. God's kingdom will not be an other-worldly, heavenly, spiritual accomplishment, but will transform the human historical circumstance so that the political and social fortunes of Israel will be restored. "The Land of Palestine will arise in a new and glorious splen-dor, forming the center of the new kingdom. Alien peoples will no longer rule over it, but will come to acknowledge God as Lord....Jesus and his faithful ones will rule over this newborn people of the twelve tribes, which will include even the Gentiles."[20] It is a powerful, universal, this-worldly realization. How-ever, it is also radically future and therefore beyond the hopes of the present human world. In a sense it is the ultimate tease, an eschatological carrot on a stick intended to maintain hope for the future even while it discourages believ-ers from thinking that any work they do can help establish or even promote that future. Thus, though it recognizes the hostile kingdom of Satan that rules the present age, the kingdom of God remains, unfortunately, a future pocket that has no power to establish present resistance.

In his *Quest of the Historical Jesus,* Albert Schweitzer found much to like in Weiss's argument. Like Weiss, he argued that Jesus was a product of his apocalyptic environment and that his kingdom of God proclamation should be interpreted out of that historical context. "The eschatology of Jesus can therefore only be interpreted by the aid of the curiously intermittent Jewish apocalyp-tic literature of the period between Daniel and the Bar-Cochba rising. What else, indeed, are the Synoptic Gospels...than products of Jewish apocalyptic, belonging, moreover, to its greatest and most flourishing period."[21]

Thus, for Schweitzer, too, Jesus' dogmatic intent was not to establish the kingdom, but to proclaim it. Though he expected its imminent arrival, it was wholly future and beyond all human control, even his own as Son of man. Only God could and would broker it. He therefore agrees with Weiss who "made an end of the modern view that Jesus founded the kingdom."[22]

An apocalyptic concept, the kingdom was meaningful only in Jesus' mytho-logical time; it had little ethical appeal for the modern human predicament. Jesus' ethics, too, were apocalyptic; Schweitzer called them interim ethics. They were not designed to establish the kingdom, but to prepare a person in the interim between the contemporary moment and the day of judgment. He there-fore, like Weiss, focused on repentance as the key to Jesus' ethics of kingdom entrance.

19. Ibid., 78.
20. Ibid., 130–31.
21. Albert Schweitzer, *The Quest of the Historical Jesus: A Critical Study of Its Progress from Reimarus to Wrede* (New York: Macmillan Publishing Company, 1968 [first published in 1906]) 367.
22. Ibid., 357.

To their credit, Schweitzer and Weiss succeeded in recovering the apocalyptic understanding of the kingdom as it is presented in the gospel texts. They understood that for Jesus the kingdom is a divinely directed and established future reality. Ironically, though, the kind of criticism they leveled against Ritschl applied to their own work. Devotion to a theological-ideological scheme, in their case that of consistent eschatology, prompted them to read the gospel texts in a highly selective manner. They considered sayings that agreed with their preconceived positions to be critical interpretive tools. They ignored or explained away those that did not. Neither gave sufficient consideration to Jesus' statements and parabolic sayings which proclaimed that the kingdom was already present.

In his book on Jesus (1926), Rudolf Bultmann followed up from Weiss's apocalyptic foundation. He believed that Jesus' conception of the kingdom was radically transcendent. It was, therefore, totally removed from human control and set apart from human ethical designs.

Bultmann defines the kingdom as the eschatological deliverance of God that ends everything earthly.[23] Confronting every human being with an ultimate choice, a divine either-or, this deliverance demands a decision. This does not mean, however, that decisive human behavior establishes the kingdom. The kingdom confronts humans in its own way, without human involvement or participation. Contrary to the opinion of social gospellers like Rauschenbusch, there is "*no 'highest good' in the ethical sense*. It is not a good toward which the will and action of men is directed, not an ideal which is in any sense realized through human conduct, which in any sense requires *men* to bring it into existence. Being eschatological, it is wholly supernatural."[24]

Though Bultmann appears on the surface to be separating the kingdom from any contemporary application, it was instead his intent to bridge the chasm that Weiss's and Schweitzer's work opened between apocalyptic kingdom thought and modern biblical interpretation. Consistent eschatologists like Schweitzer argued that because Jesus' preaching was apocalyptic, it was tied to his own mythological world and could bear no real application for the contemporary world of modern thought and science. Bultmann believed, however, that if one could remove the apocalyptic shell and interpret the kernel of truth that Jesus had hidden inside, one would see that Jesus' message was in reality a message for the modern human as well as the mythological one. It is on this premise that his program of demythologization was built.

Bultmann recognized that ancient myths could die. The myth of the kingdom of God as an apocalyptic intervention into the affairs of human lives and history certainly had. But the meaning it represented had not. It was this meaning that an interpreter had to uncover. For Bultmann, it was a meaning that centered on human existence. It was the function of the myth of the kingdom to explain and interpret for Jesus his understanding of human existence in the face of the divine and wholly transcendent. Jesus understood that humans were standing in a crisis

---

23. Rudolf Bultmann, *Jesus and the Word*, Louise Pettibone Smith, translator (New York: Charles Scribner's Sons, 1934 [first published in 1926]) 35.
24. Ibid., 35–36.

of decision before God; this is the existential reality, the hidden truth, that the apocalyptic language about the coming kingdom truly represents.

The kingdom of God, then, is a future reality which determines the present by making it a crisis moment for decision. Each "now" becomes humanity's last moment to decide against the world and for God.

> If men are standing in the crisis of decision, and if precisely this crisis is the essential characteristic of their humanity, then every hour is the last hour, and we can understand that for Jesus the whole contemporary mythology is pressed into the service of this conception of human existence. Thus he understood and proclaimed his hour as the last hour.[25]

Richard Hiers is right to point out, however, that Bultmann's ethic was more than a negative, world-renouncing one. In Jesus' demand for radical obedience in the crisis of spiritual decision for God, Bultmann also found a positive ethic of radical neighbor-love.[26] In the end, however, the edifice Bultmann built upon the foundation his teacher Johannes Weiss constructed, pushed him to see the kingdom as a wholly other entity that had little real effect in the human arena. While the future was glimpsed in the ministry of Jesus, it had no real transformative effect, except in the individual spirit of the person brought to a crisis of decision before his or her awareness that each hour was their last. There can be no present pocket moment of the kingdom beyond the spiritual life of the individual. Even if Jesus' work generated revolutionary repercussions in the lives of those he healed, exorcised, taught, and challenged, the kingdom itself was never more than a myth representing a crisis of individual spiritual existence. Because of the radical transcendence of his own kingdom reality, God could not do what Jesus did in his earthly ministry; God could not challenge the oppressive worldly powers that ruled the human socio-political circumstance.

> Despite the elegance and power of its theological criticism, Bultmann's theology seems to evade human social and political responsibility. This has dangerous implications since, as will become apparent, without the possibility of ethical construction history will be at the mercy of the dominant ideology, however malignant, and can easily become the unwitting tool for oppression. In short, history goes on regardless: to remove God from it is to leave it open for the devil.[27]

In 1935, C. H. Dodd's *The Parables of the Kingdom* attempted to correct scholarship's myopic focus on the future, otherworldly orientation of the king-

25. Ibid., 52.

26. Richard H. Hiers, Jr., "Pivotal Reactions to the Eschatological Interpretations: Rudolf Bultmann and C. H. Dodd," in *The Kingdom of God in 20th-Century Interpretation,* Wendell Willis, editor (Peabody MA: Hendrickson Publishers, 1987) 26.

27. Mark Chapman, "The Kingdom of God and Ethics: From Ritschl to Liberation Theology," in *The Kingdom of God and Human Society,* Robin Barbour, editor (Edinburgh: T & T Clark, 1993) 157.

dom. His work demonstrated that careful exegesis must reckon honestly with Jesus' sayings which presume the kingdom's present manifestation. Dodd's assessment of the sayings texts, particularly the parables, led him to the conclusion that in Jesus' life and ministry the kingdom had already arrived.[28]

Arguing against Weiss and Schweitzer, Dodd claimed that while Jesus' teachings did bear some similarities with Jewish apocalypticism,[29] for the most part he established his own theological track. His primary contribution was his belief in the present arrival of the "ultimate" kingdom.

> Whatever we make of them, the sayings which declare the Kingdom of God to have come are explicit and unequivocal. They are moreover the most characteristic and distinctive of the Gospel sayings on the subject. They have no parallel in Jewish teaching or prayers of the period. If therefore we are seeking the *differentia* of the teaching of Jesus upon the Kingdom of God, it is here that it must be found.[30]

Dodd insisted that the kingdom existed within human beings in the present, not in some incalculable future. The kingdom prevailed whenever God's rule was allowed free reign in human hearts. Kingdom ethics were not, then, limited to the interim time of Jesus' own ministry as an ethics of repentant preparation. The contemporary human could enter the kingdom by making God king in his or her soul.

> Dodd's solution was to urge that Jesus proclaimed "realized eschatology:" the kingdom of God, the Son of Man, judgment, and the ultimate blessings of life with God were already present in his own time; therefore Jesus was not mistaken as to when it would come. Moreover, Dodd claimed, the kingdom remained present ever since. Jesus' ethical teachings were meant for all who experienced the presence of the kingdom; they are therefore valid for Christians of all times; and he *meant* them "for us," not just for his contemporaries.[31]

Dodd approached the kingdom reality as a future pocket that has disrupted the proclivities of the present human moment. "The *eschaton* has moved from the future to the present, from the sphere of expectation into that of realized experience."[32] In Jesus' present ministry, where the blind see, the lame walk, lepers

---

28. In Perrin, 38.

29. At Mark 10:15, his expression, "whoever does not receive the kingdom," bears similarity to the rabbinic expression to take upon oneself the yoke of God's kingdom. The call for the kingdom to come in the Lord's prayer sounds very much like the petition in the Jewish *kaddish* prayer. As did the Jewish apocalyptists, at Mark 9:1, Jesus predicted a future and final manifestation of that kingdom. And finally, like some apocalyptists, at Mark 12:25, Jesus appears to place the kingdom in an order beyond space and time. Cf. C. H. Dodd, *The Parables of the Kingdom* (New York: Charles Scribner's Sons, 1961) 27–29.

30. Dodd, 34.

31. Hiers, 18.

32. Dodd, 34.

are cleansed, the deaf hear, the dead are raised, and the messianic representative suffers and dies, the future kingdom has appeared in the present. "It is an historical happening, to which men should respond by repentance, but whether they repent or not, it is there."[33]

Dodd is to be commended for tempering the consistent apocalypticism of Weiss and Schweitzer with his recognition of the kingdom's present qualities in Jesus' life and teachings. His work also demonstrated that Bultmann's assertions of radical kingdom transcendence do not agree with all the textual evidence; clearly, Jesus also believed and taught that this wholly future kingdom had a powerful contemporary presence. Unfortunately, however, the kingdom did not remain for Dodd a foreign pocket from the future exploding uncontrollably in the present experience. In the end, it actually merged with the present so that it lost all future potency and effect. Just as Weiss and Schweitzer had ignored the sayings about the present kingdom, Dodd, in order to justify his preconceived exegetical agenda, found reasons why he should dismiss the importance of the future oriented kingdom sayings. His primary explanation was that these sayings were the product of the early church's apocalyptic experience, and not an expression of Jesus' true thought.[34] Whatever the reason, it is clear that for Dodd the future pocket does not hold, but collapses completely into the present, so that the Gospel materials that detail present and future manifestations of the kingdom cannot be given equal exegetical weight. The texts must be interpreted and evaluated in the light of a one-sided, pre-established realized understanding.

Werner Kümmel's 1945 book, *Promise and Fulfillment,* represents an attempt to mediate between the either (present)-or (future) approaches to the study of the kingdom. Eldon Epp places him in the context of post-WWII scholarship that saw the emergence of a "consensus" position on the kingdom. Using military language, Oscar Cullmann argued that Jesus' ministry of miracle, exorcism and teaching represented the "decisive defeat of the powers of evil by the powers of the kingdom."[35] The final battle had already taken place; the future kingdom had taken hold and taken charge in the present moment. Still, however, there remained a sense of futurity which acknowledged the future orientation in many of the Gospel kingdom sayings. The final consummation had not yet occurred. In the period between Jesus' present kingdom manifestation and that final victory was the ongoing "mop-up" operation of continuing struggle.

Kümmel extended this "consensus" conclusion by arguing that Jesus held to an imminent expectation of the kingdom. Investigations of the word group ἐγγύς (ἐγγίζειν — draw near, approach), in places like Mark 13:28–29 convinced him that Jesus believed it would not be long before the kingdom dawned.[36] Texts

---

33. Ibid., 30. See also "This is the 'mystery of the Kingdom of God,' not only that the *eschaton,* that which belongs properly to the realm of the 'wholly other,' is now a matter of actual experience, but that it is experienced in the paradoxical form of the suffering and death of God's representative" (59).

34. Dodd, 35–37.

35. Eldon Jay Epp, "Mediating Approaches to the Kingdom: Werner Georg Kümmel and George Eldon Ladd," in *The Kingdom of God,* Willis, editor, 37.

36. Werner Georg Kümmel, *Promise and Fulfillment: The Eschatological Message of Jesus* (London: SCM Press, 1957) 20.

like 9:1 and 14:25 reinforced his thought. And yet, texts like 8:38 on the "day" of the Son of man also demonstrated a sense of imminent futurity for the kingdom. Schweitzer was therefore wrong to have argued that Jesus expected the kingdom to arrive prior to his death. Jesus also did not, as Dodd proclaimed, so merge the kingdom with the present that it was completely realized in his contemporary moment. Indeed, passages like 2:19 and 14:25 suggested to him that Jesus believed there would be an interval, undoubtedly short, between his own death and the coming of the kingdom. It was not yet here. The futurity of the kingdom established a this-worldly, historical orientation to Jesus' proclamations and actions. Without this emphasis the kingdom can become spiritualized, individualized and cut off from the very socio-historical concerns that haunted Jesus and his fellow Jews. "The *future* expectation is essential and indispensable, because in this form alone can the nature of God's redemptive action *in history* be held fast."[37]

But in the third chapter of his book, Kümmel dealt with numerous passages that did demonstrate a present awareness of the future kingdom. Even in some of the same texts which detailed the kingdom's future reality, e.g., Mark 8:38, there existed a present emphasis. 8:38 demonstrated how the future expectation for the kingdom caused a present crisis that demanded a present decision. The future, as Bultmann had earlier recognized, has present impact. Ethics therefore play a role for Kümmel, but they are an ethics of response to the call and word of Jesus. Humans must decide to respond positively to Jesus' ministry in the face of the present reality of the kingdom.

> Consequently men are distinguished decisively by their acceptance or rejection of the Son of Man in action even now, yet expected to be fully effective only in the near future; thus the fundamental presupposition for the future eschatological judgment was created already in the present, in which Jesus was the determining factor.[38]

In fact, the future kingdom actually made its appearance in the person and ministry of Jesus. He was himself the future kingdom intervening like a pocket into present time. Jesus' exorcisms, as the verb φθάνω (arrive, come) in Matthew 12:28 makes clear, demonstrate that, at least in the gospel narrative, Jesus thought the approaching kingdom was already showing itself in his efforts. Jesus confirmed this suspicion with his actions in Jerusalem; the entry (Mark 11:1–10) and the temple cleansing (Mark 11:15–17) both suggest that he believed his hour to be that of the eschatological savior.[39] The coming consummation had already made its way into the present moment.

> Promise and fulfillment are therefore inseparably united for Jesus and depend on each other; for the promise is made sure by the fulfillment that

---

37. Ibid., 152–53.
38. Ibid., 105.
39. Ibid., 117–19.

has already taken place in Jesus, and the fulfillment, being provisional and concealed, loses its quality as a σκάνδαλον ("offense") only through the knowledge of the promise yet to come.[40]

Kümmel's work is extremely helpful because it represents a shift in thinking that forms the foundation for an exploration into the language of the kingdom as a future pocket intruding upon the present moment. What Kümmel's argument lacked, however, was a coherent conceptualization that would hold the dissonant factions of future and present together in such a way that the reader could understand the narrative intention behind the unlikely pairing. How were the future and present held in such theoretical proximity without the force of either being diminished? And what did their connection mean — beyond the broad language of responding decisively for Jesus — for the way believers were to live their lives?

By appealing to a linguistic analysis of the gospel texts, Norman Perrin represents a powerful effort to make systematic sense of this dissonant now and not yet kingdom pairing. In his 1976 landmark work, *Jesus and the Language of the Kingdom,* Perrin thought he understood a fundamental problem in the previous work on the kingdom that allowed for the one-sided arguments about its nature and content. Previous researchers, as skilled as they were, had misunderstood what the kingdom was. They had all taken it to be a concept; it was either ethical, apocalyptic, existential, or realized. It was never a combination of two or more. Scholars looked for texts that would demonstrate the efficacy of their conceptual arguments and glossed over those texts which conflicted with their preestablished conclusions. Perrin's literary approach to the problem enabled him to avoid this critical error.

Operating from ideas about symbols and myths established by Amos Wilder, Perrin turned over new ground. The kingdom, he argued, should not be viewed as a concept, but as a "tensive" symbol which represents or evokes the myth of God's kingship. Appealing to the work of Philip Wheelwright,[41] Perrin contrasted the tensive symbol with its "steno" counterpart. He argued that a steno symbol, which most apocalyptic symbols tended to be, was exhausted by a single conceptual referent. That is to say, for example, the kingdom could be either apocalyptic or realized, but it could not be both. The kingdom of God, however, was a unique apocalyptic symbol; it was tensive. As a tensive symbol, "it can *represent* or *evoke* a whole range or series of conceptions."[42] The possibilities for interpreting the kingdom were therefore opened up immeasurably. Suddenly, the kingdom could represent both present and future realities, ethical and existential conceptualities, be wholly other and yet presently realized at the same time.

40. Ibid., 155.

41. Philip Wheelwright, *Metaphor and Reality* (Bloomington, IN: Indiana University Press, 1962).

42. W. Emory Elmore, "Linguistic Approaches to the Kingdom: Amos Wilder and Norman Perrin," *The Kingdom of God,* Willis, editor, 61.

Perrin grants to Weiss, Schweitzer and Bultmann that the context in which a symbol originally occurs dramatically influences how one should interpret its meaning. Jesus came upon the symbol as it flourished in Jewish apocalyptic thought; it is therefore inconceivable that he could have ignored its apocalyptic implications. This realization does not, however, mean that neither Jesus nor the evangelists who chronicled his narrative story could have pushed beyond the apocalyptic reference to "transcend, and even transform" how the symbol was to be conceptually realized in retelling it as part of the Jesus event.[43]

In order to demonstrate this possibility, Perrin analyzes the roots of the symbol in ancient near Eastern mythology; he begins with the Canaanites, who took it from the kingdoms of the Euphrates, Tigris and Nile, where it had developed from Sumerian times. "In this myth the god had acted as king in creating the world, in the course of which he had overcome and slain the primeval monster. Further, the god continued to act as king by annually renewing the fertility of the earth, and he showed himself to be king of a particular people by sustaining them in their place in the world."[44]

The myth was apocalyptic. Life in the ancient world was envisioned as a battle between good and evil forces. In the cycle of death and rebirth, spring represented the reinstatement of the renewed king over the evil power represented in winter. "That ancient Israel learned to think of their god in this way, and to celebrate his kingship in this way, can be seen from the so-called enthronement psalms (Psalms 47, 93, 96, 97, 98, 99), with their constant refrain, 'Yahweh has become king!' a cultic avowal often mistranslated, 'The Lord Reigns.' "[45]

By using the same symbol Jesus contextually evokes a similar myth. Perrin believes that he is intentionally summoning it in the hopes of demonstrating how the symbol and the myth it represents are coming alive in his own ministry. Through his work, God's future kingship is intervening in the human present to overcome the powers of evil.

The apocalyptic conceptuality does not, however, exhaust Jesus' use of the kingdom language. Perrin argues that Jesus owes his tensive use of the symbol to his Israelite context. Early on the Hebrews added their own emphasis to the kingship myth. He points to Psalms 93:1–2; 96:10, and 97:1–2 as examples, where the concept of salvation history enters into the make-up of the kingdom symbol. Righteousness and justice are seen as foundations of the king's throne. God will judge the people accordingly. But the ultimate lean of that judgment is toward salvation. As Deuteronomy 26:5b–10 indicates, the myth represented a *Heilsgeschichte*, "a confessional summary of the activity of God on behalf of his people."[46]

---

43. "So far as the *literary-critical question* of the nature and force of the symbol, and of the linguistic context in which it is found, is concerned, there is general agreement that the background of Jesus' use is the language and symbolism of ancient Jewish apocalyptic. But to say that is to raise a whole set of further questions, questions with regard to the possibility of a non-apocalyptic use of the symbol by Jesus." Perrin, 15.

44. Ibid., 16–17.

45. Ibid., 17.

46. Ibid., 18.

Two different conceptual trends are therefore brought together and symbolically connected in the kingdom language. The symbol represents the reality that God intervenes in the life of his people, his nation, and, that he does so for the express purpose of establishing justice and salvation. "What happened was that the two myths came together to form one, the myth of God who created the world and is active on behalf of his people in the history of that world, and the symbol evolved to evoke that myth."[47] It is a symbol that represents the hope for this-worldly, social and political transformation. The kingship is represented by the socio-political activities of the Exodus, the movement of a people to a promised land, and the establishment of a theocracy with holy city and temple. "In all this God was acting as king...."[48]

According to Perrin's analysis, Israel was able to celebrate this myth of God's kingship as long as the people remained free. Only in their political sense of national freedom did it appear that God was indeed intervening on their behalf. When national catastrophes occurred, they were explained within the confines of the myth; God was punishing the people, judging them, correcting them. God was still king and still intervening on the people's ultimate behalf. Even major setbacks appeared to reveal God's rule. Babylon's sack of the city and temple was overcome by God's intervention through Cyrus. Alexander's conquest, which eventually led to subjugation by the Seleucid kingdom, was overcome by God's intervention through the Maccabees and the Hasmonean empire they put in place. But in 63 B.C.E., when Pompey took command of Palestine, God's kingship power to intervene on behalf of the people was placed in doubt. By 6 C.E., Rome ruled Judea directly and all hope of freedom seemed misplaced. It was under such direly negative circumstances that the myth became apocalyptic. "The Jewish people continued to evoke the ancient myth, but now the formulations have a note of intensity about them, a note almost of despairing hope."[49] The people sought a deliverance from the evil powers that ruled the present age, a deliverance on the order of the past Exodus event, but they searched for it now in the ultimate future, for it was clear the present would not tolerate such a promise.

It was into such a present that Jesus came proclaiming that the kingdom of God, the representation of God's power intervening on behalf of the people of Israel, was realized in his ministry. Not only his miracles and exorcisms, but also his teachings mediated the realization of this kinship myth. Perrin points out, for example, that Jesus' proverbs and parables actually bore the reality about which they were concerned. In effect, then, everything about Jesus' ministry represents the mythic understanding that God, through Jesus, is intervening transformatively in human affairs.

> The *kingdom sayings* challenge Jesus' hearers to recognize the kingdom of God as a reality in the exorcisms, to recognize that the ancient myth of the

---

47. Ibid., 20–21.
48. Ibid., 22.
49. Ibid., 26.

activity of God as king can now be realized in their experience in various ways, and to recognize that the fate of the Baptist, and the potential fate of Jesus and his followers, are to be understood as a manifestation of the reality of God acting as king.[50]

When Jesus uses the kingdom symbol tensively he is not obligated to maintain a single conceptual referent for it throughout his ministry. It can and must be apocalyptic, given its context. But it can be more, as Dodd points out. It can demonstrate a present "pocket" viability for God's ultimate salvific actions, particularly in the ministry of Jesus. It can also, as Perrin points out, have parenetic emphases, encouraging an ethical conceptuality in response to the divine intervention promised in the future and being realized in the present. This is much more than an interim ethic.

Perrin's recognition of the symbol as tensive allows us to see the kingdom as a future pocket that has transformative effect in the present. God's kingdom strategy is tactically realized by a human agent whose teachings, miracles and exorcisms are themselves put into practice by a discipleship corps. Though Perrin himself, in pushing his parenetic response to the kingdom myth, never goes this far, I believe that his discussion lays the groundwork for envisioning human tactical activity that is more than a response to God's strategic effort.

And yet, here lies the limitation of Perrin's study. Strict loyalty to his literary approach hinders him from pursuing the socio-political options his tensive approach to the symbol opens. As Elisabeth Schüssler Fiorenza observes, though Perrin recognizes that the symbol has broad cultural range, he does not explore its other possibilities of meaning. By picking up on the vitality of the symbol in its representation of God acting as king on behalf of the people in historical events like the Exodus, but then overlooking the powerful ways in which that symbol was socio-culturally (as well as mythically) exploited in the first century, particularly by Jesus, he has failed to explore the full potential of the symbol's representative power. In the end, then, he contributes to the "steno" limitations that he himself decries. Or as Schüssler Fiorenza puts it, "The tensive symbol Kingdom of God tends to become a steno-symbol and the myth of God's kingly activity in behalf of the people of God seems to become the *content* of Jesus' message."[51]

Liberation approaches to the gospel materials have attempted to explore the full range of the symbol's potentiality by addressing the socio-political conceptuality of the kingdom as Jesus preaches and lives it. Gustavo Gutiérrez is an example of this approach. In his *God of Life*, Gutiérrez argues that though the kingdom can become manifest in the present, it only will become present when humans live out its ethics. Humans therefore have a tactical responsibility in the implementation of the kingdom by the way they choose

50. Ibid., 194–95.
51. Elisabeth Schüssler Fiorenza, "The Phenomenon of Early Christian Apocalyptic: Some Reflections on Method," in *Apocalypticism in the Mediterranean World and the Near East*, David Hellholm, editor (Tübingen: J. C. B. Mohr, 1983) 307.

to respond to knowledge of its presence. "When the grace of God's reign is not accepted, when God's demands are not met, the God of the kingdom is absent."[52]

The kingdom is a divine gift, and is, therefore, at least in its consummate form, beyond human manipulation. But it also demands a human response that not only reacts to the gift, but also in the process helps establish its present realization as justice.

> On the other hand, and closely connected with the point just made, the kingdom of God brings with it the demand for certain kinds of behaviors. The disciples of Jesus who accept the gift of the kingdom respond to it by a specific conduct. This is the ethical dimension of the kingdom. "Repent" is the demand that accompanies the gift of the kingdom and leads to a new kind of activity in relation to God and one's brothers and sisters.[53]

This means that Jesus' actions are not the only ones which represent the myth of God intervening in history as king. The response of the community of Jesus-followers can have the same representational value. That's because, "in the New Testament one sign of the kingdom is the community that develops around Jesus, for the existence of this believing people is evidence that God is acting in history."[54]

Liberation theologians extend the discussion by pushing the conceptual possibilities inherent in the tensive symbol, kingdom of God, so that it represents socio-political as well as mythic transformation. And there is a place for human ethical involvement in the tactical implementation of that kingdom. It is a future consummation that intrudes upon the present moment and invites human beings to become participants in its transformative process. It has become a pocket of transformation. Unfortunately, it has also become so politicized that its other conceptual qualities are often overlooked. I need not delve here into the criticism brought against liberation approaches to the biblical materials over the past two decades, except to agree that the emphasis on "praxis" (liberative action) often implies that the kingdom has again become a "steno" symbol with only a liberation conceptualization. In many ways, the liberation theologians have thus taken us full circle, back to the liberal-ethical arguments of Ritschl and Rauschenbusch. Operating in oppressed environments where a singular appeal to the spiritual condemns whole populations to perpetual injustice, they so hotly protest the overemphasis on the spiritual, existential and future orientations of the kingdom that they tend to exclude these narratively based kingdom conceptualities from proper review.

In fact, each of the watershed works on the kingdom we have mentioned examines a single conceptual segment of the kingdom symbol. This, of course, is

---

52. Gustavo Gutiérrez, *The God of Life*, Matthew J. O'Connell, translator (Maryknoll, NY: Orbis Books, 1991) 75.

53. Ibid., 102.

54. Ibid., 104.

the problem. Each reading declares that its particular understanding exhausts the symbol's conceptual range. The kingdom is either future (Weiss, Schweitzer, Bultmann) or it is present (Dodd). It is either an ethical way of living in a just community founded on love (Ritschl, Rauschenbusch) or a wholly other, transcendent reality (Bultmann, Weiss, Schweitzer) which can in no way be established by human action. It is either a linguistic symbol which represents a mythical reality (Perrin) or a tangible symbol which represents and demands socio-political acts of liberation (Gutiérrez). In each case the authors operated as much from methodological or ideological presuppositions as from the actual language of the text. Therefore, in arguing the viability of their particular concept, they could dismiss other conceptual realities which are just as visible in the text but did not fit their preconceived positions. It is for this reason that I propose an analysis of the Markan narrative from a methodological perspective that is, in its very theoretical construction, designed to appreciate all of the conceptualities that may arise in the narrative language from this single kingdom symbol.

I would propose a method that analyzes Mark's use of the kingdom of God in his historical context. We will find that he understands it to be a symbol filled with vast meaning potential. This means something more than Howard Snyder suggested in his models of the kingdom approach.[55] Although Snyder demonstrated different conceptual realizations of the kingdom language, in his theoretical presentation he left them isolated from one another in a way that the text would not allow. The various conceptualizations of the kingdom, though disparate and often contrasting, are held in tension throughout the narrative presentation of Mark's gospel. Although Snyder does indeed make this point, his presentation, which separates each model from the others, implies a segmentation that Mark would not have understood.

One must be careful at just this point, however. Because the kingdom symbol has a large conceptual range it is possible that its very potentiality could cause a vast amount of confusion in the minds of a reading audience. Just because the symbol *can* mean many things does not mean that it *does* mean many things. If an evangelist is attempting to establish faith and engender discipleship behavior demonstrative of that faith, one would expect him to develop his text in such a way that, given the context he shares with his audience, a particular emphasis would arise from the many conceptual possibilities. That is to say, the audience could be expected, given the signals in the text and the circumstances of the shared social location, to access a particular piece of the symbol's meaning potential. This is not to say, however, that the segment accessed by this community would be the only possible meaning conclusion that can arise from the text. It is the meaning that is significant for the persons reading from a particular communal perspective. Readers coming from other socio-historical perspectives may be expected to appropriate a different segment or different segments of the conceptual range of possibilities as meaningfully significant. It will

---

55. Howard A. Snyder, *Models of the Kingdom* (Nashville: Abingdon, 1990).

be my task to explore which part of the meaning potential the Markan community might have been expected to access as meaningful (although I admittedly
do this through the influential lens of my own socio-historical location and perspective), and then to relate its meaning conclusions (as I refract them through
that lens) to the interpretative work of the contemporary African-American
church.

Part II

Kingdom Language in the First-Century Markan Context

3

Social Location and Language

Accessing Meaning

THE POLITICS OF THE KINGDOM OF GOD

What exactly did Mark's first readers hear when his Jesus used the kingdom of God symbol? And what does my answer to that question imply for our understanding of the symbol in contemporary circumstances? These are the two questions that will preoccupy me as I consider the language of the kingdom in the earliest Gospel. Particularly, I will offer a linguistic interpretation of Mark's kingdom language in its historical context. I will subsequently argue that there are important analogies between that context and the context of the contemporary African-American church. Mark's narrative presentation of the kingdom symbol as a pocket of resistance, and the apocalyptic framework in which it sits, therefore, have powerful social, economic and political implications for the life and work of that church.

Mark's kingdom language communicates the projection of supernatural power that intervenes in human life and history. The symbol is spiritual because it demands a kind of interior trust, a belief that the kingdom whose reality is flashed into the present as a pocket moment will ultimately be consummated in full. It is social because it inspires believers to provoke other such pocket manifestations in their contemporary social and political histories. It is therefore both soteriological *and* political. Its soteriological goal is every bit as encouraging of socio-political activism as it is of redemptive spirituality. In fact, it is my contention that kingdom calls, which on the surface appear to have a singular spiritual orientation (such as the imperative "repent" of 1:15), also have dramatic socio-political implications.

One of the primary tasks of this project will be to determine the Markan parameters and characteristics of this kingdom symbol and the relationship of his Jesus-followers to it. I will therefore analyze Mark's kingdom language from a sociolinguistic perspective. Sociolinguistic theory holds that language does not convey meaning; rather, language conveys meaning potential. Individual words

conjure up a plethora of conceptual references. Conceptual references are elucidated by a host of individually distinct words. It is no wonder, then, that the
complex combination of words and conceptual references that make up a written text will play host to a variety of meaning possibilities.[1] Simply put, texts do
not harbor a single meaning possibility that can be uncovered by scientific endeavor the way a petrified Jurassic fossil is unearthed from a desert floor by an
experienced paleontologist. Instead, texts harbor meaning possibilities, meaning
potential. And this potential must be accessed contextually.

This means, in our case, that the Markan symbol, kingdom of God, is not an
objective linguistic marker with only one determinative meaning. The symbol is
filled with meaning potentiality. This potential was (for Mark's audience) and is
(for contemporary reading and interpreting audiences) accessed contextually. In
other words, the sociolinguistic location of the reader influences the perspective
from which he or she approaches a text. As a result, the reader accesses as
"meaning" that part of the potentiality that is most applicable to his or her social
and linguistic setting.[2]

At the historical level, sociolinguistic theory operates from a principle that
has been agreed upon in New Testament research since the advent of form criticism: the evangelists are not attempting historical biography when they relay
their Jesus stories. Every word placed in Jesus' mouth may not be his. The
chronology of events suggested by the Gospel outline does not necessarily agree
with the historical chronology of Jesus' actual ministry, and so on. The evangelists, in other words, are writing out of and for a particular religio-political
context. They have an interpretative agenda; their narrative about Jesus is written in service of that agenda. The material, then, is not meant to be taken as
literal "fact," but as proclamation. Indeed, "the primary intention of the biblical
writers was to awaken a commitment of faith from their readers, not simply to
inform them of events that had taken place."[3]

The fact that the evangelists write out of and for a particular religio-political
context suggests that they would have shared cultural and religious presuppositions with their intended reading audience. It is likely that they would anticipate
that, just as they were interpreting *for* their shared context, their audience would
interpret the narrative symbolic language *out of* that common environment. This
would explain why Mark could introduce a symbol as critical as the kingdom of
God without any kind of narrative explanation. Indeed, he not only refrains from
defining the symbol in chapter one, he never defines it. He apparently assumes

---

1. For an in-depth and more critical discussion of the semasiological and onomasiological re-
ality which establishes the potentiality of text meaning, see Blount, "Potential Meaning in Mark's
Trial Scenes," in *Cultural Interpretation: Reorienting New Testament Criticism* (Minneapolis:
Augsburg/Fortress Press, 1995) 89–109.

2. Ralph Fasold, *The Sociolinguistics of Language* (Cambridge, MA: Basil Blackwell, 1990).
"A possible consequence of this would be that speakers of different languages could stand side
by side and experience precisely the same event and yet understand it in profoundly different
ways....Furthermore, each would find it difficult or impossible to understand the event from the
other's perspective" (52).

3. Cf. Christopher Rowland and Mark Corner, *Liberating Exegesis: The Challenge of
Liberation Theology to Biblical Studies* (Louisville: Westminster/John Knox Press, 1989) 60.

his readers will "know what he means." He assumes they will access that part of the meaning potential that he intends because they approach the symbol from the same contextual horizon. In other words, he can write and anticipate a shared meaning experience precisely because of their shared sociolinguistic location.

In order to determine how meaning might have been contextually processed between author and reader, it is therefore critical that we delineate Mark's context as clearly as possible. We cannot understand how Mark and his intended audience accessed the potentiality of the kingdom symbol unless we first comprehend the context from which and to which he wrote.

A SOCIOLINGUISTIC APPROACH: CONTEXT IS KEY

Language is created and must be interpreted contextually because language is itself a contextual medium. It is created out of and for social circumstance. This is why at its most fundamental level biblical exegesis is a contextual enterprise. As Bruce J. Malina argues,

> Biblical scholarship is the interpretation of written language. Now written language does not live in scrolls or books. The markings on a page stand for wordings that represent meanings that can come alive only through the agency of the minds of readers.... What texts invariably communicate is information from a social system.[4]

Sociolinguist M. A. K. Halliday would agree. He observes that language is composed of signs. Only when these signs become part of a system are they capable of conveying meaning; the potentiality they represent is accessed as actual meaning through that system. A conglomeration of such systems is called a culture.[5] Because these system sets are a definitive part of a culture's make-up, and individual linguistic signs, like the marker "kingdom of God," take their meaning from these systems, the signs themselves have a cultural foundation. In order to interpret the signs and the texts they create, one must therefore approach them by way of their cultural-contextual foundation.

In other words, a text must never be studied in isolation from its con-text.

> There is text and there is other text that accompanies it: text that is "with," namely the con-text. This notion of what is "with the text," however, goes beyond what is said and written: it includes other non-verbal goings-on — the total environment in which a text unfolds.[6]

---

4. Bruce J. Malina, "The Social Sciences and Biblical Interpretation,"*Interpretation* 36 (1982): 229–30.

5. M. A. K. Halliday and Ruqaiya Hasan, *Language, Context, and Text: Aspects of Language in a Social Semiotic Perspective* (Oxford: Oxford University Press, 1990 [first published in 1985]) 4. Halliday defines culture as "a set of semiotic systems, a set of systems of meaning, all of which interrelate."

6. Ibid.

I am not advocating a simple literary analysis of the words and sentences preceding and following a designated text. I am making the more fundamental case that the performative social situation in and for which both the text and the literary con-text were fashioned must be evaluated and understood. Only then do we have our best chance of determining which particular slice of the meaning potentiality the original reading audience may have accessed as meaningful. In fact, as Halliday points out, the con-text is so critical to the interpretative process that a researcher should start there before he or she turns an investigative gaze upon the text. "I am going to talk about context first, for the reason that, in real life, contexts precede texts. The situation is prior to the discourse that relates to it."[7]

Halliday appeals specifically to the work of anthropologist Bronislaw Malinowski. Malinowski divided context into two theoretical components, the context of situation and the context of culture. "By context of situation, he meant the environment of the text."[8] Malinowski recognized that the pragmatic setting in which the text was uttered critically influenced how meaning was both vested in and accessed from that text. The more precisely one could define the context of a situation the more likely one would be able to access the text meaning in a manner appropriate to and for the original communicative situation.

Malinowski also recognized what he called context of culture. Because language is a part of the social systems which make up culture, knowing the total cultural background of the text writer/speaker and reader/hearer was as important to the interpretative process as was a knowledge of what was happening at the precise moment of communication (the context of situation).

Text is functional language; it performs a task in some particular context. It is therefore unlike isolated words or sentences scribbled randomly on a blackboard. Functionally speaking, then, a text is both a product and a process. As product, it is something that can be recorded and studied; it is comprised of a particular construction and is represented by particular system terms. It is also a process of semantic choice. That is to say, a text is not a puzzle whose interpretative solution can only be pieced together in a single way. Instead, it is a potential of meaning possibilities which are continually accessed according to the perspectives and presuppositions of its context, and (as I will argue below) the context of its interpreter. "A text, then, is both an object in its own right (it may be a highly valued object, for example, something that is recognised as a great poem) and an instance — an instance of social meaning in a particular context of situation."[9]

When analyzing a first-century text like the Gospel of Mark, a direct appeal to the contexts of situation and culture is impossible. The context must therefore be reconstructed. In the case of the context of culture, we are looking for "institutional and ideological background that give value to the text and constrain its interpretation.[10] The investigation would be historical. Various forms of

---

7. Ibid.
8. Ibid., 6.
9. Ibid.
10. Ibid., 49.

the historical-critical and literary models of biblical research have traditionally served this purpose, even if those models have traditionally failed to consider fully the consequences of subsequently interpreting the text language in light of those reconstructed conclusions.

Reconstructing the performative setting in which a first-century text found its life appears even less likely. Halliday believes, however, that, because the context of situation is embedded in the text, formulae of text appraisal can be developed which will ferret it out. He argues that if text and context are treated as "semiotic phenomena," as categories of discourse, an interpreter should be able to get at the latter from the former. He therefore devised a theoretical tool specifically aimed at evaluating the various modes of language in order to ascertain, through the language of the text itself, the context of situation in which that language took its shape.

He is concerned with three primary modes of discourse. The first is the field of discourse: what is happening in the text. Here the investigator wants to determine the particular situation in which the participants are engaged, and in which their language plays a critical role.

The second is the tenor of discourse. The tenor denotes the conversation partners who are taking part in the situation under investigation. Here the investigator would be concerned with the nature of the participants, their status, their roles and role relationships, their speech, and the relationships they form.

The third is the mode of discourse. The mode specifies what part the language is playing. Here the investigator wants to know what the participants expect the language to do for them in the situation in which they are involved. Text language, it is to be remembered, is ultimately functional in its design.[11]

In fact, Halliday argues that language, like any other tool, is shaped by its purposes.[12] Three global metafunctions are primary. The first is the ideational, the intent of language to convey sense. Concepts are symbolically encoded and communicated so that sensory data can be exchanged between language partners. The specific function of this language category, then, is the encoding of human experience in the form of conceptual content.

The second is the interpersonal. Language relays interaction between characters in a text. Narrative conversation partners are impacted and "moved" by words said or actions conveyed.

> The sentence is not only a representation of reality; it is also a piece of interaction between speaker and listener. Whereas in its experiential meaning language is a way of reflecting, in its interpersonal meaning language is a way of acting; we could in fact use that terminology, and talk about *language as reflection* and *language as action* as another way of referring to experiential and interpersonal meaning.[13]

---

11. Ibid., 12.
12. Ibid., 44.
13. Ibid., 20.

I would also argue, however, that the interpersonal metafunction operates beyond the confines of the text's semantic boundaries. The text writer/speaker and the text reader/hearer(s) (or, in the case of an ancient text, the text interpreter) are critical components of the text interpretative process. Because text language is also meant to perform some function in the reader/hearer (interpreter) on behalf of the writer/speaker, all of whom stand outside the actual text, knowing the characteristics of these text interlocutors, whether they be ancient or contemporary, is vital to the process of text interpretation. It is therefore impossible to consider how a text would be meaningfully accessed without accounting for these vital, and also *interpersonal,* but in this case, "context of culture" criteria.

Finally, the textual function specifies the text's lexico-grammatical balance, focus and intent. These are the components of language which give it its texture and coherence. While it therefore includes grammar and lexicography, it goes well beyond those limited categories; it also includes what that grammar achieves, its value and its topicality.[14]

Halliday argues that all language operations are multifunctional. Each of the three metafunctions is always operational within any context of situation and context of culture. Therefore, in order to determine how meaning was accessed from a particular context, to predict how it will be accessed from some other particular context, or to determine the influence the contextual situation of the interpreter will have on either of those interpretative processes, an investigator's text evaluation should take all three metafunctions into account. It seems to me that this has not been done in studies of the kingdom of God in the Gospel of Mark. Investigators have operated almost exclusively in the textual and ideational domains. The interpersonal, particularly as it relates to context of culture, but just as significantly in the consideration of context of situation, is given lesser priority, if it is considered at all.

"But in fact the relationship between text and context is a dialectical one: the text creates the context as much as the context creates the text. 'Meaning' arises from the friction between the two."[15] Which is to say, one cannot understand how meaning was accessed between writer/speaker and reader/hearer (or interpreter) unless one understands and appreciates the context in which a text has taken shape. The linguistic forms of the text may exist on a page or piece of papyrus, but meaning only develops from and through the forms in the midst of a context. It is for this reason that Halliday specifically relates the modes of discourse that make up the context of situation with the metafunctions of language operation. The field of discourse is expressed through the ideational metafunction. Conceptual language functions to communicate the experience of what is happening in the text. The tenor of discourse is expressed through the interpersonal function. Interpersonal language functions to communicate how characters in the text interrelate and establish role relationships. On the level of context of culture, where I also wish to push the interpersonal, the tenor involves the relationship between the writer/speaker and his or her readers/hearers (inter-

---

14. Ibid., 23.
15. Ibid., 47.

preters). The character of that relationship, particularly as that character is given shape by the cultural backgrounds of the individuals involved, will have a dramatic impact on how meaning is accessed (or how the writer/speaker will predict that it will be accessed) from the written or spoken text. Finally, the mode of discourse is expressed through the textual metafunction. Textual language functions to communicate how the text coheres in its pursuit of a particular goal or goals.

To summarize, I am suggesting that the Markan linguistic symbol, "kingdom of God," does not by itself convey meaning. Instead, it conveys a potentiality of meaning that is delimited (accessed) contextually. Therefore, given that meaning occurs as a result of the friction between text and context, in order to develop a better understanding of how Mark's original readers/hearers may have accessed his kingdom text meaningfully, and for that matter how he would have predicted they would access it (given that we agree they share the same contexts of culture and situation), we must use the sociolinguistic tools available to reconstruct both their contexts of situation and culture.

A BIBLICAL MODEL FOR SOCIOLINGUISTICS

It is my plan to apply Halliday's model to the task of biblical inquiry. I, therefore, start from the interpersonal premise that texts have the functional objective of affecting either characters who live inside the story or readers/interpreters who stand outside it. They do this by conveying information that will produce some desired effect. My task, then, if I am to access that interpersonal-functional intent, as well as the ideational and textual information used to process it, must be one of describing as definitively as possible the applicable contexts in which the three metafunctions operate. I believe that the contextual reference points Rudolf Bultmann described as life relation and preunderstanding will help me achieve exactly that end.

Although Bultmann limited his understanding of contextual influence to the existential situation of the reader/interpreter, he did recognize the importance context played in the interpretative process. Bultmann perceived that an interpreter's conclusions regarding the meaning of a text were inextricably bound to the kinds of questions he or she brought to the investigative task. He believed incorrectly that these presuppositional questions were always existential. The "meaning" conclusions reached would therefore also necessarily be existentially oriented. Bultmann consequently designated two variables which would describe how the process of existential (contextual) influence would take place. He labelled them preunderstanding and life relation.[16]

---

16. For a fuller examination of this discussion, see Blount, *Cultural Interpretation,* 31–32. For primary reading cf. Rudolf Bultmann, *Jesus Christ and Mythology* (New York: Charles Scribner's Sons, 1958) esp. 46–58; "Is Exegesis Without Presupposition Possible?" in *Existence and Faith: Shorter Writings of Rudolf Bultmann,* Schubert M. Ogden, editor and translator (New York: Meridian Books, 1960); "The Significance of 'Dialectical Theology' for Scientific Study of the New Testament," in *Faith and Understanding,* Louise Pettibone Smith, translator (New York:

While it is clear that Bultmann's existential category was not as universal as he'd thought, the variables he developed can be applied in a way that helps us understand the influence of context upon text interpretation in a more global sense. I will therefore apply his categories of preunderstanding and life relation in a manner that moves beyond existential inquiry into the realm of the more general inquiry of sociolinguistics.

Preunderstanding involves the interpersonal dialectic between interpreter and history. An interpreter cannot comprehend history, or, for that matter, a historical text, unless he or she acknowledges that part of himself/herself stands in history and is responsible for it. As Bultmann explains, we can only understand the concept "joy of Christ," or "death" because of a historical preunderstanding. Our mortality prevents us from knowing either supernatural joy or death in an absolute sense. We can, however, understand them in a limited fashion because of a preunderstanding that derives from our past history. We have experienced our own limited joys, and we have witnessed death in the finite way that it occurs in human living. In other words, we bring our own contextual history to our attempt to understand a text about supernatural joy or ultimate death. That history provides a context through which we can arrive at some semblance of understanding. That understanding is therefore contextually marked.

Life relation operates from the premise that every reader/interpreter possesses a relationship to the subject matter contained in a text. This relationship gives the interpreter a unique perspective and consequent understanding of the matter discussed in the text. From such an understanding come the conceptions that drive and radically influence exegesis. "This is, then, the basic presupposition for every form of exegesis: that your own relation to the subject matter prompts the questions you bring to the text and elicits the answer you obtain from the text."[17]

Connecting these two contextual criteria with Halliday's functional categories directs me toward the following model of biblical sociolinguistics.[18] At the first level, the historical, I want to determine how the context of situation and the context of culture in the first century influenced the manner in which Mark encoded meaning in the language of his text. I want, in other words, to reconstruct the context Mark shared with his reading audience in a way that will

---

Harper and Row, 1969) esp. 157–59, where Bultmann explains "joy" and "death" in terms of preunderstanding.

17. Bultmann, *Jesus Christ and Mythology,* 50–51.

18. Malina discusses the necessity of building such sociolinguistic models from the point of view of reading comprehension. He presses the point that psychologists and linguists conclude that human readers operate from either a propositional or scenario model of reading. The propositional model considers text to be a kind of super sentence. The focus is therefore on the level of the sentence and word of a text. A reader parses the text into propositional units and then connects those units to create meaning. Our appeal to sociolinguistic theory has already pointed out the flaw in such a model. Words and sentences, absent their contexts of situation and culture, do not convey meaning. The more contextually appropriate scenario model considers the text a succession of explicit and implicit scenes or schemes in which a mental representation is evoked in the mind of the reader. That representation consists of a series of settings, episodes or models directed by the text. The reader's task here is to identify an appropriate "domain of reference" which will call to mind an appropriate scene, scheme or model suggested by the text. The reader will then use that domain of reference as an access point (a model) in delimiting the "meaning" of the text. Cf. Malina, 229–30.

help me understand how persons within that context would delimit the meaning potentiality of a Markan text on the kingdom of God.

This *historical*-contextual reconstruction is founded upon the two categories of life relation and preunderstanding. The life relation in this case corresponds to the context of situation. Here, I want to reconstruct the performative location in which the Markan text took shape so that I can predict how language would have been meaningfully accessed from it. "The assumption is that the text represents an abridged version of a real conversation and that by detailed attention to text and context the assumed context can be re-created, leading to a new and valid understanding of the dialogue."[19]

Preunderstanding corresponds to the context of culture. Here I want to reconstruct the global environment that shaped the presuppositions Mark's first-century readers brought with them to their reading/hearing of his Jesus narrative. Given that first-century readers accessed meaning contextually, "it would seem that the best a contemporary biblical scholar can offer is a set of domains of reference deriving from and appropriate to the social world from which the texts derive and thus facilitate biblical understanding."[20]

To the degree that I am able to reconstruct the historical-contextual environment of the Markan text I should theoretically be able to predict how writers/speakers and readers/hearers in that environment would have meaningfully accessed the linguistic potentiality of his texts on the kingdom of God. The ability to make such critical predictions involves the sociolinguistic category called register.

Halliday notes that we continually hear of contemporary breakdowns in communication, sometimes to devastating effect. He argues, however, that, given the complexity of modern society, we should be more amazed at the fact that successful communication exists. How are we to explain this success? "The short answer," suggests Halliday, "is that we know what the other person is going to say. We always have a good idea of what is coming next, so that we are seldom totally surprised."[21]

Sociolinguistics is concerned with how these mostly subconscious "predictions" are made. "The first step towards an answer is: we make them from the context of situation. The situation in which linguistic interaction takes place gives the participants a great deal of information about the meanings that are being exchanged, and the meanings that are likely to be exchanged."[22] In other words, as Halliday goes on to explain, participants in any culture make use of a

---

19. Peter Cotterell, "Sociolinguistics and Biblical Interpretation," *Vox Evangelica* 16 (1986): 61. Halliday offers a brief example. "For example, you might hear something like this: 'Well, I've come to see you because I've been having this pain. Had it on and off for ever such a long time and never done anything about it. Tried to forget about it really, I suppose.' That will probably be a middle-aged or elderly woman describing her symptoms to the doctor. It is a woman's language rather than a man's language. It is an old person's language rather than a young person's. It is in a private doctor's clinic rather than a hospital; and so on. We can reconstruct a lot about the situation just by attending to that little bit of text" (38).

20. Malina, 231.

21. Halliday and Hasan, 9.

22. Ibid., 10.

close relationship between the text and context as a foundation for establishing successful communication.[23] The success occurs because, based on the fact that they are operating from a shared context, the speakers are able to predict and therefore understand what the other intends to say and mean.

> I am not saying, of course, that either the participant in the situation, or the linguist looking over his or her shoulder, can predict the text in the sense of actually guessing in advance exactly what is going to be said or written; obviously not. What I am saying is that we can and do (and must) make inferences from the situation into the text, about the kinds of meaning that are likely to be exchanged; and also inferences from the text to the situation.[24]

This is register. Halliday points out that there can be open or closed registers. A closed register utilizes restricted language. Here the range of meaning possibilities is fixed. There are, in other words, tight limits on the meaning potentiality. Interpretative conclusions ought therefore to operate meaningfully within those limits. Halliday poses the example of the international language of pilots. When communicating with ground control, airline pilots use a fixed language. They keep the total message language within a certain fixed range. They will not, he suggests, start discussing the state of high fashion design. Such talk would fall outside the bounds of the tightly limited register. As a result, an interpreter of a text conversation between a French pilot and his or her ground controller whose exegetical efforts concluded that the pilot's language indicated an interest in the latest fabrics taxiing across a Paris fashion runway would be operating from the start on shaky ground.

The register limits the range of meaning potentiality. Within those limits communication can occur because the limitations provide for the possibility that conversation partners can predict what the other is going to say. Interpretative investigations should operate freely within those contextual boundaries. Everyday conversation is more open-ended, of course, so here the suggested boundaries would be more expansive (open registers). Still, boundaries do exist, and interpretative procedure must operate within them if it is to access the meaning of conversation partners within those originally shared boundaries.

> There is no situation in which the meanings are not to a certain extent prescribed for us. There is always some feature of which we can say, "This is typically associated with this or that use of language." Even the most informal spontaneous conversation has its strategies and styles of meaning. We are never selecting with complete freedom from all the resources of our linguistic system. If we were, there would be no communication; we understand each other only because we are able to make predictions, subconscious guesses, about what the other person is going to say.[25]

---

23. Ibid., 36.
24. Ibid.
25. Ibid., 40.

We make that prediction about a biblical text by attending as closely as we possibly can to the situational and cultural text environment. The historical-contextual reconstruction, in other words, helps us limit the meaning potentiality, and therefore makes it more likely that we will access it in the way the first-century Markan audience would have.

RECONSTRUCTING MARK'S CONTEXT: APOCALYPTIC INTERVENTION

It is my contention that a reconstruction of the socio-historical context (of culture) and story-world context (of situation) in which Mark situated his kingdom of God language can be described with two words: apocalyptic intervention. Apocalyptic intervention, in other words, conveys the register which bounds the language potentiality for Mark and his community. By understanding this register we will have the best opportunity to predict how these two conversation partners would have accessed the symbol, kingdom of God.

The adjective "apocalyptic" refers to the context of culture, the mythological preunderstanding that shaped the climate in which Mark and his readers lived. Mark operated within a Palestinian-Syrian, Jewish environment whose expectations of ultimate deliverance by God were mythically realized through the language of apocalyptic story. While the mythical stories themselves could be quite uniquely narrated, they operated from the common premise that God would imminently establish a holy reign. That supernatural rule would deliver and vindicate the "elect" people from their persecutors and persecutions. Mark wrote and should be interpreted with this preunderstanding in mind.

The noun "intervention" refers to the context of situation, Mark's narrative life relation. The historical preunderstanding that God was imminently about to break into human history was encoded in the story in the form of boundary intervention. Human boundaries are demolished as Jesus preaches and enacts his kingdom message. Though we do not see the ultimate deliverance and vindication of the faithful elect, we see its foreshadowing as Mark narrates the story of Jesus and his disciples whose very lives embody the shattering of conventional cultic, social and political margins. The Markan characterization of these boundaries as overwhelming barriers that are themselves overwhelmed by Jesus represents for Mark's readers what the bizarre symbolism of apocalyptic mythology represented for the wider Jewish-Palestinian world of the first century: supernatural, kingdom intervention into human history and affairs.

A BRIEF TEST CASE

The Markan language of repentance provides an opportunity to test my model. Because an appeal to the context of culture would draw me too far afield at present, demanding a consideration of how the language of repentance was used in the ancient world, as well as analyzing related ideologies and institutions of the time, I shall, in this example, confine my inquiry to the context of situation.

Even this limited sample evaluation will prove helpful to the defense of my argument that Mark's kingdom of God symbol was accessed socio-politically as well as spiritually by his readers. Because socio-political activity is a manifestly human endeavor, I would need, as a first step, to demonstrate that Mark considered humans capable of directly wielding supernatural kingdom power. An analysis of the context of situation establishes that Mark and his readers would have accessed the potentiality of his repentance language in this way.

Mark uses the language of repentance only three times in his text. In the first instance, 1:4, he narrates the mission of John the Baptist as one of preaching a baptism of repentance for the forgiveness of sins. The other two uses are verbal. At 1:15, Jesus, who has submitted himself to John's baptism of repentance, preaches that because the kingdom of God has drawn near, humans should repent and believe in the gospel. Finally, at 6:12, following Jesus' authorization of his disciples to go forth and exorcise unclean spirits, we learn that besides exorcisms, anointings, and healings, the disciples preached that people should repent.

How might Mark have expected his readers to access the meaning potential of "repent"? A first step toward answering that question is the reconstruction of the context of situation of the word repent. Mark does not define it. There is no definitive preparation for its use in 1:4, and his subsequent uses in 1:15 and 6:12 do not offer any clarifying discussion. We can only surmise that either he didn't care whether his hearers/readers understood what he was trying to say when he used it (which would be counter to the functional understanding: that he was using his language to "do" something), or we can presume that because he shared a common context with his hearers/readers he realized that the potentiality would be sufficiently limited so that they would be able to access the meaning he intended.

The latter presumption suggests that if we are to have a reasonable expectation of accessing that same meaning we must reconstruct the context of situation in which the communication between Mark and his audience took place. I will therefore take each of the texts in turn.

In the first episode, which centers on 1:4, the field of discourse is clear. John, the one who baptizes, is being introduced. However, the introduction occurs only after a proclamation that the text is going to be about a certain Jesus Christ, Son of God. John's story, then, is obviously not the central story. We must therefore determine what role it has to play in relationship to the Jesus story.

We know immediately that the story is framed by Mark's citation of the Exodus event (23:20) and the messages of the Hebrew Prophets, Isaiah (40:3) and Malachi (3:1), at 1:2–3, even though only Isaiah is cited. Indeed, one might speculate that because Mark quotes from both prophets but only credits Isaiah, he expects his readers to be unaware that he has offered a hybrid prophecy. They must not, therefore, be well versed in Hebrew prophetic history. In the end, such a speculation could neither be proven nor disproven (the body of Hebrew prophecy is vast enough that it would not be remarkable that a reading or listening audience did not know which prophet proclaimed which statements), and thus becomes contextually irrelevant.

What is clear, however, is that whether they know their prophetic history or not, Mark's readers trust his representation of it. Mark's voice is an authoritative one, and the evangelist knows it. He therefore conjoins the statements of two different prophets and presents them as a single prophecy which related specifically to this Jesus Christ, Son of God, knowing that his readers would not quibble about accuracy of representation, but would instead seek the *meaning* behind the fact that a revered prophetic conveyance of God's word applied to Mark's central narrative figure. Our task, therefore, is to bypass analysis of the hybrid nature of the prophecy in favor of a concentrated effort to determine the *meaning* behind the "fact" that the life and story of this Jesus figure, not to mention the mission and ministry of John the Baptist, were supernaturally foreordained from the time of classical prophecy.

The quotation (1:2–3) declares that one shall come as a messenger to prepare the way of the Lord. Both the primary characters, Jesus Christ, i.e., the Lord of 1:1, 3 (cf. related prophecy in 1:2: προσώπου σου — your face; τὴν ὁδόν σου — your way), and John the Baptist, the messenger whom 1:2 claims will prepare the way of the Lord (cf. related prophecy at 1:3: φωνὴ βοῶντος ἐν τῇ ἐρήμῳ — a voice of one crying in the wilderness), are promised in this prophecy of preparation.[26]

We are therefore led to infer that John's character functions to prepare Jesus' way. This point is confirmed when John's pronouncement that a mightier one comes after him (1:7–8) segues without pause into Mark's narrative introduction of Jesus at verse nine. It is here in verses seven and eight that we also learn about John's baptism; it is a symbolic, ritual act implemented with water. The proclamation and execution of this act are John's narrative priority. Hordes of people came out to him and submitted to it. They did so as they were confessing their sins. Jesus, the one who follows John (literally, as far as Mark's character presentation is concerned), will perform a similar ritual. His feat, however, will be consummated with the Holy Spirit.

The tenor of discourse tells us who is acting in the scene. There are two primary actors. The son of God is the first one mentioned at 1:1. When he appears

---

26. We connect Lord with Jesus Christ, Son of God, because of the semantic parallelism between verses 2 (τὴν ὁδόν σου) and 3 (τὴν ὁδὸν κυρίου). Joel Marcus also appeals to balance between "your way" in 1:2 and "the way of the Lord" in 1:3. He, too, concludes that the parallelism indicates a literary relationship between Jesus and the Lord. "It is obvious from the Markan context, moreover, that John the Baptist, the messenger who prepares the way of Jesus (1:2), is also the voice that speaks of preparing the way of the Lord (1:3). One path, therefore, seems to be described in 1:2–3 under two names: 'your [Jesus'] way' and 'the way of the Lord.' A very close connection between Jesus and the Lord is thus implied by 1:2–3." Cf. Joel Marcus, *The Way of the Lord: Christological Exegesis of the Old Testament in the Gospel of Mark* (Louisville: Westminster/John Knox Press, 1992) 37–38.

Mary Ann Tolbert makes a different kind of still textual argument. She appeals to the chiastic structure of 1:1–13, which she understands to be the prologue of the gospel. The rhetorical balance between 1:1–3 and 4:11–13 indicate that Jesus is the central figure in both sets of verses. Cf. *Sowing the Gospel: Mark's World in Literary-Historical Perspective* (Minneapolis: Fortress Press, 1989) 112. For an extended textual and ideational discussion leading to the same conclusion, cf. 239–48.

in the flesh in verse nine, it is clear that Mark intends to narrate a story whose working premise is that a supernatural figure has, in accordance with ancient prophetic witness, intervened in human reality. In this single person two mutually exclusive realities, the supernatural and the mortal, have intersected in a very intimate way.[27] It is this reality of supernatural intervention (1:1–3, 9) that not only provides the foundation not only for Jesus' own baptismal efforts (1:7–8), but also offers an explanatory preface and thematic basis for John's baptism of repentance (1:4–6).

John, the real protagonist of this scene, is the second character. The field of discourse emphasizes a relationship between his baptism of repentance and the cessation of sins (1:4–5). This sense of negation is narratively confirmed by the tenor of John's character (1:6). Even without a cultural knowledge of the dress and living habits of the time, we can conclude that he has rejected woven clothing and prepared food and has chosen an occupational domicile in the wilderness. John thereby consciously avoids the very centers of human population where one would think potential candidates for his baptismal rites would have been more plentiful. His very character embodies the role of negation.

Here, of course, we are entering into the mode of discourse. The purpose of the activity in this text is directed toward getting people who have been properly motivated by an awareness of the supernatural intruding upon human space to confess (and thus presumably cease) their sins, seek John and submit to his baptismal rite of repentance.

The preliminary conclusion from the context of situation surrounding 1:4 is that both Jesus and John baptize. John clearly baptizes into repentance. The inference from verse eight is that Jesus does so as well. The situation which necessitates this activity is the intimate intervention of the supernatural into human history in the form of a human person.[28] For John this repentance involves a negation.

The second text, which centers on 1:15, establishes Jesus as the protagonist. The field of discourse instructs that Jesus, the one who will baptize with Holy Spirit, comes from Nazareth in Galilee and is baptized by John (1:9). The narration affirms Jesus' baptism by citing the opening of the heavens and the descent

---

27. Marcus notes how this exclusivity will be presented dramatically in the baptism scene. Appealing to E. Lohmeyer, he recognizes that the tearing of the heavens, which Mark indicates with the verb σχίζειν, is based upon a dualistic understanding of the human and divine realms. "[The tearing of the heavens] is rooted in the view that heaven and earth are shut up against each other, so that God can no longer associate with his people in an unmediated manner, or they with him, as once happened. It is therefore a sign of unusual grace when the heaven opens. This occurs in a miracle that embraces the entirety of the people or of the world; not accidentally, the motif is found almost solely in apocalypses." Ibid., 56.

28. This conclusion is all the more probable since Matthew and Luke agree against Mark by citing the Isaiah 40:3 text only *after* they have introduced John the Baptist and his baptism into the repentance of sins (Mt 3:1–6; Lk 3:1–6). The Malachi quotations have been, in both cases, removed from the John the Baptist context altogether. If Marcus is correct in his conclusion that Mark is responsible for placing the material *before* the introduction of John the Baptist, rather than after as it appeared in Q, then it appears even more likely that the evangelist was using the material to stress to his readers that John's person and role be evaluated against the background of divine intervention in the person of Jesus as Lord. Ibid., 11–17.

of the Spirit in the form of a dove. A heavenly voice then confirms what Mark narrated at verse one: Jesus is the son of God.

Immediately after the supernatural declaration of affirmation comes an action by the Spirit. It pushes Jesus out into the wilderness for forty days where Satan, another supernatural figure, tempts him (1:12–13), and where Jesus interacts with angels, yet more supernatural figures. John is later arrested, and afterward Jesus comes to Galilee preaching, "the time is fulfilled, the kingdom of God is at hand, repent and believe the gospel" (1:15).

The immediate scene comes to a close when Jesus, who *will* baptize, follows up his preaching (1:14–15) declaration, just as John, who *has been* baptizing, followed up his preaching — by interacting with inhabitants of the region. In Jesus' interaction, however, there is no call for a confession of sins. In fact, the language of sin is missing altogether. Instead, he calls the inhabitants, who are fishermen, to follow him by extending their fishing enterprise to luring and catching humans.

The tenor of discourse provides us with several characters. Jesus and John we've already met. Jesus' representation as a supernatural figure intersecting human reality (1:1–3, 7–8) is confirmed in this second scene. The heavens open for him. The supernatural voice speaks to him. The Holy Spirit descends upon him. In fact, this intersection between the human and supernatural realms becomes almost commonplace by the time the scene ends. The Spirit acts historically again, as does Satan, who tests Jesus, while angels consort with him in the wilderness. Just as John's preaching of baptism into repentance took place against a backdrop of supernatural intervention, so does Jesus' preaching to the similar end of repentance (1:15) take place against the backdrop of the supernatural intervening intimately, and now routinely, in human affairs. This fact of intervention stands behind the evident urgency of John's and Jesus' calls. It is an urgency evidenced by the fact that John negates a life of normalcy, and Jesus declares that time itself has been filled up.

In the mode of discourse, though, a striking dissimilarity between the characterization of Jesus and John develops. Repentance means something different for the two of them. Although both demand it as the appropriate response to the intersection of supernatural and human realities, for Jesus it is a new kind of behavior. It is no longer the negation (i.e., ἄφεσιν, leaving behind), the confession of unacceptable, but already accomplished, sinful behavior. It is instead the affirmation and acceptance of a new life of "fishing" discipleship. Indeed, while the ideational language of sin surfaces twice (1:4–5) in the Johannine context of situation, it is noticeably absent in this second narrative situation. This is all the more remarkable given the fact that the Jesus context deploys all the other language of preaching, baptism and repentance. The two contexts encourage two distinct ways of accessing the meaning potential of the same linguistic marker.[29]

---

29. No wonder, then, that the Son of God would submit to a baptism of repentance. As far as the characters and readers are contextually concerned, where the Son is involved repentance should be accessed as a positive, affirming response to the realization that the divine is operating within the boundaries of human reality. It is a positive orientation of obedient discipleship. This kind of response is as appropriate for the Son of God (who therefore submits himself to a baptism

Mark also uses this new context to clarify what he means by supernatural intervention. While in the John scene intervention occurs indirectly — the Lord's presence and mission is predicted (1:1–3, 7–8), in the Jesus scene intervention occurs in the narration, through the direct speech of God, and through the characterization of the primary player. Jesus proclaims that the kingdom of God, his father, is at hand. Therefore repent. But we already have the contextual sense that Jesus demands repentance against the same background as John; the supernatural has intervened into human reality. And we know that according to the context of situation this intervention takes place primarily through the character of Jesus himself. All the other supernatural interventions are projected at his character and exist in the story not independently, as he does, but in relationship to him. The kingdom of God language, for example, does not occur independently in this context of situation, but in relationship to Jesus' prophetically ordained mission of baptizing into repentance (1:7–8).

The contextual meaning therefore seems to be: (A) Repentance operates from the foundational realization that the supernatural is intervening in human reality. (B) Jesus Christ, the Son of God, the Lord, is that act of intervention (cf. vv. 1–3, 7–8, 10–13). (C) Therefore, when, at 1:15, this same repentance operates from the foundational realization that the kingdom of God (which only occurs in the con-text because Jesus preaches) is at hand — which is to say, is intervening into human reality — the narration can only make contextual sense if (D) Jesus also represents that kingdom. The symbol, kingdom of God, is for Mark contextually manifested and, therefore, given narrative content in this situation by the characterization of Jesus Christ, Son of God, Lord.

Immediately after his programmatic proclamation that the kingdom of God was at hand and that humans should respond with repentance and faith, Jesus calls disciples to follow him. Immediately after the call narrative, Mark demonstrates the kind of authority Jesus projects. The man who proclaims the kingdom wields kingdom power. Indeed, through Jesus' person and activities the future kingdom is making a present appearance. The litany of miracle stories that ensue in chapter one is a clear illustration of Jesus' kingdom might. He represents the incursion of supernatural force breaking into human reality. His healings are "pockets" of wholeness which resist the brokenness of disease that has as much a foundation in cosmic defiance as it does biological disturbance. And in each pocket moment the power, the authority, and the hope of the future kingdom are revealed. It is not just that the future kingdom is being previewed in Jesus' healings; in a very tangible way, in the transfiguration from dis-ease to wholeness the kingdom is concretely present. In the wider context of chapter one's Jesus situation, it becomes increasingly clear that supernatural reality is intruding upon the human circumstance and that its power is being administered by a human agent.

The third appearance of the repentance language occurs at 6:12. In this field

---

of repentance) as it is for followers whom he would evidently baptize with Holy Spirit. Indeed, Mark's appeal to the divine phrase "in you I am well pleased" (ἐν σοὶ εὐδόκησα) indicates that Jesus' obedience to God as son is being showcased. Cf. Gottlob Schrenk, "εὐδοκέω, εὐδοκία," G. Kittel, ed., *Theological Dictionary of the New Testament* (hereafter *TDNT*) G. W. Bromiley, translator (Grand Rapids, Mich.: Eerdmans, 1964–76) 2:738–50.

of discourse, Mark narrates Jesus' authorization of his twelve followers to evangelize and have authority over unclean spirits. He charges them to carry little on their missionary journey. And incredibly, he tells them that if they are not received, they must leave the place and shake the dust of its habitation from their feet as a testimony against them. We are then told that their primary role (i.e., fishing) was also one of preaching toward repentance, 6:12. Also, like Jesus, they cast out many demons and healed. In other words, in this field of discourse, as it was in the Jesus context of situation, repentance language is followed up by the language of affirmation. Indeed, even their direction of discipleship, as opposed to John's positioning of his ministry, suggests affirmation. "The radicality of discipleship as Mark pictures it is evident in the demand of Jesus that all ordinary human ties and obligations be set aside, *not in a retreat to the desert*, however, but to go out into the world-wide mission."[30]

We have, of course, already introduced the tenor of discourse by discussing the parallel roles of preaching for repentance that Mark accords to John the Baptist, Jesus, and Jesus' disciples. But the tenor of discourse focuses more sharply on the interaction between Jesus and his twelve (3:14), and the subsequent interaction between the twelve, the inhabitants of the land, and spiritual powers. Once again there is supernatural intervention. Unclean spirits and demons populate the countryside. The disciples utilize their Jesus-authorized power to protect the inhabitants of the land from demonic force. This protection forms the background for their preaching toward repentance. That is to say, the language of supernatural intervention, and human activity in light of that intervention, still forms the backdrop for the language of repentance. The urgency of the time is also on display in the interaction between the twelve and any who reject their message. The mission of the twelve is so important that they are not to weigh themselves down with unnecessary baggage. They must move quickly. Most importantly, they must offer a choice to the persons they meet. The choice is so important and must be proclaimed so rapidly that they are not to stay and bicker with recalcitrant inhabitants, but must present their message of repentance and leave. The supernatural kingdom is at hand. Time cannot be wasted.

In the mode of discourse, therefore, we find that the twelve are to preach with the same goal that preoccupied Jesus' and John's preaching: repentance in the face of supernatural intervention (6:12). And the follow up to that preaching is, as it was in Jesus' case, the enactment of affirming behavior (6:13). The disciples' actions, then, do what Jesus' presence does, effect the intersection of supernatural power into human reality.[31] While John's actions could only witness to that intersection in the form of John's proclamation of the one to come, in the Jesus material, Jesus' person attracts the activity of supernatural characters

---

30. Howard Clark Kee, *Community of the New Age: Studies in Mark's Gospel* (Philadelphia: Westminster Press, 1977) 89. Emphasis mine.

31. Adela Collins makes a similar point by appealing to the miracle language of chapter 9 and suggesting a comparison of the material here with the teaching on prayer at Mark 11:22–25. "Further, by portraying Jesus in the context of a miracle story as saying, 'All things are possible for the believer' (9:23), the Gospel implies that ordinary humans may share the omnipotence of God." Adela Yarbro Collins, *The Beginning of the Gospel: Probings of Mark in Context* (Minneapolis: Fortress Press, 1992) 40.

like Satan, the angels in the wilderness, the demon at the synagogue in 1:21–28, and, most importantly, the heavenly voice of God at 1:11. Jesus also demonstrates his ability to bring human reality into the reality of the supernatural by healing various infirmities. At 1:32–34, Mark makes it clear that the healings and the exorcisms are all pieces of the same cloth. In each case Jesus' actions are representative of supernatural power intervening into human reality. Jesus, who, according to the context of situation, represents the kingdom, is therefore capable of drawing the power of the supernatural kingdom into the realm of human conflict and illness at will.

At 6:7, Jesus appoints the disciples to the very same task. It is no wonder, then, that their preaching activity (3:14, κηρύσσειν; 6:12, ἐκήρυξαν) is described in terms very similar to Jesus' preaching activity (1:14, κηρύσσων), including the seldom used verb "repent" (6:12, μετανοῶσιν; 1:15, μετανοεῖτε), the recognition of exorcism (6:13, ἐξέβαλλον; 1:34, ἐξέβαλεν) and healing (6:13, ἐθεράπευον; 1:34, ἐθεράπευσεν). Their proclamation of repentance, too, is backed up with an ability to interject supernatural power into human activity. Indeed, an examination of the context of culture would tell us that their "dusting off" activity is so dramatically connected to the in-breaking power of the supernatural that those who do not heed their preaching word are deemed subject to a highly convicting symbolic act of judgment.[32]

When we consider the three scenes together we come to the following context of situation resolutions. The field of discourse narrates the intersection of supernatural and human realities. The supernatural intervened. Recognition of this intrusion demands repentance, in the form of John's confessions, and in the form of following Jesus, which is, in essence, a call to call (fish) others to follow.

The tenor of discourse, though it also deals with the roles of John the Baptist and various supernatural figures and forces, centers primarily on the relationship between Jesus, his disciples, and the inhabitants of the land. We are particularly interested in how Jesus' ability to manipulate the kingdom power in his person and through his behavior becomes the ultimate foundation for the call to repentance. Jesus authorizes his followers to make the same call, and then empowers them to back that call up with actions that, like his, manipulate the same kind of power. In the confines of these three scenes, it can only be kingdom power. Mark presents no other. Just as Jesus' interpersonal activities with the inhabitants of the land are contextualized by the intersection of the supernatural and the human realities, so now it appears that the interpersonal interactions of Jesus' disciples with the inhabitants of the land operate within the same contextual domain.

The mode of discourse makes this clear. Their "following" behavior, which is in itself a repentant response to the realization that the kingdom is at hand and intruding into human reality, has an explicit purpose: to effect repentance. Every time they call for repentance (6:12), back that repentance up against the realization that supernatural power is intruding upon human reality (6:7–11), and affirm

---

32. D. E. Nineham, *The Gospel of Saint Mark* (New York: Pelican Books, 1979 [first published in 1963]) 170 and Eduard Schweizer, *The Good News According to Mark* (Atlanta: John Knox Press, 1970) 130–31.

that realization with the kingdom power of healing or exorcism (6:13), they establish an alarmingly tense intersection between the power of the kingdom and the reality of human existence that demands radical decision. This is what their "repent" interaction with the "inhabitant" characters of the text is all about.

This study of the context of situation demonstrates, then, how we should access the meaning potentiality of the linguistic marker "repent." Repentance is the proper response to the realization that the kingdom of God is at hand. It is an impetus of affirmation for Jesus and his twelve, rather than the impetus for negation that it was for John. When Jesus calls for repentance, he does not demand the confession of sins. Instead he calls disciples to follow. Their following leads them to do what Jesus does, preach repentance, and, as a demonstration of the gravity of the choice before listeners, preach that repentance against a backdrop where they manipulate the power of the kingdom.

Human disciples, therefore, participate in mobilizing the supernatural power of God's intervening kingdom. If the convergence of supernatural and human realities can only be effected through either Jesus' person or through the wielding of the power of God's kingdom (which also occurs through Jesus' person, as in Jesus' healings and exorcisms) then it appears contextually apparent that the twelve must be in some way manipulating the power of the kingdom. Though they are not, of course, given Jesus' stature as the Son of God, they are, like Jesus, capable of governing the power of God's kingdom in such a way that their language of repentance, too, is backed up by moments of supernatural intervention *which they themselves enact*. In other words, in their *human* efforts, *supernatural* kingdom pockets of power flare up and resist the brokenness of human reality. This is what their *repentance*, their affirmation and empowerment, is all about.

A CORRESPONDENCE OF RELATIONSHIPS

A complete sociolinguistic study does not end with the historical-contextual findings. Interpersonal involvement with a biblical text extends beyond the characters in the text and the hearer/readers to whom the text was intended in the first century. The interpretative process is also influenced by the interpersonal perspective and identity of the *contemporary* interpreter. This is the contemporary-contextual level. Once again life relation and preunderstanding play pivotal roles. At this level, however, the life relation designates the academic context (or lack thereof) of the researcher or interpreter. All investigative methodologies are driven by certain interrogative presuppositions. Those presuppositions, as Bultmann recognized, play a powerful role in determining the manner in which an interpreter accesses the meaning potentiality offered by the language of a text. Preunderstanding, which denotes the context of culture of the interpreter, includes the personality, biases, emotional content, ideological perspective, and cultural presuppositions any interpreter brings to the interpretative task.

I would argue that every interpreter's contemporary-contextual relationship to the text affects the manner in which he or she accesses the meaning potential resident in that text. Indeed, because this process cannot be avoided, I not only recognize it, but encourage it as an interpretative avenue through which a text can be brought to meaningful life in the midst of a contemporary communal situation. Modern interpreters should both admit and foster the same kind of interpretative relationship to the text that the biblical authors assumed existed between themselves and the traditions they creatively interpreted in their process of writing their biblical narratives.

> Scripture is itself very much a development of church tradition. It represents the response of the early church communities to the challenges of their day, one which could speak to their present reality only through a "creative fidelity" to the words and work of Jesus.[33]

In other words, the interpretations of the early church which led to the formation of texts like the Gospel of Mark were achieved in light of *their* contemporary-contextual reality. Our historical-contextual investigation helps us understand the parameters of that creative interaction. Which is to say, the relationship between the Markan church and the Jesus and Jewish traditional materials which prompted the kind of kingdom of God language that occurs in his text corresponds to the kind of relationship that currently exists between contemporary faith communities and that text language. The same creative fidelity in interpretation not only occurs on a subconscious level, but should be consciously encouraged if the text is to live in contemporary community the way the traditions came to life in the communities of the first century.

It should also be encouraged for a second reason. If, indeed, Mark's text language about the kingdom of God is a potentiality of meaning to be accessed contextually rather than a single meaning to be discovered, interpreters from different communities are liable to, because of their unique perspectives, perceive different segments of that potentiality as meaningful. We will begin to appreciate the full potentiality of any text only when we recognize the value of each community's contextual conclusions. Since I cannot demonstrate this quality for every possible community I will limit my contemporary-contextual evaluation of Mark's kingdom language to the single community of the African-American church. My procedure, however, will not be restricted to descriptive analysis. While I will demonstrate the process whereby the contextual situation of the African-American church influences its interpretation of Mark's kingdom language, it will also be my task to fathom the imperative meaning of Mark's message for the life of this contemporary community.

As I have argued, language is functional. It intends to "do" something. Mark's kingdom language intended to "do" something in the lives of his readers. I would contend that a similar intention remains for any contemporary readers who pick up his text, no matter how many centuries they are removed from the evangelist's actual writing. Since, however, the context of the latter day

---

33. Rowland and Corner, 60–61.

interpreter has changed dramatically, he or she will tend to access Mark's imperative language in a way that can be quite distinct from the way a first-century community would have meaningfully accessed it.

My task will be to consider how the African-American community, given its unique contextual reality in the United States of the latter twentieth and early twenty-first centuries, might find a point of access that brings the potentiality of Mark's kingdom language to meaningful imperative life. Specifically, I will argue that the socio-political potentiality resident within the Markan kingdom language has particular application for the life of the contemporary African-American church. There is a dramatic correspondence of relationship between the manner in which the contexts of situation and culture of the Markan first-century community sanctioned a political access to his soteriological kingdom of God language, and the manner in which the life-relation and preunderstanding of the contemporary African-American community in the United States has supported and continues to mandate a comparable socio-political meaning approach.

This argument does not suggest, however, that the African-American community, or any contemporary community for that matter, can take the text to mean whatever it believes is most advantageous for its religious or political purposes. I am instead encouraging a contextual meaning access which operates within the boundaries of potentiality that were established between Mark and his original audience. This is the point of doing the historical-contextual investigation. If Mark's words and meaning intentions are to be authoritative for the contemporary church, respect must remain for the boundaries established by this text. I intend to apprehend the contours of those boundaries through the historical-contextual investigation.

At the first level I will access meaning through a critical reconstruction of the context of situation for Mark's kingdom language. Even scholars who approach biblical inquiry from a standpoint that is not sociolinguistic have begun to appreciate the value of this kind of analysis. As Gerd Theissen writes, "Simultaneously with the crumbling of the form-critical consensus, hermeneutical reflection has rehabilitated the 'cohesive text' as the object of exegesis. The new 'axiom' is that meaning constitutes itself in the synchronic text, not in the diachronic text."[34] This context of situation, Theissen agrees, is a necessary check on the historical-critical tendency to believe that historical inquiry is sufficient contextual analysis. "Approaches to evaluation of Gospel texts in terms of historical and cultural context have a common problem of method: they leave the world within the text in order to look 'outside.' "[35]

Theissen realizes, however, that what I call a complete historical-contextual investigation must use the context of situation as a starting point, not a conclusion to analysis. The context of culture is an important corroborative tool.

---

34. Gerd Theissen, *The Gospels in Context: Social and Political History in the Synoptic Tradition*, Linda M. Maloney, translator (Minneapolis: Fortress Press, 1991) 6.
35. Ibid., 12.

Without knowledge of everything within the context of the texts as they now stand — their prehistory, their situation, the historical association and presumptions of the period — an interpretation of "cohesive texts" would be arbitrary. It would lack that corrective historical knowledge that shields us from distorting backward projections of our own problems and values into the past and at the same time enables us to discover analogies between then and now that make possible an appropriate encounter with the texts.[36]

Indeed, quite significant here is Theissen's realization that these contextual inquiries have value that extends into an interpretative use of the historical-contextual findings for contemporary edification and parenesis.

The contemporary-contextual indicative and imperative meanings accessed by the African-American church that I will use as an example will arise from an interaction between the contemporary context and the meaning potentiality of the text in light of what the historical-contextual investigation tells me are the boundaries of that potentiality. I will, then, be roaming free across a wide expanse of interpretative territory that nonetheless registers, in the end, a restricted range.

---

36. Ibid., 6.

4

Establishing the Context

Mark's Social Location

An examination of Mark 13 reveals that the evangelist wrote in response to the historico-political crisis occasioned by the Jewish-Roman war of 66–70 C.E. Joel Marcus argues that "it seems likely that the prophecies of false messiahs, war, persecutions, and betrayal in vv. 6–13 (cf. 21–22) are part of the present experience of Mark's community."[1] He concludes that Mark wrote just after the climactic event of that war, the 70 C.E. fall of the Jerusalem Temple. Adela

---

1. Joel Marcus, "The Jewish War and the *Sitz im Leben* of Mark," *Journal of Biblical Literature* 111 (1992): 447. Marcus notes that contemporary scholars, operating from clues in Mark 13, are evenly divided as to whether Mark wrote just before or just after the destruction of the Temple in 70 C.E. (460, fn. 90.) He opts for the latter temporal location because the language of the Temple's destruction at 13:1–2 appears to resemble the actual historical circumstance of the event too closely. He points out that unlike 14:58 and sayings like John 2:19, what he calls the *ex eventu* prophecy of 13:1–2 conforms to the events of 70 by not adding a prophecy of Temple restoration to that of Temple destruction. He then points to Pesch's argument that the remark "no stone upon a stone" confirms Josephus's report of the razing of the Temple (447–48).

Marcus does not address the fact, however, that unlike Luke's recording of the destruction (cf. Luke 21:5–7, 20), which details the surrounding of Jerusalem by armies, Mark's account remains rather general. The "no stone upon a stone" remark is simply Jesus' response in rhetorical kind to the disciples' initial observation, which initiates the critical "stone" vocabulary, that the Temple is a magnificent institution (13:1). And the omission of a Temple restoration prophecy is not surprising given the fact that the overall theme of Mark 13 is about the consequences and response to destruction, unlike the Passion narrative which is as ironically focused on vindication and restoration in a new way as this section is mythically focused on the decimation of the old way.

Adela Collins makes a stronger case for a writing just before the Temple's demise. (Adela Yarbro Collins, *The Beginning of the Gospel: Probings of Mark in Context* [Minneapolis, Fortress Press, 1992].) She argues that had Mark been written after the fall of the Temple, there would have been little reason to warn his readers about their particular apocalyptic slant on the events of the time. She also notes that verses 7–8 suggest an earlier writing date. The vocabulary of rumors of wars, an end still to come, and birth pangs suggest that "the war will be long and hard rather than resolved immediately by divine intervention or indicate that the war has been in progress already for sometime. If the war were already over, it would hardly have been necessary to point out that the end had not yet come. It would have been clear to all that the war did not issue immediately in the end time" (82). Collins continues to press her case that the text was written prior to the fall of the Temple in her commentary on the chapter verses. She follows this process specifically through page 87.

Collins disagrees. She asserts that Mark writes just before the Temple's destruction. There is, however, agreement on the more general, but just as significant point. Collins's analysis of Mark 13 brings her to the comparable conclusion that the "present experience" of Mark's community was the Jewish-Roman war. "Taken together, these factors suggest that Mark was written after the outbreak of the war, after the appearance of at least a few 'false messiahs' and 'false prophets,' but before the destruction of the temple."[2]

An understanding of this messianically tinged, combative socio-political background helps us better appreciate the evangelist's use of an apocalyptic-interventionist strategy to make his narrative point about the meaning of Jesus' message for his believing community. Apocalyptic language fueled the nationalistic-patriotic zeal that ignited and sustained the Jewish war effort. The false prophets and messiahs were those who counseled taking up arms and joining in God's alleged martial campaign-intervention against Rome. Mark took up the language in order to redirect the fervor of his community so that their expectation of God's imminent intervention would encourage a "Jesus" response of transformative service and sacrifice rather than a "Zealot" response of military engagement. In other words, as Ched Myers points out, Mark was caught up in a kind of "war of apocalyptic myths" with messianic pretenders like Menahem, who returned from Masada in 66 C.E., proclaiming himself the anointed one of God who would restore Davidic independence to Israel.[3]

In fact, Mark was fighting his "war of apocalyptic myths" on more than a single front. A provisional government of conventional Jewish leaders took control in Jerusalem just after the onset of war in 66. Members of the high priestly and scribal ranks were seduced by the heady, but ultimately deceptive, lure of success after the Roman forces who initially responded to the uprising were defeated and expelled. By either accommodation or force, these provisional leaders were determined to secure the reestablishment of institutional Israel. Their goal, then, was not unlike the goal of the more radical Zealot forces. Their differences

---

In any event, it is not my aim to resolve the issue of pre- or post-Temple-fall dating. However, the fact that the debate about Mark's timing focuses so carefully on a specific point in time, and around a specific event in history, demonstrates clearly that there can be no question that the broader context of Mark's writing was the 66–70 war with Rome.

2. A. Collins, *The Beginning of the Gospel*, 86.

3. Ched Myers, *Binding the Strong Man: A Political Reading of Mark's Story of Jesus* (Maryknoll, NY: Orbis Books, 1988). Collins appears to agree. "The most likely historical allusion here [13:6, 21–22] is to the Jewish messianic pretenders who come forward during the Jewish war with Rome, beginning with Menahem in 66 C.E. According to Josephus, he returned from Masada to Jerusalem in that year like a king. From the point of view of Mark, these pretenders were competing with Jesus for the title and role of God's anointed" (A. Collins, *The Beginning of the Gospel*, 82).

Marcus is even more specific: "We will see that the postulated situation of tension with Jewish revolutionary groups provides a plausible setting not only for Mark's Gospel in general but also for his exegesis of certain Old Testament passages in particular. Some of the same scriptural prophecies that appear to have galvanized the anti-Roman revolutionaries turn up in Mark's Gospel as testimonies to a different sort of holy war with different enemies and a different sort of Messiah as its standard-bearer. Mark's exploitation of these testimonies is probably in part a polemical response to their use by the Jewish revolutionaries; his Old Testament exegesis appears to be forged in the fires of a warfare that is both military and theological" (Marcus, *The Way of the Lord: Christological Exegesis of the Old Testament in the Gospel of Mark* [Louisville: Westminster/John Knox Press, 1992] 11).

were methodological; the Zealots were convinced that the reconstitution of Israel could only be secured through the spilling of Roman blood. Mark's apocalyptic narrative challenged that both of these tactical agendas were out of step with God's strategic kingdom intent.[4]

The evangelist's focus, one which he shared with the false prophets and apocalyptic pretenders, was on the intervention of God's kingdom through messianic agency (13:24–27). But it was intervention of a radically different type. While the messianic revolutionaries proclaimed that the war was God's actual intervention into human history, and would reestablish an independent Jewish state, Mark pronounced, from 13:1–2 onward, that God's kingdom would be prefaced by an intervention of destruction and punishment for national behavior inimical to the divine ways. The war was not the kingdom, but the prosecutory prelude (13:7–8) to it.[5]

---

4. Cf. Josephus, *The Jewish War, Books I–VII,* H. St. J. Thackeray, translator, E. H. Warmington, editor, 9 vols., Loeb Classical Library, Vol. II, *Josephus* (Cambridge: Harvard University Press, 1968); Josephus, *The Works of Josephus,* William Whiston, translator (Peabody, MA: Hendrickson, 1968). Richard A. Horsley, "High Priest and Politics in Roman Palestine," *Journal for the Study of Judaism* 17 (1986): 23–55; David M. Rhoads, *Israel in Revolution, 6–74 C.E.: A Political History Based on the Writings of Josephus* (Philadelphia: Fortress Press, 1976); E. M. Smallwood, *The Jews Under Roman Rule from Pompey to Diocletian* (Leiden: E. J. Brill, 1976), esp. chapter 12, "The War of A.D. 66–70"; Doron Mendels, *The Rise and Fall of Jewish Nationalism* (New York: Doubleday, 1992); Emil Schürer, *The History of the Jewish People in the Age of Jesus Christ,* G. Vermes and M. Black, editors, New English edition, 4 volumes (Edinburgh: T & T Clark, 1979).

Following an attempt by the Roman procurator Gessius Florus (64–66 C.E.) to expropriate 17 talents from the Temple Treasury in 66 (*War* 2:293), actual fighting broke out. Florus's forces plundered the city (*War* 2:305), and attempted to capture and control the Temple (*War* 2:328–31). But Florus's attempts failed, and he was driven from the city. Eleazar ben Ananias, captain of the Temple, then led the lower priests, with the support of the revolutionary groups, in a refusal to offer gifts or sacrifice to Rome. They took control of the Temple area and the lower city. Meanwhile, the chief priests overwhelmed the upper city and called in reinforcements. Responding quickly, Cestius Galluis, the Syrian legate, sent reinforcements of his own to quell the revolt. But his forces, too, in a much more humiliating defeat for Rome, were driven back. Although the high priests, ever seeking accommodation, had initially sought to open the city to Cestius, when his maneuver failed, a provisional government was formed under the leadership of the high priests themselves (*War* 2:562). As Schürer points out, the chief priests and eminent Pharisees were the ones responsible now for the organization of the city's defenses (*War* 1:491).

Soon after Cestius's defeat, certain radical revolutionaries of the Zealot party (e.g., Eleazar ben Simon [*War* 2:564]), who were excluded from the provisional government, took control of the Temple and elected their own high priest by lot. Suspecting the provisional government of moderation, they later accused it of plotting to turn the city over to the Romans (*War* 4:228). The provisional government, then, appears to have been made up of high priests, Sadducean rulers, and some revolutionaries, even though it excluded the more radical of them. There also seems to have been some leading Pharisees who participated in the provisional government. Josephus, for instance, mentions Simon ben Gamaliel (*War* 4:159–60). According to Rhoads (155), because he was of the house of Hillel, he probably worked to find some way to reestablish the peace. There seems, then, to have been a mix of those who thought that war with Rome was winnable and those who joined the provisional government to work toward some kind of settlement while keeping the more radical elements in check.

5. Marcus makes the intriguing proposal that the Zealot leaders had gone so far with their messianic pretension as to actually desecrate the Temple (Marcus, "The Jewish War...," esp., 447–62). It is his contention that at 13:14, Mark writes with their behavior, particularly that of Eleazar, son of Simon (67–78), specifically in mind. Occupying the temple in the interests of establishing a new, revolutionary Davidic kingdom, they have turned it instead into a den of brigands (σπήλαιον λῃστῶν). Brigand (λῃστής), in fact, is the very term Josephus uses to

Mark, therefore, counseled a different kind of human response to God's apocalyptic activity. This "war of apocalyptic myths," then, paints the socio-cultural landscape in which he locates his Gospel. The evangelist, the messianic pretenders, and the provisional leadership are all using interventionist imagery and language to broker specific kinds of behavior in the context of war. Therefore, "Instead of speaking vaguely of the Gospel's context as one of 'persecution,' we may specify the context of intra- and intercommunal tension produced by the upheaval of the Jewish war."[6]

The location where the effects of this war would have its greatest impact, and thus, one would expect, fuel the most explosive contrasts and battles of apocalyptic-interventionist myth language, is Palestine.[7] The texture of Mark's narrative language supports such an hypothesis. Mark's field, tenor and mode of discourse militate against a Roman provenance and in favor of an Eastern Mediterranean rural or village culture, one akin to the kind we find in the region just north of the upper Palestinian border. Howard Clark Kee notes that "the accurate reflection of practices having to do with agriculture, housing, employment, and land-ownership and taxation that are characteristic of the whole

---

describe the zealot forces of the war period. Referring back to Jesus' Temple cleansing actions, where this language, den of brigands, surfaces (11:17), Marcus therefore concludes that in Mark's opinion, the Temple, a place intended to be a house of international prayer, has been turned into a nationalistic front for revolution. "The redactional verse Mark 11:17, then, can plausibly be viewed as the superimposition upon the tradition about Jesus' cleansing of the Temple of some features of an event that occurred during the Jewish War, the occupation of the Temple by the Zealots in pursuit of their military aims and their theology of purificatory war against the infidel." (Ibid., 451. See also 454–55, for Josephus's citations which Marcus uses to demonstrate that the actions of Eleazar were viewed as a defilement of the Temple. *War* 4.9.1, #486–90.) In other words, the revolutionary false prophets demanded allegiance from those who sought to respond appropriately to the realization that God was about to intervene in human history. Unfortunately, they were using the Temple as a staging ground for revolutionary behavior that included the purification of the Temple, the place of *international* prayer, from Gentile presence. It is for this reason that God's intervention will result in Jerusalem's destruction rather than its restoration. With Jesus' temple cleansing and parable of the vineyard ringing in the background, Marcus thus concludes, "In response to the Zealot occupation of the Temple and similar acts of 'purification' of the holy land from Gentile influence, Mark tells his community — which perhaps has experienced at first hand the drastic effects of these acts — that the revolutionary purge is actually a defilement, that it will precipitate divine judgment, and that the inheritance of Israel will be taken away from the Jewish leaders and turned over to a new people that prominently includes Gentiles in its ranks (12:9)" (ibid., 455–56). In fact, Marcus argues that Mark, in his war of myths, is attempting to reclaim the use of Zechariah 9–14, an apocalyptically oriented section of the prophetic work, from the Zealots. He hypothesizes that the Zealots have interpreted Zechariah 14:21 literally. An expulsion of all Gentile influence and presence from the Temple is therefore demanded; this expulsion becomes their key tactical objective. Mark attempts to reshape the Zecharian influence by utilizing Zechariah 9:9–13 at his 11:1–11 text, climaxing with the key verse, 11:17, which clarifies the divine wish that the Temple should be a house of international prayer.

6. Ibid., 462.

7. Ibid., 441. Marcus's footnotes one and three detail the list of scholars on each side of the debate. His careful work need not be repeated here. As he notes in his article on the location of the Gospel, although most scholarship continues to argue that Mark was written at a distance from the combat in Rome, a growing number of scholars are positioning the writing in the province of Syria just north of the upper border of Palestine. The bloc of Hellenistic cities ringing Palestine's northern border would provide an ample audience base for the predominantly Gentile readership to which Mark was most likely directed (ibid., 441–42, fn. 4).

of Syria-Palestine in this period do indeed speak for that larger area as the place of origin and against Rome."[8]

The region's concentrated Gentile population complements the argument for a southern-Syria, northern-Palestine Gospel provenance. Mark's apocalyptic positioning of himself against the nationalistic proclamations made by "false prophets and messiahs" is logical if he is operating in and indeed speaking to a Palestinian community heavily populated with Gentiles. Marcus argues that, because of their literal interpretation of Zechariah 14:21, the revolutionaries adopted the expulsion of Gentile influence and presence as a key tactical objective.[9] Therefore, "A mostly Gentile Christian community in such a location would have had good reasons to fear the Jewish revolutionary movement."[10]

Marcus continues with the observation that since Hasmonean times the Hellenistic cities at the southern Syria, northern Palestine border were in constant conflict with their Jewish neighbors. In fact, it was not until Pompey's incursion into the region in 63 B.C.E., that Hasmonean control over the cities was broken. But Marcus believes that tensions remained high enough even after that point that the conflict here was one of the major contributing factors to the 66–70 war. "Indeed, as U. Rappaport points out, most of the fighting in the first year of the war was not between Jews and Romans but between Jews and the inhabitants of the Hellenistic cities."[11]

Josephus notes that at the outset of the war, Gentiles massacred Jews. Jews retaliated by returning fire against Gentiles.[12] It would be in this kind of volatile, multi-ethnic setting that the controversy Mark assumed (13:9–13) would result from his message of kingdom openness to Gentiles (cf. 12:1–12, esp., verses 9 and 12) would make the most narrative sense. In this kind of environment it is plausible to suggest that Mark would want to transform the objective of divine intervention, particularly as it issues forth messianically through his char-

---

8. Kee, *Community of the New Age,* 102. Cf. also Marcus, "The Jewish War," 442–46, for a comprehensive argument against a provenance in Rome. Though Galilee, with its rural village structure may also appear to be a possibility, Kee, Marcus and others quickly reject it. Kee carefully points out how the text language reveals an inadequate understanding of Galilean life proper. "But the specific details of the locations are not accurately perceived by the author, who represents Jesus as travelling back and forth in Galilee and adjacent territories in a puzzling fashion" (Kee, 103). Kee goes on to mention key passages of geographical concern. There are unknown sites mentioned by the author (8:10), improper designations of regional locations (5:1), and improbable travel itineraries (7:31). Marcus adds that it is unlikely that a Jewish audience, which would be the case should Galilee proper be Mark's writing location, would need the kind of information Mark feels compelled to provide at 7:3–4, 14:12, or 15:42.

It is clear that Galilee does have an importance for the evangelist. I would agree, however, that its significance for Mark is more historical and theological than geographical. "Galilee is important to Mark, but not necessarily because his community is situated there; his emphasis on the region may result from a combination of historical memory (Jesus actually *did* perform much of his ministry there) and theological utility (e.g., Galilee is a setting in which, and from which, the Marcan Jesus can plausibly interact with Gentiles, since it is contiguous to Gentile regions)" (Marcus, "The Jewish War," 461).

9. Marcus, *The Way of the Lord,* 160.

10. Marcus, "The Jewish War," 451.

11. Ibid., 451–52. Cf. also U. Rappaport, "Jewish-Pagan Relations and the Revolt against Rome in 66–70 C.E.," *Jewish Cathedra* 1 (1981): 81–95.

12. Ibid., 452.

acterization of Jesus, from one that targeted the destruction of Rome to one that envisioned the shattering of faith boundaries that existed between Jew and Gentile. In this kind of environment it is also understandable, however, why Mark would counsel that anyone who followed his universalist kingdom understanding would encounter resistance, and even persecution. It therefore makes sense that in the tenor of discourse Jesus' primary conflicts are not with Romans but with his own religious and political leaders who would have had a stake in preventing this international mission agenda by appealing to an apocalyptic mythology based in nationalistic fervor. The apocalyptic war of myths took on a decidedly sectarian character.

> Mark is confronted with an Israel that has taken up the cudgels against the non-Jewish world in a desperate fight for survival. In the heat of the war, and fired by apocalyptic visions of victory by a purified Israel, some Jews are prepared to take drastic steps against Gentiles and against Jews who advocate coexistence with them — that is, the sorts of people who make up Mark's community.[13]

There was also a marked history of socio-economic tension in the region. Radical economic differences have often provided a platform for either establishing or heightening appeals for divine intervention.

> Closely related to political alienation is the question of *money*. Burridge, for instance, stresses that money "seems to be the most *frequent* and *convenient* axis on which millenarian movements turn." Money, like cargo, represents wealth, power, and above all a symbolic measure of human worth. Thus the introduction of money into a previously unmonied culture (the Melanesian situation depicted by Burridge and others), or the hoarding and control of money by a colonial power in a monied land (the situation of Palestine under Roman rulers), creates a crisis not just of finance but of human dignity as well.[14]

In such a climate, wealth is viewed as a sign of corruption and decay. Binary oppositions develop within the interventionist mind set: poor-rich, good-evil, pious-hypocrite, elect-damned. The interventionist hope is for a situation of imminent reversal whereby the socially devalued, but religiously esteemed, are economically and socially vindicated.[15]

This appears to have been the social circumstance of upper Palestine and southern Syria during the time of Jesus' ministry *and* that of Mark's writing. E. P. Sanders rejects the work of scholars like Richard Horsley and Marcus Borg who argue that massive and redundant Roman, Herodian, and High Priestly tax demands sparked a downward spiral of apocalyptic violence which ultimately

---

13. Ibid., 453.
14. John G. Gager, *Kingdom and Community: The Social World of Early Christianity* (Englewood Cliffs, NJ: Prentice-Hall, Inc., 1975) 24.
15. Ibid.

triggered the nationalistic war.[16] However, even his more conservative financial estimates concede that the socio-economic predicament was dire.

> Nevertheless, the people were hard pressed. Modern scholars are in one sense right to speak of their "oppression." The wealthy did not sit down each night and try to devise ways of making the peasantry more comfortable. The populace was a resource to be utilized. Not all rulers managed their greatest national resource with equal wisdom and moderation. No ruler wanted a tax revolt, but the general tendency was to press the populace as hard as possible without causing one.[17]

Given this hypothesis of economic "oppression," two factors would contribute to interventionist leanings. A novel Jewish combination of theology and patriotism was first. Tribute to a foreign power offended religious sensibilities and, therefore, ignited zealous feelings of revolt, and hopes for divine, revolutionary intervention. "Any disregard of national tradition was offensive to God, and people loyal to God knew that he would save them."[18] It is no wonder that many of the bandit leaders, who cultivated a particular loyalty among the poor, presented themselves as messianic, kingly figures commissioned to usher in God's kingdom moment of revolution against Rome.[19] But again, this is not the kind of transformation that Mark's kingdom portrait of Jesus counseled.

A second factor would be the chasm that separated the wealthy and the poor. Martin Goodman points to the key problem of debt which accentuated an already contentious social divide. Instead of investing their wealth in manufacturing or trade, the aristocracy increased capital through usury. The poor who took the loans were rarely able to meet the established terms. Whatever they'd placed in collateral holding, usually the family land, was therefore eventually acquired as payment. "The wealth that flowed into Jerusalem led in this way to the indebtedness of many of the poor of both city and countryside.... And rural debt was no less serious. Peasants were reduced to selling off or forfeiting their farms and becoming part of a rural proletariat of growing size and volatile political ambitions."[20]

At the same time that the poor were becoming poorer, the aristocracy was spending lavishly on itself. The subsequent stress that developed between the social groupings is well represented in the role relationships characterized in the Markan text.[21] Mark makes the aristocracy and their scribal and priestly re-

---

16. E. P. Sanders, *Judaism: Practice and Belief 63 BCE–66 CE* (London: SCM Press, 1992) 158–59.

17. Ibid., 168.

18. Ibid., 168–69.

19. Blount, "The Social World of Bandits," in *The Good Samaritan (Luke 10:25–37): An American Bible Society Interactive CD-ROM for Windows* (New York: American Bible Society, 1996). The article considers the social issues surrounding banditry, particularly the bandits' relationship with the peasantry who often perceived them as rebel heroes.

20. Martin Goodman, "The First Jewish Revolt: Social Conflict and the Problem of Debt," *Journal of Religious Studies* 33 (1982): 423–24.

21. Richard L. Rohrbaugh, "The Social Location of the Marcan Audience," *Biblical Theology Bulletin* 23 (1993).

tainers (the Herodians, high priestly Sadducean families, scribes, and Pharisees) Jesus' primary opponents. His message of kingdom intervention, which they reject, was directed squarely against their social, political, and economic authority. Even more intriguing for our discussion is the fact that the rural inhabitants who made up some ninety percent of the population (the tenant farmers, day laborers, fishermen, artisans, craftsmen, etc.) are the only Gospel characters (as opposed to the aristocracy and religious leadership) who see in Jesus the interventionist power of God.[22] Jesus' transformative power, in other words, would therefore represent, in this context of situation, a reversal designed to shatter (that is to say, intervene against) social boundaries established by human fiscal reality.

Cultic transformation is also a key interventionist concern. The same persons who were economically "oppressed" were victimized by purity and holiness codes (that is to say, boundaries) whose mandates virtually guaranteed that these "people of the land," would be considered perpetually unclean and therefore, cultically speaking, unholy. Here, the foundational work of anthropologist Mary Douglas, and the subsequent efforts of biblical scholars to build upon and critique it, is most illuminating. Douglas argues that the purity code is a way of structuring society. "Defilement is never an isolated event. It cannot occur except in view of a systematic ordering of ideas."[23] A cultic code thereby becomes a method of structuring how humans order themselves and their lives in community. In this way, religious tradition maintains a direct political end. This is particularly important in the establishment of boundaries that separate those who are insiders from those who are not, those who are, in other words, acceptable within the community of the faithful, and those who are considered unacceptable and are, therefore, excluded from the religio-political process centered in the Temple.

The primary concern was holiness. Appealing particularly to the Levitical codes which emphasize the refrain, "Be holy, for I am holy," Douglas makes the point that, "since each of the injunctions is prefaced by the command to be holy, so they must be explained by that command."[24] At its root, holiness means to set apart. Those who do God's will are set apart from those who do not; they are, therefore, holy, and will achieve God's prosperity. "Set apart" is augmented in the Israelite understanding by the sense of wholeness or physical perfection. This sense of wholeness as completeness becomes a way of ordering the society as well as the cult. "Holiness requires that individuals shall conform to the class to which they belong."[25]

As Jerome Neyrey recognizes, this means that boundary lines must be drawn, lines which will tell us "... *what* and *who* belong *when* and *where*."[26] Some forms of Judaism within Israel, in other words, institutionalized cultic codes of

---

22. In fact it is clear from texts like 3:22–27 that the leadership believes Jesus' authority to be demonically inspired and empowered.

23. Mary T. Douglas, *Purity and Danger: An Analysis of the Concepts of Pollution and Taboo* (London: Routledge and Kegan Paul, 1966) 41.

24. Ibid., 48.

25. Ibid., 53.

26. Jerome Neyrey, "The Idea of Purity in Mark's Gospel," *Semeia* 35 (1986): 93.

purity so that holiness became a mode of mapping out the ways in which human beings were societally ordered and, therefore, accepted or dismissed as unacceptable. Helpfully, Neyrey specifies three specific ways in which boundaries were established based on purity mandates.[27] First, there were the external boundaries established by some forms of Judaism which distinguished Jews from other people of the time. Those who operated on the proper side of these boundaries — kosher diet, circumcision and Sabbath observance — were acceptable; others, Gentiles, were not.[28] I have already argued that in the Markan presentation the Jesus story represents an inclusion of the Gentiles in the cause of God's kingdom intervention. Mark's language, at least in the manner in which he portrays these cultic boundaries, is therefore boundary breaking.

Second, there were the physical margins. Those lacking bodily wholeness like lepers, the blind, the lame and eunuchs were considered unholy, even if they were Israelites. "They are marginal to the covenant people, residing on the fringes or borders of Jewish society."[29] Interestingly enough, Jesus' actions in the Gospel also represent a transgression of these boundaries. His character constantly interacts with, rather than avoids, such marginalized persons.

Third, there were the internal boundaries which operated from what Neyrey called a map of the body. This human map replicated the map of the social body; both operated from the principles of purity and holiness. This is particularly important given the demands of wholeness. A complete body would be considered pure. A broken one, as in the lame or the blind, would not be. Indeed, anything that leaked from the skin, mucous, blood, etc., would make a body impure and would necessitate social quarantine. The ill and women, again persons Mark narrates as being continually in Jesus' presence, were obviously singled out by such a ruling.

> The appropriate strategy in this type of world is defensive. What is called for is: (a) avoidance of contact with what is either too holy or marginal or unclean (see Luke 10:31–32; Acts 10:14 & 28) or (b) reinforcement of boundaries and purity concerns (see Mark 7:1–4 and the rabbis' "fences"). People who continually have even passing contact with sinners, lepers, blind, lame, menstruants, corpses and the like are perceived as spurning the *map of persons.* People who show no respect for holy places such as the temple (see Mark 11:15–17) are crossing dangerous lines on the *map of places.* People who "do what is not lawful on the Sabbath" disregard the *map of times,* and would be rated as unclean. Not only are they themselves polluted, they become a source of pollution to others.[30]

---

27. Ibid., 99–103.

28. David Rhoads, "Social Criticism: Crossing Boundaries," in *Mark and Method: New Approaches in Biblical Studies,* Janice Capel Anderson and Stephen D. Moore, editors (Minneapolis: Fortress Press, 1992) 153. "The boundary of Israel distinguishes Jew from Gentile. Only male Jews who are circumcised and without blemish are considered pure. Jews who have contact with Gentiles become unclean, intermarriage is strictly prohibited. Generally speaking, Jews guard the social boundary to keep Jews in and Gentiles out."

29. Neyrey, 100.

30. Ibid., 105.

Given Neyrey's remarks, it seems evident that Mark wants to portray the majority of people who consort with Jesus as beyond the boundaries of social acceptability. In fact, Mark goes out of his way to demonstrate that Jesus keeps himself in the presence of tax collectors and sinners.[31] The controversy materials portray him acting against the wishes of the societal authorities, in the company of and on behalf of those who exist outside the bounds of purity acceptability. Mark is narratively suggesting that his readers must at the very least restructure the manner in which they relate socially to such "impure" persons. It is also likely, given the fact that among Jesus' followers and beneficiaries are tax collectors, sinners, fishermen, those who eat bread on the sabbath, etc., and particularly Gentiles, that Mark understands that his reading audience is composed of those who would be considered of "impure" pedigree.

It seems certain, then, that Mark has a particular apocalyptic point to make: Jesus' kingdom ministry appears in the evangelist's narratively constructed social location of second temple Judaism, to cross the mapping boundaries (ethnic, economic, cultic) that order the way Palestinian-Jewish society, as he characterizes it, is supposed to be constructed.

---

31. Note, for example, the intentional repetition of the phrase "tax collectors and sinners" at 2:15–17.

5

The Context of Culture

Apocalyptic Intervention

Given the contentious socio-political realities of his location and the apocalyptic responses to them, it is no wonder that Mark, too, would choose to paint his narrative story in an interventionist hue.[1] In this battle of apocalyptic myths it is imperative that he convince his readers that Jesus' interventionist perspective is the one that most appropriately fulfills prophetic expectations, and, therefore, is the one that should be zealously followed. He begins by using authoritatively accepted apocalyptic books as the literary background for his own narrative Jesus story. Daniel is key. In fact, Howard Clark Kee argues that Mark picks up on Daniel's narrative strategy and imitates it in his narrative telling of the Jesus event. Like Daniel, in the first half he concentrates on miracle, and in the second, on suffering and martyrdom, punctuating it all with personal and cosmic moments of revelation.

Whether Kee is completely correct about the intentional structural similarity, the statistical evidence is clear; a disproportionate number of Mark's quotations from the Hebrew scriptures comes from the book of Daniel. "Daniel alone among all the Old Testament books is quoted from every chapter...."[2] Not only in the clearly apocalyptic material of chapter thirteen, but also, and especially, in the material that details Jesus' ministry and death, Mark operates from the same kind of interventionist perspective that energized the apocalyptic work of Daniel. Most significant for our purposes is Kee's realization that Mark uses this interventionist frame for the same objective as the writer of Daniel, to convince

---

1. In fact, N. T. Wright makes the important point that apocalyptic characterized the entire Second Temple period. Not only Judaism, but other ancient Mediterranean and Near Eastern religions thought in terms of imminent divine intervention. N. T. Wright, *The New Testament and the People of God* (Minneapolis: Fortress Press, 1992).

2. Kee, *Community of the New Age,* 45. Kee points out that of Mark's direct quotations, eight come from the Torah, two from the historical writings, twelve from the Psalms, twelve from Daniel and twenty-one from the prophets. Of some 160 allusions to the Hebrew writings, one-half come from the prophets, and one-eighth each from Daniel, the Psalms, the Torah and non-canonical sources.

his "persecuted" readers that, because this-worldly, communal vindication was imminently forthcoming, they should wait on God in active endurance.[3]

Mark's use of canonical apocalyptic materials does not end with his heavy dependence on Daniel. As Ched Myers notes, the evangelist also displays a strong interest in apocalyptically oriented prophetic texts. "Indeed, quite aside from Daniel, Mark's use of the prophets draws equally 'disproportionately' from texts that modern scholars attribute to late prophetic 'proto-apocalyptic,' such as Isaiah 24–27, 34–35, and 56–66 ('Trito-Isaiah'); Ezekiel 38–39; Joel 3–4; Zechariah 9, 12–14; and Malachi 3–4."[4]

Marcus makes the helpful point that right from the outset the evangelist wants the reader to understand that he is operating from an apocalyptic frame that has deep prophetic roots. The reference to Deutero-Isaiah 40:3 at 1:3 makes this quite clear. Having already argued that Deutero-Isaiah is the "father of apocalyptic," Marcus goes on to explain that by appealing to his language and imagery so early in the narrative, Mark must want his readers to perceive his work, particularly his opening narrative preoccupation with the wilderness and the presentation of his central character, from an Isaian-interventionist perspective.[5]

Kee adds that the apocalyptic-mythological imagery in these prophetic pieces represents contemporary historical realities. Cosmic transformation, and the language of redemption and resurrection that are connected with it are, therefore, representative of socio-political reversal. And it is most notable that this interventionist-oriented reversal takes place on behalf of those Mark's gospel seemed peculiarly interested in, the poor and powerless. Speaking directly in reference to Isaiah 24–27, but keeping all the so-called "proto-apocalyptic" prophetic works in mind, Kee therefore argues,

> Here the recurrent phrase "in that day" (25:8; 27:1) refers to the time when God will execute judgment (26:21) on the creation, wreaking destruction in the earth (24:1, 18) in a manner that recalls Gen. 4 and the days of Noah. The result will be the overturning of the entire social and religious order (24:2) in judgment for violation of the covenant and adoption of a profligate, sensual mode of life (24:5). The faithful, righteous ones who will be vindicated in that day (26:2, 7) are identified as the poor and needy in 25:4 and 26:6. The overturning of the social order and the religious power structure will be accompanied by the defeat of both political and

---

3. Ibid., 66. Kee points out that this kind of writing has two central modes of discourse. The first is what he calls "eschatological-historical." In this mode the reader is alerted to the reality that God's purposes for creation have been overwhelmed by demonic forces; this cosmic reality has deleterious effects on the lives of human believers. The second is literary. The cosmic crisis sparks narrative and poetic interest in the eschatological endpoint, God's consummate vindication. But primary concentration lies not on that consummate end itself, but on the "present penultimate critical moment" which demands current endurance rather than future speculation. "Can Mark be appropriately understood on the basis of these dual modes, with what might be called an apocalyptic philosophy of history as its presupposition and with the literary strategy of apocalypse as providing its structure? Both parts of this question must be answered in the affirmative."

4. Myers, 102.

5. Marcus, *The Way of the Lord*, 19–29.

cosmic enemies (24:21), with the image of the dragon from the cosmic waters utilized as the symbol of diabolical evil (27:1)[6]

In this kind of interventionist-prophetic frame, it is no wonder that an interpreter could access the language of resurrection (25:8; 26:19) as representative of social and political transformation.

There is, however, some debate as to whether apocalyptic works of the period were concerned with historical transformation. Skeptics have pointed out that they were generally so preoccupied with otherworldly journeys and vindication located in otherworldly realms that there was little room, not to mention concern, for contemporary crisis realities. The apocalyptic writer attempted to relocate his readers' attentions to a world where justice will, and, in fact, already did mythologically prevail. Connecting Mark with this kind of interventionist preunderstanding would therefore seem, on the surface, to militate against the claim that he might expect his readers to access his language as a hope for this-worldly, socio-political transformation.

In his careful work on the genre of apocalyptic, however, Collins has noted that not all apocalyptic works are so exclusively otherworldly. Daniel and the aforementioned prophetic works from the Hebrew tradition are illustrative examples. These works, like later Jewish apocalyptic works which shared with Mark an interest in the human realm (cf. 1 Enoch: The Apocalypse of Weeks; 1 Enoch: The Animal Apocalypse; 4 Ezra; 2 Baruch), are historical apocalypses.[7] The character traits that set these apocalypses apart were an abiding interest in the problems and persecutions that occurred within human history, and a determined — one might even say "deterministic" — assurance that God would intervene historically to overturn them.[8] Indeed, according to Wright, this hope for historical liberation at the national level, which he defined as vindication, was not an ancillary, but a primary concern.

> It was a book which, in a complex blend of myth and metaphor, told the story of Israel's history, brought it into the present, and pointed forward to the moment when the forces of (this-worldly) evil would be routed and the (this-worldly) liberation of Israel would finally take place. It offered the clue to the *interpretation* of history, not the escape from it.[9]

No wonder, then, that Mark, who is so heavily indebted to and preoccupied with historical-apocalyptic works like Daniel, demonstrates God's divine kingdom authority moving through a human figure caught up in historical confrontation

---

6. Kee, *Community of the New Age,* 80.

7. John J. Collins, "The Jewish Apocalypses," *Semeia* 14 (1979): 22. Cf. also his *The Apocalyptic Imagination: An Introduction to the Jewish Matrix of Christianity* (New York: Crossroad, 1984) 206. "In both illustrations [Paul's apocalyptic and the Son of man Gospel passages], the major affinities of the New Testament are with the 'historical' apocalypses of Daniel's type rather than with the otherworldly journeys of Enoch."

8. J. Collins, *The Apocalyptic Imagination,* 206.

9. N. T. Wright, *The New Testament,* 393.

with the human authorities and cosmic forces of his time. Indeed, in his most explicit apocalyptic section, the sermon of chapter thirteen, the evangelist connects the movement of God to a review of the historically significant circumstances surrounding the sad denouement of the Jewish-Roman war.

The historical-interventionist perspective also offered a unique dualistic angle from which the evangelist could perceive the movement and structuring of time. The approach helped provide the faithful with an answer for the problem of theodicy. Faith asserted that God was in control of human history and destiny. God was also benevolent, particularly toward the faithful. These two principal thoughts caused dissension in the mind of a suffering believer. How could it be true both that God was in control and that God cared for the faithful, if the faithful were suffering?

In Mark's case, as I have reconstructed it, adversity was caused by two separate and competing forces: the occupying Roman forces and the false prophets and messiahs. If indeed Mark counseled his readers to reject both sides, they were liable to a double portion of persecution. But if their "non-aligned" following of Jesus was the proper response of faith to God's movement in the world through the divine Son, how was it that this very response attracted such suffering? This was the question a dualistic understanding of time helped answer in the historical apocalypse in general and Mark's Gospel in particular. The answer lay in the reality of two ages. In the present age evil had been allowed free reign; but in the age to come God would destroy the cosmic forces and human representatives of evil and vindicate the faithful and righteous. As Mark 13 makes clear, the evangelist understood that his community lived in the present age, but that the suffering of this age was itself a sign, the birth pangs, in fact, of God's coming intervention.

Wright points out that the concept of apocalyptic dualism is a rather complex one. There are, in fact, several distinct ways to approach the topic. Instead of considering all the facets of dualism that he considers, I want to consider those categories that are most meaningful to my own project. I would therefore appeal to a distinction between eschatological and cosmological dualism. Though both can be found in apocalyptic writings, it is my contention that it is the former that most appropriately represents Mark and the historical apocalypses and apocalyptic-prophetic materials upon which he bases his interventionist approach. Cosmological dualism opposes the two ages in such a way that the present age is so wicked as to be thought irredeemable. It must therefore be utterly destroyed before a "different and better" world can take its place. In this scenario transformation cannot be this-worldly, because, by definition, everything associated with this world is evil and must be demolished. The intervening God will, and indeed must, in the final age, start anew.

Eschatological dualism recognizes a distinction between the present age and the age to come, but does not necessarily see the present age as one beyond divine redemption. It is, in fact, this type of dualism that is most representative of Jewish writings, particularly, as Wright points out, the rabbinic and prophetic. It is no wonder, then, that Jewish writers, both prophetic and rabbinic, while appealing to God for the establishment of the new age, would do so with the expectation that the moment of divine intervention would transform rather than annihilate the present age.

> The great bulk of apocalyptic writing does not suggest that the space-time universe is evil, and does not look for it to come to an end. An end to the *present world order,* yes. Only such language, as Jeremiah found, could do justice to the terrible events of his day. The end of the space-time world, no.[10]

Wright points out that one could only take the apocalyptic imagery to mean an annihilation of the present age if the symbolism was taken literally. Historical-apocalyptic language is, however, representative rather than literal. The monsters, demonic figures, etc., represent the evil reality of the social and political forces that rule the present age. Their defeat represents the conquest of that evil and, therefore, the transformation into a new, liberated age. "This sense of 'representation' is common and well known. It is a standard feature of the genre."[11] The often bizarre metamorphoses that occurred in the mytho-logical arena, therefore, represented the apocalyptists' hope that God's kingdom intervention would transform the contemporary socio-political circumstance.

This representative process is on dramatic display in the eschatological du-alism of Daniel. The author's grandiose and shocking imagery corresponds to the social and political realities of Israel under Seleucid domination. God's di-vine intervention would not bring about the destruction of the present occupied age, but its transformation. This-worldly Israel would be liberated. Thus Kee can agree,

---

10. Ibid., 299–300. N. T. Wright goes on to make the persuasive case that cosmological du-alism, which implies that the created order is so evil as to require destruction, would contradict Israel's understanding of creational monotheism where creation, according to God's own review, was assessed to be "good."

11. Ibid., 289. To make the case N. T. Wright points to a poetic example from the "Testament of Moses," where this-worldly transformation is represented through the language of graphic turmoil in the heavenly arena. "It should be clear from the context of this poem that its meaning is not to be found by taking the cosmic imagery 'literally'. Sun, moon and stars function within a poem like this as deliberate symbols for the great powers of the world: to speak of them being shaken or dimmed is the kind of language a first-century writer might use quite naturally to express the awesome significance of great political events, such as the terrifying year (A.D. 68–69) in which four Roman emperors met violent deaths, and a fifth marched from Palestine to claim the throne" (N. T. Wright, *The New Testament,* 305). Though separated, the two worlds, the heavenly and the earthly, are in fact close enough that they can, like the two ages, the present and future, be interconnected when the boundaries between them are intervened by God or one whom God chooses as divine agent. In that way, the liberating reality of the heavenly and future age, mythologically represented, can invade and subsequently impact, in a radically transformative fashion, the socio-political circumstances of the earthly present. "This examination of 'representation' within apocalyptic literature helps to explain, I think, why the genre is what it is. Because the heavenly and the earthly realm belong closely with one another — which is a way of asserting the presence of the creator god within his creation and in the midst of his people — it makes theological sense to think of penetrating the mysteries of the heavenly realm and emerging with information that would relate to the earthly realm" (291).

What is remarkable in all this literature is that the apocalyptists move easily from the metaphorical representation of their historical enemies (the Seleucids; the corrupt priests) to demonic opponents, to cosmic powers. The political problems — involving both civil and religious authorities — will not be resolved until the demonic and cosmic powers are also brought under control (cf. The Song of Moses, Ex. 15, especially 4–10). The very fact that the imagery used to depict the political powers is drawn from the cosmic mythology of the ancient Near East — raging waters, mysterious mountains, falling stars, earthquakes — underscores the interconnection between present realities and unseen powers.[12]

In using this apocalyptic framework of eschatological dualism as the context of culture for his own historical-interventionist presentation, Mark has a particular point to make. God's intervention, as taking place through the Jesus event, represents its transformative challenge to the present socio-political age through its mythological language. It is no wonder that the controversy narratives (2:1–3:6; 11:27–12:44, which is introduced by Jesus' only negative miracle — the cursing of the fig tree), which highlight Jesus' direct confrontations with representatives of the Jewish leadership, are infused with stories of miracle, healing, and exorcism. In fact, Mark makes the connection explicit at 3:20–27, where a conflict between Jesus and some scribes is represented in the mythological language of conflict with the power of Satan. Jesus' defeat of Satanic power, represented by his miracle, exorcism and healing activity, indicates that he is taking control of the present age and, as the intercalation of the temple cleansing within the fig tree miracle makes clear, transforming it. It is interesting that, from Mark's point of view, this mythological struggle has specific socio-political implications. It represents a direct threat to the structure of Jewish society as the scribes have helped order it.

> The old order — its definition of sacred space, social status, and cultic/ political authority — is confronted and subverted through the narrative vehicle of conflict and exorcism stories. The new order — its imperatives of inclusivity, equality, servanthood, and suffering patience — is mediated through stories of conversion, miracles and healing, symbolic action, and parenetic teaching.[13]

The new order promised historical vindication. And while the objective of this intervention was on a more global scale the liberation of Israel from the powers that "exiled" her, there was always a more narrowed focus on a particular group in Israel. The apocalyptists were particularly concerned for those who remained faithful to God during times of great crisis and persecution. It was this particular "Israel" that would be vindicated when God's divine rule crossed the boundaries of human history. This faithful "remnant" was often characterized as socially,

---

12. Kee, *Community of the New Age,* 71.
13. Myers, 102.

politically, and economically oppressed. Intervention was envisioned and petitioned on its behalf. [14] In fact, Wright is so convinced of apocalyptic's concern for the poor and persecuted that he can say, "On all accounts, [it] can function, and we may suppose was intended to function, as the subversive literature of oppressed groups...."[15] In second temple Judaism these "oppressed" were particularly represented by the people of the land, the poor who were shut out of the economic, political and cultic administration of a Palestine under Roman control, and therefore sought a divinely initiated transformation of their present age.[16]

Considered in the light of this kind of interventionist preunderstanding, language that otherwise appears exclusively personal in its orientation can be accessed in a decidedly socio-political way. Because this vindication is narrated in the representative language of the new age and the forgiveness of sins, the apocalyptist makes it clear that at the center of this historical transformation is a foundational theological meaning. A theological strategy backs up the tactical change in the political situation of faithful Israel and the nations who persecute her. It is never a merely political transformation, but is always a historical situation that reflects an ultimate theological reality. It is for this reason that the language, while representative of socio-political realities, appeals to the "apparently" otherworldly imagery of a divine kingdom and the cosmic forces who array themselves against it. This is why, appealing to apocalyptic poetry in the "Testament of Moses," Wright concludes, "The language and imagery of the poem is designed to *denote* future socio-political events, and to *invest* those events with their full 'theological' significance."[17]

When accessed from this kind of interventionist preunderstanding, the interpretative possibilities surrounding the language of sin and resurrection widen dramatically. Mark highlights the vocabulary of sin-forgiveness in his presentation of John the Baptist. Though this language most often conjures up reflections of personal redemption, in the context of the historical apocalypse its representative force is most closely linked with a hope for national restoration: "if this [restoration] was to happen Israel's god had to deal with her sins. The end of the exile, in fact, would be seen as the great sign that this had been accom-

---

14. Shea, 86.

15. N. T. Wright, *The New Testament,* 288. J. Collins agrees, though he points out that one must allow for the fact that the kind of distress perceived by these 'oppressed' groups is not of a single kind. Indeed, D. Hellholm was so convinced that apocalyptic literature has the specific concern for groups in distress that he suggested an addition to the definition of apocalyptic literature (a genre of revelatory literature with a narrative framework, in which a revelation is mediated by an otherworldly being to a human recipient, disclosing a transcendent reality which is both temporal, insofar as it envisages eschatological salvation, and spatial insofar as it involves another, supernatural world [J. Collins, *The Apocalyptic Imagination,* 4]) that Collins and others had established from their *Semeia* 14 collaboration. He recommended that the addition read that the apocalypse was "intended for a group in crisis with the purpose of exhortation and/or consolation by means of divine authority" (J. Collins, *The Apocalyptic Imagination,* 31).

16. Kee, *Community of the New Age,* 79. But the lack of social concern about certain parts of society on the part of the political powers and their exclusive concentration on economic exploitation served only "to exacerbate the situation of the lower strata of the population. It prepared the ground for apocalyptic speculation and the later revolts, which had increasingly strong social elements, right down to the time of the Bar Kochba rebellion."

17. N. T. Wright, *The New Testament,* 306.

plished. The promise of forgiveness and that of national restoration were thus linked causally, not by mere coincidence.... "[18]

Appealing to Daniel, Wright points out that the resurrection language of 12:1b–3 represents the hope for national deliverance from persecution and suffering.[19] Despite the "apparently" otherworldly imagery of personal rejuvenation in a heavenly, non-physical existence, Wright refocuses the reader's attention. Resurrection language is a metaphor, a literary representation of a historical, social and political transformative hope.[20] Thus, John Collins can write,

> This aspect of apocalyptic language has not been adequately appreciated by theologians. The apocalyptic literature does not lend itself easily to the ontological and objectivist concerns of systematic theology. It is far more congenial to the pragmatic tendency of liberation theology, which is not engaged in the pursuit of objective truth but in the dynamics of motivation and the exercise of political power.[21]

---

18. Ibid., 300.

19. Ibid., 322.

20. Ezekiel's dramatic imagery of the rejuvenation of corpses is a case in point. Here the mythological symbolism clearly represents a hope not for personal immortality, but for the return of the people from exile. Once again, the intent of the author is to invest a present socio-political hope with theological significance by using cosmological, interventionist language. (Ibid., 322, 332.) The literature of Second Maccabees provides ample evidence for such a claim. The narrative describes seven brothers who are vainly tortured in an attempt to have them submit to an edict by Antiochus Epiphanes. Their hope beyond suffering and death is for a physical resurrection, a future bodily life in a new creation, not an immortal soul in an otherworldly realm. In other words, as was the case for forgiveness of sins, the hope for resurrection is placed in the context of national restoration in a new age. (Ibid., 323. Cf. 2 Maccabees 7:9, 14, 21–23, 29, 33, 36–38.) N. T. Wright agrees, however, that later some Jewish authors spiritualized (the expectation of an immortal soul) this hope for physical resurrection due to Hellenistic philosophical and religious influences. He provides the work of Josephus on pages 324–28 as an example. Still, he concludes that the majority of Jews during the period were still influenced, when discussions of resurrection arose, most critically by this apocalyptic preunderstanding of national restoration. "Rather the eschatological expectation of most Jews of this period was for a renewal, not an abandonment, of the present space-time order as a whole, and themselves within it. Since this was based on the justice and mercy of the creator god, the god of Israel, it was inconceivable that those who had died in the struggle to bring the new world into being should be left out of the blessing when it eventually broke upon the nation and then the world" (*The New Testament,* 331–32).

"As good creational monotheists, mainline Jews were not hoping to escape from the present universe into some Platonic realm of eternal bliss enjoyed by disembodied souls after the end of the space time universe. If they died in a fight for the restoration of Israel, they hoped not to 'go to heaven,' or at least not permanently, but to be raised to new bodies when the kingdom came, since they would of course need new bodies to enjoy the very much this-worldly *shalom,* peace and prosperity that was in store" (286).

21. J. Collins, *The Apocalyptic Imagination,* 215. Cf. N. T. Wright, *The New Testament,* 282–84 for examples of this-worldly intervention in Jewish Apocalyptic. Wright points, for instance, to the Apocalypse of Abraham (12:1–10: "This is the essence of apocalyptic: to Abraham are revealed secrets of all sorts. As a result, he learns new ways of worshipping the true God, and finally glimpses [chapter 31] the future deliverance of Israel." [282]), 2 Baruch (36:1–37:1: "[The vision] assures the faithful that the kingdom which is presently oppressing them will be overthrown, and Israel restored.... The writer of 2 Baruch was clearly not writing, in the last analysis, about forestry and viticulture: living after the disaster of A.D. 70, he intended to say something about Israel, her oppression and her future hope." [282]), and 4 Ezra ("So, too, it is possible and even likely that a book such as 4 Ezra, written like 2 Baruch after the destruction of the Temple in A.D. 70, contains actual visions seen during actual mystical experience, and *at the same time* regularly intends to speak of actual Israel, her present suffering and her future hope" [284]).

While Daniel's otherworldly language represented the concern of the faithful that God would intercede on their behalf against Seleucid oppression, in the second temple period, Jewish apocalyptic imagery envisioned that God's interventionist activity would confront Roman occupation. In fact, each of the Jewish responses to Roman rule catalogued by scholarship demonstrates some type of interventionist orientation. Like Jesus, the Zealots used a theological slogan to motivate followership. Where Jesus had appealed to "the kingdom of God," these nationalistic and violent revolutionaries operated from the premise that there was "no master but God."[22] It was this mythological faith premise that formed the foundation for their demand that all faithful Jews should join the revolt. God was about to act historically in a very socio-political way, and those who stood with God should show their allegiance through a very specific kind of participatory response.

Even passive Jewish resistance aimed at this-worldly, socio-political intervention. The situation surrounding Caligula's ill-advised attempt to erect a statue of himself in the Jerusalem Temple is a case in point. Josephus records how the Jews who resisted the move were willing to subject themselves to voluntary execution rather than allow the abomination of the sacred place. The resistance, in other words, had a transformative objective; it was not a case of fatalistic surrender. There remained, despite the apparent futility of their situation, the certainty that God would physically intervene.

> According to Josephus, the men who faced Petronius, at the time of the crisis precipitated by Caligula, reasoned that, for those who were determined to take the risk "there is hope even of prevailing; for God will stand by us if we welcome danger for his glory" (Antiq. 18.267). They hoped, that is, that if reason did not prevail God would intercede, either fighting on their side, or producing a miracle that would confound the enemies of his temple.[23]

Sanders also mentions a kind of response to Roman domination that was intermediate to the aforementioned two. In this case the faithful were prepared to take up arms and initiate a confrontation with the Romans, assured that their actions would prompt God's direct socio-historical involvement. God would finish the fight and restore faithful Israel's political fortunes. The man Josephus calls "The Egyptian" is a case in point. During the time of Felix's procuratorship (52–59 C.E.), the Egyptian gathered a multitude and marched on Jerusalem (*War* 2.261–63). Following the prophecy of Zechariah 9–14, he asked the people to join him on the Mount of Olives, where he claimed that, at his command the walls would fall (*Antiquities* 20.169–72). Sanders is justified in concluding that the Egyptian was never so deluded as to think that he could himself prevail against the superior force of the Romans. And yet he could still expect the

---

22. Cf. Sanders, *Judaism: Practice and Belief,* 282.
23. Ibid., 284.

kind of political transformation that would come from a victorious confrontation because he believed that God would finish the fight he started.

> The statement in the *Antiquities,* that he and his followers expected the walls to fall down, probably points in the right direction, at least in part. His followers had not counted swords, spears and armour, and concluded that they could outman and outfight the Romans; they thought, rather, that if they would take the first step, if putting their lives at risk would strike the first blow, God himself would see to the rest.[24]

Common to each kind of response to national oppression and political domination was the expectation that God would intervene. Mythological imagery and apocalyptic symbol were used in the service of motivating hope and often action for a divinely directed socio-political intervention. It is a constituent element of the kind of preunderstanding that characterized the cultural context of second temple Judaism.

> What is much clearer is the widespread hope of a *new age* on this earth, one in which the God of Israel will reign supreme, being served by loyal Jews, and possibly by converted Gentiles, in purity and obedience. This is a main theme, which runs from the biblical prophets to such diverse later sources as the Qumran scrolls and Philo. The hope that God would fundamentally change things was a perfectly reasonable hope for people to hold who read the Bible and who believed that God had created the world and had sometimes intervened dramatically to save his people.[25]

Roman domination was not, however, the only target of this interventionist preunderstanding. Usually when one thinks of the kind of socio-political transformation anticipated by Jews of the second temple period, it is agreed that the overturning of Roman occupation was the singular objective. But the expectation for God's intervention was also directed at socio-political transformation within Israel. This is particularly important to remember given the earlier realization that apocalyptic expectations were not established on behalf of Israel as a whole, but on behalf of the faithful within Israel. Interventionist agendas were often sectarian. These "faithful," as Mark's Gospel (in the case of Jesus and his followers) and the separatist Qumran community clearly demonstrates, often found themselves at odds with priestly and scribal authorities.

In Qumran there was the adamant call for a more rigorous application of the purity and holiness codes of the Israelite tradition. Convinced that inadequate attention to divine demands provoked God's judgmental anger, followers of the Teacher of Righteousness held to a strict code that vigorously set them apart from the interpretation of the ruling Temple authorities. Because of their more rigorous position on the law, this community felt itself oppressed by the authorities. This sense of persecution and oppression motivated them to withdraw

---

24. Ibid., 285.
25. Ibid., 303.

from Jewish life as directed by what they perceived to be a corrupt "... coalition of pagan political power: Jewish collaborationists, the priestly bureaucracy, and a largely indifferent local populace."[26] Their subsequent interventionist visions were therefore directed not only against Rome, but just as provocatively against the corrupt priestly leadership of their own people and religious heritage.[27]

4 Ezra provides a similar interventionist perspective. Because of the people's iniquities, when God intervenes he will punish Israel as a whole and provide transformative comfort only for those within the community who have remained faithful. Ultimately, that intervention, because Israel as a whole has become so corrupt, turns its positive emphases even toward responsive Gentiles. Key again, though, is the fact that God's this-worldly interventionist behavior can target its transformative behavior against corruption and oppression in Israel as well as against the domination of an outside force like Rome.[28]

What is of vital significance in this discussion of the historical apocalyptic context of culture is the realization that God will intervene on behalf of the faithful among God's people. This intervention will inaugurate a this-worldly transformation of a communal, socio-political nature. It is preunderstood in the writing of the historical apocalypse that God's historic intercession not only encourages this-worldly endurance, but promises a new age which will revolu-

---

26. Howard Clark Kee, "The Social Setting of Mark: An Apocalyptic Community," *SBL Seminar Papers* (1984) 247.

27. Craig A. Evans, "Predictions of the Destruction of the Herodian Temple in the Pseudepigrapha, Qumran Scrolls, and Related Texts," *Journal for the Study of the Pseudepigrapha* 10 (1992): 89–147. In terms of the perceived corruption of the priesthood, Evans points out that one has to decide whether references to the "Wicked Priest" also represent the views of the community in the later period, i.e., the time of Jesus and the time of the writing of Mark. Evans makes the point that the eschatological interpretation of the Qumran community makes it likely that the criticism of the original Wicked Priest also represents the critical attitude toward the priesthood of the first century community (130–31). In any event, the Wicked Priest is accused of robbing the people, including the poor (1QpHab 8.12; 9.5; 10.1; 12.10) and amassing wealth (1QpHab 8.8–12; 9.4–5). This material also speaks of judgment of the Wicked Priest, though it is not clear whether this entails destruction of the Temple as well. (96–7) As 1QpHab states, *"Because you have plundered many nations, all the remnant of the peoples shall plunder you:* interpreted this concerns the last Priests of Jerusalem, who shall amass money and wealth by plundering the peoples. But in the last days, their riches and booty shall be delivered into the hands of the army of the Kittim, for it is they who shall be the *remnant of the peoples."*

28. Cf. James H. Charlesworth, editor, *The Old Testament Pseudepigrapha*, Volume I: *Apocalyptic Literature and Testaments* (Garden City, New York: Doubleday & Company, 1983) 525–29, 538–39. "Go and declare to my people their evil deeds, and to their children the iniquities which they have committed against me, so that they may tell their children's children that the sins of their parents have increased in them, for they have forgotten me and have offered sacrifices to strange gods" (1:4–6).

"What shall I do to you, O Jacob? You would not obey me, O Judah. I will turn to other nations and will give them my name, that they may keep my statutes. Because you have forsaken me, I also will forsake you" (1:24).

"Thus says the Lord to Ezra: 'Tell my people that I will give them the kingdom of Jerusalem, which I was going to give to Israel. Moreover, I will take back to myself their glory, and will give to these others the everlasting habitations, which I had prepared for Israel'" (2:10–11).

"So also will be the judgment which I have promised; for I will rejoice over the few who shall be saved, because it is they who have made my glory to prevail now, and through them my name has now been honored. And I will not grieve over the multitude of those who perish; for it is they who are now like a mist, and are similar to a flame and smoke — they are set on fire and burn hotly, and are extinguished" (7:60–61).

tionize the human historical circumstance. That intervention, whether facilitated by a messianic agent or by God,[29] is not otherworldly and escapist in its agenda, but targets the oppressions of this world and seeks to reverse them, so that those who wait upon the strategic movement of the Lord will be socio-politically as well as spiritually vindicated. The mythological language of intervention, then, can represent the firm expectation of socio-historical change.

---

29. There has been a great deal of material written on the matter of making a distinction between God's direct intervention and intervention initiated and orchestrated by a messianic representative. While this discussion would take us too far afield of the primary concern of the fact of the intervention itself, it is useful to mention the recent discussion N. T. Wright presents on the issue (*The New Testament,* 307–20). Helpful appeals are made to primary texts which elucidate the various passages which appeal to intervention directly by God and/or by a messiah figure.

Part III

The Kingdom of God in Mark

Crossing Boundaries

An Excursus

Strategy and Tactics

My contemporary-contextual perspective has been forged from the social and political involvement of the African-American church in the United States, particularly its participation in the Civil Rights struggle of the sixties and early seventies. To be sure, the contemporary African-American church became sufficiently fragmented that social and political activism are no longer essential components of its communal life. Still, given the continued struggle for socio-political equality and economic achievement for the majority of its black constituency, a political edge remains in much of its rhetoric. Scholarship continues to ask whether this edge has been honed by the witness of the biblical texts or inappropriately grafted onto the text by preachers and teachers who force it to speak to alien issues. That is to say, when an interpreter's evaluation of a biblical text yields a socio-political meaning, has that interpreter correctly assessed the text, or, feeling the need to speak to the social and political plight of his or her people, has that interpreter forced the text to say something that was originally beyond its range of interest?

I would argue that such an interpreter, because of his or her contemporary-contextual perspective, may well see (access) a part of the text's meaning potential, in this case its socio-political component, that other readers miss. I am convinced that this is indeed the case for an interpreter operating from a contemporary-contextual perspective like mine. I am also convinced that it is the case with the community that originally accessed the language in the Gospel of Mark, since that community approached the language from a contemporary-contextual perspective of apocalyptic intervention.

There is, of course, a problem. Because scholarship inappropriately confuses the strategic goal with the tactical actions devised to implement it, the socio-political implications of Mark's text have been downplayed or dismissed. Mainstream Markan interpretation focuses on the strategic goal of God's intervening kingdom as represented in the ministry and person of Jesus. In Mark's narrative the reader can only gauge God's strategic intent by studying Jesus'

tactical activity. That intent is redemptive, the reestablishment of broken relations between God and humans. Humans will be brought near and into the
kingdom. It is for this reason that in the first controversy story of 2:1–12, Jesus'
healing of the paralytic represents the larger goal of forgiving sin. In his activity and person, Jesus provides an opening to God's forgiveness that need
not detour through the institutionalized provisions of the Temple cult and the
religio-political leadership who maintain it.[1]

Consider Mark's careful choice of salvation language. In his world view,
Jesus' mythological healings represent God's strategic intent for the salvation
of broken, that is to say, sinful humankind. At 3:4; 5:23, 28, 34; 6:56; and 10:52,
it is the language of "to save" (σώζω) that describes Jesus' cures, the same language Mark's Jesus uses at 8:35, 10:26, and 13:13, 20, passages which clearly
indicate that being saved means being drawn into the kingdom presence of God.
Jesus' tactical actions represent and accomplish the redemptive-strategic goal
("saving") of God's kingdom.

But a tactic need not be of the same essence as the strategic goal it wants to
implement. Defeat and victory are not synonymous, and yet a careful strategist
can tactically utilize the former to achieve the latter. Defeat can be, and often
has been, used to accomplish victory. Jesus' own crucifixion is one of history's
most intriguing examples. The early church used his scandalous end as the impetus for inaugurating its successful, universal program of spreading the gospel
about him. Chess champions routinely deploy the tactical sacrifice of pawns or
other lesser pieces in a strategic design to obtain victory. Military strategists
have, with considerable success, either planned or exploited a loss in battle to
orchestrate conditions favorable for success in the larger war. One might consider the tactical interpretation of the Battle of Dunkirk in World War II. The
decisive defeat of the British by the German forces could well have been even
more crushing than it was had a suddenly over-cautious Hitler not restrained
his forces from prosecuting the kind of complete pursuit and annihilation that
his commanders desired. As it developed, however, the hesitancy of the German
leader allowed the beaten and retreating British forces a spectacularly legendary
escape. Tactical use was made of that flight and the heroism associated with it
to spur the Allied forces in a way that a victorious engagement there probably
could not have. The tactical use of the defeat therefore helped accomplish the
strategic goal of victory. It is fair to say, then, that although the Allies went on
to victory in the global conflict, the defeat at Dunkirk represented the spirit of
the war. The defeat represents the ultimate victory, what the victory stood for,
the price that was paid to achieve it, and the indomitable character and spirit of
the men and women who realized it.

Examples are, of course, voluminous. While Jesus' tactical preaching activities are never in such direct contrast with the strategic kingdom goal he
seeks to accomplish, it is the case that his tactical activities are not always

---

1. This appears to be Mark's emphasis at 15:38, when he narrates the tearing of the temple
veil from top to bottom. The powerful proclamations of 10:45 and 14:24 reinforce the narrative
perception that Jesus is a wedge whose life and death open the believer to the possibility of God's
kingdom salvation.

of the same material essence as the strategic goal he hopes to accomplish by them. In fact, I will argue that in Mark's presentation Jesus often tactically utilizes a socio-political (boundary-crossing) religious agenda in order to represent and accomplish what many consider its exact opposite, a redemptive-religious strategic end.

6

Preaching the Kingdom

In Mark's literary strategy every narrative theme develops from the primary assertion that in Jesus Christ God has intervened into human history. That mythological reality is represented historically in the text by Jesus' assault against oppressive political, economic and cultic boundaries. That is to say, Jesus' narrative crossing of political, social, and religious constraints, and the challenge this "intervention" represents to the leaders who maintained and interpreted them, elucidates tactically what God was doing strategically.

One of the primary reasons many scholars argue against a Markan sociopolitical concern is that Mark does not narrate a Jesus who promotes revolution against Rome. In fact, Mark intended to convince his readers that the Zealot path was counseled by false prophets and counterfeit messiahs. His political objective, then, was certainly not the overthrow of Roman authority. And yet, there were religious groups in Palestine operating from an interventionist perspective who believed that fellow Jews were also, and perhaps primarily, responsible for cultic abuse and social oppression. "Sects like the Essenes believed that the present order, in which the wrong Jews held power, would come to an end, and a new world order would be inaugurated in which the right Jews, i.e., themselves, attained power instead."[1] Surely, such a sectarian, religious-mythological vision would have represented a realistic socio-political threat if the Essenes had not withdrawn into the desert.

Jesus, who certainly did not withdraw, had, at least in Mark's presentation, such a "sectarian-religious" agenda in mind. The evangelist's interventionist design was based upon the premise that God must act through his son because the leaders of the people had led them astray. This is no doubt why, speaking about the parable of the vineyard at 12:1–11, Rhoads and Michie make the point that "the story implies that the human authorities have been ruling for themselves rather than God. . . . It is at this point in the story world that the narrative opens, with the Lord of the vineyard beginning something new by sending his son to the vineyard."[2] In the Markan field of discourse, that new "religious" vision,

---

1. N. T. Wright, *The New Testament,* 333.
2. David Rhoads and Donald Michie, *Mark as Story: An Introduction to the Narrative of a Gospel* (Philadelphia: Fortress Press, 1982) 74.

because of its potent challenge to Israel's cultic-political rulers, has dramatic "political" consequences.

Mark's tenor of discourse lends personality to the story's interventionist agenda. Mark characterizes what it means for God to intervene in the human arena by the way he positions his characters in relationship to one another. Therefore, when we understand the meaning behind their dialogues and the roles they play, we get a clearer sense of God's kingdom strategy as Mark understands it. God's process of kingdom intervention is not limited to the character Jesus. While Jesus is the only one who represents the kingdom in his person, others in the text have the distinct honor of representing the power and reality of the kingdom in their behavior. That is to say, humans play a role in the ushering forth of the kingdom rule.

Finally, Mark's mode of discourse clues us in to the ultimate aim of the kingdom stratagem. The grammatical texture and rhetorical flow of the language indicate the message the author wants to leave with his readers. Mark is doing more than merely representing and characterizing God's intervention; he is also relating that divine act to human living and discipleship in such a way as to leave his readers with an "apocalyptic" ethic for action. It is my contention, then, that Mark wants to do much more than explain how God is intervening through the "act" of Jesus; he is using that explanation as the foundation for an apocalyptic appeal. He wants his readers to position themselves so that they, too, can be tactical conduits through which the power of the mythological kingdom can find a tangible, historical point of flow. In other words, his readers are to do what Jesus did, wield the power of the future, divine kingdom in the present, human circumstance.

JESUS' PROGRAMMATIC KINGDOM STATEMENT: MARK 1:14, 15

[1:14] After John was betrayed, Jesus came into Galilee *preaching* the gospel of God [1:15] and *saying,* "the time is fulfilled, and the kingdom of heaven has drawn near; repent and believe in the gospel."[3]

Beginning with the immediate kingdom statement and moving out into the broader context of situation as the evidence warrants, I find that the text establishes the concept of preaching as its principal access point. Preaching, particularly the preaching of Jesus about the kingdom, acts as the literary mechanism through which God's future kingdom power intervenes in the present moment. Jesus' proclamation is an event which in its very speaking inaugurates, at least in the form of a present pocket, the thing it declares, the imminently coming kingdom. It is not, however, an act/event unique to Jesus. His preaching

---

3. Translation mine. Μετὰ δὲ τό παραδοθῆναι τὸν Ἰωάννην ἦλθεν ὁ Ἰησοῦς εἰς τὴν Γαλιλαίαν κηρύσσων τὸ εὐαγγέλιον τοῦ θεοῦ καὶ λέγων ὅτι Πεπλήρωται ὁ καιρὸς καὶ ἤγγικεν ἡ βασιλεία τοῦ θεοῦ· μετανοεῖτε καὶ πιστεύετε ἐν τῷ εὐαγγελίῳ.

is presented by Mark as both the successor to John's proclamation of God's intervention through him, and the prototype for the preaching of those who follow him as disciples. Their contemporary preaching in the Markan community is to do what Jesus' preaching did a generation before, establish the kingdom of God as a "pocket" that resists the oppressive social, religious and political boundaries that litter the landscape of human living. Mark dramatizes this accomplishment through the presentation of his text characters. Their "preaching" achievements become the tactical models which establish the ethical mandate for the disciples in the Markan community.

FIELD OF DISCOURSE

Mark establishes this theme by the way he structures his story. The broad field of discourse has a story segmentation of ten principal parts. Each part contributes to the overall theme of apocalyptic intervention that bonds the story into a narrative whole.

The first part, 1:1–3, indicates that Mark's literary effort is a presentation about God's historical appearance in the form of the Lord (v. 3), who is defined in verse one as the Messiah, and identified more informally as Jesus. And whether one accepts the appellation, son of God, as textual or not,[4] it is certain, given the declaration of the heavenly speaker in verse eleven (you are my beloved son), that Mark presents his protagonist as the manifestation of God's prophesied intervention into human reality. This is the good news; Jesus represents in his person the mythological movement of God, as Lord, into human space and time.[5] There is no talk of kingdom yet. Indeed, the kingdom dis-

---

4. Cf. Mary Ann Tolbert, *Sowing the Gospel: Mark's World in Literary-Historical Perspective* (Minneapolis: Fortress Press, 1989) 110, n.43. Tolbert's discussion acknowledges the textual problems and the textual evidence that strongly support both an inclusion and exclusion of the phrase. Her chiastic structural argument for chapter 1, however, adds literary weight to the argument for believing the phrase to have existed in the earliest manuscript copy.

5. This argument presumes my understanding that εὐαγγελίου Ἰησοῦ Χριστοῦ is being used here as an objective genitive. There is, of course, a wide variety of opinion on the matter. A listing of authors who consider it to be a subjective genitive include: Georg Strecker, "Das Evangelium Jesu Christi," in *Jesus Christus in Historie und Theologie: Neutestamentliche Festschrift für Hans Conzelmann zum 60. Geburtstag*, ed. Georg Strecker (Tübingen: J. C. B. Mohr, 1975) 503–48: 535. C. E. B. Cranfield, *The Gospel According to Saint Mark* (Cambridge: Cambridge University Press, 1959). Because he takes the subjective genitive as primary with the objective as an implicit undertone, he could also be taken to view the usage as a combination of subjective and objective uses. G. Dautzenbert, "Die Zeit des Evangeliums: Mk 1:1–15 und die Konzeption des Markusevangeliums," *Biblische Zeitschrift* 21 (1977): 219–34. Others consider it an objective genitive: Robert H. Gundry, *Mark: A Commentary on His Apology for the Cross* (Grand Rapids: William B. Eerdmans Publishing Co., 1993) 31–32. Eduard Schweizer, *The Good News According to Mark*, Donald H. Madvig, translator (Atlanta: John Knox Press, 1970) 28. Robert A. Guelich, *Mark 1–8:26, Word Biblical Commentary* (Dallas: Word Books, 1989) 9. However, in an earlier article, he states, the objective genitive in 1:1 expressed as "the gospel about Jesus messiah, Son of God," subsumes as integral to it a subjective genitive expressed "in the gospel of the kingdom proclaimed by Jesus." The thrust of his argument against a subjective reading is that it reads 1:1 in light of 1:14–15 rather than the reverse, placing too much emphasis on the latter. "'The Beginning of the Gospel' Mark 1:1–15," *Biblical Research* 27 (1982): 5–15. Cf. also E. Klostermann, *Das Markusevangelium*, HNT 3 (Tübingen: Mohr, 1950); W. L. Lane,

cussion that will come some twelve verses later, must, as regards the field of discourse, be seen from this interventionist perspective. Mark's focus is on God's intervention in Jesus. It is on this emphasis that he both begins his narrative here and concludes it at 16:8. He wants his readers to recognize first and foremost that Jesus is the literary (in his story) and historical (in the tradition) representation of that intervention. The preached statement, "the kingdom of God is near," is a way of sloganizing that principal reality. The kingdom message, then, is not Mark's primary focus; God's movement through Jesus is. We must therefore, when we get to the kingdom statement, see it in the light of this overall structural theme. It may well have been, as even Mark's story presents it, that Jesus' central message was the preaching of the kingdom. But we are not dealing with the historical Jesus here. We are focusing on the story of Jesus presented to us by the Markan account. In this account, Jesus' kingdom message does not open and close the story. The realization that God has entered human reality through Jesus does.

The second principal part, verses four through eight, maintains this focus. The introduction of John the Baptist obviously initiates a new section in verse four. Given that verses one through three prepare us for the introduction of either the prophesied lord or the one who will preface him as messenger, we assume immediately that John fits one of these two character designations. In verses four through six, Mark hints that John is the precursor to the messiah when he tells us that he is preaching in the wilderness/desert. The prophecy he recounted at verse three has already warned us that the messenger who is to prepare the way of the Lord will raise his voice in the wilderness/desert. John preaches a baptism of repentance into the forgiveness (leaving behind — ἄφεσιν, v. 4) of sins. People heed his voice, come out to him, confess their sins, and submit to his baptism.

Mark has not yet, however, delivered all that is important about John's preaching. In verses seven and eight, he declares that his preaching has an important content. Using the phrase "and he preached, saying," he defines it. The point is that John's baptism does not stand alone; it is based on his preached declaration ("saying") that someone comes after him who is stronger than he is, someone who will baptize the people in Holy Spirit.[6] The return to mythologi-

---

The Gospel According to Mark, New International Commentary on the New Testament (Grand Rapids: Eerdmans, 1974); R. Pesch, *Das Markusevangelium,* Herders theologischer Kommentar zum Neuen Testament, 2 vols. (Freiburg: Herder, 1976/7); R. Schnackenburg, "Das Evangelium im Verständnis des ältesten Evangelisten." *Orientierung an Jesus,* J. Schmidt, ed. (Freiburg: Herder, 1973) 309–24; V. Taylor, *The Gospel According to Mark,* 2d ed. (London: Macmillan/New York: St. Martin's Press, 1966); J. Wellhausen, *Das Evangelium Marci,* 2d ed., (Berlin: Raeimer, 1909). Finally, there are those who perceive the usage to be a combination of subjective and objective uses. John G. Cook, *The Structure and Persuasive Power of Mark: A Linguistic Approach, SBL Semeia Studies* (Atlanta: Scholars Press, 1995) 155–56. Joachim Gnilka, *Das Evangelium nach Markus* (Neukirchen-Vluyn: Neukirchner Verlag, 1978). Gerhard Friedrich, "εὐαγγελίζομαι, κτλ," *TDNT* 2:707–37, 728. Willi Marxsen, *Mark the Evangelist: Studies on the Redaction History of the Gospel,* James Boyce, Donald Juel, William Poehlmann, Roy A. Harrisville, translators (Nashville: Abingdon Press, 1969). H. Anderson, *The Gospel of Mark* (London: Oliphants, 1976).
    6. Note the parallel use of the verb "preach" from verse 4 where John is preaching a baptism

cal language implies a return to Mark's opening theme, divine intervention. He baptizes in order to prepare the people for the introduction of God's messiah.

The language, "one who comes after me," does not, in this field of discourse, suggest discipleship. Owing to verses one through three, it confirms instead that John is the forerunner who is to prepare the way for the Lord, the Messiah, who is evidently the one John now proclaims will be stronger than he is. And John's strength, at least as far as the narrative now discloses, is that his charismatic preaching and baptizing with water attract people from all of the Judean countryside and all of Jerusalem (v. 5).[7] Certainly, as many commentators have recognized, Mark is here appealing to hyperbole. One cannot imagine that every single person in the surrounding Judean countryside and Jerusalem literally came out to John. The literary inference, though, is that all of the people of God in the land of God's people come out to hear this man preach, and be baptized by him. This preacher represents a strong and powerful interventionist truth to which people respond in a powerful way. That is his strength. And yet, the baptismal purpose of his preaching is the announcement that someone will follow who will be even stronger.

The implication, then, is that John has a role to play in the acting out of God's intervention through Jesus. His role is to prepare the way for the Messiah by preparing the people, that is to say, by getting them to repent. Their repentance in this case is the negation (which is to say, leaving behind — ἄφεσιν, v. 4) of their sinful ways; that negation is symbolized by their submission to his baptismal rite. Mark's overall message is clear: human repentance is the appropriate response to the realization that God is intervening in human reality through the protagonist who has been identified in verse one as Jesus, and is now being preached by the charismatic John as one who is stronger than he is. The interventionist focal point, then, is not on the baptism, but on the preaching about the coming one of God whose coming makes the baptism necessary.

Principal part number three, verses nine through thirteen, introduces the stronger one to the drama of the story. Jesus enters and, in scenes saturated with apocalyptic imagery, is baptized by John.

1:14–15 forms the fourth principal part. Jesus' work is now introduced in the same way as John's, through the use of the verb "preach" (κηρύσσω). The difference is that, instead of preaching a baptism of repentance based on the realization that the Messiah is coming, Jesus, who is the Messiah, comes into Galilee preaching the good news of God. But I have already argued that Mark's good news is that God has intervened in Jesus. Jesus, therefore, apparently has the dubious and somewhat shameless honor of preaching himself.

Before the reader can be caught up in this problematic realization, Mark defines the content of Jesus' preaching in the same way that he defined the content of John's, with the masculine, singular, nominative participle "saying"

---

of repentance into the forgiveness of sins. Here at verse 7, Mark defines the content of that preaching with the participle, "saying."

7. Some might suggest that John's strength lies in the baptism which leads to a forgiveness of sins. But, as 2:7 indicates, only God was understood to have the capability of sin-forgiveness. John's act, then, is celebratory and symbolic of someone else's strength (God's), not his own.

(λέγων, v. 15), which, this time, occurs under the direct literary supervision of the masculine, singular, nominative participle "preaching" (κηρύσσων) in verse fourteen. In other words, Jesus' behavior, his coming, his intervention into the scene and the Galilean landscape, is contextualized by, and therefore given meaning through his act of preaching. Jesus, who is God's intervention, *comes* preaching that the kingdom of God, which is a metaphorical way of describing God's intervention, has *come* near.

When we analyze Mark's tenor of discourse we will develop a better understanding of the complexities involved. For now, a logical equation will help clarify what Mark's language is suggesting. The formulaic expression is as follows: if A equals B, and A equals C, then B must also equal C. In this Markan scenario, A is God's intervention into human reality. This is the primary message, the good news. B is Jesus, who in verses 1–3 and 9–13 is identified as that intervention. A equals B. C is the kingdom of God, which Jesus comes preaching as God's intervention in 1:15. A therefore also equals C. The formula therefore requires that B equal C, or, to put it more clearly, that Jesus, at least in Mark's field of discourse, equals the kingdom of God.

There is, of course, an immediate problem with time. Jesus stands in the present moment of the Markan story world, while the kingdom is portrayed in the story world through Jesus' preaching as a future reality. And yet they are narratively equal. In the Markan story Jesus, then, must represent in the present moment the reality of God's future intervention into human space and time. He is, so to speak, a manifestation of the future that has formed a pocket of personal identity and preaching in the present.

Principal part number five, verses sixteen through twenty, continues Jesus' preaching from part four. Jesus, who in verses fourteen and fifteen was preaching (κηρύσσων), saying (λέγων) "the kingdom is at hand, repent and believe," is now passing (παράγων) alongside the Sea of Galilee. The narrative suggestion is that the soon-to-be disciples' recognition of that intervention, in both his message and person, prompts their positive response to Jesus' radical invitation that they leave their former lives and accept his invitation to become fishers of people, that is to say, disciples.[8]

Four disciples in tow, Jesus turns his interest in the sixth principal part, verses twenty-one to twenty-eight, to a synagogue in Capernaum. The action in verse twenty-one initiates from another participial formation, "after entering the synagogue, he taught" (εἰσελθὼν εἰς τὴν συναγωγὴν ἐδίδασκεν). Once again, the continuation of the masculine, singular, nominative participles in the introduction of the section suggests that the ensuing activity, his teaching, should be interpreted in light of the central metaphorical "preaching" (κηρύσσων) about God's kingdom intervention.

The description of Jesus' movement with the participle is even more striking since Mark opens verse 21a with an announcement in the third person plural

---

8. Jesus' call, come follow me (δεῦτε ὀπίσω μου), and Mark's narrative description of their response, they followed and they went behind him (ἠκολούθησαν and ἀπῆλθον ὀπίσω αὐτοῦ), are both relayed in the technical language of discipleship.

that "they," meaning Jesus and the four just-called disciples, entered Capernaum. However, when it is time to introduce Jesus' movement in relationship
to his teaching (v. 21b), the disciples are awkwardly left behind, and only Jesus
is narrated, via the participle, as entering the synagogue where he taught. The
disciples seem to disappear from the narrative at this point, as if they did not go
into the synagogue with Jesus. But this cannot be Mark's intent since, at verse
twenty-nine, he tells us that all of them left the synagogue together and entered
the house of Simon and Andrew with James and John. The awkward move from
the third person plural of the group (21a) to the singular, participial focus on
Jesus (21b) must suggest instead that Mark is continuing the narrative train of
thought that he began at 1:14, 15 with the controlling participle "preaching."
What happens in the synagogue happens in the context field of participles that
derive their meaning from Jesus' kingdom preaching. In other words, because
his teaching surfaces as a manifestation of that larger preaching (κηρύσσων,
v. 14) context, it should be read in the light of that more primary activity.[9] This
teaching, which must therefore be Jesus' kingdom gospel, amazes the synagogue
congregation because it is presented with an authority their normal teachers, the
scribes, never show.

Verse twenty-three begins a new subset of this sixth principal part. While
teaching authoritatively about the kingdom Jesus is confronted by a man with
an unclean spirit. The mythological standoff once again redirects the reader's
attention to the fact that Jesus represents God's intervention in human time. The
unclean spirit confirms this reality by his testimony of Jesus as the holy one
from God. It is no doubt this identity which gives his preaching-teaching such
amazing authority (ἐξουσία). Mark now makes this clear. Jesus rebukes and
silences this mythological figure using the same language (rebuke — ἐπιτιμάω,
muzzle, silence — φιμόω) he will later use to control the mythological forces
of wind and wave (4:39). He then forces it to leave the man it has occupied.
The man who represents God's intervention into human reality has *this* kind
of authority. According to verse twenty-seven, that authority derives from his
teaching, which is itself narratively linked (via the context field of masculine,
singular, nominative participles) to his kingdom preaching. Mark has thereby
connected Jesus' kingdom preaching to the exorcism of an unclean spirit. The
exorcism is, of course, a mythological occurrence which demonstrates the reality
that God is and will be victorious over demonic forces. The exorcism, then, is
a literary representation of the narrative belief that God can and will (through
Jesus' preaching) intervene victoriously over the powers that rule human reality.

When word of Jesus' authority spreads it goes everywhere, to people from all
of the surrounding countryside of Galilee (πανταχοῦ εἰς ὅλον τὴν περίχωρον
τῆς Γαλιλαίας [1:28]), just as it had reached all of those in the Judean countryside (πᾶσα ἡ Ἰουδαία χώρα [1:5]) who had once come to John. Although
the location of his ministry has shifted to northern Palestine, Jesus, evidently, is
becoming just as popular in his preaching of God's intervention as his forerunner, John the Baptist, had once been. The only difference is that we have not

---

9. Cf. Gerhard Friedrich, "κῆρυξ . . . προκηρύσσω," *TDNT* 3:683–718, esp., 713.

yet been told that those who hear about Jesus flock to him in the way that those who heard about John sought out his desert preaching.

The seventh principal part of the field of discourse begins at verse twenty-nine where Jesus and his four disciples enter the house of Simon and Andrew. We are told that Simon's mother-in-law lies ill with a fever and that this fact is relayed to Jesus. Once again, when Mark specifically narrates Jesus' movement he does so with a singular, masculine participle. Despite the fact that his disciples apparently are constantly following behind him, once again only Jesus is narrated as approaching the sick woman. The "approaching" (προσελθών) is meant once again to rekindle thoughts of Jesus' preaching (κηρύσσων) context. The actions that follow his movements take place in relationship to the fact that he preaches the intervention of God's kingdom. Just as the kingdom preaching (as teaching) has just prior to this episode been linked with the mythology of exorcism, here it is linked to miraculous healing. The preaching of the kingdom, in effect, realizes that which it proclaims, God's miraculous intervention into human reality. In this case, the healed woman gets up from her sick bed and serves (διακονέω) them all, just as the angels had in the desert served (διακονέω) Jesus.

Mark has, in other words, grammatically demonstrated throughout the field of discourse in parts four through seven that Jesus' preaching actions represent the in-breaking of God's rule. Everything that he does, the "saying" (λέγων) about the kingdom (v. 15), the "passing" (παράγων) alongside the sea in search of disciples (v. 16), the "entering" (εἰσελθών) into the synagogue to teach and exorcise (v. 21), and the "approaching" (προσελθών) of Peter's mother-in-law with healing intent (v. 31) must be seen in light of the fact that his primary task is the "preaching" (κηρύσσων) of the good news of God, i.e., the news that God is breaking into human reality.

The summary statement of verses thirty-two through thirty-four forms the eighth principal part. People of every kind of infirmity were brought to Jesus, no doubt from everywhere in the surrounding countryside of Galilee (v. 28), so that he might heal them. Mark makes it clear in verse thirty-four that he did heal (ἐθεράπευσεν) and he did exorcise (ἐξέβαλεν) successfully. Through him God intervened; the result was a wholesale trespass across oppressive lines of medical illness and demonic possession.

Indeed, his fame has reached such levels that in the ninth principal part, verses thirty-five through thirty-eight, he seeks the solace of a desert/wilderness place of prayer. But even there he is sought out. Simon tells him that they all (πάντες), presumably from Galilee (v. 28), sought him. Jesus' response is to go forth and preach, for that is why he came. By the time verse thirty-eight comes to a close Mark has neatly packaged Jesus' opening days of ministry into a tidy unit bracketed by the verb preach (κηρύσσω, vv. 14, 38). This, as Mark makes clear here at the close of the section, is his function. In his present preaching, what he proclaims, the future intervention of God, actually occurs.

The final principal part opens at verse thirty-nine with what functions as a kind of postscript to what has gone before. Mark opens by repeating the key points of the aforementioned narrative. Jesus is "preaching" (κηρύσσων) in their synagogues and exorcising and reaching all of Galilee. This postscript also functions to tie Jesus' preaching mandate to his activities in the controversy narrative of 2:1–3:6. In 2:1, Jesus' initial movement (εἰσελθών) is introduced as a participial continuation from the preaching of 1:39. I would argue, therefore (though at this point a detailed discussion takes us too far afield), that the participle "after entering" (εἰσελθών) at 2:1 designates that the ensuing discussion where Jesus trespasses numerous social and cultic laws should be seen in the light of his ministry of preaching (κηρύσσων, 1:14, 39) the good news of God's intervention.

The validity of this hypothesis is strengthened by the fact that already in the postscript to chapter one Jesus breaches a cultic code of purity by touching a leper before he heals him. This is what God's kingdom intervention looks like. Certainly this kind of behavior would have had dramatic social bearing. Had it been emulated, it would have transformed the way an entire grouping in the society was treated and housed. Mark extends the witness of God's transformative presence through Jesus' teaching ministry by relaying the man's actual healing. The impetus to community suggested by Jesus' inappropriate touch is now given closure in a healing which would allow the man's actual reintroduction to community.

Mark describes the result of this activity with his last use of the verb "preach" (κηρύσσω) in chapter 1. The healed leper, inspired by Jesus' interventionist act, takes up the mantle of preaching. In this case, no doubt, it is a preaching about Jesus, precisely what Jesus had done for him, and how Jesus had demonstrated God's intervention in the power of his touch and healing. What is even more interesting, however, is Mark's return to the kind of language that surrounded John. Because the response to the healed leper's preaching is so great, Jesus is so besieged that he can no longer openly enter a town. Instead, like John, he must operate — that is to say, preach — in the desert/wilderness. And, as with John, people come to him from all over. Except in this case there are no qualifiers. With John people came from all over the Judean countryside. At 1:28, Jesus was like John in that a report of him went out to people from all over the Galilean countryside. At 1:35 and 37, Mark initiates the explicit geographical comparison with John. Jesus, too, has entered the desert/wilderness. And, as with John, all (πάντες) in the surrounding area of Israel (v. 28) seek him there. But now, after the preaching of the leper, people come to the desert seeking Jesus from "everywhere" (πάντοθεν). In this geographical regard, the notoriety that attracts people to Jesus' preaching charisma is greater than that which surrounded John.

Before moving on to the tenor of discourse, it would be helpful to summarize the key things we have learned from our field of discourse inquiry. The first is that intervention is the constant element that runs throughout the field. This is the good news. However, the context of culture suggests that for the community to which Mark wrote, the times were anything but good. Threatened by the false messianisms of nationalism, the colonial domination of Rome, the economic subjugation of subsistence living, and the institutional controls of a holiness/cultic ideology, the proclamation of a good news to the people of the land suggests some form of outside intervention. This intervention occurs in the text through preaching.

A second conclusion is that preaching is central to Mark's opening narrative. A numerical accounting makes this clear. Mark uses the verb twelve times in the text of the entire gospel that ends at 16:8; fully fifty percent of those uses are found in this single chapter. He obviously has a point to make right from the outset of his Jesus story, and he chooses to relay that point through the vocabulary of preaching.

The action of each distinctly mentioned character is represented as a preaching about God's intervention into human reality. 1:7 explains that John's preaching of a baptism of repentance is based on his expectation that God was about to intervene in the form of one stronger than himself. 1:14 establishes that Jesus' speech about the kingdom, his movement in search of disciples, his teaching and exorcising in the synagogue, and his healing of the fevered woman and the outcast leper all occur under the aegis of his preaching of God's intervention. Finally, 1:45 directs that we read the response of the leper as a preaching about God's intervention into his life through the miraculous ability of Jesus.

Preaching is Mark's central focus in this chapter, and specifically, preaching about the intervention of God. And interestingly enough, by the way Mark describes the circumstances that follow immediately upon the preaching acts, we see that the proclamation not only declares the intervention, it also effects it.[10] Transformation follows immediately. When John preaches a baptism of repentance into God's intervention as forgiveness, people flock to him from all Judea and Jerusalem to confess their sins. And immediately after John preaches the coming one, he appears. Immediately after Jesus preaches the good news of God, disciples leave their former lives and follow, worshipers recognize the introduction of an unusual authority in their midst, demons are exorcised, and the sick are healed. And immediately after the former leper preaches the power of Jesus, people flock to Jesus in search of the in-breaking of God's healing power.

Indeed, mythology surrounds Jesus most of all. In his person he represents God's divine intervention. He compels people to leave their pasts and follow him. He speaks authoritatively with demons. He teaches with supernatural authority. He exorcises and heals. But these are not the ways he represents the kingdom. *They are the manifestations of his preaching.* The preaching is the way Jesus intervenes. Preaching, in Mark's narration, is what shatters the boundaries. It is the form of God's intervention. Even the person of Jesus is preached, as the coming one, as the good news. And it is his preaching that compels disciples to follow, demons to vacate, illnesses to disappear, and leprosy to be cleansed.

---

10. This understanding about Mark's portrayal of preaching fits the overall synoptic presentation of the concept. Cf. Friedrich, 704. "Emphasis does not attach to the κήρυγμα, as though Christianity contained something decisively new in content — a new doctrine, or a new view of God, or a new cultus. The decisive thing is the action, the proclamation itself. For it accomplishes that which was expected by the OT prophets. The divine intervention takes place through the proclamation. Hence the proclamation itself is the new thing. Through it the βασιλεία τοῦ θεοῦ comes."

The preaching represents on a tactical, human level what God is doing on the mythological level, entering human reality with the purpose of transforming it.

The mythology of preaching, then, ultimately has a social-communal focus. The exorcisms, healings, unusual authority, and hyperbole of people flocking in from everywhere represent the crossing of boundaries that oppress the readers in Mark's community. In John's case it is the trespass of the boundary of sin that separates humans from God. John preaches a baptism of repentance into the forgiveness of sins. Mark 2:7 indicates that forgiveness of sin is an act of God. And if, indeed, God chooses to intervene through the human-John's preaching, then a significant soteriological boundary has been crossed.

Soteriology becomes the foundation for sociology as Jesus' preaching implies the crossing of boundaries of possession, illness, and cultic purity that separate humans from one another. Nowhere is this shift more dramatic than in the story of the leper. But even the boundary he crosses, the move from communal outcast to healed participant, is no match for the crossing implied in the response to his own preaching. In a world where the scope of proper ministry was limited to the people of God in the land of Israel, Mark clearly states that those who seek out Jesus in the aftermath of the leper's preaching come from everywhere. Gentile peoples from Gentile lands are not specifically mentioned. Still, one must ask how a person from Mark's context of culture, where the Gentile mission was already in full swing, and apparently quite controversial, would access this term "everywhere," particularly in light of its comparison with earlier passages which limited the response to God's intervention to all the lands of Judea or Galilee? Such a likely Gentile access would make this final act of preaching the most socially, politically, and religiously dramatic of all.

TENOR OF DISCOURSE

An appeal to the tenor of discourse helps us build upon this point. Each of the three preachers in this text represents God's intervention in a very human way. John the Baptist's preaching actions represent God's forgiveness of sins and God's intent to come to the people in the form of a messiah. Jesus' preaching reflects upon the fact that he himself is the act of God's intervention. But that preaching also lives itself out as authoritative calling, teaching, exorcising and healing. Finally, the preaching of the leper represents the spread of the preached word about Jesus to such lengths that people come from everywhere, not just Judea and Galilee, to experience God's intervention through Jesus. In the living out of their narrative roles each preacher effects God's mythological intervention in a very human way.

Jesus, the protagonist, is obviously the most intriguing character. This is in no small part due to the fact that he is both the subject and the object of the verb "preach." Just as important, however, was Jesus' expectation of a response to his interventionist preaching. Like John, he preached with the anticipation that those who recognized the reality of God's intervention would respond with repentance and faith. That response is signalled initially and most forcefully when his preaching ministry brings him across the path of Simon, Andrew, James and John. Whereas John had only expected a response of negation, the leaving behind of sins, Jesus expects both a negation, the leaving behind of former lives, and, more importantly, an affirmation, a following of his preaching ministry (it is not explicitly termed as discipleship until 3:7, 9). Jesus calls it a fishing of people. But it is clear from Mark's continuation of the narrative that their fishing is in reality a re-presentation of Jesus' own task of preaching the good news of God's intervention.

The language of transformative intervention is already implicit in the phrasing of the call to become fishers of people. In fact, Mark's Jesus has selected and reinforced the meaning of an appropriate metaphorical image already widely used in the ancient Jewish world.[11] Biblically, the image has strong linguistic ties with Jeremiah 16:16, Amos 4:2, Habakkuk 1:14–15, and Ezekiel 29:4.[12] In each case the prophetic metaphor of fishing people is used negatively to suggest censure and judgment. Israel as a whole is censured in Jeremiah, the rich in Amos and the powerful in Ezekiel. In Habakkuk the Chaldeans, symbolized as fishermen, are again agents of judgment against Israel. Because of the negativity surrounding the metaphor in the Old Testament, Nineham does not believe that Jesus would have used it as it was traditionally understood.[13] I would hold with Smith, however, that those who argue for a positive connotation of the metaphor miss not only the Old Testament influence, but the logic inherent to the symbolism. "Fishing is a congenial diversion and perhaps occupation — for the fisherman, but scarcely for the fish. For them his coming is ominous."[14]

The image of fishing is an image of judgment that demands an immediate response. Wuellner's detailed investigation is helpful. In his work he broadens his analysis of the metaphor by analyzing contemporary uses of the fisherman image alongside the Old Testament prophetic uses. In each case he finds a common *positive* denominator: the censure implicit in the act of fishing does not have an ultimate design of destruction, but one of transformation. He notes that the divinely commissioned fishers were historically military aggressors and conquerors like Assyria in Amos or Babylon in Jeremiah. In each case, the goal of the intervening "fisher" was to effect a dramatic change in the identity of the "fished."[15]

In the prophetic messages of ancient Israel the desired transformation was of a specific type. In each of the categories noted above, particularly the Old Testament prophetic categories, the word of judgment was meant to provoke *the*

---

11. Cf. William H. Wuellner, *The Meaning of "Fishers of Men"* (Philadelphia: Westminster Press, 1967) 8, 64. Also Charles W. F. Smith, "Fishers of Men," *Harvard Theological Review* 52 (1959): 188.

12. Cf. also Ezekiel 47:10, 19:4.

13. Cf. D. E. Nineham, *The Gospel of Saint Mark,* 72. See also Eduard Schweizer, *The Good News According to Mark,* 48. He argues that Jesus used the metaphor in a primarily positive Hellenistic sense: "the Greek speaking church appears to have formulated the metaphor 'to catch men,' following the Greek peripatetic philosophers who spoke in a similar manner."

14. C. Smith, "Fishers of Men," 187–88.

15. Wuellner, 94.

choice that transforms a sinful, recalcitrant "fished people" back into being the obedient people of God.[16]

This conclusion drawn from the context of culture is supported by the way Mark later develops the characterization of his Jesus disciples. These fishers of people operate in the same way as John the Baptist, Jesus, and the leper. They preach. The goal of their preaching is the repentance of the people. Mark has two principal sections where he describes Jesus' institution of his discipleship corps. In the first, 3:13–19a, Mark records that Jesus appointed them to the specific task of preaching. And, interestingly enough, this preaching is connected, as it was in Jesus' case, with the power of exorcism. Their preaching, like Jesus', represents the power of God's liberative intervention into the human realm. This appointment is confirmed in the second primary discipleship scene, 6:7–13, where Jesus sends the appointed twelve out on their first discipleship journey, two by two. 6:12 notes specifically that they preached that people should repent. 6:13 reaffirms that this preaching effects the transformative intervention it betokens. Healings and exorcisms accompany their proclamation. Certainly 13:10 and 14:9 relay that the content of their preaching is the εὐαγγέλιον, the good news of God's intervention, the same good news that Jesus himself represented and preached. The transformative kingdom power, resident in preaching, that Jesus wielded resides effectively now in the hands of his appointed disciples.

The Holy Spirit is a character mentioned by John the Baptist at 1:8. All we know at this point is that part of Jesus' strength (his role as Messiah is obvious) as compared to John is related to his ability to baptize in the Holy Spirit. In his overall narrative Mark uses the term spirit some twenty-three times, most of which apply to an unclean or human animation. There are several other significant places (1:10, 12; 3:29; 12:36; 13:11), however, where Mark specifically points out the Holy Spirit as a divine agent. Only in the latter two citations is the Holy Spirit credited with a function: it teaches persons to speak. At 12:36, the Spirit helps David speak presciently about the identity of the Lord, the one who intervenes on God's behalf. At 13:11, the Spirit leads disciples who have been hauled before the courts on account of their gospel preaching to speak as

---

16. Ibid., 103–6. Here Wuellner describes the examples from the Old Testament and concludes that whether the fisher is king, judge, prophet or priest, the ultimate aim is to turn Israel back to God. "The true prophetic fisher of men is one who would have turned Israel from its evil way, from the evil of its doings (Jer 23:22)" (104). Cf. pages 95–99 where Wuellner discusses each of the highlighted prophetic examples individually. "Convinced of the real presence or immanence of Yahweh in the world, the priests sought in their men-fishing to bring men back to the full dynamic of the divine life. The priestly men-fishing was designed to serve those in sin and error by catching them through the purification, sanctification, healing and enlightenment of body, mind and soul" (104). Wuellner also appeals to the use of the metaphor in Qumran. In the psalms of Thanksgiving (cf. 1QH3:24ff and 1QH5:7f), the Teacher of Righteousness and his followers are commissioned as fishers of men. Once again all the initial indications are judgmental (cf. also Smith, 190). But after analyzing the passages in context Wuellner observes: "That his [Teacher of Righteousness] commission to fish was essentially a constructive, positive, or soteriological function, and not exclusively judgmental, has been emphasized among others by G. Jeremias" (129). An analysis of Rabbinic Judaism elicits a similar conclusion. "To win back, to gather, or to fish a Jew meant to bring him back under the wings of the *Shekinah,* which is another way of saying that the omnipresence of God was to become a living, life shaping reality to him again" (114).

they should. The Holy Spirit's role, then, according to Mark, is to teach persons, particularly those who are preaching the gospel of God's intervention, how to speak. If Jesus baptizes persons with this Spirit, one would assume, given this singular Markan role of the Spirit, that, in this narrative field of discourse, he imbues persons with the ability to speak about God's interventionist work in the world. This is certainly Mark's understanding when he explains at 3:13 and 6:12 that Jesus appoints his disciples to the task of preaching.

This assertion finds support in the realization that Mark never directly explains what John the Baptist means by his 1:8 statement that Jesus will baptize with the Holy Spirit. How did the evangelist expect his readers to access this part of the Johannine proclamation? In the text's context of situation there appears to be no explanation at all. In fact, Jesus never does baptize, unless one can euphemistically term his calling of the disciples a kind of baptism, as 10:38–39 might lead one to think. Indeed, the passive construction of those texts suggests that Jesus understands that the Spirit will baptize his followers into their role of obedient and even suffering discipleship, just as the Spirit participated in his own baptism into his obedient and suffering sonship role (1:10). We have already determined that the role (tenor) of discipleship is preaching. In the context of situation that is the Markan narrative, then, baptism in the spirit refers to discipleship (which would fit the context of cultural understanding of baptism in the early Christian communities), which is effected through fishing (1:17), which is in turn defined as preaching (3:13; 6:12), which is, finally, a task several lesser characters in the text also perform.

All of which brings us to the final character presentation in the preaching discourse of chapter 1, the cleansed leper. We have already noted that Jesus' interaction prompts him to speak, preach, in fact, about God's healing intervention in his life. This preaching creates such a storm of interest that knowledge of Jesus pushes beyond the expected geographical and ethnic boundaries so that persons from everywhere seek out God's kingdom power as it is represented in Jesus' ministry.

Not only the appointed disciples, then, but also an unheralded, unnamed interloper to the narrative wields the power of the kingdom. Geographical boundaries are trespassed in the transformative wake of his preaching. And, interestingly enough, in Mark's narrative he does not stand alone. Other uses of the verb "preach" apply to the preaching of two other unnamed, textual interlopers. At 5:1, when Jesus moves across the sea of Galilee into the Gentile territory of the Gerasenes, he meets a man with an unclean spirit. Jesus' interaction with the man leads, as it does in the case of the leper of 1:40–45, to his healing. And in the wake of that healing Jesus specifically charges him to speak to others about God's transformative intervention in his life (5:19). Mark narrates that speaking in 5:20 with the verb "preach." The exorcised man preached in the Gentile Decapolis about Jesus' representation of God's divine intervention in his life. Again, Jesus is pictured by Mark as stronger than John; he empowers a preaching of God's intervention that knows no geographical limitation.

As if to make the point conclusively, Mark adds a third citation where an unnamed character is transformed by Jesus (7:31–37). Indeed, the transformation is so complete that even though Jesus commands the healed man and the witnesses of the event to silence, they all preach about his interventionist power. And once again, it is a preaching in Gentile territory (7:31).

The verbal linking of the leper's preaching to the preaching of these other unnamed, interloping characters leads us into the mode of Mark's discourse. Mark has patterned the language of his opening text so that it builds from the preaching metaphor. In each preaching case the interventionist result is heightened. John's preaching directs the reader to the coming one, Jesus. Jesus' preaching directs the reader to the gospel of God's kingdom intervention as it lives itself out in the discipleship call, the synagogue teaching and exorcism, the healing of Peter's mother-in-law, and finally, the cleansing of the leper. But even then Mark has not reached his climax. There remains one more instance of preaching, inspired by Jesus, but enacted by a human of little textual reputation. This final preaching brings to Jesus people from everywhere. This universal realization is literally the last word of the opening discourse field.

I believe this progression to be purposeful on Mark's part. He has told us that Jesus is stronger than John. Jesus represents God's kingdom intervention. And because he does, he can baptize with the Holy Spirit, which, Mark shows us, functions to teach persons how to speak about God's intervention. But Mark will never, at least on first sight, tell us what this Holy Spirit baptism is. But he does leave a clue. Although both Jesus and John preach the intervention of God, and they both call for transformation, i.e., repentance in the face of that intervention, only Jesus, precisely because he represents that intervention, inspires his transformed listeners to act in the affirmation of discipleship and preaching that overwhelms the greatest of all boundaries, the geographical one that separates Jew from Gentile. This certainly appears to be Mark's rhetorical aim as far as preaching is concerned. The final two citations of the verb, 13:10 and 14:9, both testify that the gospel will be preached in all the world. The process has already begun with the proclamation of the leper here in 1:45.

MODE OF DISCOURSE

Commentators have long agreed that readers would identify with the twelve disciples of Jesus. The fact that the disciples are commissioned to preach the good news of God's intervention would also be understood as a commission for members of the community. Thus if the disciples are to be a guide, the most powerful way a person can respond to God's intervention in Jesus is by preaching, metaphorically introduced as a fishing of people. The goal of that preaching is transformation.

It is just as certain, though, that the disciples' constant failures of faith are meant as a warning to the members of the Markan community. Though Jesus mandates faith as a response to the realization of God's kingdom intervention, the disciples are constantly chastised for lacking faith (e.g., 4:40; 6:52; 9:19). It is the disciples who misunderstand Jesus' mission after each of his three passion predictions (8:31; 9:31; 10:33–34). And sadly, these same chosen ones abandon him at the moment he needs them most. In a world where discipleship is defined by the act of taking up Jesus' cross and following, the scattered disciples all fall short. The burden falls upon a previously unknown interloper who just happens upon the text and this critical discipleship role at 15:21.

In fact, this interloper fits the narrative pattern which starts with the preaching of the cleansed leper of chapter 1. The response Jesus demands for the realization of God's intervention is described by the imperative "have faith!" (πιστεύετε) of 1:15. Called by Rhoads and Michie "the little people" of Mark's story, these interlopers represent the realization of faith in the narrative. In fact, Mark uses the noun πίστις only five times in the text. Once he uses it to tell the disciples they need faith (11:22). Another time he laments that they have no faith (4:40). And on three separate occasions, so-called "little people" exhibit faith (2:5; 5:34; 10:52). Their actions demonstrate for Mark the kind of behavior that believers in his community ought to exhibit. Mary Ann Tolbert is convinced; she argues persuasively that the parable of the sower ends climactically with these characters in mind when it speaks of the good soil that offered up an abundant yield.[17] Rhoads and Michie agree that these so-called "little people" demonstrate for Mark the kind of faith believers in his community should exhibit, character traits his readers ought to possess.[18] Again the first trait, if the "interloping" leper is any guide, is that of preaching. That task according to 13:10, is instrumental to the task of witnessing to the Jesus event. It is a trait that Mark pointedly notes is also attributed to other notable narrative "interlopers": the exorcised Gerasene demoniac (5:20) and the inhabitants of what clearly appears to be Gentile territory who witness Jesus' healing of a speaking- and hearing-impaired man (7:36).

It is not simply a preaching that reaches into all of Judea and Galilee. Jesus inspires preaching that reaches and affects people everywhere. The leper is key here, to be sure. But both the Gerasene demoniac, who preaches in the Greek Decapolis at 5:20, and the preaching witnesses to the healing in Gentile territory at 7:31–37 are also important narrative examples. Where Jesus is concerned, preaching relates not to a particular baptismal rite, but to a speaking power that ultimately issues from the Spirit, the power of preaching that Jesus inspires in the leper. It is a power that crosses the greatest of boundaries, from old life to new life of discipleship, from old teaching to new teaching in authority, from possession to liberation, from disease to wholeness, from exclusion to community, from all of Israel to everywhere. This is the power the preaching of God's intervention through Jesus represents and makes real. And it is a power wielded not only by Jesus but by those whom he commissions (the disciples) and those whom he inspires (the leper).

Mark acknowledges that Jesus directed his preaching only to his own people (cf. 7:24–30). But Mark also knows he is writing to a community of Jesus-followers who are reading from a perspective where the gospel is already reaching out beyond those earlier self-imposed boundaries. It intervenes into

---

17. Tolbert, *Sowing the Gospel,* 124, 148–72.
18. Rhoads and Michie, 129–34.

the Gentile world. Mark represents this reality in this text through the preaching of the leper (not to mention the Gerasene and the miracle witnesses of 7:31–37 later on). By connecting his work to Jesus' own preaching, Mark legitimates not only the leper's efforts in the text story, but the communal mandate for his own universally oriented preachers.

It would be natural for believers living in northern Palestine/southern Syria to access Mark's language in such a way, particularly since conflicts between Jew and Gentile had been heightened by the 66–70 c.e. war. In such a climate, where nationalist Jews fought Gentiles and persecuted fellow Jews who offered Gentiles safe haven, it makes perfect sense that a believing community of Jews and Gentiles being persecuted for its engagement in a Gentile mission (cf. 13:9–13) would receive the encouraging word that their preaching beyond geographical and ethnic boundaries was inspired right from the start by Jesus himself. If Mark does indeed hold the leper up as a model for his community of readers, it must be in his role as preacher that he has a word for them.

Finally, if indeed the leper participates in this transformative preaching, it is clear that his actions, too, represent the power of God's kingdom intervention. If, as Mark wants to say, the transformative force in chapter 1 comes from preaching, and the disciples and the leper are imbued with this ability by Jesus, then it is clear that these humans participate in the representation of God's kingdom movement on earth. That is to say, their preaching transformatively to people *everywhere* represents in a tactical way what God is doing strategically at the mythological level. And if their actions, particularly those of the leper, are to be presented in order that they might be emulated by the Markan preaching community, then it appears certain that this community, too, represents that power precisely in its discipleship act of preaching that ultimately knows no geographical boundary. By centering his interventionist focus on preaching, and allowing that humans not only can but must preach in discipleship response to the realization that God has intervened in their lives through Jesus' preaching, the evangelist has established a scenario where every disciple is called to represent in the pocket moment of their preaching the transformative reality of God's future kingdom. And Mark makes it clear that it is not merely preaching as the sounding forth of words, but preaching that transgresses the boundaries, *particularly those of geography and ethnicity,* that separate humans from God and one another. It is a religious message with a sharp political edge, one which no doubt many, particularly nationalistic, zealot messiah figures and their followers would find difficult to swallow (cf. 13:9–13, esp. vv. 9, 13). Any disciple who obeyed the call mandated in such a message would, given Mark's context of culture, contribute to a dramatic socio-political transformation of the religious landscape in northern Palestine/southern Syria. Such an understanding of this intent of God's divine intervention, is, as we have seen from our study of the context of culture, quite in line with the themes emphasized in the historical apocalypses that served as a model for Mark's own interventionist work.

7

Dismantling Satanic Rule

Mark's second kingdom reference occurs in a setting of conflict. Having just been maligned by scribes who have come down from Jerusalem, Jesus defends himself against their allegation that Satan is the source of his authority. They charge that his tactical activity of preaching, with its exorcism, healing, and teaching manifestations, represents the strategic design of an evil dominion. Jesus reacts with a parable whose opening line encourages the impression that the kingdoms of God and Satan are locked in immortal combat.

[3:23] And after he had called them [crowd][1] together, he spoke to them in *parables,* "How is Satan able to cast out Satan? [3:24] And if a <u>kingdom</u> is divided against itself, that kingdom is not able to stand."[2]

FIELD OF DISCOURSE

Once again the story theme is established structurally. The field of discourse has a segmentation of five principal parts, each of which contributes to the overall theme of mythological conflict living itself out on a practical, human level. The conflict between Jesus and the scribes represents the mythological clash of God and Satan.[3]

3:7–12 opens the discourse by summarizing key themes from the narrative past. Seeking escape from the crowds, Jesus has withdrawn to the sea. Because his charisma and authority are stronger than John's, the crowds that seek his interventionist work are larger. Jesus' audience is also more global; those who throng to him come from Galilee *and* Judea.

---

1. Cf. Mark 3:20, 32.
2. Translations for all following kingdom texts are mine.
3. Cf. David Rhoads and Donald Michie, *Mark as Story: An Introduction to the Narrative of a Gospel* (Philadelphia: Fortress Press, 1982) 74. "The conflicts that result occur in part because of what God is doing; in part, the conflicts occur, too, because people do not recognize God's rule or submit to it. The result is a power struggle between Jesus and those who resist or oppose him."

But they also come from Idumea, a region of non-Jews until the Hasmonean ruler John Hyrcanus (134–104 B.C.E.) forced the Jewish religion and its physical symbol of circumcision upon them. Mark goes even further. The crowd is also exemplified by people from "across the Jordan." If he is referring to the lower Jordan, his phrase might well imply a Judean location. But such a reference would be redundant. Mark has already mentioned Judea and the area around Jerusalem. More likely the phrase designates the new geographical location of the upper Jordan. In this case, "across the Jordan" would point the reader east toward the Greek territory of the Decapolis (cf. Mt. 4:15, 25).

The mention of the Greek cities Tyre and Sidon extends the reach. While Jews were certainly settled in the two cities, as they were in cities throughout the Hellenistic Diaspora, where Israel was concerned, the locales are foreign rather than familiar territory. Taken together, as Eduard Schweizer recognizes, "This enumeration [of geographical locations] is meant to portray the impact of Jesus as world wide."[4]

Verse 8 explains why. People from everywhere seek Jesus for the same reason they sought him in the discourse field surrounding 1:14, 15; they hear about his healing, exorcising, and teaching activities.[5] In Mark's narrative, these "interventionist" activities are manifestations of Jesus' kingdom preaching. This preaching is how he represents the invasion of God's transformative future into the present. The individuals in the geographically diverse crowds want God to "intervene" through that preaching on their behalf.

Mark makes it clear, though, that Jesus does more than exorcism and miracle. His interventionist preaching is also actualized in boundary-breaking social and cultic activities that occur in the same narrative space as his mythological activities. Along with 1:39–45, the controversy cycle of 2:1–3:6 is controversial precisely because Jesus intentionally violates widely accepted social, cultic, and purity conventions. He then makes the outrageous claim that these violations represent God's strategic intent for human living (cf. 2:10, 11, 17, 27; 3:4).

> In each case, Jesus seems to be making the same point, that the distinct needs of human beings in every special moment in time always take precedence over the established rules, rituals, and customs dictated by tradition.... Custom, law, and ritual are not condemned, but they are subordinated to the changing requirements of people in ever-new situations.[6]

Because this summary passage suggests that massive crowds follow Jesus because of the things he has been doing in chapters 1 and 2, these boundary-crossing socio-cultic activities must be as narratively critical to their motivation as were his mythological activities. And the fact that Jesus' popularity with the crowds was based as much on his socially transformative behavior as on his

---

4. Eduard Schweizer, *The Good News According to Mark*, Donald H. Madvig, translator (Atlanta: John Knox Press, 1970) 79.

5. Cf. 3:8b: ἀκούοντες ὅσα ἐποίει ἦλθον πρός αὐτόν (After they had heard what he was doing, they came to him).

6. Tolbert, *Sowing the Gospel,* 133–34.

supernatural abilities would necessarily, at least in the language of the narrative, have engendered political concerns from any leadership opposed to him. It is no wonder, then, that his tactical representation of God's kingdom intervention initiates conflict with those, like the Jerusalem scribes, who represent social and cultic leadership in Israelite society (2:1–3:6).

In 3:9 Mark underscores the size of the crowd; it is so massive that Jesus fears it will crush him. The evangelist then reiterates Jesus' mythological authority to heal and exorcise (3:10–12). In so doing, he prepares a neat segue into the section's principal theme of conflict.

The unclean spirits, prime targets of Jesus' preaching activity, know that his authority comes from God.[7] Thus, they treat him with respect. Mark notes that whenever they saw him they "fell down before" him. In the only other instances where Mark uses this particular verb (to fall down before — προςπίπτω), he refers to two admirable "interlopers": the woman with the twelve-year issue of blood (5:33) and the Syrophonecian woman (7:25). Both clearly approached Jesus believing that his interventionist authority could operate on their behalf.

Mark's use of language has created an awkward and potentially confusing circumstance for the characters who inhabit his narrative. They do not know what the unclean spirits know. Therefore, the spectacle of persons possessed by unclean spirits deferring respectfully to Jesus could reasonably lead those opposing him (and even some predisposed toward him, cf. 3:21) to suppose that his mythological backing came from a force other than God. The leaders who have been sparring with Jesus in 2:1–3:6 pick up on this possibility and attempt to extend it to their advantage in their rivalry with him (3:22). The summary text, then, not only recapitulates conflict past; it anticipates conflict to come.

But now, in the second principal part, 3:13–19a,[8] Mark oddly, it seems, changes his narrative train of thought. Before he climaxes the conflict, he pauses to narrate what appears to be a wholly unrelated story. Jesus forsakes his seaside escape and heads for a mountainside one where he will establish the core of his discipleship corps. The evangelist, then, has mixed the conflict themes into his discipleship account. The tactical activity of discipleship making, which I have already argued is directly related to Jesus' interventionist task of representing the kingdom of God (1:16–20), is suddenly bound up with the conflict that Jesus' activities ignite on both the mythological and social levels.

---

7. When they cry out before him they address him as Son of God (σὺ εἶ ὁ υἱὸς τοῦ θεοῦ), the same title Mark used to open his account at 1:1, and the divine voice verified at 1:11. However, like the divine voice at 1:11, the unclean spirits address Jesus personally. The crowds, then, do not know that the unclean spirits approach Jesus out of fear rather than admiration. 3:12 makes this clear; here Jesus admonishes the unclean spirits not to reveal their knowledge that he is God's son to the crowds. Such an order only makes sense if their declarations of his sonship in 3:11 have not made his relationship to God known to the crowds.

8. The NRSV and RSV both open the third principal part of the text at verse 19b, "Then [Jesus] went home." Verse 19a concludes the section on discipleship with the recognition that Judas Iscariot would be the disciple to betray Jesus. The Nestle-Aland 26th Greek edition, however, ends verse 19 with the recognition of Judas's future betrayal and begins what I am calling the third principal part of the discourse with verse 20's statement that Jesus went home. In this case the second principal part would be 3:13–19, and the third, 3:20–27. In recognition of the fact that many readers may not be working from the Greek text, I will follow the English translations.

Jesus is establishing a community. But he does so in a very provocative way. The mountain imagery and the number twelve pique the reader's memory of Moses constituting the people Israel at Sinai.

> Both the number of disciples chosen and the location on the mountain have strong symbolic overtones from Jewish tradition: the twelve tribes of Israel, the mountain of the covenant, or the mountain of divine revelation, and so forth.[9]

Mark's wording is significant. He tell us that Jesus "made" (ἐποίησεν) twelve.[10] A focus on the word "make" (ποιέω) helps clarify the narrative emphasis. Where Jesus is concerned Mark uses the term in connection with miracle-interventionist activities.[11] Its only other two Jesus occurrences are at 1:17 and 3:14, where Jesus acts out his interventionist mandate by "making" disciples.[12] At the earlier citation, Jesus' preaching tour takes him before Simon and Andrew, whom he promises to "make" fishers of people. These two fishers are among those who are "made" twelve at 3:14. No wonder Herbert Braun argues that "ποιεῖν is used generally for the appointment of the disciples by Jesus . . . in the sense of an authoritative act of creation."[13]

Obviously, though, there is more. The dual emphasis of the verb in its Markan connection with Jesus allows a reader to access this constitution of the discipleship community as a creative act on a par with Jesus' miracles, exorcisms, and boundary-crossing behaviors. Each of those "preaching" behaviors was vital to his representation of the future kingdom in the present moment. So, too, then, is this act of "making" twelve.

At 3:14b Mark explains why Jesus "made" the twelve; they were to be with him. But they were also "made" to "preach." Mark then explains that their preaching is interventionist; it is accompanied by mythological expressions of divine power. That is, they exorcise (3:15). Their preaching has the kingdom authority to create radical, mythological transformation.

Mark unleashes the full-blown conflict of the third principal part, 3:19b–27, only after Jesus has commissioned the core of a discipleship community to represent (preach) the transformative power of the future kingdom in the present

---

9. Tolbert, *Sowing the Gospel,* 143.

10. The dubious textual value of the repetition of the phrase, "he made twelve," at the opening of verse 16 is indicated by its enclosure in brackets in the Greek text. Metzger agrees that it is quite likely that the words entered the text through the scribal carelessness of repeating the opening words of verse 14. However, because internal evidence also suggests the need for such repetition ("to pick up the thread of v. 14 after the parenthesis ἵνα . . . διαμόνια"), the words were retained and bracketed. Cf. Bruce Metzger, *A Textual Commentary on the Greek New Testament* (Stuttgart: United Bible Societies, 1971) 80–81.

11. Cf. 3:4, 8; 5:19, 20; 6:5; 7:37, 37; 10:51. These occurrences, which make up the bulk of "make" (ποιέω) citations that refer to Jesus, deal specifically with his miracles.

12. A third case would be 3:16, depending on one's conclusion of the text-critical concerns involved with it.

13. Herbert Braun, "ποιέω . . . ," *TDNT* 6:474. Cf. also Schweizer (81), who appeals to texts from the Hebrew Bible. He compares Mark's use of the verb at 3:14 with its use at 1 Kings 12:31 and 2 Chronicles 2:17. Both use "make" (ποιέω) in such a way as to suggest a formulaic understanding of "constituting" a people.

human circumstance. First, though, he tells us, just as he told us prior to the narration of discipleship "making," (3:7–12) that a formidable crowd pursues Jesus (3:20). In fact, this crowd is even more solicitous. Its constituents follow him home, apparently right inside a house, with such reckless abandon that Jesus and his disciples don't even have room to eat.

Just as the evangelist mixed the discipleship "making" scenes with conflict imagery, he also connects them to narratives that show crowds reacting positively to Jesus. It is as if Mark wants to add this newest creative act of Jesus, disciple-making, to the list of accomplishments (3:8) that excites an enormous following. Immediately after he "makes" this twelve, this communal preaching witness to and representation of God's kingdom intervention in the human realm, what appeared impossible just a few paragraphs earlier actually occurs. Popular response intensifies.

So does the level of conflict. First up are those who apparently formed Jesus' familial circle (3:21). Like the crowds in verse 8, Jesus' family approaches him because of what they have heard (3:8, 21). They, however, want to snatch him away. They fear he has gone mad.

But why? Why, from what the evangelist has previously narrated, should a text character think Jesus had lost his mind? It was not because he had become so popular with the crowds, or because he was preaching the imminent coming of the kingdom. The Baptist also attracted large audiences preaching this theme. There is no narrative indication that either his charisma or his preaching topic warranted such a negative personal assessment. And since at this point in the narrative no one, not even the disciples, understands Jesus' role to be that of the intervening Son of God, this messianic identification would also not appear to have been the root of the problem. One would also suspect that it was not due to his ability to perform mythological acts of exorcism and miracle, as others who were reputed to have had such ability in the ancient world were not targeted as "beside themselves." In fact, Mark himself narrates such a case at 9:38 without any indication that the man so miraculously predisposed was thought of in such a way. The disciples, too, heal and exorcise in the text without attracting such suspicion.

Since there is no narrative reason why Jesus' mythological activities should warrant such an assessment, the character (and the reader through the character) is necessarily directed back to the practical activities that Jesus associates with his supernatural ones. In the controversy cycle of 2:1–3:6, Jesus' cultic, purity, and social boundary-crossing activities sparked the most intense conflict. No wonder, then, that at just this point, representatives of Israel's cultic, purity, and social leadership arrive on the scene to challenge Jesus. Mark makes a point of noting that these are not village scribes from Galilee. They come from Jerusalem, the center of cultic and social power. And they come to challenge Jesus' source of authority.

Given that the scribes who have come down from Jerusalem cannot disprove the reports about Jesus' abilities (3:8), and that they, too, believed in the interventionist power of the supernatural, they take the only course available. They attribute Jesus' mythological authority to possession by Beelzebul. If he is possessed by Beelzebul, then, yes, he does have unusual authority. In fact, he even has a kind of authority that the scribes themselves do not possess (1:22, 27). But it is demonic authority. Consider how demons obey him, or that unclean spirits approach him with genuflected respect. Yes, he represents the intervention of a supernatural power. But it is Satan's power, not God's. Everything he does as a practical (boundary-crossing) result of that mythological reality must therefore be against God's strategic design for God's people.

Were this allegation true, Jesus' creation of twelve to serve as the core of a discipleship community at 3:13–19a, not to mention his abrogation of cultic, purity, and social convention in 2:1–3:6 and 1:39–45, would appear as not simply mad, but evil. A community representing the mythological rule of Satan in its activities would have to be stopped at all costs. The scribes no doubt hoped to school the crowds on just this point. So educated, even a crowd formerly predisposed toward Jesus would have to turn against him.

It is clear that Mark's Jesus knows the stakes. As does any politically astute operative, he understands the importance of popular opinion. He cannot allow the crowds to be turned. He therefore calls them to him and speaks to them for the first time in parables. The parable surfaces in Mark's narrative, then, not just as a story meant to edify and instruct; it is also a conflict-oriented tool meant to influence opinion and retain support.

The parable's content expands the narrative thesis that practical activity represents mythological reality. Jesus uses the language of kingdoms poised against kingdoms and households set against households to explain a strategic mythological truth. If he does represent Satan, his behavior is self-destructive; his actions lead to the expulsion of Satan's agents from their human hosts. It would be as if a kingdom had turned against itself.

The truth is, as 3:27 explains, Jesus represents an interventionist power that is directly opposed to the rule of Satan. Satan dominates the present human circumstance; it is his house. The epidemic of illness and demon possession proves the point. Jesus, however, is the tactical representation of God's opposing mythological force. His mythological and boundary-crossing behavior represent the binding up of Satan's forces and the plundering, the liberation, of Satan's historical holdings. This is what the exorcisms are all about. Jesus' preaching activities do not represent a kingdom turned in upon itself; they represent God's kingdom arrayed against Satan's. They represent the rule of God breaking into the human realm in order to set it free from Satan's grip.

There is more. There are only two kingdom options available from the parable, God's and Satan's. If Jesus' preaching accurately represents God's strategic design to transform the human predicament, then those who oppose Jesus must lay their loyalties in the camp of the opposing kingdom power. Therefore those, like the scribes who come down from Jerusalem, who oppose Jesus' mythological and boundary-breaking activities must, by narrative definition, represent the strategic intent of Beelzebul, a.k.a., the strong man.

The parable leaves the crowds in the narrative, and the reader, with a choice. They can lend their support to Jesus or to the scribal authorities who oppose him. But they must know, as Jesus and the authorities appear to agree, that their very human decision will align them with, and therefore support and represent, either God's or Satan's supernatural strategy.

In the fourth principal part, 3:28–30, Mark's Jesus reaffirms the claim that his life and preaching ministry represent God's kingdom rule. In verse 28, he claims to know the divine mind regarding the act of forgiveness. As only God can bestow forgiveness (2:7), the fact that Jesus knows how it is to be dispensed implies an intimate relationship with God. In fact, Jesus is animated by the Holy Spirit. Therefore, to call his spirit unclean is to blaspheme the Holy Spirit. For this one crime there is no hope of forgiveness. And since the narrative makes it clear that the Jerusalem scribes have blasphemed the Holy Spirit by alleging that Jesus has an unclean spirit (v. 30), the reader must target them as the characters worthy of such punishment. The tactical choice for the text character is now clear. It has been clear for the reader, who has known Jesus to be God's Messiah from 1:1, all along. But now the reader finds confirmation in Jesus' remarks to his narrative listeners. Whoever wants to represent God's kingdom strategy in his or her tactical, human endeavor must make his or her stand on Jesus' mythological and boundary-crossing side.

3:31–35 makes up the final principal part of the discourse field. Here, Jesus opens the door to membership in the discipleship community anchored by the twelve. But his community, like his tactical behavior, is radically different from the one represented by the Jerusalem scribes. Mark makes his point in the strongest possible terms. Jesus' biological family, represented here by his mother and brothers, call for him. Jesus, sitting in the midst of a crowd (and crowds come to him from everywhere, 1:45; 3:7–8), and specifically targeting the crowd with his eyes (v. 34), responds to his "family" by establishing a new associative ruling. Those who are related to him, and, because he is the son of God, are no doubt a part of the family ("community") of God, develop that relationship through obedience to the will of God.

Once again Jesus is shattering boundaries. This time it is the socio-political boundary that defines the make-up of God's community. Jesus' twelve-centered community is not based on blood, ethnic, or national ties. It is tied instead to a principle of behavior that Jesus will himself teach and emulate, obedience to God's will.

A reader accessing this text language from the cultural context I have proposed would very likely have interpreted Mark's language as allowing and even encouraging the inclusion of Gentiles into the Markan community as a tactical way of representing God's kingdom strategy for humankind. In the northern Palestinian, southern Syrian context of the 70s, this is a boundary crossing that would have, and my research argument maintains did have, dramatic social and political as well as cultic ramifications for the Markan community. Mark's narrative helps the reader understand why. Sectarian sides were taken. Tensions were high. For Mark and his readers the choice was clear; Jesus' side represented God's intent. But Jesus' side also opened up membership in the kingdom community to all comers. In a cultural context given narrative flavor by the characterization of a scribal leadership whose actions in 2:1–3:6 (also 1:39–45) demanded allegiance to cultic, purity, and social conventions that would have maintained strict separation between Jew and Gentile, it is no wonder that such a community anticipated hostility and perceived persecution (cf. 13:9–13) for their universal approach to discipleship. However, since the tactical track of Mark's Jesus represented God's kingdom intent, it is also understandable that a leader like Mark would encourage the readers in his community to stay the course.

TENOR OF DISCOURSE

The tenor of the narrative reinforces the field of discourse conclusions. Consider Mark's characterization of the crowd.[14] Mark offers the crowd as a consistent character type.[15] Primarily, they are positively disposed toward Jesus. Indeed, as late as 12:37, after the shadow of the passion has been steadily creeping across the path of Jesus' ministry, the crowd hears his teaching gladly. And, interestingly enough, it is a teaching that directly contradicts the theological instruction of the scribes (12:35). In matters of conflict with the scribal leadership, the crowd, as Mark portrays it, consistently aligns itself with Jesus.

Mark makes this point graphically clear at 11:18 and 12:12, where the leaders, who conspicuously include the scribes, fear moving against Jesus precisely because the crowd sympathizes with him and his mythological and boundary-crossing activities. At 11:18, Mark records the crowd's favor with Jesus after his mythological cursing of the fig tree frames and thereby represents his boundary-crossing exploit of temple cleansing as an act of divine judgment. At 12:12, though representatives of these same leaders (cf. 11:27) seek to arrest Jesus for teaching a parable that implies God's divine disfavor with their religious and political leadership, they cannot move against him for fear of the supportive crowd. On numerous occasions they are described as a large group hovering about Jesus,[16] or as a group so attentive to his teachings and leadership that they follow and listen in the fashion of discipleship.[17] Indeed, at the critical teaching juncture of 8:34, where Jesus defines discipleship as the taking up of one's cross and following, Mark makes it clear that his pupils are made up of the crowd with his disciples.[18]

---

14. The scribes are also a key characterization in this text. However, as their role had to be addressed in the field of discourse inquiry, I shall not deal with them separately here.

15. Cf., for example, Elizabeth Struthers Malbon, "The Jewish Leaders in the Gospel of Mark: A Literary Study of Marcan Characterization," *Journal of Biblical Literature* 108 (1989): 259–81, and "Disciples/Crowds/Whoever: Markan Characters and Readers," *Novum Testamentum* 28 (1986): 104–30. See also Rhoads and Michie, 134–36.

16. Cf. 2:4; 3:9,20; 4:36; 5:21,27,30,31; 6:45; 7:33; 8:1,2,6; 9:14,15,17,25; 11:32; 12:41.

17. Cf. 2:13; 3:32; 4:1; 5:24; 6:34; 7:14,17; 8:34; 10:1,46; 11:18; 12:12,37.

18. Indeed, this connection between the characterization of the crowd and the disciples is so strong that Malbon offers an extensive discussion which highlights the parallel Mark wishes to develop between the two character types throughout his narrative. "It hardly needs to be said that there are crucial differences between the disciples and the crowd — in terms of both narrative roles and theological significance. The concern here has been to illustrate the narrative and theological points of contact between the two groups. That both the disciples and the crowd are portrayed in positive and negative ways in relation to Jesus is indicated by the various — and parallel — kinds of activities that characterize each group's relationship with Jesus. That the disciples and the crowd are more complementary than competing groups in the Markan narrative, contributing to a

The presence of a large crowd in the present discourse field reinforces Mark's narrative point that when large masses of people from wide geographical regions perceive the conflict brewing between Jesus and the scribal leaders, they find Jesus' position not only more authoritative (1:22, 27), but also more convincing.[19] This ability to sway the crowd to his side is presented by Mark as a political advantage that Jesus carries with him throughout the story. The scribes and other leaders recognize astutely that if his power base cannot be assaulted he will grow stronger, and his message will establish greater and greater transformative impact. This is political language that describes a very real sociopolitical fear on the part of the characterized social and cultic leadership, as that leadership is represented by the scribes who have come down from Jerusalem.

The relationship of both Jesus and the leadership to the crowds, then, is narrated as one of political as well as religious persuasion. "The chief priests, scribes, and elders raise also what must be called political objections, based on their struggle with Jesus for authority and influence over the people."[20] Indeed, it is only after they have been able to "turn" the crowd against Jesus that their religio-political control is confirmed to the point that they can reestablish cultic and political command and have Jesus destroyed (14:43, 56 [πολλοί]; 15:8, 11, 15). What remains clear, however, is that both Jesus and his adversaries recognize the political value of the crowd. Jesus, like the leaders, realizes that his tactical representation of God's strategic design will not have the transformative impact he desires unless he can achieve the political objective he needs, the sympathy of the "crowd." He seems to know that if he cannot, as he does not, the exorbitant price of failure will be paid in blood (8:31; 9:31; 10:33–34).

This political representation of the crowd makes sense in the Markan context of culture as I have reconstructed it. If indeed there was conflict within the ranks of various Jewish factions regarding the way God was intervening at the moment of the war with Rome, each faction would have necessarily needed to sway the general populace to its side in order to achieve its objectives. In that apocalyptic war of myths, the community that professed a more universal approach to evangelism, one that included even the acceptance of Gentiles, would have been the least likely to maintain such support. Given the realities of Roman occupation and conflict with Gentiles in general throughout Palestine, it would have been far easier to convince ("turn") fellow Jews that the path of traditional leadership was the correct one. The traditions would have to be protected at all costs.

The counter-message that God, through Jesus as representative, was establishing a non-traditional discipleship community composed of Gentiles, "unclean" Jews, as well as any others of Israel who desired inclusion, would have been as provocative as Mark portrays it in his narrative. And yet, this is the mes-

---

composite portrait of followers of Jesus, is suggested by the distinctive — but compatible — kinds of activities that characterize each group's relationship with Jesus" (Malbon, "Disciples/Crowds/ Whoever," 124).

19. Following Malbon, I take the references to the great multitude, πολὺ πλῆθος, at 3:7, 8, to be a variation on the way Mark describes his characterization of the crowd. Cf. Malbon, "Disciples/Crowds/Whoever," 126–27.

20. Malbon, "The Jewish Leaders in the Gospel of Mark," 267.

sage that Mark's community continues to profess to the "crowds" of his own time (13:10). It is a message that draws the price of hostility (13:9–13), and perhaps even death. But it is, in the end, the correct message, for it is the message "preached" by Jesus himself. This is the message Mark's Jesus offered the crowds that besieged him, the one Mark's community must offer the crowds in its own historical moment, even in the face of certain persecution.[21]

If the characterization of the crowd helped Mark's community understand its audience and its relationship to that audience, the evangelist's characterization of the twelve disciples guided them in an understanding of themselves. The disciples are sent by Jesus as Jesus was sent by God, to represent the mythological kingdom strategy in the mythological/boundary-crossing activities of their tactical preaching ministry. Their mythological activities of healing and exorcism have already been noted. It is also clear, however, from texts like 2:18, 23 and 7:1–5, that the disciples follow Jesus in crossing the boundaries of cultic and therefore social expectation.[22] Indeed, in their very identities, as well as their actions, they represent the tactical reality of boundaries crossed. "Decisive here is the fact that He calls to Himself disciples who do not seem to enjoy the necessary qualifications for fellowship with Him, e.g., the tax-gatherer Levi...."[23]

The disciples are, however, prone to missteps. Literary and narrative critics call their characterization by Mark "round." That is to say, instead of flatly representing one character trait throughout the narrative, the disciples are fully rounded characters who sometimes succeed and sometimes fail miserably in their attempts to tactically represent God's kingdom strategy in their following of Jesus.[24] In fact, because their failures were so prominent, Theodore Weeden argued that Mark used them polemically in order to portray a mistaken group of

---

21. Ibid., 262. "This study of the general element of persecution, set within the more specific context of the synagogue, and illustrated by the very specific issues of controversy by the opponents of Jesus, gives support to the hypothesis that the Markan editorial use of the opponents reflects a *Sitz-im-Leben* in which the followers of Jesus have experienced opposition from the Jewish community, are being disciplined at the hands of that Jewish community, and now find themselves on the verge of being thrust out of that Jewish community as the Jews begin to involve secular/political authorities in their opposition to the followers of Jesus."

22. Ibid., 266. What bothers both the scribes and the Pharisees about the Marcan Jesus is that he challenges tradition — the tradition of the elders (7:5). What bothers the elders — and the chief priests and the scribes and the whole council — is that the Marcan Jesus appears to be attracting a large following in this challenge. Thus the challenge of the Marcan Jesus is not merely theoretical; it has practical consequences.

23. K. H. Rengstorf, "μανθάνω, καταμανθάνω, μαθητής..." *TDNT* 4:444.

24. Mark offers a conflicting portrait. When introduced at 3:13–19a, the discipleship corps is presented in a highly positive light as Jesus' new community of faith. The fact that Jesus renames the central three discipleship figures suggests that he has established them as a community. And yet, even in this moment of triumph, we get a preview of coming failure. Jesus renames Simon "Πέτρος" (Peter), a name which on the surface suggests a rock solid foundation. However, by the parable of the sower, at 4:5, Jesus describes rocky soil (πετρώδης) as a ground which hears the word of God, initially accepts it, but disallows it a full rooting, and thereby ultimately fails to profit from it. In the end, it is not the disciples who are therefore pictured in the parable as the most worthy characters, but the little people, who are described as good soil which hears the word and allows it to grow and multiply. The rest of the narrative is an accounting of just how "rocky" is the faith of the disciples. For a more detailed analysis of this argument, cf. Tolbert, *Sowing the Gospel*, 142–48.

contemporary believers who advocated that Jesus was a hellenistic divine man (θεῖος ἀνήρ).[25]

The realization that Mark features the disciples in the ebb and flow of both positive and negative expression has discredited Weeden's thesis. Nowadays, instead of seeing the disciples as a consistently unfavorable characterization his readers were to avoid emulating, consensus has developed around the thought that Mark narrates them as a foil for the teaching community.[26] Precisely because they have shortcomings and experience lapses in their discipleship tasks they more appropriately serve as a model for the Markan community. Because their portrait is sketched in a realistic hue, the Markan community can better cope with their own fears, weaknesses and doubts, for they are assured by the record of Jesus' own story that even followers with such evident shortcomings can participate in the tactical representation of God's kingdom rule.

Despite how magnificently they fail (falling asleep at Gethsemane, running for cover during the crucifixion, misunderstanding the role of Jesus' messi-ahship, seeking glory while Jesus was approaching his passion, denying him while he stood trial, etc.), there is always the hint in the text that they will be redeemed. Indeed, the hopeful insinuation is on display at 3:13–19a, where Jesus establishes them as the foundation of a non-traditional community that will tactically represent God's strategic design for humankind in the future. It begins with Jesus' promise to make them fishers of people and develops in their preaching ministry which is a mythological emulation of Jesus' own. It ends with the words of the divine man who meets the women at the tomb at 16:7, words that echo the promise Jesus made at 14:28, that he would go before them, as a restored discipleship community, to Galilee after his death.

> The young man at the tomb says to the woman, "Go tell his disciples, even Peter, 'He's going ahead of you to Galilee. There you will behold him just as he told you.' " Everything about this statement suggests the possibility of restoration. Simon is again called Peter, his discipleship name (Jesus addressed him as Simon at Gethsemane!). Jesus is still "going ahead" of them and they are to follow. Furthermore, the instruction to go to Galilee points to the possibility of a new start, a movement from rejection in Jerusalem toward proclaiming the good news to gentiles.[27]

And yet, 16:1–8 also offers the reader who has taken comfort in the hope that the disciples will be restored cause for concern. For the text is never certain as regards this positive outcome. Indeed, it presents as powerful an opportunity for failure as for success by the way it ends at 16:8 with the fearful silence of the women. What will they do? Knowing that the regathering of the disciples hinges

---

25. Theodore J. Weeden, Sr., *Mark: Traditions in Conflict* (Philadelphia: Fortress Press, 1971).

26. Cf. Robert C. Tannehill, "The Disciples in Mark: The Function of a Narrative Role," *The Journal of Religion* 57 (1977): 386–405. Also Joanna Dewey, "Point of View and the Disciples in Mark," *Society of Biblical Literature Seminar Papers* 21 (1982): 97–106, and Malbon, "Disciples/Crowds/Whoever."

27. Rhoads and Michie, 97.

on their making this angelic declaration known to them, will they overcome their fear and convey the message? Despite the fact that the disciples have continually misunderstood Jesus' teachings on his death and resurrection, will they have enough faith to trust his 14:28 promise and return to Galilee to await him? In the words of Rhoads and Michie, "the reader remains uncertain."[28]

But it is just here, in this uncertainty, that the message to the readers in the Markan community comes alive. The fate of the promise hinges on the activity of the disciples. And yet, their narrative is in fact closed. They cannot act further. Someone outside the narrative must act in their stead, someone for whom the disciples have played the role of foil all along. That someone would be the Markan reader.[29] The narration of an uncertain fate for the disciples, then, becomes a way of issuing a call to the Markan community. They, as the contemporary disciples of Jesus, must finish the story in their preaching behavior. They must act the role of a community that invites hostility and persecution from traditional authorities precisely because it shatters the old traditions, particularly the tradition that limits membership in God's community to persons of particular nationality and ethnicity. God's strategic design is now lived out in the call that reaches out intentionally to anyone willing to submit himself or herself to a life of obedient discipleship (3:35). This is the tenor of the message behind Mark's juxtaposition of the discipleship texts of 3:13–19a/3:31–35 with the conflict material of 3:19b–30. It is as social and political as it is cultic.

The community of faith that wields God's future rule in the present human circumstance is not closed, but universally open. The one criterion, that of obedient discipleship, can be observed by anyone. It is a transparent narrative message spoken obliquely by Jesus to his hostile scribal opponents, his attendant disciples, and the following crowd, but meant explicitly for the readers in Mark's community. If in fact they were enduring persecution and conflict because of an already underway evangelistic mission that was inclusive of Gentiles, it would not be surprising for them to access Mark's parabolic language in such a manner. Indeed, it would be precisely because of such a theologically interpretative process that they would have found themselves in the business of establishing a new, globally inclusive kind of socio-religious community of faith in the first place.

MODE OF DISCOURSE

I have, then, already anticipated the mode of discourse. How is Mark's language functioning? The scribes and the disciples present two behavioral options. The disciples are the tool through which the readers in Mark's community can learn how they can tactically represent the kingdom rule in the present time as

---

28. Ibid., 97.

29. Cf. Malbon, "Disciples/Crowds/Whoever," 126. "What the Markan narrative says about discipleship it says to all. Both separately and together, the disciples and the crowd serve to open the story of Jesus and the narrative of Mark outward to the larger group — whoever has ears to hear or eyes to read the Gospel of Mark."

Jesus did. The disciples must first, however, come to grips with the realization that Jesus', and therefore God's, community is a universal community open to anyone who demonstrates obedient discipleship. Second, they must recognize their mandate to act tactically as Jesus has acted on both the mythological level of exorcism and healing and, most especially, the boundary-crossing level that rejects and overturns restricting tradition. They have been "made" for a reason: to exorcise, heal and preach. But they have also been "made" the core of a community whose constituency breaks all the traditional cultic and purity boundaries, particularly, in this case, the boundary of acceptable membership. They must not simply be the core of a community; they are called to anchor a new, more inclusive kind of community. And, they are warned (through the narrative "mixing" of discipleship and conflict themes in this discourse field) that the newness they promulgate will bring them into conflict with the leadership responsible for maintaining the boundary of membership tradition which their very existence overturns.

What does this intentional language for the text characters mean for the text readers?[30] The lesson the narrative impresses upon the disciples is the same message the evangelist proclaims to his readers. A choice must be made. Either one follows the example of the disciples who are "made" to initiate tradition-transforming community, or one follows the example of those who oppose Jesus and demonize his tactical activity. The apocalyptic challenges Jesus and the scribes make against each other illustrate just how crucial a choice Mark thinks the reader is making. To follow the leadership of the scribes who have come down from Jerusalem is, in Mark's narrative, not only a mistake, but a situating of oneself on the side opposing God. It is no wonder that the language of Mark 13 refers to them as false prophets and counterfeit messiahs. The tactical decision to provoke war with Rome and civil strife with Gentiles, or to make accommodations that allow traditional boundaries to remain (the scenario represented by the "scribes"), thereby promoting division rather than inclusion, does not represent God's kingdom strategy; instead, both provocation and accommodation are seen as directly opposing God's interventionist intent. Even if it might remain a debatable issue for the Markan characters, whom Jesus is at this very discourse point trying to rally to his side, it is clear which choice the readers (who already know Jesus to be God's son) should take, on whose side the readers should stand, and, therefore, what kind of community the readers should make.

---

30. "The Marcan reader would have perceived that character portrayal and the events in which the major characters are involved are the points of focus from which one understands the message of the Gospel." Malbon, "The Jewish Leaders in the Gospel of Mark," 260, quoting T. Weeden.

8

Teaching Intervention

Teaching, like exorcism and healing, is a manifestation of Jesus' interventionist preaching.[1] That is to say, it is one of the tactical maneuvers Jesus uses to represent the incursion of God's future kingdom into the human present. In chapter 4, Mark calls this teaching a "mystery."

> [4:11] And [Jesus] said to them, the *mystery* of the <u>kingdom</u> of God has been given to you; but everything occurs in *parables* for the outsiders.

FIELD OF DISCOURSE: THE TACTICS OF TEACHING

The first two verses of chapter 4 set the stage for the parable teachings in the way a good musical score prepares a movie audience for important developments in the plot. In 4:1–2, Mark is using a kind of literary "score" to foster the anticipation of conflict even as he narrates Jesus' seaside teaching before an apparently sympathetic crowd (ὄχλος).

A clue lies in the text's second word, again (πάλιν). "Jesus *again* began to teach alongside the sea." Mark is directing the reader back to situations that have already occurred in order that the emotions stirred in those earlier circumstances might stimulate a similar kind of reader-response here.[2]

Teaching is, as I have argued, just one of the ways in which Jesus' interventionist-preaching ministry manifests itself in Mark's Gospel. In each previous narrative case, whenever there was a confluence of a preaching manifestation, the sea, and a crowd, conflict between Jesus and the leadership was

---

1. Cf. Morna D. Hooker, *A Commentary on the Gospel According to St. Mark* (London: A & C Black, 1991) 119. Hooker points out that although Mark doesn't have as much content of Jesus' teaching as the other Synoptists, he clearly sees teaching to be as critical to Jesus' ministry as the miracles and exorcisms. "This [lack of teaching content] does not mean, however, that Mark considered Jesus' teaching in any sense unimportant: he has already emphasized its authority and effect, and it is clear from his vocabulary — the word διδαχή (teaching) is used five times, διδάσκω (to teach) seventeen — that he regards teaching as one of Jesus' main activities."

2. Cf. Tolbert, *Sowing the Gospel,* 131–32. "Moreover, the use of 'again' (πάλιν)...serves to remind the audience that they have heard similar material before and encourages them to remember the earlier episode while hearing this new one."

also on dramatic display. The first occurrence was 2:13: "And he went out again beside the *sea;* and the entire *crowd* was coming towards him, and he was *teaching* them."[3] The teaching reference is immediately followed up by the call of Levi the tax collector, a scene which finds its denouement in the conflict between Jesus and the scribes of the Pharisees over the fact that Jesus crosses institutional boundaries of cultic purity, and therefore social structuring, by associating himself with such inappropriate kinds of people. The second prior intersection between preaching manifestation, the sea, and a crowd occurs at 3:7–12, whose context of conflict with the scribal leaders builds from the controversy cycle of 2:1–3:6 and anticipates the heightened tension of 3:13–35.

Mark accentuates the preface's premonition of conflict by appealing to the term parable (παραβολή) for only the second time in verse 2.[4] The one other time this narrative stimulus occurred in the text, 3:23, Jesus used it to elicit crowd support for his preaching activities in a context of conflict.[5]

Principal part number two, 4:3–9, is, as is the larger parable teaching section, framed by the verb "to hear" (ἀκούω). It recounts the telling of the parable of the sower amidst this background score of conflict and the larger theme of apocalyptic intervention. Joel Marcus makes a valuable contribution by recognizing the similarities between Mark's Sower parable and the apocalyptic text of 4 Ezra 4:27–29.[6] There are many obvious parallels. Both texts utilize seed imagery. Both identify the seed with the word and soil with humans who hear the word.

In 4 Ezra 4:27–29, a good and an evil sowing are in conflict. While Mark's parable offers four types of sowing, it is nonetheless clear that Jesus' narrative listeners and Mark's readers are encouraged to emulate only one. This is because, in both Mark and 4 Ezra, although the good and bad soil coexist, the bad predominates.[7] In effect, then, as far as the 4 Ezra text is concerned, the kingdom of God, represented by the good soil, exists as a kind of future pocket of what will and must be that resists the complete domination by evil in the present. The parable of the sower, with its good and bad soils, when read

---

3. The first occurrence of a Jesus action by the sea is, of course, 1:16, where Jesus, passing alongside the sea, encounters Simon and Andrew. In this case, however, there is neither a crowd nor an overt manifestation of Jesus' preaching ministry.

4. Cf. Schuyler Brown, "The Secret of the Kingdom of God (Mark 4:11)," *Journal of Biblical Literature* 92 (1973): 73. "We see, then, that the Marcan parables have but one thing in common: When they are delivered in public, as all of them are, with the exception of 13:28, 34, they are Jesus' response to the hostility or culpable incomprehension of his hearers with respect to himself and his ministry."

5. Though in verse 23 Jesus calls them (plural — αὐτούς) to him, it is clear from 3:20, 32, 34 that he is teaching within the context of the crowd (presented in the text in the singular). In fact, at 3:34, the crowd, ὄχλος, is designated with the plural phrase "the ones sitting encircled around him" (τοὺς περὶ αὐτὸν κύκλῳ καθημένους), and at 2:13, the singular "crowd" (ὄχλος) is specifically referenced by the plural pronoun "them" (αὐτούς).

The only times that Mark uses the term "parable" (παραβολή) outside of chapter 4 (7:17; 12:1, 12; 13:28) are also instances of conflict. The first two clearly involve the same theme of direct engagement with the leadership. In fact, in both cases it is also clear that Jesus and the leaders are competing for the affection of the crowd (ὄχλος). As at 3:23, that support swings in Jesus' favor, much to the chagrin of the authority figures.

6. Joel Marcus, *The Mystery of the Kingdom of God* (Atlanta: Scholars Press, 1986) 47–51.

7. Mark makes this point structurally by narrating three kinds of bad soil to only one kind of good.

through an apocalyptic lens, presents a similar kind of "pocket" understanding. In a world filled with internal division (13:6, 21–22) and persecution (8:35–38; 10:30, 32–34; 13:8–13, 19), the understanding that God's kingdom was breaking in rather than in control would have made narrative sense to the readers in Mark's community who were experiencing such difficulties.

> As V. Fusco puts it, then, our parable speaks of the kingdom of God "not as a sudden overturning which puts an end to the old age, substituting for it the future one, but as the irruption of the new age *within* the old. Such a vision of the kingdom of God, although it goes beyond anything found in the OT or Judaism, is consonant with the Semitic concept of "mystery," which can denote the strange reality that God's action in the world meets with opposition.[8]

The parable, however, presents more than just the ambience of difficult times into which the kingdom has intervened like a pocket of resistance. It also delivers the demand that readers make a choice.

As Hooker and Marcus point out, Jesus is the sower.[9] His preaching ministry actualizes the "good news" (εὐαγγέλιον); it is the sowing of which the parable speaks.[10] The parable, however, is principally concerned with response to Jesus' sowing. In Mark's narrative presentation thus far the "good" response is defined by the terms repentance and faith (1:14, 15), which is to say, obedient discipleship. The reader must therefore choose which kind of soil to be. Given the preferential presentation of the "good" soil, the choice should not be a difficult one to make. But one only makes this choice "with Jesus" to be "good" soil if one believes that his activities represent the strategic design of God's kingdom intent. We know for certain, however, that the scribal leaders in the narrative do not. When they hear (ἀκούω) Jesus or hear about him they reject him. Indeed, in some cases they attempt to arrest or attack him (3:22; 6:2; 11:18; 14:58, 64), whereas the disciples and the crowd (at least until the passion narrative) hear and respond by seeking his interventionist power (2:1; 3:8; 5:27; 6:55; 7:25; 10:47; 12:28–29). When Jesus connects his parables to the imperative "listen" (ἀκούω), he is, then, as far as Mark's narrative is concerned, initiating the kind of conflict that forces a choosing of sides.

It is with such an understanding in mind that we approach the critical third principal part of this discourse field, 4:10–12, the text that gives Mark's explanation for Jesus' use of the parable as his primary teaching tool. Mark introduces the theme of conflict almost immediately when he repeats his emphasis on "parable" (παραβολή) in 4:10. Then, in the following verse, he redundantly hammers

---

8. Marcus, *Mystery,* 49.

9. Hooker, *A Commentary,* 122. "Although Jesus does not preach himself, or announce himself as the Christ, the effect of his teaching, as presented to us by Mark, is to do precisely that. Jesus confronts the reader as the one who brings salvation: to accept or reject his teaching about the kingdom is to accept or reject both the kingdom itself and the one who brings it." Also Marcus, *Mystery,* 38.

10. Cf. Marcus, *Mystery,* 50. "The use of seed as a metaphor for the word in 4 Ezra, as well as the juxtaposition of 4:1–2 with 4:3, means that Mark's readers, even before they reached 4:14, would have interpreted the seed as the word."

his conflict point home by connecting "parable" with his insider/outsider language. Indeed, it is clear by the way Mark writes, that "parable" not only exists in a setting of conflict where Jesus attempts to obtain the support and enthusiasm of the crowd, its use *heightens* that conflict.

The conflict that occurred in Mark 3 between Jesus' tactical representation of God's kingdom strategy and what Mark perceived as the scribal leaders' tactical representation of a Satanic kingdom strategy spills over into and therefore radically influences the teachings that occur in chapter 4. The theme is the same; Jesus continues the use of an authoritative manifestation of his preaching to demonstrate that his present work represents God's strategic intent for humankind. The difference is that the manifestation this time is parable teaching; in chapter 3, it was exorcism. Indeed, 4:10–12, with its climactic emphasis on an unceasing lack of forgiveness, may well be perceived as a restatement of the admonition about the eternal absence of forgiveness found in 3:28–30. Because the leaders persist in their challenge that Jesus' actions represent the rule of Satan there can be no forgiveness for them. Jesus' teaching use of parables makes this realization final. While it is implied (4:12) that if they turned there would be the possibility of exoneration, it is clear that they won't. In fact, given the apocalyptic dimensions of the conflict, they can't. Though they recognize the presence of a supernatural authority behind the parable teachings, just as they recognized an authoritative power back of the exorcisms and miracles, they consider that leverage evil. Jesus' use of the parables to further what his miracles and exorcisms were already doing, that is, to amaze, and, more importantly, to influence the crowds, convinces them, therefore, that he represents a significant, satanic danger (cf., for example, 12:12).

Indeed, for the leader there is no real choice. In an apocalyptic environment, there can be no turning from their position as long as they are convinced of Jesus' authoritative lineage. If Jesus' power does represent Satanic rule, he *must* be challenged; the kingdom strategy he represents must not be allowed practical realization. Every time he heals, exorcises, accomplishes a nature miracle, or, in the case of Mark 4, teaches a parable, his authoritative influence over the crowd grows stronger. If the crowd is swayed not only by the manifestations of his preaching ministry, but also the boundary-crossings that attend them, cultic, purity, and social traditions will be irreparably damaged. Every parable must therefore be met with the same resolute opposition applied against Jesus' healings and exorcisms (3:22). It is here that the inevitably circular pattern of response and counter-response turns vicious. The more often Jesus must defend himself, thereby appealing to more parables, the more vigorously the attack against his power source *must* be made. Ironically enough, then, it is the leaders' sincerity of conviction about Jesus that guarantees both their hostility at the manifestations of his preaching, like the parable teachings, and their consequent identification as eternal sinners (3:22, 28–30; 4:12). It is a feedback loop of apocalyptic proportions.

Consider Mark's use of the term "mystery" (μυστήριον). Although Joel Marcus's 1984 article, "Mark 4:10–12 and Marcan Epistemology," suffers from a lack of detailed attention to the context of situation, it recognizes the need to interpret "mystery" out of the apocalyptic context in which Mark wrote and his intended audience read.[11] Marcus states early on that the most vital truth in Mark's Gospel is the secret of Jesus' identity. He does not believe, however, that this messianic secret is the "mystery" referred to in 4:11, for, like Schuyler Brown, he argues that this identity is not given to the disciples until chapter 8.[12]

Of what, then, does this "mystery" consist? Here Marcus appeals to the parallels between Mark's language and the language of Jewish apocalyptic. Of particular concern is the concept of dualism. "The motif of concealment from the many and revelation to a few is also a commonplace in Jewish apocalyptic."[13] God is the one who authors the "eye-opening" and the "blinding" in both Mark and Jewish apocalyptic material by allowing the existence of two Spirits, that of Truth and that of Falsehood.[14] Indeed, anyone, not just the leaders, can be subject to the deceptive powers of the Satanic Spirit. Peter, for example, though privy to the secret of Jesus' identity at 8:29, is dominated by the spirit of Satan at 8:32–33.

Other key parallels exist. At Qumran (CD 8:32–34), there is a similar emphasis on hearing the precepts of the teacher,[15] and the belief that the blindness of outsiders is "linked with the fact that they do not obtain forgiveness from God."[16]

Marcus points finally to the work of Raymond Brown, whose research into the term "mystery" in Jewish apocalyptic literature yielded the conclusion that "the real parallel to the Synoptic usage [i.e., in Mark 4:11 and parallels] is where divine providence and its workings in reference to man's salvation are referred to as mysteries."[17] This has been my point about Mark's narration exactly. In other words, in apocalyptically charged settings, "mystery" refers to God's interventionist actions in the realm of humankind. Amazingly, while these actions, like Jesus' parables in Mark's presentation, lead some to salvation, they incite in others the kind of hardening that guarantees destruction. Brown pointed to examples in the literature of Qumran which highlighted the mysterious fact that while some people responded faithfully to God's interventionist actions others, hardened, turned away.[18]

As do I, Marcus suggests that Mark presents a similar kind of mysterious response to God's interventionist activity, this time as it takes place through the preaching activity of Jesus. He points out that the plural references to parable in 4:10, 11 (τὰς παραβολάς) connect the parable of the sower with the parable of Satan's kingdom (3:23–26) and the parable of the strong man (3:27).[19] Since

---

11. Joel Marcus, "Mark 4:10–12 and Marcan Epistemology," *Journal of Biblical Literature* 103 (1984): 557–74.

12. Cf. Schuyler Brown, 66.

13. Marcus, "Mark 4:10–12," 560. Marcus cites as examples, 2 Bar 48:2–3; 4 Ezra 12:36–37; 1QS 9:17 among others.

14. E.g., Enoch 41:8; 1QH 1:19–20 and CD 2:13; 1QS 3:18–21.

15. Marcus, "Mark 4:10–12," 562.

16. Ibid., 563.

17. Ibid., 564.

18. Cf. ibid., 364 for citations.

19. Ibid., 566–67.

Jesus remarks that the mystery of the kingdom has been given in the parables (emphasis on the plural), Mark must understand him to be referring in this context to all three parables and the circumstances surrounding each. Here is where Marcus's appeal to context of culture lends support to the context of situation argument I have been pursuing. Mark could assume that his readers would access his language at 4:10–12 with the same sense of conflict evidenced in 3:22–30 because 4:10–12 points back to the contexts surrounding all three parables narrated thus far in the text. Given their apocalyptic setting, it would be natural to assume that his readers would access the two very different kinds of responses to Jesus' parables as commonplace, though still mysterious, occurrences in the dualistic frame in which God's interventionist activities took place.

While Marcus, then, may continue to insist that "mystery" does not refer in 4:11 to Jesus' identity as Messiah, his "context of culture" research leads him ever closer to the realization that it does deal with Jesus' role as the tactical representative of God's interventionist kingdom strategy. "The 'mystery of the kingdom of God' thus has to do with God's strange design of bringing his kingdom in Jesus Christ, yet unleashing the forces of darkness to blind human beings so that they oppose that kingdom."[20] It is a context of culture conclusion that is very much in sync with the context of situation argument I have been making about the Markan field of discourse here in chapter 4.

In this case the perfect passive verb "it has been given" (δέδοται) fits. Tuckett points out that Marcus's conclusions must be challenged from the perspective of the context of situation. For while he believes that the mystery of the kingdom "has been given" in the parables, it is clear that it cannot be confined there. The comment in 4:11 suggests that while some have been given the mystery, others have been denied it. Tuckett makes the powerful point that the parables, to this point, have all been delivered publicly. Thus, everyone has had access to them.[21] The mystery, then, must be something resident within the parables, yet, at the same time, independent of them, something which "the ones around Jesus, with the disciples," are privy to, but not the outsiders. I would argue that the only component that fits such criteria is Mark's characterization of Jesus as tactically representing the interventionist power of God's kingdom.

Whether they accept him as the Messiah yet or not, "the ones around Jesus, with the disciples," and indeed, even the crowd, have been given the knowledge that Jesus' preaching ministry effects a positive divine interventionist authority (ἐξουσία) in the midst of human living (e.g., 1:22, 27, 32–34; 3:7–12). In this apocalyptic setting of dualistic choices, the positive connotations would necessarily indicate a representation of God's kingdom power. This is precisely the "mystery" that the leaders do not have; in point of fact, they reject the very possibility that Jesus' actions represent God's kingdom intent. They believe instead that he represents the "other" kingdom power (3:22).

---

20. Ibid., 567.
21. Christopher M. Tuckett, "Mark's Concerns in the Parable Chapter (Mark 4:1–34)," *Biblica* 69 (1988): 16.

Their negative reaction shows them to be indeed "outside," seeing at one level, but at another level blind and refusing to end their hostility to Jesus. It is thus hard to deny that the "mystery" which the disciples have been given is to be closely correlated with the claim that Jesus is inaugurating the Kingdom of God.[22]

The identification of Jesus as the tactical representation of *God's* kingdom strategy is, then, the mystery which the parables clarify. Through the sowing (preaching) activity of Jesus, God has intervened in human history. Some will respond like good soil, some will respond like bad soil. Those who respond like bad soil will be so hardened in their rejection of the sower's activity that they will challenge the sower himself, thereby refusing a grasp of the "mystery," and, simultaneously, dismissing any possibility that the salvific kingdom authority intrinsic to Jesus' work can ever be used on their behalf.

The fourth principal part, 4:13–20, begins with Jesus' reprimand of "the ones around him, with the disciples." It is clear since he now speaks in the singular ("you do not know this parable" — οὐκ οἴδατε τὴν παραβολὴν ταύτην) that he is concerned specifically about the sower parable. Once again the parable occurs in a context of conflict; this time, however, the clash is between Jesus and his followers. But it is certainly not because they attribute his actions to the power of Satan. Jesus' problem is that those who have been given the "mystery" do not understand the parable which explains his role in relationship to their role as respondents. It is one thing to have been given the secret that Jesus represents the power of God's kingdom in his preaching ministry, quite another to comprehend what that representation means for how one must live one's life.

Mark therefore offers the widely recognized allegorical interpretation of the parable at 4:14–20.[23] One could, on this basis, make the case that Jesus' censure of 4:13 applies as appropriately to the evangelist as it did to those who first misunderstood it. While there is no doubt that Mark has offered a kind of interpretation that Jesus probably did not intend, it is still helpful to consider the two pieces not in isolation and opposition, but as works falling within the same contexts of situation and culture. Response, then, would be the interpretative key. This is the part of the parable content that the disciples evidently did not, as 4:13 suggests, understand. Mark therefore uses this allegorical interpretation of it to make it clear that "the seed represents the word proclaimed by Jesus, the crop the response of men and women to him."[24]

In fact, to this point Mark has used "word" (λόγος) only twice, at 1:45 and 2:2, and in both cases it refers to either the kingdom proclamation of Jesus or

---

22. Ibid., 17.

23. The general scholarly consensus is that the parables were allegorized in order to adapt them meaningfully to situations in the early church. Because the parables were handed down in the tradition without any connections to places and situations (contexts) in Jesus' ministry, their original meanings are no doubt lost forever. Recognizing this problem, interpreters in the early church connected the material to their own communal contexts and thereby "adjusted" the meaning of the material. "It was natural, once the parables seemed unduly puzzling, to add explanatory comments: application to a new situation often involved allegorization" (Hooker, *A Commentary*, 121).

24. Ibid., 122.

the proclamation about Jesus, i.e., that he represents the kingdom power.[25] The parable explains that while some will respond appropriately to this word (the good soil) others will reject it (the bad soil). In order to make his point Mark connects the language of seed and soil to characterizations in his text. Mary Ann Tolbert's work, *Sowing the Gospel,* looks at these connections in detail.[26] The seeds that fall along the path and in the clutches of Satan are the leaders who allege that Jesus' interventionist power comes from Satan. The seeds that fall along rocky ground and grow up fast, but without the foundation of deep roots, are the disciples who follow Jesus but scatter whenever trouble arises. The seeds that fall among the thorns and are choked by the cares of the world are hearers like the man of 10:17–22 who wished to follow Jesus but could not bear to part with his worldly possessions. In each case, the group represented falls within the apocalyptic category of "bad" soil. Finally, the seeds that fall upon good ground and multiplies are characterized by "interloping" characters (Rhoads and Michie's "little people") who are the only ones in Mark's text who actually respond to the word with faith (2:5; 5:34; 10:52).

Jesus, then, is offering the listeners and Mark's readers an opportunity to recognize the various ways whereby they can, through their response to the mysterious word, manifest themselves as bad or good soil. He is offering them, if they can understand the parable, the ability to see the difference and make a choice. The positive presentation of the narrative interlopers as good soil gives narrative preference for this characterization as the type the readers should emulate. Because they have been given the mystery, they can make the appropriate choice.

The strange case of 4:21–25 makes up the fifth principal part of this discourse field. It seems clear to me that the first three verses about a lamp's place on a lamp stand rather than under a bed or a bushel, and the statement that nothing is hidden except to be made manifest, should be understood within the apocalyptic mindset of the mystery that is revealed at the kingdom moment in the last day. But in this context of situation, Mark has given the apocalyptic saying an intriguing new twist.[27] In Jesus' activities the future kingdom dawns, like a pocket of resistance, in the present moment. The secret now is, as it were, hiding in plain sight. The mystery that Jesus represents God's divine kingdom strategy is constantly being revealed as if it were a lamp on a stand and yet it remains a mystery precisely because the evidence is being misread.[28] The leaders see the authority (ἐξουσία) but assign it an evil pedigree. The mystery is therefore not

---

25. Cf. also G. Schrenk, "λέγω, λόγος...," *TDNT* 4:69–193, esp., 120–22. In addition, see Werner Kelber, *The Kingdom in Mark: A New Place and a New Time* (Philadelphia: Fortress Press, 1974) 33. "*Logos* is aptly rendered with 'message,' for it entails Jesus' fundamental program and is but a different term for the 'gospel' of the Kingdom."

26. Cf. Tolbert, *Sowing the Gospel,* 124, 148–72.

27. The fact that the sayings are not in the same setting in the so-called Q source, but are scattered throughout Matthew and Luke, suggests that Mark has a specific contextual intent by including them in his parable chapter. (Cf. Schweizer, 99; Hooker, *A Commentary,* 133).

28. Hooker points out that the active tense in 4:21 suggests that Jesus is the lamp (*A Commentary,* 134). I would agree, but then, following Mark's lead, connect Jesus and the lamp imagery to the "mystery." The lamp, then, would refer to Jesus' mysterious role as the representative of God's divine kingdom strategy in the human arena.

given to them, because it cannot be given to them; they refuse to accept it. The crowd and the disciples see it but don't connect it with the understanding that Jesus is the Messiah until chapter 8, and even then the issue is not fully clarified. They certainly don't, as 4:13 makes clear, understand the kind of demand the mystery makes upon them. The leaders reject the secret, the disciples and the crowd hold onto it, but none of them understands what it means for the living of their lives.

Still, this does not thwart the function of a mystery, to become visible to all, which is why it is in plain sight to be seen by anyone who witnesses Jesus' powerful interventionist actions. Perhaps, then, the refrain, "whoever has ears, let him hear," is not a negative, cryptic challenge which implies that if you have ears to hear something everyone else misses, then act on it. Perhaps instead Jesus means precisely what he says, that is, that the mystery is visible to all, like a light on a lamp stand. *Whoever* has ears to hear this mystery, hear it. Boundaries are crossed; there are no restrictions. That is to say, *whoever* can hold the mystery and understand that it demands a response, let them respond, no matter who they are, tax collector, sinner, synagogue ruler (Jairus), scribe (12:28–34), beggar (Bartimaeus), or Gentile (Syrophonecian woman). *Whoever* can grasp the mystery, which is offered freely to all, though it is rejected by many, has the opportunity to respond appropriately, like the good soil, to the realization that in Jesus' activity the occasion for inclusion into the power and salvation of the kingdom has intervened into the human moment.

Verses 24–25 are even stranger still. And yet the contexts of situation and culture provide us with interpretative clues. In this environment of conflict, we should determine against whom Mark directed his polemic. In the narrative it has clearly been the scribal leaders who attribute Jesus' authority to Beelzebul. Hooker therefore seems justified in concluding that the verses sum up what Mark has been offering in the first twenty verses of chapter 4: "those who accept the word — who have the secret of the kingdom — will receive all the joys of the kingdom, but those who do not have this secret will lose even what they had — the word which was offered and rejected."[29] At least until this point, the leaders have had Jesus' powerful presence among them, even if they blasphemed him by attributing his power to a satanic source. Still, they have in their midst the representation of God's kingdom intervention, even if they reject it. But even this will now be taken away from them.

It is all about entrance into the kingdom. Given Mark's context of culture where the chief opposition to the actions of his readers occurred because of their interest in and promulgation of a Gentile mission, we might posit a concluding remark about how this polemical language might have been accessed by the evangelist's audience. Hooker provides a clue when she writes, " . . . the saying might refer to those on the one hand who possess the kingdom and those on the other who imagine that they are in within the community of Israel, but who will find that they have lost that privilege."[30] Those who hold the mystery, no matter

---

29. Hooker, *A Commentary*, 134.
30. Ibid.

who they are, have the key to salvation. But the situation is different for those who do not have the mystery, those who reject it. Even what they think they have through the provisions of Israel's cultic and social traditions, i.e., entrance into the kingdom, will be taken from them.

Principal parts six and seven offer the two final kingdom parables of chapter 4.[31] The first similitude deals with the automatic growth of the seed planted by the sower. Mark is explaining to his readers, it appears, that Jesus does not know who will respond positively to the presentation of God's kingdom strategy in his preaching ministry. His task is to preach; the manifestations of that preaching will inspire the response of good soil in some, and rejection by others. What is clear is that those who respond positively are drawn into the harvest imagery of God's kingdom salvation.[32] What has been implied before is now made clear; one's response to the mystery of Jesus has to do with much more than mere understanding. As the language of unforgiven sin at 3:28–30 and 4:12 suggests, salvation itself is on the line.

Here, once again, context of culture will help us understand how Mark's readers may have further interpreted the evangelist's words. Helmut Merkel and D. E. Nineham remind us that Mark was polemicizing against the position of the Zealots. These false prophets proclaimed that God was now fighting against the Romans and that those who wanted to participate on God's side should respond, not as Mark's Jesus requested, but by joining the revolt. Mark explains that the kingdom's arrival will not come because of human activity, but automatically, the way seed breaks open in the ground and grows into the full plant. "Just as the husbandman cannot advance the moment of the harvest (αὐτομάτη ἡ γῆ καρποφορεῖ), so neither can anyone force the kingdom of God to come."[33] The proper response to the mystery of the kingdom, then, is faith in the preaching ministry of Jesus, not the joining of revolution against Rome. Indeed, the consequences of the two reactions will prove to be dramatically different. While the Zealot path leads to the exclusion of Gentiles and a reaffirmation of cultic and social traditions, Jesus' leads to a kind of radical inclusion that trespasses these very same traditional boundaries.

The background score of conflict surfaces once again in the mentioning of "parable" (παραβολή) at 4:30. Images of sowing and seed continue, but this time the reference is comparative. While it is certainly true that Mark intends his readers to compare the relatively insignificant present stature of the kingdom

---

31. For a more comprehensive discussion of the kinds of parables found in the Gospel materials and the distinctions between their categorizations as similitude, parable in the strict sense, allegory, and exemplary story, cf. Jan Lambrecht, *Once More Astonished: The Parables of Jesus* (New York: Crossroad, 1983) 1–23. Lambrecht deals specifically with the parables in Mark 4 in his fourth chapter (85–109).

32. Cf. Synoptic use of "harvest" (θερισμός) clearly refers to the understanding of the kingdom as the moment of salvation at the close of the age: Matthew 9:37, 38; 13:30, 39; Luke 10:2. The salvation imagery is particularly concrete when the symbolism of wheat (Mark 4:28) is used (Matthew 3:12; 13:25, 29, 30; Luke 3:17. The echoes of Joel 3:13 pointed out by Hooker (*A Commentary,* 136) make the reference to the final judgment certain.

33. Helmut Merkel, "The Opposition between Jesus and Judaism," in *Jesus and the Politics of His Day*, Ernst Bammel and C. F. D. Moule, editors (Cambridge, MA: Cambridge University Press, 1984) 143. Cf. also Nineham, 143; Hooker, *A Commentary,* 136.

as it is mysteriously represented in Jesus' preaching ministry with its ultimate manifestation at the last day, there is also an (allegorical) emphasis that can be drawn uniquely from the intersection of this context of situation with the Markan context of culture. It is the Markan community itself, as compared with the Zealot forces now engaged in battle against Rome and its Gentile representatives, that is initially small and fragile, but shall yet become the greater force, the only force capable of sheltering those, even, and perhaps particularly the Gentiles, who are in search of God's kingdom. Mark's use of the image of birds nesting in the shade of a great tree, which historically referenced Israel's ultimate kingdom relationship to the Gentiles, makes such a hypothesis all the more tenable.[34] The message to the persecuted Markan community would therefore be clear; despite how small and fragile it and its Gentile mission now appear to be, it will become what Israel itself was always intended to be, the great tree with branches capable of sheltering all the nations.

Mark now closes the parable discussion proper with 4:33–34. Verse 33 underscores what we have already learned, the parables are decipherable without special instruction, even if it remains clear from verse 34 that Jesus does give private instruction of some kind to the disciples. If our reading of the chapter is accurate, Mark's conclusion here amplifies his contention that what must really be clarified about the parables is that they are not secret indicative statements whose contents can only be understood by the discipleship community. They are instead imperative demands which require a response of faith and actions which replicate the kind of kingdom behavior that Jesus' preaching ministry has made manifest. This is what must be explained, what, apparently, the disciples either can't or won't understand. That is to say, the disciples have been given the mystery that Jesus' preaching ministry represents God's kingdom intent. They must now be taught that it is necessary to adjust their lives in response to that intent. They must be the "good" soil.

TENOR OF DISCOURSE

The tenor of discourse offers support for the conclusions I have drawn thus far. Two new characterizations have surfaced, or at least have apparently surfaced. In truth, the critical language of "outsider" (ἐκείνοις τοῖς ἔξω) and "insider" (ὑμῖν) at 4:10–12 applies specifically to characters Mark has already

---

34. Cf. Hooker, *A Commentary,* 136, who refers to Ezekiel 17:23; 31:6; Daniel 4:12, 14, 21. "If the Markan parable also is interpreted allegorically, the birds may represent the Gentiles, who will one day have a place in the kingdom — and indeed in Mark's day, are perhaps already flocking in; but the important point is the contrast between the almost invisible seed and the enormous bush." Cf. also Marcus, *Mystery,* 214–15. "This interpretation is confirmed by the observation that Mark 4:32 alludes to Old Testament texts in which a tree shading birds and beasts symbolizes a great king or kingdom that protects subject peoples. These passages were apparently the basis for the equation of birds with Gentiles in some later Jewish texts (1 Enoch 90:30; Midr. Psalms 104:13). Furthermore, the verb found in Mark 4:32 [κατασκηνοῦν] ("to dwell or settle") is used in Zech 2:11 and in a variant of Joseph and Aseneth 15:6 to speak of the eschatological gathering of Gentiles to the God of Israel."

introduced. This is because the conflict established in chapter 4 is a part of the overall conflict scenario that Mark has been developing since the opening of his text when it became apparent that Jesus' authority was not only of a type that was different from that of the scribes, but was indicative of boundary transformations that would spark a contentious rivalry with them. But by the time Mark arrives at 4:10–12, the membership ranks of the outsider category have swelled. At 3:31–35, the evangelist identifies Jesus' family as standing outside (ἔξω) the circle of the new kingdom community. At this point it becomes clear that the key to kingdom inclusion is an obedient discipleship to the preaching ministry of Jesus. Blood relationship (3:31–35), national kinship (6:1–6a), and traditional leadership roles (12:1–12) are not as important as proper response (obedient discipleship, 1:14–15) to what God is mysteriously accomplishing in Jesus' life and activities (1:14, 15; 3:35).

In fact, it is this fear of Jesus' accomplishments, and the possibility that they will be perceived as indicative of God's strategic kingdom design, that makes the outsiders outsiders. Outsiders, in effect, choose their position! Consider the way Mark has developed his personality profiles. When Jesus says the parable of the sower at 4:3–9 he says it to everyone. But apparently, in this case, neither side understands it (4:10–13), just as at 4:33 it appears that both sides may possibly have the capability to understand the parables. And yet, the verb "has been given" (δέδοται) suggests that the insiders do have something the outsiders do not. But that can't have anything to do with the explanation of the parable, since at 4:11 that has yet to take place. It must instead deal with the fact that Jesus and his preaching ministry represent the present in-breaking of God's future kingdom. This the insiders apparently believe; the outsiders, according to 3:21–22, do not.

The outsiders choose their precarious stance because of the social, political, and cultic ramifications that go along with supposing that Jesus' preaching represents God's kingdom intent. If the parables are a manifestation of Jesus' preaching, they are a party to the interventionist design of that preaching. This suggests that the parables, too, ultimately have a transformative design. This seems clear from the interpretation of the sower parable, which demands a response of faithful obedience to the kind of kingdom presentation Jesus' ministry represents. Indeed, the second parable (4:26–29) makes it clear that only those who "bear fruit" by responding faithfully as the good soil to Jesus' preaching (sowing) ministry will find a place in the kingdom harvest. Those who are a part of this kind of kingdom strategy (the insiders) will find that though this ministry may seem small now, it will become the definitive representation of God's kingdom power and intent. And the ultimate manifestation of that representation will live itself out as the ultimate transformative act, the opening of kingdom salvation to the Gentiles. It is this kind of vision espoused so far in Mark's radical presentation that not only convinces some that Jesus is mad (3:21) and others that he is satanic (3:22), but compels them to position themselves against, that is to say, outside, what Jesus' ministry intends.

The insiders, then, are, simply put, those who respond positively to the manifestations of Jesus' preaching ministry. Their membership is drawn much more broadly, however, than just the circle of disciples. These are they who accept the mystery that Jesus represents the strategic intent of God's kingdom power. As we saw from the tenor of discourse discussion in our last chapter, Mark portrays the crowd as responding as positively to this representation as the disciples. They recognize the positive supernatural authority in the healing, exorcising, and teaching manifestations of Jesus' preaching. Indeed, Mark reaffirms this characterization in the parable chapter. When he writes at 4:11, "to you has been given the mystery of the kingdom of God," his hearing audience consists of crowd elements along with the disciples. Marcus points out that there is an integral connection between the groups in 3:31–35 and those in 4:10–12. At 3:32 a crowd is seen sitting around Jesus. It is from that crowd that Jesus says that members of his family, his new kingdom community, are to be found. As Marcus clarifies, at 3:34, the evangelist describes this crowd as "those around him [Jesus]," which is precisely the way he describes the listeners he is addressing at 4:11. The conclusion: "Mark's addition of *hoi peri auton* to 4:10, therefore has widened the 'in' group so that it includes not only the Twelve, but also those from the crowd who have been stimulated by Jesus' teaching to further inquiry."[35] 4:13 makes clear that it is also to this "in" group of disciples and crowd that Jesus addresses his explanation of the parables. The crowd, then, not only holds the secret that Jesus represents the kingdom power of God, but also the instruction that those who would enter into that kingdom must respond positively to that power by following Jesus' tactics in obedience and faith.

MODE OF DISCOURSE

All of which brings us to the mode of discourse. Mark is using his language to "do" something in the context of his community's culture. The first thing he must get across is that Jesus' preaching activity, in its manifestations of healing, exorcism, and in this case, teaching, represents God's kingdom intent. Those who accept this mystery will find kingdom salvation, no matter who they are. The way one accepts is, as Jesus explains to the "insiders," by responding faithfully to that intervention, that is to say, by becoming the good soil that grows in Jesus' tactical image. The allegorization of 4:3–9 at 4:14–20 suggests that they do this first of all by becoming sowers themselves, sowers who realize that there will be many difficulties which will produce many different kinds of responses to their preaching activity.[36] They must trust, however, that there will be positive growth from good soil. They cannot manufacture that growth through violent actions, like those of the Zealots, but must be assured that God will provide it. The fruit of their labors will grow until, ultimately, they become the door through which even the Gentiles move toward kingdom salvation.

---

35. Marcus, *Mystery,* 91.

36. Commentators have long noted that the allegorization of the parable places the Christian preacher in the role of the sower. In fact, most tend to see this development as evidence that Mark has dramatically transformed, as to say, disfigured, Jesus' original intent. Cf. Nineham, 140; Dodd, 145; Lambrecht, 97–98; Hooker, *A Commentary,* 129–30.

Such a vision, in the Markan environment of the Jewish-Roman war, was bound to have created conflict. As Jesus' preaching activities envisioned transformation that invited conflict, so the community's actions of sowing would likely invite conflict and persecution; they envisioned similar transformations, particularly as regards the inclusion of Gentiles in the kingdom vision. Despite the hostility his work generated Jesus continued to preach and offer the crowd an opportunity to make a choice between his representation of the kingdom and the traditional one that opposed him. The Markan community, by allegorically being assigned the sower position that Jesus had originally assigned himself, is given this same task. Their continued preaching of the mystery of the kingdom not only created conflict with the leaders of the time, it intensified it. But they too must offer the crowd a choice between the kingdom vision of Jesus that their ministry represents and the vision of the leaders whose most pressing call at the moment was for either a successful revolution against (Zealot) or some kind of accommodation with (provisional government) Rome that would reestablish Israel in all its cultic, social and political traditions.[37]

---

37. Mark's decision to end chapter 4 with the miracle on the stormy sea indicates that this demand for an obedient and faithful following of Jesus' preaching path in the face of the conflict it would engender is indeed his intended message in the parable chapter. Many commentators have noted that Mark chronologically connects the sea events with the parable teachings by having them occur on the same day (4:35). In 4:35–41, as in the allegorical interpretation of 4:14–20, Mark is using his Jesus narration to speak directly to his persecuted reading audience. Believing the mystery, following it, representing its transformative presence in the way they choose to live their lives (e.g., as in a mission to the Gentiles) will place them in situations of difficulty and struggle (storm) precisely because of the kinds of transformations their tactical activities will represent.

9

Discipleship as Apocalyptic
Intervention

Scholarship has long recognized that 8:27–10:52 is a self-contained Markan unit. It identifies Jesus as a suffering, Son-of-man kind of Messiah, and then suggests what this characterization means for the life of the disciple who chooses to follow him. It is also the context of situation where Mark next chooses to unleash his proclamation about the kingdom of God. Even a superficial reading demonstrates the evangelist's interest in connecting his kingdom vocabulary to the language of discipleship. At 9:43–47, he proposes that a disciple should be willing to sacrifice everything in order to achieve the refuge of the kingdom. At 10:14–15, he demonstrates the child-like demeanor that is necessary for kingdom entrance. And, at 10:23–25, he carefully instructs the disciples to treat material, earthly possessions as an albatross around the neck of the person seeking the salvation of the kingdom.[1] The Son of God on his way to the kingdom gives his disciples a behavioral road map that will allow their successful passage to the same strategic goal even after he is no longer around to lead them.

The first kingdom reference in this larger context occurs at 9:1.

> And he said to them [the crowd with his disciples — 8:34], "truly I say to you, there are some standing here who will surely not taste death until they see the <u>kingdom</u> of God having come in power."

It is an odd text that appears to have broken the narrative train of thought. Previously, the narrative concerned itself with the meaning of Jesus' suffering messiahship for the life of the disciples (8:31–38). Afterward, even though the narrative presses on with the account of an apocalyptic transfiguration (9:2–8), the connection between Jesus' suffering and his followers' discipleship continues. What, then, is 9:1 doing in the middle of this otherwise nicely scripted

---

1. In the interests of space, because these kingdom texts operate from the same contextual themes and mandates, instead of dealing with each of them, I choose to analyze the one that I suspect is the most intriguing, 9:1. The insights we garner from this investigation, I believe, apply equally well to the other kingdom texts that inhabit this narrative domicile.

messiahship-discipleship narration? Or to put it in the language of strategy and tactics that I have been using thus far, does 9:1 help us answer the question that 8:27–10:52 as a whole, and 8:27–9:8 specifically, are concerned about: i.e., what does it mean for the tactical mission of the disciples that Jesus' messianic tactics represent the strategic resolve of the kingdom of God?

FIELD OF DISCOURSE

The first principal part of this context of situation, 8:27–33, connects the language of kingdom and discipleship through the metaphor of "the way" (ὁδός). As Marcus, following Ernest Best, points out about the broader context, "this section is the center of Mark's instruction to his readers on the meaning of Christ and their own discipleship, and it would be no exaggeration to say that the phrase 'on the way,' which appears at its beginning, middle, and end (8:27; 9:33–34; 10:32, 52), could well stand as its title."[2] In fact, half of Mark's total use of the term "way" (ὁδός) occurs in 8:27–10:52.[3] And it seems clear that these uses are placed emphatically in this context by Mark himself.[4]

But what does the evangelist want to say with his use of the term? Working from the lead of Werner Kelber and William Swartley, Marcus comes to the conclusion that Mark develops his understanding of "way" from the Deuteronomic tradition of Israel's journey from the wilderness toward entrance into the land (Exodus 23:20). It is for this reason that Mark opens his gospel at 1:2–3 with a quote from Exodus 23:20 via Malachi 3:1, in combination with Isaiah 40:3. "In both texts the key word for Mark is *hodos*. The destiny of both John the Baptist's and Jesus' ministries is the *hodos* to the kingdom of God."[5] In other words, Mark takes over the Old Testament imagery and heightens it with an eschatological emphasis. Thus, whereas the obedient journey of the people Israel looked toward the strategic goal of the promised land, Jesus travelled the road to the kingdom.

Marcus goes beyond Kelber and Swartley by emphasizing this "eschatological transformation" of "way" in the gospel. Mark, he argues, has taken the Deuteronomic tradition, combined it with a Psalmic cultic emphasis on entry and fused and transfigured them via the eschatological emphasis of Deutero-Isaiah.[6] The result is that "way" signals the present irruption of God's kingdom

---

2. Marcus, *Way of the Lord,* 32.

3. Mark 8:27; 9:33–34; 10:17, 32, 46, 52.

4. Cf. William M. Swartley, "The Structural Function of the Term 'Way' (Hodos) in Mark's Gospel," *The New Way of Jesus: Essays Presented to Howard Charles,* William Klassen, editor (Newton, KS: Faith and Life Press, 1980) 73–86. Swartley points out that of the seven uses of the term in 8:27–10:52, only two are paralleled in Matthew or Luke. And while Mt. 20:17b roughly parallels 10:32, Mt. 20:30/Lk. 18:35 follow 10:46 exactly. Thus, because of this lack of synoptic parallelism, the fact that the term is used at key structural points in the text (for instance, as opening and closing brackets of the overall section), and Mark's consistent use of the imperfect verb in connection with it, Swartley concludes that the use of "way" (ὁδός) in this section is redactional.

5. Swartley, 79.

6. Cf. Marcus, *Way of the Lord,* 32–37.

power into the human arena. God has projected the force of divine authority into human history, and is powering God's way toward Zion. And what's more, Yahweh's return to Zion also implies the kingdom return of the King's people. In other words, when God moves, God's people are drawn up in the procession. "Read with this background in mind, the Synoptic sayings about entering the βασιλεία conceive of the βασιλεία not as a *place* but as God's eschatological extension of his kingly power into a lost world, and human beings are invited *to enter into* — that is, participate in — this divine extension of power."[7]

Here is where Marcus makes his dramatic turn away from the arguments of Kelber and Swartley. While the latter argue that Mark develops the metaphor "way" (ὁδός) as the way of disciples moving toward the kingdom of God, Marcus contends that it is instead the way of God moving to God's kingdom, the disciples in tow. In other words, while Kelber and Swartley believe the metaphor focuses on tactics (discipleship), Marcus argues that it focuses on strategy (God's movement of divine kingdom power). My own study of the Markan context of situation up to this critical narrative point suggests that the evangelist stresses both themes simultaneously. As Marcus argues, Mark has made it clear from 1:2–3 onward that the way of Jesus is the way of the Lord,[8] the way of extending God's kingdom power into the human arena. In the language I have been using, Jesus tactically represents the power and authority of the future kingdom in his present preaching ministry. As Jesus journeys on his (Lord's) way of preaching, God's kingly power extends itself into the human arena like a pocket of resistance. But Mark also wants to make it clear, as Marcus himself recognizes, that those who follow Jesus in a discipleship preaching ministry "participate" in the divine extension of the future kingdom power into the present moment. Their preaching, I have argued, like Jesus', represents the power and reality of God's divine kingdom authority. What better way to make this point explicit than by connecting Jesus' own messianic understanding of his preaching ministry with his teaching about discipleship, as Mark does here in 8:27–10:52. This is why, at one of the most critical moments in his gospel, 8:27–33, where Jesus prepares to explain what his messianic identity means for their discipleship identities, Mark opens with the language of the way. "The way of Jesus is the way of the disciples, and discipleship consists in walking the way of Jesus. This is the meaning of *akolouthein,* to follow, in the gospel of Mark."[9]

The narrative has made it clear that the Lord's way is tactical preaching that projects the power of the strategic kingdom into the present moment. In this text Jesus is inviting his disciples to join him on this preaching way to the kingdom where God, through their (as well as Jesus') tactical preaching activity, projects God's kingly power into the human present. The way, then, is not just what God is doing to project God's power; it is also the role the Lord and his disciples play in tactically representing and realizing that power projection as they journey

---

7. Ibid., 33.
8. Cf. ibid., 35.
9. Werner Kelber, *The Kingdom in Mark* (Philadelphia: Fortress Press, 1974) 71.

toward Jerusalem and beyond. Mark keeps the strategic goal and the tactical activities (of Jesus and the disciples) that help accomplish it closely linked as the narrative unfolds along the way.

The discussion that occurs "on the way" (8:27) is critical for it is the first time that someone, Peter, correctly connects Jesus' interventionist power with his interventionist identity. At 8:29, Peter declares what Mark told the reader from the very outset: Jesus is the Messiah. The "people" to whom Jesus refers in 8:27 already know that Jesus is something special. Even Jesus' enemies (3:22) knew that he possessed a special interventionist power. What they don't know, as 8:30 makes clear, is that his power is messianic. Peter realizes, however, that this power connects Jesus in a particular way with God's kingdom authority. And yet, Peter has really not progressed far enough beyond the thinking of "people," even at this critical stage. For it will become apparent that though he sees Jesus differently, it is a quantitative rather than a qualitative difference. For Peter, Jesus is *more* powerful than "people" thought. And in a sense, of course, this is correct. But Jesus also represents a different *kind* of power. This difference, and what it will mean for the preaching ministry of the disciples, forms the basis and central content of the teaching that begins at 8:31.

Jesus is once again about the tactical business of preaching, that is to say, teaching about the necessary suffering of the son of man. At the moment of this teaching, then, as at other moments where Jesus' preaching manifested itself in healing or exorcism, the strategic reality of the kingdom of God extends like a pocket in the midst of the human present. Jesus teaches his listeners that his suffering is a part of the way in which the kingdom tactically makes its transformative move into the human circumstance. We must determine how suffering and rejection, which conjure images of defeat, can represent what appears to be an exactly opposite strategic goal, the ultimately victorious kingdom of God.

Mark makes his point in 8:31 by connecting the reality of messianic suffering with a characterization of the institutional rulers of Israel, the elders, high priests, and scribes. The verb form "it is necessary" (δεῖ), then, should be read in connection to the narration that has taken place so far. The pertinent question becomes, why is it so necessary that the leaders make Jesus suffer and ultimately die?

In other words, 8:31 should be interpreted in light of the context of situation in which it sits, and not in isolation from it. Thus, when we talk about his suffering as necessary, it should not be in the sense that his suffering is an objective on a par with preaching as the tactical means to representing the kingdom reality and power in the human circumstance. It never has been. The tactical strategy has consistently been that of preaching, with its manifestations of healing, exorcism, and, like here in verse 31, teaching. Because the future kingdom won't extend into the present without Jesus' preaching, he must preach.

I would therefore continue the argument that my context of situation analysis has developed thus far; Jesus' preaching ministry presumes and even demands boundary crossings that transform the traditions and institutions over which the leadership has charge and control (1:39–45; 2:1–3:6). And, as 4:10–12 made clear, if Jesus continues to preach in the kingdom representative manner that he does, the leadership will necessarily act against him in order to preserve institutional stability and control. The pattern is inevitable.

Inevitability and necessity have different nuances, both of which are caught up in Mark's use of "it is necessary" here at 8:31.[10] Jesus' preaching, because of the cultic and social boundary crossing that it represents, makes it inevitable that he will clash with those in power. Because they have power, more social and political power than Jesus at this point, the end result will necessarily be Jesus' suffering. The necessity, thus, operates from the perspective of the rulers who have no other option if they want to curtail Jesus' boundary-trespassing preaching. If he will not stop, they must destroy him. Indeed, the parable of the vineyard at 12:1–12 explains that Jesus understands his predicament all too well. His preaching, like that of the prophets before him, demands an end to the unjust leadership of the people. In order to preserve their position the leaders have no other recourse but the rejection of each messenger the vineyard owner sends, even when that messenger is his own son. His coming, like Jesus' parable teaching, is pure provocation. They must resist and reject him. And yet, if a kingdom transformation is to occur, the son must come even though he must surely know that, given the circumstances, his arrival will lead to an inevitable rejection.

I have already noted how this leadership grouping functions with the earlier presentation of the scribes as a characterization opposed to Jesus' preaching ministry. In fact, they are opposed to Jesus precisely because of his preaching ministry and the boundary crossing it both achieves and inspires. Already at 3:6, just after the first kingdom context of situation, and immediately prior to the second, Mark informs his readers that those who represent the ruling groups, all of whom fit into the characterization of the outsider at 4:10–12, are determined to make Jesus suffer for his preaching. At 3:22, the leaders attempt to initiate Jesus' downfall by turning the crowd against him. They suggest that his interventionist abilities and transformations are satanically inspired and empowered. Mark narrates and his Jesus character anticipates throughout the first half of the gospel that his preaching provokes a hostile response from those characterized as institutional leaders. It is only here at 8:31, however, that for the first time he teaches directly (as I mentioned, he implies it at 4:10–12) that this rejection is inevitable and that it will grow more hostile.

As Mark presents it, then, Jesus' plight is not an act of redemptive, vicarious suffering which atones for the sins of the world, but a socially and politically

---

10. That "it is necessary" (δεῖ) possesses the semantic potential to be interpreted in such a manner can be seen from two uses of the verb form in the broader Hellenistic world. In Appian's *Roman History of the Punic Wars*, chapter 8 (Appian, Liby. 122, #578) we find the sense of the inevitability of Carthage's capture (ἁλῶναι ἔδει Καρχηδόνα).

Josephus provides another example. *Ant.* 6, 108 (κἄν ἀποθανεῖν δέῃ). Saul and his high priest, Achias, sit on a hill and watch the devastation the Philistines wreak on their country. They are in deep anguish because of the gravity of the situation. Meanwhile, Saul's son proposes to his armor-bearer that they go secretly into the enemy camp to sow confusion and panic. The armor-bearer replies that he will go, even if his going inevitably (necessarily) leads to his death. In other words, he knows that his actions may inevitably cause his death, but he also knows that the situation is grave enough that the course must be pursued.

motivated response by a leadership bent on halting his transformative preaching ministry. As Tolbert recognizes,

> For Mark, Jesus' death is *not* the innocent sacrifice demanded by a right-eous and angry God to atone for the sinful state of humankind; instead, Jesus' suffering and death are the inescapable [inevitable] results of challenging the authority of the present tenants of the vineyard in order to sow the good news of the nearness of God's kingdom to the nations.[11]

Tolbert reads Mark's language correctly from a contextual standpoint, but misses the socio-political implications this kind of interpretation surely would have aroused in Mark's readership. Jesus' preaching-directed boundary crossings would transform the cultic, social, and, therefore, political life of his people. The official leaders of his people had to respond. This is the narrative cause of the (Son-of-man kind of) Messiah's inevitable suffering.

Surely, this is how Mark interprets what happens at Jesus' trial. As Kelber points out, "An air of fatefulness and inevitability hovers over this whole journey. But despite the divinely ordained necessity of Jesus' passion and resurrection, the realm of freedom and personal decision remains untouched. Jesus himself takes the initiative and wills his fate."[12] Jesus, in other words, could avoid his fate by ceasing the preaching ministry. Instead, as at 4:10–12, he continues knowing what a provocation his preaching is. Nowhere is this clearer than at 14:62 where Jesus answers the high priest's question that comes to him in the exact same grammatical form as Peter's confession in 8:29. The high priest asks exactly what Peter answered, "you are the Christ" (σὺ εἶ ὁ χριστός). At this point in Jesus' trial the proceedings are in disarray. The attempt to stack witnesses against Jesus has failed. Credible evidence does not exist. The last-ditch effort by the prosecuting priest is to get Jesus to become the sole witness against himself. Jesus could outmaneuver him by simply answering "no." Instead, he does what he has been doing throughout Mark, he preaches that he is the one who represents the power and reality of God's kingdom. His vocal "I am," finally announces what his kingdom preaching throughout the Gospel has been claiming all along. And it is only then that the leadership has the goods they need to destroy him. But it was not their investigative or sophistic skill that doomed Jesus; it was Jesus' determination to preach despite the inevitable consequences he knew such preaching would bring. It is in this manner that one should read Mark's statement in 8:31 that it is necessary for the Son of man to suffer, be rejected, and killed by the institutional leaders of the people.

Suffering, then, in Mark's context of situation is a consequence of the preaching tactic. It is not a tactic like preaching. Mark does not start his story by building from a suffering Messiah; he begins foundationally with a preaching Messiah. The suffering, then, I would argue, should be interpreted in light of that preaching.

---

11. Tolbert, *Sowing the Gospel,* 262.
12. Kelber, 70.

How, then, does Jesus represent the future kingdom of God as a present pocket? By being on the Lord's way of preaching. That preaching manifests itself as healing, exorcism, and, like here in verse 31, teaching. These manifestations incorporate institutional boundary transformations that inevitably result in Jesus' suffering. It is for this reason that Jesus must now define his messiahship through the lens of the suffering Son of man.

The problem with all of this, of course, is that to "people," even people like Peter, the inevitability of suffering for a messiah figure sounds suspect. It is therefore interesting that Mark's emphasis on "people" brackets this important text. The people who realized Jesus' power in verse 27 but did not understand how it lived itself out through a preaching that invited and even mandated suffering, would not accept a messiah who had to suffer. And when Peter rebukes Jesus for connecting such a saying to his own preaching ministry, it is obvious that he is thinking more like "people" than like a Jesus disciple. Indeed, the fact that Jesus rebukes Peter only after he has turned toward all the disciples suggests that they too were thinking the things of "people" with Peter. Therefore, in a disturbing use of the language of discipleship ("behind me" [ὀπίσω μου; cf. 1:17, 20]), Jesus tells Peter to assume the position of following in preparation for departure from his way rather than continuation upon it. In fact, the language is so biting that Jesus identifies Peter with Satan. The identification helps the reader understand Mark's message. The only ones in the text thus far who have been linked with Satan (3:22–30) are the scribal leaders. And their conflict with Jesus resulted because of their self-protecting refusal to accept the boundary transformations Jesus' preaching ministry anticipated. Peter's satanic identification here at 8:33, I believe, bears the same kind of implication. Anyone who wishes to preserve the status quo, *even the status quo of messianic expectation*, cannot follow on the Lord's way to the kingdom. Even that boundary must be trespassed. And unless Peter is willing to make such a transgression he will not be able to travel the arduous path on which Jesus is set. Jesus says as much in the second principal part of the context that begins at 8:34.

When Jesus' message becomes one of explicit discipleship, he wants everybody to be in on the teaching. He therefore beckons the crowd (ὄχλος) to join with his disciples. Having explained who he is, Jesus can now tell his followers who they must be. And, as was the case in 3:31–35, Jesus speaks universally; discipleship is based not on blood or national kinship, but on obedient following. If *any*one wishes to follow behind (ὀπίσω μου) him, as opposed to depart from behind him, that person must obediently deny himself, take up his cross, and follow on the Lord's preaching way.

The most striking language at this point, because it is the only language in 8:34 that has not appeared before in the context of situation, is that of the cross.[13] On the surface there is no justification for its use. To this point it is totally for-

---

13. Although the verb "to deny" (ἀπαρνέομαι) arises first here, its sense occurs as early as 1:16–20 where the four chosen fishermen deny their livelihood and their family relationships in order to follow Jesus. Indeed, Peter will later make this point clear at 10:28; the disciples have left everything to follow. And in 14:30, 31, 72, it is used in the dramatic retelling of Peter's denial. Suddenly, the image of crucifixion materializes as a prerequisite for Jesus discipleship.

eign to the context of situation; the reader would have no obvious access point for interpretation. He or she would therefore need first to consult the context of culture shared with the evangelist. Here there was clarity.

> The cross was the Roman supreme penalty. It was the standard form of execution of slaves and was also employed against those convicted of political offenses such as treason, insurrection, and banditry (usually associated with insurrection in Palestine).... It follows that if Jesus had expected death by crucifixion he must have anticipated being charged with something serious, in his case treason, since brigandage would hardly fit.[14]

I have also argued, however, that Jesus' political target was the institutional leadership of Israel, not Rome. However, the cross would still apply as a natural, though Roman, form of challenging Jesus' boundary trespasses, because the Jewish leadership would have needed the help of the Roman governor to precipitate capital punishment.[15] No doubt, since the Roman leadership desired the same socio-political stability coveted by the Israelite leadership, it would not have been too difficult for the scribal and high priestly leaders to convince the Romans that Jesus' boundary trespasses were as much a threat to them as to the traditions in Israel. And, given Mark's narration of the crowd support Jesus received, it makes good contextual (of situation) sense that Roman police authority was as necessary to the execution of a plot against Jesus as was the death sentence of a Roman court.

> With the city full of Galileans a public stoning may have been impossible, or very dangerous for those who organized it [14:2]. Recourse to Pilate, therefore, may have been advisable for more than legality's sake. If Pilate could be persuaded to take action against Jesus there would be less chance of an uprising of popular feeling against the Jewish leaders, and, with the execution guaranteed and safeguarded by Roman military power, less chance of a sudden reversal or a later backlash against the Sanhedrin.[16]

I am suggesting then that the access point back from the context of culture into the context of situation for the Markan reader must have come at the point of Jesus' preaching-inspired boundary trespasses. These cultically and socially, and, therefore, politically important boundary infractions are the only possible motivators consequential enough to have warranted the narrative Jesus' expectation of crucifixion. Indeed, they are the only motivators that make sense from both the context of culture and context of situation perspective. Jesus, in other words, knows that his preaching will inevitably lead to conflict with the leaders of Israel (8:31), and that, because this preaching effects and inspires institutional

14. David P. Seccombe, "Take Up Your Cross," in *God Who Is Rich in Mercy: Essays Presented to Dr. D. B. Knox*, Peter T. O'Brien and David G. Petersen, editors (Grand Rapids: Baker Book House, 1986) 142–43.
15. Cf. John 18:31.
16. Seccombe, 144.

transformations that will destroy the old Israelite power base (14:58; 15:29), trespass cultic, legal, and economic boundaries (cf. 2:1–3:6, the first controversy cycle; 5:1–8:21, material comprising the so-called "Gentile cycle"; 11:1–12:44, the second controversy cycle), and establish a new kind of discipleship, and, therefore, faith community (3:13–19a, 31–35), it must ultimately bring him to a Roman cross.

There are two points of concern here that need to be highlighted before I move on. First, the context of situation has given the reader a clear cause for Jesus' suffering, his kingdom preaching. When he preaches, the kingdom extends like a pocket of resistance. That resistance takes the form of boundary trespasses which have dramatic socio-political implications. Therefore, second, because those boundary infractions are resisted by the leadership, Jesus must suffer and ultimately die. His passion, therefore, at least in the narrative context of situation, has a clear socio-political foundation.

All this has a particular meaning for Jesus discipleship. Those who would follow must be willing to take up their cross, that is, to preach in an interventionist way that invites the same kind of end, because it agitates the same kinds of boundary transformations. It is easy to read verse 8:35 as a mandate for martyrdom. It appears, given Jesus' earlier mandate to pick up the cross, and now this directive to give up one's life, that he is calling his disciples to suffer. I would argue that such a conclusion misreads the contextual (of situation) case that Mark has all along been carefully piecing together. Even Jesus' way, the Lord's way, is not one of suffering. His primary task is not martyrdom, but preaching. The suffering comes as a result of the kingdom preaching he insists on transmitting. Disciples who are called to follow him on the Lord's way are called, therefore, not to suffering, but to interventionist preaching. Mark makes this explicit at 13:10 when he ties in the verbal form "it is necessary" (δεῖ) with the task of preaching the gospel *to all the world*. This is the final, and, for Mark's readers, great boundary trespass, the move outward into the despised Gentile community in search of kingdom citizens. The disciples, from the fishing metaphor that is ultimately defined in terms of preaching, are called to preach. But as the context of 13:10 (13:9–13) makes clear, as does 8:34–9:1, anyone who preaches the kingdom transformative message that Jesus preaches, given the context (of culture) in which they are preaching, will inevitably suffer. At 13:10, directly addressing the Markan community that has begun its preaching move into Gentile territory, the evangelist specifies that the problem is the Gentile mission for which his reading community was already undergoing persecution. At 8:34–9:1, the provocation is still primarily located in the context of situation, where, building directly from Jesus' narrative preaching (and therefore boundary-trespassing) activities, the narrative disciples are called to follow Jesus' narrative preaching pattern.

8:38, then, comes as both warning and promise. The disciples, and no doubt the community through the disciples, are warned to stand fast to Jesus' transformative preaching way, to commit themselves to following that way despite the sufferings that will inevitably come as a result. But the negation in the verse, that the Son of man come in his glory will deny those who deny him in their human circumstance, also proposes a kingdom affirmation. The judging Son of man who has the power to condemn at the end time also has the power to save. As the emphasis upon "saving" (σῴζω) in verse 35 makes clear, that salvation will be directed toward those who follow, and keep following even if the way should lead to a cross.

Interesting here is the narrative implication that salvation occurs not as a result of Jesus' death, but as a result of holding fast to his preaching tactic. Indeed, throughout the context of situation thus far, the language of suffering has not been causally connected with that of salvation. When Mark uses the language of "saving" (σῴζω), he has two primary emphases in mind. First, he connects the language to the reality of the kingdom (8:35; 10:26; 13:13, 20). This, of course, makes sense; he wants his readers to understand that God's kingdom means salvation for the believer. His only other use of "saving" language connects not with suffering but with Jesus' preaching manifestations. At 3:4, Jesus' boundary-trespassing healing of the man with the withered hand is connected with the language of saving. At 5:23, when Jairus seeks Jesus' help in healing his daughter, he tells the teacher that if you come you can "save" her. At 5:28, 34, when Jesus heals the woman with the twelve-year issue of blood, the cure is described with the language of saving. At 6:56, the summation of Jesus' healing and exorcisms are described as saving. At 10:52, Bartimaeus's healing is described in terms of saving. Finally, at 15:30, 31, when Jesus is mocked by the leaders because, though he saved others, he cannot save himself, the question is begged, how has he saved others in the narrative? The answer is already evident; he has saved them through the manifestations of his boundary-trespassing preaching. It is the tactic of preaching that leads to the imagery of "saving," no doubt precisely because it is preaching that represents the kingdom of God, and it is in the kingdom that saving occurs.

This realization has particular importance for the life of the disciple following Jesus. If it is indeed preaching that is connected to kingdom "saving," as the narrative suggests, then their call to follow Jesus in preaching (6:7, 12–13; 3:13–15; 13:10) takes on even more dramatic implications. The drama unravels at the mysterious text of 9:1: there are some standing here who will not taste death before they see the kingdom of God come with power.

Has Jesus wandered off on an apocalyptic tangent? Even worse, has his wandering taken him into an area of discussion that prompts him to offer a prophecy that will not be fulfilled? Most argumentation on the text has approached this as though it were isolated from its context of situation, and therefore fretted more about its apocalyptic miscalculation than its meaning for Markan messiahship-discipleship. As Hooker points out, some, like C. H. Dodd, have argued that Jesus was not in error because the kingdom had already come in Jesus' ministry. Still, since the kingdom was not fully present, Jesus could speak of it as if it had yet to come. Others have argued that the transfiguration scene that follows in 9:2–8 is a prolepsis of that final kingdom and therefore Jesus' prediction was immediately fulfilled. Skeptics have pointed out that the transfiguration, though certainly a preview of the parousia of the Son of man enthroned in glory, did not equal the expectations of the consummate kingdom. Dodd's realized kingdom expectation has already been shown to be problematic because of his under-appreciation of the many future sayings about the kingdom in the gospel. Hooker counsels that the reader should simply realize that Jesus made a mistake, and that such a mistake was very much in keeping with the doctrine of the incarnation and the limits of human knowledge that such a doctrine implies.[17]

Hooker's advice is well taken, particularly when she points out that the evangelist has more in mind here than calculations about the arrival of the end time anyway. That is most certainly not his primary concern. "But this problem of the non-arrival of the kingdom in power has tended to obscure the fact that the saying is not so much a prediction of a particular event as a confident declaration of the final establishment of God's purposes."[18] The declaration is a fitting conclusion to 8:34–38, where Jesus is challenging his disciples — and Mark, his readers — to remain steadfast to the preaching way despite the suffering that such preaching will inevitably bring. In this cultural context of an apocalyptic "war of myths," Mark wants his readers to know that this Jesus way is the right (Lord's) way toward the kingdom. And when the kingdom dawns, when the Son of man has come in power (prefigured in 9:2–8), this way will be vindicated. It is this future assurance that the evangelist hopes will facilitate the endurance of his readers, just as Jesus narratively used it to cultivate it in his disciples.

But there is more. There is no doubt that in the sense of a kingdom consummation Jesus' prediction in 9:1 was wrong. But neither the claim nor the interest is ever made in terms of the consummate kingdom, but in terms of *the kingdom come in power*, which the narrative suggests has already begun as an invading pocket in Jesus' preaching, and can be anticipated in the preaching of the disciples. In this context it seems to me that the language should connect with the imperative message that comes from 8:34–38, and therefore be interpreted in terms of messiahship-discipleship rather than end-time calendar calculation which, according to Mark 13:32–37 (where the text places discipleship preparation over end-time prognostication), was never one of Jesus' preaching interests.

Precisely because there is a merging here of the narrative context of situation and the message for Mark's readers in their context of culture, so that what is happening in the story has a direct message for those reading the story, we can in the end see that 9:1 belongs in this context where the evangelist explains discipleship in terms of kingdom messiahship. The disciples who have been invited to preach now know that as Jesus' preaching was connected with the "saving" of the kingdom, so will theirs. Through their preaching, too, the "saving" reality of the kingdom will extend powerfully like a future pocket invading present time. They heal, they exorcise, and according to 6:30, as dull as Mark pictures them to be, they teach. But, as 8:27–9:1 makes clear, their preaching is not as transformative as Jesus'; theirs does not invite the hostility that his does. Their preaching, then, does not yet do what Jesus' does, extend the full

17. Cf. Hooker, *A Commentary,* 212.
18. Ibid.

power of God's future kingdom into the present circumstance. However, this entire text on discipleship assures that those who follow Jesus on the preaching way — to the extent that they preach the kingdom of boundary trespass that Jesus preaches — *will* invite the suffering (cross) that he invites. It is, according to 8:35, in this way that they will find kingdom saving. It is also, if verse 34 has been interpreted correctly, the way they will extend that kingdom saving to others. Preaching — the kind of preaching that is so transformative that it guarantees a hostile response from institutional leaders and therefore suffering on the part of the preacher — is the transformative discipleship tactic that will establish the kingdom in all its *power* as a pocket in the present moment.

In 9:1, Mark is telling his readers, as the narrative Jesus is telling his disciples and the crowd, that there are those of their respective generations who will actually see discipleship tactics usher in the kingdom as a pocket of *power* in the same way that Jesus' tactics have ushered it in as a powerful pocket of resistance. And while we do not see the suffering of the disciples in the narrative itself, although it is prefigured as a result of preaching at 13:9–13, we do know from our context of culture discussion that it is already taking place in the Markan community because of their boundary-trespassing preaching of the kingdom to the Gentiles. That kingdom pocket invasion into the present is already beginning and will see powerful realization in the generation of Mark's readers if they do not allow the persecution their actions are provoking to push them off "the Lord's [preaching] way."

The recounting of the transfiguration story in the section's third principal part, 9:2–8, lends weight to the claim that Jesus' way is the way of the Lord, the way of extending the power of God's future kingdom into the present human circumstance. The picture of Jesus glorified verifies that despite the suffering and death his preaching attracts, it is the kind of preaching that God desires.

The heavenly voice (9:7) confirms Jesus' enthroned future status, which validates his present kingdom preaching ministry, when it designates him as divine son while ignoring the presence of eschatological heavyweights Elijah and Moses. The second half of the divine statement directly applies to the kind of discipleship that should be practiced in light of Jesus' present Son-of-man messiahship and future enthronement as Son of God. The disciples are told to listen to him. The directive points back to Jesus' difficult message in 8:34–9:1, the one about discipleship that must be ready to endure the cross, that inevitably stands on the horizon of the preaching way. At the climactic moment of the most starkly apocalyptic text in the narrative, then, the reader is directed toward the message of what it means to be a disciple who follows Jesus on the Lord's way. To be sure, the evangelist wants the readers to understand who Jesus is and what Jesus will become, but it is just as important that they understand what that present/future identity means for them as disciples. Just as Jesus' preaching extends the power of the future kingdom into the present, a fact certified by the transfiguration scene, so, too, is the disciple called to preach in a way that the transformative, boundary-crossing reality of the kingdom extends its powerful and saving presence into the human circumstance. This is the message to which the heavenly voice wants them to listen.

TENOR OF DISCOURSE

The characterizations Mark develops in 8:27–9:8 reinforce my thesis that suffering is an inevitable consequence of the Son of man's tactical preaching activity, but neither a tactical nor a strategic goal of the Lord's way. The tactical goal remains what it has been through Mark's context of situation thus far, the extension of the future, and transformative, kingdom into the present human circumstance. Preaching, not suffering, even on the cross, is the tactical activity that leads to it. The strategic goal is the consummate kingdom that is prefigured in the parousia prolepsis of the transfiguration. Mark's presentation of Jesus as Son of man explains exactly how this is so.

8:27–9:8 includes all three of the primary titles, messiah, Son of man, Son of God, accorded Jesus thus far in the context of situation. In fact, what may on the surface sound as if it is the most important, Son of God, is the least significant as far as my present thesis presentation is concerned. Mark's implicit use of the title through the heavenly voice at the transfiguration (9:7) does, however, support the contention that the evangelist uses the transfiguration as a prolepsis of the parousia. As Boers points out, the title smacks of royal enthronement themes. "Son of God was an appropriate title for the Messiah who was to have been, like the kings of Israel and Judah, adopted by God as his son (cf. Ps. 2:7, 'You are my Son: this day I have generated you')."[19] The divine voice's designation of the transfigured Jesus as "son" in such a highly charged apocalyptic setting gives Mark the opening he needs to suggest narratively that even though this messianic figure's preaching will inevitably draw the kind of conflict that will lead to his earthly suffering and death, he will, at the end time, be vindicated. He will be enthroned as God's one true eschatological agent.[20]

Unfortunately, such a heady vision of Jesus' enthronement could mislead the reader into the wrong impression of his earthly messianic work. The evangelist meets the problem head-on at 8:31. Jesus' response to Peter's confession clarifies precisely what kind of messiah will ultimately be enthroned at the end of time. Mark's Jesus understands himself to be a Son-of-man kind of messiah. 9:2–8 and 14:62 contend that this Son-of-man is also the Son of God who will be enthroned beside God as judge in the consummation of the kingdom (cf. also 8:38; 13:26). But as other critical texts (8:31; 9:9, 12, 31; 10:33–34; 10:45; 14:21, 41) also reflect, this Son-of-man is destined to suffer. This Son-of-man messiahship, not the false messiahship (13:21–22) of militant revolution which is already under way, is the kind the disciples are beckoned by Mark, to follow.

Many of these conclusions are, of course, commonplace in Markan research. The critical question for me is, how is this suffering of the Son of man to

19. Hendrikus Boers, *Who Was Jesus? The Historical Jesus and the Synoptic Gospels* (San Francisco: Harper & Row Publishers, 1989) 268.

20. Howard Clark Kee, "The Transfiguration in Mark: Epiphany or Apocalyptic Vision?," in *Understanding the Sacred Text: Essays in Honor of Morton S. Enslin on the Hebrew Bible and Christian Beginnings,* John Reumann, editor (Valley Forge: Judson Press, 1972) 149. "...[T]he transfiguration scene is not a theophany *to,* nor an epiphany *of,* Jesus, but a proleptic vision of the exaltation of Jesus as the kingly son of man granted to the disciples as eschatological witnesses."

be understood in Mark's context of situation? Was it a redemptive suffering whose tactical accomplishment was the express intent of Jesus? Or was it a suffering that resulted as a consequence of the Son-of-man's intentional tactic of transformative preaching? Which endeavor, the suffering or the preaching, was the tactical activity that extended the power of God's future kingdom into the present moment, and therefore anticipated the strategic realization of the consummate kingdom?

It is interesting that in his work on the title as it is used by Mark, Frank Matera finds three categorizations. We have already cited the ones which deal with the Son of man's suffering and future enthronement. Matera's third category deals with the way Mark portrays the Son of man's earthly activity. There are only two such citations, and interestingly enough, both (2:10, 28) occur in the initial controversy cycle where Jesus' preaching message draws fire from the leadership. In the first case, it appears that the Son-of-man's role is one of forgiveness. To be sure, this is indeed Jesus' express sentiment. But one must also interpret this sentiment in light of its preaching context of situation. Or, as Paula Fredriksen puts it, "the Son of Man exercises authority in defiance of the norms of Jewish piety (2:2–23)."[21] This text initiates the controversy cycle precisely because Jesus' claim to forgive sins trespasses a vital cultic boundary that has been long institutionalized in Israelite religion. Only God can forgive sins (2:8), and God has done so for generations through the sanctioned cult which is administered by the cultic leadership. Jesus' attempt now to do directly what has heretofore been supervised by the cultic apparatus denotes a transgression that, as Mary Douglas's work has found, would have had dramatic implications for the socio-political structuring of Israelite society. Jesus' preaching demonstration of interventionist healing validates his claim to make this kind of boundary trespass and encourages the surrounding crowd to acknowledge both the religious and socio-political authority this kind of action, as Son of man, asserts.

The only other occasion where Jesus' earthly activity is described as the activity of the Son of man occurs at 2:28. In this case Jesus allows his disciples to do what is not considered institutionally lawful on the sabbath. When he is challenged he makes the rather presumptuous claim that he, as Son of man, has dominion even over the very critical institution of the sabbath. In this case the trespass is so obvious as to need no further comment. No wonder, then, that by 3:6, the representative leaders who have witnessed these transgressions seek a way to put an end to the man who initiates them. The preview of the Son of man's suffering is clear; it comes because of a preaching ministry that takes direct aim at the boundaries established to order and institutionalize Israelite cultic and, therefore, socio-political society.

The one verse that allegedly offers difficulty for such an interpretation is 10:45. Here Jesus proclaims that the Son of man has come to give his life as a ransom for many. The word "ransom" (λύτρον), in its connection with the title

---

21. Paula Fredriksen, "Jesus and the Temple, Mark and the War," *Society of Biblical Literature 1990 Seminar Papers*, David J. Lull, editor, 29 (1990): 294.

Son of man, has too often been incorrectly read to mean vicarious, redemptive sacrifice.

There is broad agreement that Mark's apocalyptic use of Son of man comes from Daniel 7. There, the title represents the extension of God's kingdom power on earth. The primary concern is about power. Who will be in historical control, the representative of the Most High, the Son of man and the saints who represent him, or the beasts who are represented by the kings of the earth? It's about control, tactical control that represents strategic-mythological control. The saints, as Son of man, are persecuted by the kings. Their hostile efforts are an attempt to gain tactical control for the mythological beasts whom they represent. This is why the saints, as Son of man, are persecuted, because they tactically represent the control of the Ancient of Days. The beasts desperately want this control on the historical level. In such a way the conflict between the beasts and the Ancient of Days at the mythological level boils down on the tactical level to combat between the Son of man/saints and the kings of the earth.

No wonder, then, that Kee, after having compared the opening chapters of Daniel to the narration of Jesus' ministry, can assert, "In the opening chapters of Daniel, his sufferings and those of his companions are *necessary* to prove their moral merit and to demonstrate their fidelity to Israel's God in the face of opposition from the pagan ruler (cf. Daniel 2:28 and Mark 13:7)."[22] The first half of Daniel appears to set up the suffering motif in a way quite similar to the "preaching" set-up found in Mark. Daniel's suffering, and that experienced by his colleagues, occurs because they lived a life that was in contradiction to the life set for those living in the empire. If they stopped living their lives in this way, which represented God's kingdom design for the living of his faithful people, they could have escaped the suffering that befell them. The suffering was therefore inevitable given the kind of challenge their lifestyle represented for the way the society they lived in was structured. That is to say, their lives, which represented God's kingdom design, crossed boundaries, exactly as Jesus' preaching did (cf. Daniel 3:1–18; 6, esp. 6:5, 10).

My argument, then, does not preclude that Jesus' death will have the saving value that 10:45 implies. Indeed, his death is a part of his preaching ministry; it is the inevitable consequence of it. And the text has demonstrated that the preaching ministry has saving value; it brings the future kingdom into the present moment. Through preaching, then, salvation, as the extended power of the future kingdom, becomes a pocket of resistance operating transformatively in the present historical circumstance. Everything associated with that preaching ministry, including the inevitable suffering and "life-giving" of the Son of man, leads to the extension of that kingdom power. It is the Son of man's preaching, and his choice to continue in that preaching despite the conflict he knows it will provoke, that inevitably costs him his life. But, as the resurrection and parousia imagery confirms, it is not a cost he will pay in vain. His way is the way that extends the power of the kingdom presently and assures its consummation imminently. It is his way that will save humans from the mythological control that

---

22. Kee, *Transfiguration in Mark,* 141.

even now Satan attempts to make historically realizable in the institutional controls against which Jesus fights. It is for this reason that Mark ties the language of "saving" (σῷζω) so significantly to the healing and exorcising manifestations of Jesus' preaching. It is through and because of his preaching ministry that the Son of man will inevitably give his life in a way that ransoms (releases) humans from the mythological and institutional control of the satanic strongman.[23] In other words, the pocket his preaching creates extends the kingdom power that can successfully resist the dominion Satan attempts to exert.

The community that follows Jesus does so, then, not as a martyr community called to suffer, but as a community called to preach. But they can be certain that if they preach transformatively, in a way that represents the interventionist power of the mythological kingdom extending itself into the human historical circumstance, they will inevitably suffer. It is this narrative message that explains the persecutions that are presently plaguing the community as it goes about its transformative preaching across the once impenetrable boundary of the Jewish/Gentile ethnic divide (13:9–13).

MODE OF DISCOURSE

Mark's mode of discourse in 8:27–9:8 begins from just this point. My concern is particularly with the message Mark wants to give his reading community. "The members of Mark's community would easily read themselves into his portrait of the disciples on their way up to Jerusalem."[24] Their discipleship is to be of the same type as Jesus' messiahship. This means that they are to represent God's kingdom strategy in their preaching way, even though they realize that the very prosecution of that preaching will necessarily result in their suffering. Indeed, they are already seeing this occur in the persecution the community is suffering because of their transformative preaching mission to the Gentiles, in this very anti-Gentile, revolutionary context of culture.

Mark, in other words, is not telling his readers to go out and suffer; he's telling them (cf. 13:10) to go preach. If the readers are to take their cue from the Jesus mandate given to the disciples, then this conclusion is certain. Throughout the context of situation the disciples' task has been that of following Jesus, a task that is given narrative shape in their preaching that emulates Jesus' own preaching. As was the case with Jesus, so it will be with the community, their preaching will lead them to suffering. But because their preaching is the only way in which the kingdom finds its tactical extension into the present human circumstance, the preaching, as it did in Jesus' case, must continue. It is there-

---

23. Cf. Walter Bauer, William F. Arndt, and F. Wilbur Gingrich, *A Greek-English Lexicon of the New Testament and Other Early Christian Literature,* second edition (Chicago: The University of Chicago Press, 1979) 482. The fact that λύτρον has the sense of the price of release for a slave allows it the semantic range to be interpreted in such a way if the contexts of situation and culture allow such an access point, as they do in the case of the Markan narrative.

24. Marcus, *The Way of the Lord,* 37.

fore necessary that, despite the threat, the readers, like the disciples, put aside concern for their own lives and well being and follow on Jesus' preaching way.

The community's preaching discipleship will do what the "incomplete" preaching activity of the narrative disciples could only anticipate, for their preaching will be of the type that completely fulfills the qualifications of 8:34. The disciples' preaching in Mark's narrative fulfilled only the two of self-denial and following, but not suffering. Indeed, in an effort to avoid suffering Peter will deny Jesus, the other disciples will scatter, and the women who follow him all the way to the tomb will turn silent at the precise moment when they are ordered to speak.

But Mark's community is called to preach (most particularly, to the Gentiles) in an interventionist manner that fully realizes the kinds of social, cultic and political boundary crossings (transformation) that Jesus' preaching represented. Their preaching will therefore not only guarantee suffering, it will also, as 9:1 makes clear, effect the contemporary representation of the future kingdom. In their generation, then, through their interventionist preaching, the future kingdom will extend tactically with all its power into the present moment, like a pocket of resistance. For those who harbored doubts, Mark's text offers the assurance of the resurrection and the transfiguration, apocalyptic moments which not only preview the future, but guarantee that the present path of preaching is the path that tactically represents God's strategic kingdom intent.[25]

Such an evaluation of 8:27–9:8, in light of the context of situation to this point, rather than an interpretation in light of a preconceived notion about the vicarious efficacy of undeserving suffering, suggests that the matter and consequences of interventionist messiahship/discipleship is the theme Mark wants to get across in this crucial mid-narrative narration.

---

25. Cf. Marcus, *The Way of the Lord*, 93. "For the members of the Markan community, the images of Jesus robed in light, conversing with Moses and Elijah, and being proclaimed Son of God by a heavenly voice probably function as a counter to other, profoundly unsettling images: images of dark days of tribulation fallen upon the church (see 13:19); images of beatings in synagogues, perhaps on the grounds of apostasy from the tradition symbolized by Moses (see 13:9; 7:5; 10:4); images of eloquent and militant personalities who are persuading many, even within the community, that *they* are the successor of Moses whose coming was prophesied of old (see 13:6, 22)."

10

Enter the Kingdom

Jesus never corrects them.

At 8:29, when Peter declared that Jesus was messiah (χριστός), Jesus immediately reconfigured the identity and function of his messiahship (8:31–34). But this time, when once again Mark narrates a situation that reveals Jesus as messiah, in a context that suggests an overtly political and militaristic nature, there is no counter-narration.[1] Indeed, as Hendrikus Boers discerns, "One would have to concede, however, that if Jesus had allowed his followers to acclaim him as they are presented to have done when he entered Jerusalem, the conclusion would have been unavoidable that he himself had contributed to the impression that he was a messianic pretender."[2]

Boers is dealing with concerns about the historical Jesus. His interest is to ferret from the text a better understanding of the Jesus behind the narrative of the synoptic materials. My task is to read the Markan text as it stands. I, therefore, look not for what lies behind Mark, but what is revealed in Mark. And I agree that in this narration, regardless of what one thinks about the historical Jesus, Mark presents Jesus as a messiah whose "preaching" confrontation with the established leadership in Israel is overtly social and intensely political. The kingdom that enters Jerusalem on the colt with him is a kingdom that implies a tangible socio-historical, political transformation.

[11:10] Blessed is the coming <u>kingdom</u> of our father David; Hosanna in the highest.

---

1. Cf. David R. Catchpole, "The 'Triumphal' Entry," in *Jesus and the Politics of His Day*, Ernst Bammel and C. F. D. Moule, editors (Cambridge: Cambridge University Press, 1984) 319–34. Mark has crafted a marvelous parallel between this narration of Jesus' entry into Jerusalem and the story of Peter's confession. Just as the confession of 8:27–30 followed the healing of a blind man at 8:22–26, so this entry, whose very narration confirms what Peter confessed, follows the healing of a blind man at 10:46–52. In both, the way is mentioned (10:46, 52; 11:8). In both Jesus is acclaimed in Davidic terms (10:47–48; 11:10). In both there is a reference to "clothing" (ἱμάτιον) (10:52; 11:9). In both the theme of salvation is prominent (10:52; 11:9). And finally, in both acclamation and following are joined (10:52; 11:9). No wonder that Catchpole concludes, "The 'triumphal' entry, therefore, matches the confession and has to do with the disclosure of Jesus's identity and status" (319).

2. Hendrikus Boers, *Who Was Jesus? The Historical Jesus and the Synoptic Gospels* (San Francisco: Harper & Row Publishers, 1989) 90.

FIELD OF DISCOURSE

The first principal part establishes the preaching theme. The entry narrative opens with a miracle-preaching manifestation. Jesus sends two disciples off into an unknown situation. Still, he appears to know how everything will unfold, as if the occurrences are themselves inevitable. The grammar highlights structurally what the narrative wants to deploy thematically; the future unfolds in just the way Jesus, standing at his perch in the present, predicts. At 11:2 he declares: "you will find a colt tied" (εὑρήσετε πῶλον δεδεμένον). At verse 4 we find the prediction grammatically realized: "they found a colt tied" (εὗρον πῶλοω δεδεμένον). At verse 3 he predicts that someone may well ask them a particular question as they are taking the animal: "why do you do this?" (τί ποιεῖτε τοῦτο;). This prediction is subsequently realized in verse 5. Bystanders make the particular inquiry: "why do you release the colt?" (τί ποιεῖτε λύοντες τὸν πῶλον;). Finally, in verse 6, when the two disciples respond as Jesus instructed, the result is exactly as he predicted; the bystanders allow the strangers to walk away with the animal.

The miracle establishes that what follows is a part of Jesus' preaching ministry, his tactical representation, and, therefore, extension of Kingdom power. The entry, then, reflects not only on Jesus, but on how the kingdom, as represented in Jesus, aims to intervene in the human present.

The timing is crucial. In the second principal part, 11:7–11, Mark agrees with John (John 2:13; 12:1, 12) when he narrates that the entry occurred in anticipation of the Passover (cf. 14:1).[3] This is a critical narrative alignment. Passover was celebrated as a remembrance of socio-political liberation. Jesus' entrance personifies the extension of God's kingdom power into the holy city at the time when the people were celebrating the historical extension of God's liberative power through the Exodus event. A new kind of liberation is about to take place. If I might paraphrase the words of Paula Fredriksen:

> In sum: Jesus' gesture [triumphal entry] near the archetypical festival of "national" liberation (Passover) in the context of his mission ("The Kingdom of God is at hand!") would probably have been readily understood *by any Jew [reading]* as a statement that the ... present order was about to cede to the Kingdom of God.[4]

---

3. Hooker points out that many scholars suggest that the actual entry must have occurred during the Feast of Tabernacles, in Autumn, rather than at the Passover, since the narrated procession fits the kind of procession held at that time: "the people carried branches of greenery (presumably cut in the countryside near Jerusalem), which were waved during the recital of the Egyptian Hallel (Psalms 113–18, the psalms of praise recalling the Exodus); according to the Talmud (B. Sukkah 37a-b), these branches were waved at the word 'Hosanna' (Ps. 118.25)" (*A Commentary*, 256). However, Hooker goes on to point out that a similar ceremony was also held during the *Hanukkah* (Festival of Dedication), which celebrated the cleansing of the temple by Judas Maccabaeus in 165 B.C.E. Further conjecture is made regarding the timing of figs, so that Jesus' expectation of fruit on the tree would fit a certain season. Attempts are therefore made to find the time when the historical Jesus most probably entered the city, and under what specific kinds of circumstances.

4. Fredriksen, 299.

The celebratory words shouted by Mark's crowd support such a conclusion. It is widely recognized that the acclamation comes from the Hallel, Psalms 113–18. Only, in this case, they refer not to an Israelite king, but to Jesus. It is an image of Davidic kingship that the words bring to mind, not that of vicarious suffering.[5] And, I say again, neither the narrative nor Jesus steps in to offer a counter-perspective. In fact, as Hooker's careful analysis shows, the grammar pointedly affirms that Jesus has the task of instituting the strategic kingdom in his present tactical activities. Between the two Hosanna brackets, are the critical texts of 11:9 and 10. "In Greek, the two greetings are clearly parallel (εὐλογημένος ὁ ἐρχόμενος [blessed is the one who comes]...εὐλογημένη ἡ ἐρχομένς βασιλεία [blessed is the coming kingdom]...), confirming that the one who is welcomed also brings the kingdom."[6] That one, of course, would be Jesus. Jesus' present preaching ministry tactically represents the strategic design and intent of the future kingdom of God. Mark apparently wants his readers to access his entry language with this understanding in mind.

It is language filled with meaning potential. The question we must consider is, how would someone, Jewish or Greek, have accessed it given the context of culture in Mark's northern Palestine/southern Syria of 70 C.E.? The form of his narrative entry provides us with a vital clue. As Mark has narrated it, Jesus' entry fits exactly the kind of behavior exhibited by royal and/or messianic figures who entered a city amidst the celebratory pomp and circumstance of a victorious, socio-historical transformation they had already accomplished. Catchpole demonstrates, for example, that there was a standard form for such triumphal entry stories in the first-century world. The form had several standard features which were always present, and other, less recurrent ones, which nonetheless augmented the emphasis or triumph. The standard features included a victory already achieved and a status already recognized by the central figure; a formal and ceremonial entry; greetings and acclamations; entry to the city climaxed by entry to the Temple (if the city in question had one); and cultic activity of either a positive (offering sacrifice) or negative (expulsion of objectionable persons) type. All of these standard features are included in Mark 11, plus several other illuminating recurrent features, such as the reference to a royal animal (1 Kings

5. Cf. Catchpole for argument that Mark crafted 11:1–10 in order to establish a particular kind of identity for Jesus. Indeed, Catchpole further argues that Mark's intent in this endeavor was to present Jesus as Davidic king and link his crucifixion to this royal identification. "At the hands of Mark the historical fact of the crucifixion of Jesus has been subordinated to the less historical idea of the crucifixion of Jesus the king of the Jews. And that in turn means that the historicity of Mark 11:1–10 cannot be sustained, either on the basis of the tradition of an earlier event in the pre-Easter sequence (8:27–30), or on the basis of an appeal to the ground of his ultimate execution (15:26). That Jesus went to Jerusalem is certain, and to that minimal extent one could affirm historicity. Whether he was greeted like all other pilgrims with the words of Psalm 118:25f, and/or whether an intensity of expectation of the kingdom of God was apparent in his companions, must remain speculative and uncertain" (330). Catchpole's historical reconstruction notwithstanding, I would agree that Mark's presentation as we have it in the narrative specifically determines to present Jesus in a royal/messianic pose.

6. Hooker, *A Commentary,* 259–60.

1:35; Zech 9:9), the use of the language of the (Hallel) psalms, and the use of the "lord" (κύριος) word group.[7]

In other words, any ancient reader familiar with the form would be led by its presence in Mark's narration of chapter eleven to access the language in a particular messianic-political way. In fact, Boers points out that the German scholar Hugo Gressmann was convinced that Mark's story of the entry so exactly matched the entry of the zealot leader and messianic pretender Menahem ben Judah as reported by Josephus in the *Jewish War* (2.17.8–9) that it had been creatively "applied" to Jesus.[8] It is certainly clear that Mark's story bears an intriguing resemblance to the account of Simon Maccabeus's final consolidation of power in 1 Maccabees 13:49–53 (cf. also 2 Mac 10:1–9). "These events are not repeated exactly in the story of Jesus' entry into Jerusalem and the cleansing of the temple; many differences are evident. Nevertheless, there are enough similar features to associate the two incidents in which Jesus had reportedly been involved with the grasping of messianic-political power."[9]

In the third principal part, 11:12–14 (20), Mark frames the story of yet another preaching manifestation, the miraculous cursing of the fig tree, around Jesus' transformative actions in the Temple. As Jean Comay points out, the Temple was the center of life in institutional Judaism. Politically, it was the seat of the Sanhedrin. Economically, it was not only the site for money exchangers and traders, but also the central financial storehouse that collected economic resources from all over the world. Redemptively, it was the center of cultic purification and sacrificial offering to the Lord.[10] Any of Jesus' actions which made a transformative, messianic statement about the life of the Temple would therefore necessarily have broad socio-political as well as religious implications for the life of institutional Israel.

The fig tree action is the only negative miracle in the Gospel, and it is certain that Mark applies it here with a particular boundary-crossing intent. The miraculous (preaching) cursing interprets the "cleansing." That is to say, it is the strategic intent of the kingdom of God, as tactically represented in Jesus' preaching ministry, that the Temple, now fruitless, will be destroyed. It is a symbolic message that very much fits the literal statement by Jesus at 13:1, 2, and the ironically true "false" accusations and taunts of 14:58 and 15:29. The parable of the vineyard at 12:1–12 explains exactly how the Temple leadership failed to bear just fruit for its people and its God. The required transformation was so radical it had to begin with destruction.

Because of the text's symbolic nature, it obviously harbors a great deal of meaning potential. Once again we must consider how a reader in Mark's context of culture may have accessed it. Telford offers direction when he points out that ancient Israel was often symbolically represented as a tree sown by God.

---

7. Catchpole, 321. Catchpole provides extensive examples from both the Greco-Roman and Jewish worlds on pages 319–25.

8. Boers, 86.

9. Ibid., 90.

10. Jean Comay, *The Temple of Judaism* (New York: Holt, Rinehart, and Winston, 1975) 158.

Religious literature on the whole knows very little, in fact, of non-symbolic trees. The tree in the Old Testament may stand for the righteous and the wicked, but more often it is an image for *the nation itself*, its growth/blossoming or devastation/withering symbolizing the nation's fate. *Israel is God's tree or "planting,"* established in the Promised Land by his act of redemption, and watered and nourished (as long as she is faithful) by his grace.[11]

Even more fascinating is the direct link between the fig tree and Israel in the Hebrew scriptures. Telford highlights five primary prophetic "fig" passages: Jeremiah 8:13; Isaiah 28:3–4; Hosea 9:10, 16; Micah 7:1; and Joel 1:7, 12. And although he agrees that no single one of them provides the foundation for the Fig Tree cursing in Mark, it does seem likely that they together furnish the background from which the evangelist figured his readers would access his narration. It is principally an eschatological background. In these Old Testament images, the fig is an emblem of security, peace and prosperity, particularly, as Telford goes on to point out, in the golden age of Israel's past (Eden, Exodus, Wilderness, Promised Land), or the glorious age of her imminent future (Messianic Age). The image operates from the twin themes of blessing and judgment, supernatural responses to human endeavor.

The blossoming of the fig-tree and *its giving of its fruit* is a descriptive element in passages which depict Yahweh's visiting his people with *blessing,* while *the withering of the fig tree,* the destruction or withholding of its fruit, figures in imagery describing *Yahweh's judgment* upon his people or their enemies.[12]

This being the case, it would be unremarkable that when Jesus, as the tactical representative of God's future kingdom, curses the fig tree, Mark's readers would access the act as a verdict of divine judgment against the Temple and the institutions of Israel represented by it. This seems even more likely given the fact that "Very often the reason given for God's wrathful visitation is cultic aberration on the part of Israel, her condemnation for a *corrupt Temple cultus and sacrificial system.*"[13]

According to Telford's research even Gentile readers could be counted on to access Mark's narration as an omen of divine judgment against the Temple and the institutions it represented. Having discussed how the fig tree symbolized prosperity and hope in the Greco-Roman world, he turned to legends and myths which narrated the fear and apprehension that surrounded the withering of such a tree, particularly in the capital city of Rome. As in the world of the Hebrew Scriptures, so it was in the Greco-Roman climate: "The withering of a fig tree at the Roman metropolis was seen as a portent of disaster for that city."[14] It is

---

11. William R. Telford, *The Barren Temple and the Withered Tree: A Redaction-Critical Analysis of the Cursing of the Fig Tree in Mark's Gospel and Its Relation to the Cleansing of the Temple Tradition* (Sheffield: JSOT Press, 1980) 162.

12. Ibid.

13. Ibid.

14. William R. Telford, "More Fruit from the Withered Tree: Temple and Fig-Tree in Mark from a Graeco-Roman Perspective," in *Templum Amicitiae: Essays on the Second Temple Pre-*

therefore quite likely, then, that the withering of the fig tree in the Jewish capital would have provoked a similar symbolic interpretation.

Mark gives his readers an unmistakable signal for such an interpretative move when he declares through the narration that it was not the season for figs.[15] "It may be that this is a deliberate hint to us to take the story symbolically."[16] It is, I think, the continued symbolism of boundary trespass. For there are, considering Mark's overall narration, other options available to the Jesus character who tactically represents the interventionist power of God's divine kingdom. In this case, a positive miracle could have provided the sustenance he sought, that is, if sustenance was really the point of the narrative. Were his character to be read consistently the reader would have anticipated that the Jesus who multiplied food for famished thousands could have produced fruit (especially given the fact that nature had already provided the head start of the leaves) rather than destruction. This act of destruction by a man who has heretofore only acted miraculously as a creative force mandates a pause for reflection.

Mark says, Jesus hungered (ἐπείνασεν). Though the evangelist has other occasions to describe the hunger of his characters, most notably in the two separate feeding miracles, he uses this verb in only one other place, and in that case, in the exact same form. At 2:25, David, in whose name Jesus' kingdom is now proclaimed at 11:10, also hungered (ἐπείνασεν). Mark obviously has a point to make here, and part of that point includes invoking the name of David. Hooker notes that the phrase, "our Father David," is unexpected, since it is unknown in Judaism. The designation Father was usually applied to the patriarchs. Similarly unusual is the reference to David's coming kingdom, even if there was widespread hope for the coming of a Davidic king.[17] Mark's intent, evidently, is to create a narrative atmosphere in which David's person and the Davidic kingdom are kindled together in the mind of the reader; he will accomplish this task

---

sented to Ernst Bammel, William Horbury, editor (Sheffield: JSOT Press, 1991) 300. See pages 289–300 for accounting of actual myths and legends.

15. Some scholars attempt to ascertain at what botanical season a fig tree would have had leaves but no fruit in order to determine the dating of the cursing and its significance. Cf., for example, Douglas E. Oakman, "Cursing Fig Trees and Robbers' Dens: Pronouncement Stories Within Social-Systemic Perspective. Mark 11:12–25 and Parallels," *Semeia* 64 (1994): 253–72. Wendy J. Kotter offers a more imaginative solution. She proposes that the final edition of the Markan narrative has a grammatical problem that must be rectified in order to make sense of the material. Because the γάρ (because) clause that begins verse 13d does not explain the material that comes before it, but does explain the material in verse 13ab, it should follow there more naturally. The resulting text would read, v. 13ab. καὶ ἰδὼν συκῆν ἀπὸ μακρόθεν ἔχουσαν φύλλα ἦλθεν εἰ ἄρα τι εὑρήσει ἐν αὐτῇ ... v. 13d. ὁ γὰρ καιρὸς οὐκ ἦν σύκων. (And after he'd seen from a distance that the fig tree had leaves, he went to see *if* he might find something on it, because it was not the season for figs.) In other words, knowing it was not the season for figs, Jesus approached the tree cautiously, figuring there might not be any fruit, despite the fact that the tree had leaves. It was not uncommon for the fig tree to have leaves but no fruit. ("For It Was Not the Season for Figs," *Catholic Biblical Quarterly* 48 [1986] 62–66.) While Kotter's formulation is intriguing, it doesn't deal with the text as it stands before us; her interpretation requires grammatical reconstruction. Indeed, even with the reconstruction, no real motive is given for Jesus' cursing of the tree. In fact, one would expect that Jesus would in this case have less motivation. Why would he curse a tree for not having what he already knew, even from afar, it might very well not have?

16. Hooker, *A Commentary*, 262.

17. Ibid., 260.

even if he has to tinker with tradition to do so. He therefore narrates this second praise statement of blessing (Blessed is the coming of the kingdom of our Father David) in such balance with the first from the Hallel (Blessed is the one who comes in the name of the Lord) that it appears both are scriptural chants even though the former is not. Still, he succeeds in bringing up David's name and directing the reader's attention toward his acknowledged royal, and even messianic, scriptural authority. Why the need to establish such a link with David in such a context?

David, the reader will remember, hungered too (cf. 2:23–28). And his hunger, too, was connected with the "house" (οἶκος) of God. The temple, in the material that is framed by the fig tree cursing, is described as the "house" of God. In David's case, the hunger prefaced an institutional boundary crossing. He and his men did in the house of God, on the Sabbath, a work that under normal circumstances was prohibited. But the need of human wholeness outweighed the demands of the institution (the law) and therefore a transformation, if only a momentary one in that case, was warranted. The conclusion Jesus draws from that momentary trespass, however, allows for a perpetual transformation whereby human need is always placed above institutional requirement (2:27).

In this context Jesus' hunger, likewise, would be accessed as a narrative symbol utilized by Mark to preface and portend a radical boundary trespass. Once again it will become clear that the institutions, as they exist, do not meet the needs of the people. Indeed, as they exist, as representatives *not* of God's kingdom strategy, but of a satanic kingdom strategy (cf. 3:22; chapter 8 above), they *can't* meet the needs of the people any more than a fig tree can give fruit out of its season. Their strategic allegiance destines them to be as fruitless for the people of God as they are hostile to the preaching of God's son. Even though their institutional designation and mandates make them appear fruitful, just as the leaves on the fig tree make it appear so, because they represent the wrong kingdom strategy, they will be tactically unable to satisfy the hunger of God's people. Transformation is therefore required.

The fourth principal part, 11:15–19, defines the nature of Jesus' transformative action as a boundary trespass of institutionalized Temple activity. The reader knows that the Temple, because of its leadership, bears no fruit. The crucial question is, how is that fruitlessness to be understood? On the surface it appears from verses 15 and 16 that Jesus dislikes the commercialism taking place in the court of the Gentiles.[18] He casts out the sellers and the buyers, overturns the tables of the money exchangers and the seats of those who were selling doves. As a final act he prevents persons from carrying vessels through the Temple.

Craig Evans makes the traditional argument that the act should be viewed as a cleansing or purification by the historical Jesus.[19] Jesus was operating against what he saw to be rampant corruption in the priesthood. David See-

---

18. Cf. Comay, *The Temple of Judaism.* Comay provides a helpful description of the second temple and connects its various activities (such as the commercial activities connected with sacrifices and the temple tax) with the areas in which they most likely occurred.

19. Cf. Craig A. Evans, "Jesus' Action in the Temple: Cleansing or Portent of Destruction?," *Catholic Biblical Quarterly* 51 (1989): 237–70.

ley objects that "there is no other ancient testimony to this particular financial abuse."[20] I. Abrahams, making the argument that the monetary establishment in the Temple facilitated rather than hindered the ability of pilgrims to perform their pilgrim rites, agreed that there is no record of moneychangers taking exorbitant profits for private ends.[21] This is not to say that there was never any evidence of abuse in the system. But, Abrahams argues, such abuse should be seen as aberrations rather than as systemic, commonplace occurrences. He concluded that such abuses occurred not during the time of Jesus, but during the time that led up to the war with Rome and the destruction of the Temple, in other words, during the time that Mark wrote. "It was only under the aristocratic regime of the Temple's last decades that we hear of oppression."[22] Perhaps, then, Mark's Jesus was dealing with a problem specific to Mark's time, the abuses of the cultic system allegedly perpetrated during the time which led up to the Jewish revolt.

E. P. Sanders raises a necessary caution. He agrees with Abrahams that the buying and selling in the Temple were necessary to the sacrificial system. What concerned him was Abraham's willingness to allow that Jesus was attacking an external understanding of religion, which fostered the abuses of the Temple's last decades, in favor of a more genuine religious interiority. He therefore rejects Abraham's conclusion that in turning over the money-changers' tables and ejecting the sellers, Jesus did a service to Judaism. Jesus, Sanders maintains, was not attempting to purify the Temple, which is to say, take it back to some more pristine form where its worship was not bound up with the externalism of sacrifice and offering. Sacrifice and offering, and the monetary mechanisms set in place to facilitate them, had been a part of Temple worship from the beginning.

> The most important point to recognize here is that the requirement to present an *unblemished* dove as a sacrifice for certain impurities or transgressions was a requirement *given by God to Israel through Moses*. The business arrangements around the temple were *necessary* if the commandments were to be obeyed. An attack on what is necessary is not an attack on "present practice."[23]

Jesus' boundary crossing, then, was much more than an attack on "some present abuses" of a good system. It appeared to be an attack on the entire system itself. If this is indeed how a Markan reader would have accessed the narration of the event, one must therefore ask a follow-up question, in what way did Jesus understand that system to have become problematic, particularly as it related to commercial activity and the movement of vessels back and forth?

---

20. David Seeley, "Jesus' Temple Act," *Catholic Biblical Quarterly* 55 (1993): 265–68. Quote on 268.

21. I. Abrahams, *Studies in Pharisaism and the Gospels* (New York: KTAV Publishing House, Inc., 1917), especially 82ff.

22. Ibid., 86.

23. E. P. Sanders, *Jesus and Judaism* (Philadelphia: Fortress Press, 1985) 65.

The answer lies in the climactic 17th verse where once again Jesus is presented by Mark as preaching the kingdom. Jesus *teaches* the crowd (11:17, ἐδίδασκεν; 11:18, διδαχῇ αὐτοῦ) how to interpret his actions by an appeal to the Hebrew Scriptures. Interestingly enough, he does not appeal to the scripture that would appear to make the most sense in this apocalyptically flavored context, namely, Zechariah 14:21b, "And there shall no longer be a trader in the house of the Lord of hosts on that day." Certainly, the allusions to Zechariah 9:9 in the entry narrative suggest that the prophet's message was percolating in the background of the narrative. If his concern was directed exclusively at the commercial enterprise and its abuses, this text would have provided the narrative crowd and Mark's readers with the best opportunity of correctly interpreting his behavior.

His preaching manifestation opens instead with a quote from Deutero-Isaiah (56:7), "My house shall be called a house of prayer for all the nations." In fact, the more one considers Isaiah 56:7, the more it appears that Jesus was not interested in halting the sacrificial system. A key element of Isaiah's context of situation is that the *sacrifices* of the Gentiles were to be accepted equally with those of the Jews on the holy mountain.

In fact, this eschatological emphasis on the Gentiles and their equal inclusion into the worship of the Lord is, I would argue, Jesus' primary interest. Throughout the Markan narrative Jesus' preaching has represented the kingdom of God through its interventionist crossings of important institutional boundaries. The Jew/Gentile divide is one of the most significant, indeed, probably the most fiercely supported boundary at this critical juncture in the life of an Israel at war with Rome. Mark, I believe, and I have tried to show, established Jesus' interventionist intent with regard to this boundary in an implicit way early on in the Gospel. He continued to develop it in the narrative until this climactic presentation here at 11:17. He therefore explains that Jesus' anger with the institutions that support the ongoing viability and presence of the Temple is not due to the fact the institutions are inherently wrong, but because they perpetuate the maintenance of an ethnic boundary whose time of trespass has come. The future kingdom, in the "pocket" of Jesus' person and present preaching ministry, and the preaching ministry of the disciples and believers who follow behind him on the Markan landscape, has arrived. Messianic transformation is therefore warranted. The house of Jewish prayer must become a house of prayer for all the nations. This is the eschatological fruit the temple-tree must bear. If it does not, it if *will* not, it will, like the fig tree, experience destruction. Such a conclusion forms a natural fit with the later Markan narrations that the Gentiles, beneficiaries of God's just anger, will gain divine favor (12:9), that the Gentiles will be the target of discipleship preaching (13:10), and that the first to confess Jesus as divine son will be a Gentile (15:39).

This is, of course, a hostile picture that taken from its context of culture could become fodder for contemporary readers interested in promulgating exclusivist and racist interpretations. It is not Mark's intent here to say that God has now accepted Gentiles and rejected Jews because of a Jewish rejection of Jesus. Indeed, it is clear from verse 18 that the *Jewish* crowds are enthusiastically receptive to Jesus' message. It is the leadership that resists the boundary-crossings his preaching ministry demands. And the second half of the verse makes it quite clear precisely why this is so.

At 11:17b, the evangelist demonstrates that the natural opposition to "house of prayer for all the nations" is "cave of robbers." It is in this opposition that we are to determine the foundation for Jesus' anger at the refusal of the Temple infrastructure and leadership to make the boundary crossing that his messianic presence demanded. The instrumental reference comes from the prophecy of Jeremiah 7:11. And, as Hooker explains, in its Old Testament context, "The phrase 'a robber's den' is... a denunciation of those whose moral behaviour was repugnant to God, but who nevertheless came to the temple to worship."[24] But why use the odd terminology "cave of robbers" (σπήλαιον λῃστῶν)? As Don Juel points out, "What is striking about the terms... is how inappropriate they are in the present context."[25]

I would argue, however, that what appears inappropriate on the surface becomes a precise fit when the material is appraised in light of Mark's own context of culture. The first move should be a careful clarification of terminology. This move demands that I now break up my analytic categories in a way that I have not done up to this point. As the information on the issue of the robbers, a tenor of discourse discussion, is particularly relevant at this point rather than later, I will draw it directly into the field of discourse discussion here.

I prefer the translation "cave of robbers" because this language fits more precisely what Mark is describing than the traditional "den of thieves." Mark had two nouns available for his use; each has its own unique social reality. The first is "thief" (κλέπτης). Though Mark never uses it in his narrative, it is found at Luke 12:33, when he cautions readers against laying up earthly treasures which a thief can steal. Luke also uses it at 12:39, when he warns that Jesus will return like a thief in the night, stealthily and unexpectedly. It is used 17 times in the Septuagint and 16 times in the New Testament. Consistently, it describes a nonviolent offender who commits his crimes in secret. Though Josephus never uses the noun, he does use the verbal form. He also uses it to refer to a clandestine act.[26]

Mark does not choose this form for his description of what has been happening in the temple. It is, therefore, not his intent that the phrase be accessed in a way that refers to a corrupt Temple hierarchy "stealing" profits that do not belong to them. Something else is at stake. Mark therefore chooses the term "robber, bandit" (λῃστής). This term, used some 42 times by Josephus, 9 times in the Septuagint, and 15 times by New Testament writers, describes armed bands of marauders who are intentionally brutal when they carry out their activities.[27] The distinguishing marker is violence. While "thief" (κλέπτης) typ-

---

24. Hooker, *A Commentary*, 268.

25. Donald Juel, *The Messiah and the Temple: A Study of Jesus' Trial before the Sanhedrin in the Gospel of Mark* (New Haven: Yale University Dissertation, 1973) 199.

26. Buchanan, "Mark 11:15–19: Brigands in the Temple," *Hebrew Union College Annual* 30 (1959): 170–71.

27. Ibid., 171. See footnotes 5–9 for citations from *Jewish Wars*.

ically describes a stealthy person who deprives another of his property, "robber" (ληστής) denotes a bandit who operates outdoors in the company of a gang.

This differentiation still allows a great deal of interpretative potential. We must therefore analyze the choices a reader in Mark's community would have had when coming upon this term, and determine which he or she would most likely have settled upon as "meaningful" in the context of culture I have reconstructed.

A preliminary investigation suggests that there were two principal types of bandits: the highwaymen who robbed purely for personal gain, and the guerrilla warriors who directed their aggression against Roman authorities and/or the Jewish authorities and persons who collaborated with them. Josephus complicates the matter by also using the term in connection with the Zealots who maintained a more formal anti-Roman political program.[28] Even though they may well have been perceived by the Romans as bandits and outlaws, they are bandits of a different, politically organized type. In fact, they spearheaded the war with Rome in 66–70 c.e. from inside the besieged city walls of Jerusalem.[29]

---

28. Joel Marcus, "The Jewish War and the *Sitz im Leben* of Mark," *Journal of Biblical Literature* 111 (1992): 449–50. See his n. 42 which references other key sources.

29. Cf. Josephus, *The Jewish War, Books I–VII,* H. St. J. Thackeray, translator, E. H. Warmington, editor, 9 vols., Loeb Classical Library, Vol. II, *Josephus* (Cambridge: Harvard University Press, 1968); Josephus, *The Works of Josephus,* William Whiston, translator (Peabody, MA: Hendrickson, 1968); Martin Hengel, *The Zealots: Investigations into the Jewish Freedom Movement in the Period from Herod I until 70 A.D.,* D. Smith, translator (Edinburgh: T & T Clark, 1989). Richard A. Horsley, "The Zealots: Their Origin, Relationships and Importance in the Jewish Revolt," *Novum Testamentum* 28 (1986): 159–92. Doron Mendels, *The Rise and Fall of Jewish Nationalism* (New York: Doubleday, 1992). U. Rappaport, "John of Gischala: From Galilee to Jerusalem," *Journal of Jewish Studies* 33 (1982): 479–93. David M. Rhoads, *Israel in Revolution, 6–74 C.E.: A Political History Based on the Writings of Josephus* (Philadelphia: Fortress Press, 1976), "Zealots," *Anchor Bible Dictionary,* 6 (New York: Doubleday, 1992) 1043–54. Morton Smith, "Zealots and Sicarii: Their Origins and Relation," *Harvard Theological Review* 64 (1971) 1–19.

Josephus first mentions the Zealots as a distinct movement during the winter of 67–68 c.e. when conflict erupted between the Zealots and the provisional government over the conduct of the war (*War* 4.161). The continuity between this coalition and the early priestly group, who in 66 c.e. stopped the daily sacrifices in behalf of Caesar and took control of the temple area, is a matter of some discussion. (For the view that the later Zealot coalition has roots in the earlier group responsible for the cessation of Roman sacrifices in the temple, see Rhoads, *Israel in Revolution,* 101–4, and "Zealots," 1043—54. For an opposing view, see Horsley, "The Zealots," 159–92. Horsley argues that there is little evidence for continuity and that the Zealot coalition was made up largely of rural peasants who fled the Roman advance.) It is clear, however, that in 67–68 c.e., the Zealot coalition seized control of the temple. The inner courts remained under their control until near the end of the war in 70 c.e. Having taken control of the temple, the Zealots fortified it and used it as a fortress (*War* 4.151). It is at this point that they set up their own egalitarian government with a collective leadership and elected a new high priest from among their own number, an uneducated peasant from Judea (*War* 4.153–57).

While serving as intermediary between the provisional government and the Zealots, John of Gischala informs the Zealots, fortified in the temple, that the government is planning to turn the city over to the Romans (*War* 4.216–29). In response, the Zealots bring the Idumeans into the city and, with their help, take control of the city and begin a reign of terror. Eventually, the Zealots, deserted by the Idumeans because of Zealot excesses and opposed by John of Gischala because of his failure to assume control over them, withdraw into the inner temple (*War* 5.6–8) with John in control of the outer precincts. Eventually the remaining Zealots come under the control of John of Gischala when he penetrates the inner precincts of the temple (*War* 5.98–105), and they assist in the defense of the city against the Romans (while continuing to fight among themselves as well,

Indeed, Horsley and others note that Josephus does not use the term Zealot until after the hostilities of 66 have begun. Their existence is particularly tied to the revolt and subsequent war. Their locus of operation was Jerusalem, and they headquartered their resistance in the Temple.[30]

There are, then, three possible realities which can legitimately come to mind when one accesses the term "bandits" (λῃστῶν) at 11:17: highwaymen, guerrilla warriors, or zealot revolutionary forces. We must remember that Mark is writing the story at the climactic moment of the 66–70 war. At this time, politically minded revolutionaries attempted to use every resource, particularly the Temple, as a weapon in the war against Rome. They are the ones who would have offered the most attractive messianic position as an alternative to the one represented by Mark's Jesus. They are also the ones, then, whom Mark's readers would most likely have identified when, at 11:17, they accessed the term "bandit."

In fact, Marcus makes the intriguing proposal that the Zealot leaders had gone so far with their messianic pretension as to actually desecrate the Temple. It is his contention that at 13:14, Mark writes with their behavior, particularly that of Eleazar, son of Simon (67–78), specifically in mind.[31] He therefore insists that 11:17 should be read with the emphasis of 13:14 in mind. The Temple, a place intended to be a house of international prayer, had been turned into a nationalistic front for revolution. "The redactional verse Mark 11:17, then, can plausibly be viewed as the superimposition upon the tradition about Jesus' cleansing of the Temple of some features of an event that occurred during the Jewish War, the occupation of the Temple by the Zealots in pursuit of their military aims and their theology of purificatory war against the infidel."[32]

In other words, in this "apocalyptic war of myths," the revolutionary false prophets demanded allegiance from those who sought to respond appropriately to the realization that God was about to intervene in human history. Unfortunately, they were using the Temple as a staging ground for revolutionary behavior that included the purification of the Temple, the place of *international* prayer, from Gentile presence. It is for this reason that God's intervention would result in Jerusalem's destruction rather than its restoration.

> In response to the Zealot occupation of the Temple and similar acts of "purification" of the holy land from Gentile influence, Mark tells his community — which perhaps has experienced at first hand the drastic effects

---

according to Josephus) (*War* 5.248–57). It is interesting that, according to Josephus, John is able to gain access to the inner temple because Eleazar, during a lull in the conflict, opens the inner courts for those who want to worship (*War* 5.98)!

30. Cf. George Wesley Buchanan, "Symbolic Money-Changers in the Temple?," *New Testament Studies* 37 (1991): 288–89. "At that time [68–70 C.E.] the zealots unquestionably had control of the temple mount, and might have been accused of having made it a 'cave of brigands' or a zealot stronghold (*War* 4.146–61). Josephus said they made the sanctuary (τό ἅγιον) a place of tyranny, and the temple of God itself had become a fortress (φρούριον) (*War* 4.151)."

31. Marcus, "The Jewish War . . . ," esp. 448–60.

32. Ibid., 451. Cf. 454–55 for Josephus citations which Marcus uses to demonstrate that the actions of Eleazar were viewed as a defilement of the Temple.

of these acts — that the revolutionary purge is actually a defilement, that it will precipitate divine judgment, and that the inheritance of Israel will be taken away from the Jewish leaders and turned over to a new people that prominently includes Gentiles in its ranks (12:9).[33]

This supposition is all the more credible given the fact that the term Mark uses with "bandit" (ληστής), "cave" (σπήλαιον), is the same term Josephus used when he described the caves where the zealot bandits hid during the initial periods of the revolt.[34] Catchpole points out that even the language in verse 16 has the potential to fit this kind of interpretative solution. While most interpreters tend to view the verse that says Jesus stopped anyone from carrying a "vessel" (σκεῦος) through the Temple as an indication that Jesus hindered the movement of cultic materials, he allows for another intriguing possibility. Citing an extensive *TDNT* article by Maurer, he writes that ". . . σκεῦος should not be over-interpreted as a reference to any of the holy vessels, as if Jesus is here interfering with regular cultic activity. The term is frequently used in an entirely secular sense, carrying a range of meanings which includes military equipment, jewelry, baggage, undefined property in general, and containers which may be used for any purpose."[35] The fact that the range of interpretative meanings can allow a reader to access it as "military equipment" in the cultural context which I have cited allows for the possibility that the "zealot" interpretative solution may be a correct one. In fact, it is the only one which enables all of the various details of the text to make meaningful sense to a reader in the Markan cultural context of the 66–70 war *and* the Markan situational context of 11:1–25. Jesus, the one who enters Jerusalem as Messiah now approaches the temple in a way that will indicate the quality of that messiahship. It is only now that we have the narrative correction that was so sorely missing before. Jesus, Mark's narration now tells us, is not the kind of political messiah who foments revolution and comes to the Temple as other messianic pretenders, in order to use it as a base of revolutionary support and nationalistic opposition. Instead, though he is the messiah who represents a kingdom strategy that intends a transformation that remains socially and politically relevant, the new historical reality is one that diametrically opposes the vision proclaimed by the messianic pretenders. It is a vision whose realization symbolizes what the prophetic Temple vision had intended all along, a house where all the nations could gather to worship God.

I therefore argue that the most meaningful access of the language for a reader in Mark's context of culture would have been "cave of robbers." To Mark, the

---

33. Ibid., 455–56.
34. Cf. Buchanan, "Brigands in the Temple," 172. "It is quite clear that Josephus [*War*] blames the bands of marauders who revolted against Rome for his country's misfortunes. When Herod was first made King of the Jews, his immediate task was a 'campaign against the cave dwelling brigands (ἐπὶ τοὺς ἐν τοῖς σπηλαίοις ὥρυντο ληστάς) who were infesting a wide area and inflicting on the inhabitants evils no less than those of war' [I(304)]. These λησταί were difficult to conquer because they lurked in caves [τὰ σπήλαια] in the mountains where their guerrilla methods were most effective, and they would accept suicide rather than submission to Herod."
35. Catchpole, 331.

house of prayer for all the nations had become an enclave dedicated to the military resistance of Gentile rule and Gentile presence in Palestine. The Son of man, and the Markan community who followed him, preaching a narrative message of inclusion, and therefore representing the kingdom of God as an inclusive reality of the future taking hold as a "pocket" in the present, had run up against, in the Temple, what had become the most powerful of all symbols for nationalist and exclusivist resistance.[36]

TENOR OF DISCOURSE

It is at this point that the text directs us to an immediate consideration of the tenor of discourse. When Mark closes his fourth principal part at 11:18–19, he mentions several critical characterizations. The leadership, represented by the scribes and high priest, respond as they do throughout the narrative; rejecting Jesus' words, but fearing the influence those words have over the crowd, they seek a secret way to destroy him. The crowd, too, plays to form, responding with amazement at Jesus' preaching manifestation (the teaching of 11:17 which interprets his Temple "cleansing"). But it is the new characterization that occurs in this section that gives me the greatest reinforcement for the argument I have been developing thus far. It is the characterization introduced at 11:11. It is the central focus of verse 15, and later the teaching centerpiece of verse 17. It is the Temple.

I am well aware that Mark does not develop the Temple as a character in the same way that he develops the scribes, the crowd, Jesus or the disciples. It is neither personified nor given an action role. It is, however, given an "active" characterization as the seat of Jewish social, cultic and political life. It is characterized as the place where the intent of God's kingdom strategy comes alive as either nationalist exclusion or universal inclusion.

The Temple's tactical interests are represented in the language "cave of robbers." Because those interests conflict with Jesus' preaching interests, transformation is required. Furthermore, because its present state is symbolized as defiant fruitlessness, transformation equals destruction. This is the characterization that begins at 11:11 and continues to the final mentioning of the Temple at 15:38, where the tearing of its curtain presents another apocalyptic symbol of its impending destruction.[37] As Seeley points out,

---

36. For a larger discussion of these issues cf. Brian K. Blount, "The Social World of Bandits."

37. It should be pointed out that when "temple" occurs in the text two different Greek terms are used to make the reference. 11:11, 15, 16, 27; 12:35; 13:1, 3; 14:49 all use the term ἱερόν. 14:58; 15:29; 15:38 use the term ναός. A lengthy debate is not necessary given the parameters of our study. No matter how one interprets the reasons Mark may have had for using the different terminology it is certain that he is referring in either case to the Jerusalem Temple. For one of the principal opinions, cf. John Donahue, *Are You the Christ?: The Trial Narrative in the Gospel of Mark* (Missoula, MT: Society of Biblical Literature, 1973) 104–5. "Mark uses two terms for temple, *hieron* in 11:11, 15, 16; 12:35; 13:1, 3 and 14:49, and *naos* in the above contexts [14:58; 15:29]. The difference does not indicate a difference between the whole temple area and the sanctuary proper, but rather connotes a difference between tradition and redaction since Mark uses *hieron* in those places that show his strongest redaction." Juel takes the opposite opinion and

the end of the temple service constitutes a powerful motif running through the last chapters of Mark. It is almost as though the last movements of Mark's story had been charted in terms of the temple's projected demise, for its fate and that of Jesus seem tightly interwoven.[38]

It is particularly noteworthy that the most specific remarks about the temple's demise are narrated as Jesus statements. At 13:1–2, Jesus forgoes the symbolism of cursed fig trees and proclaims outright that the temple will be destroyed. At 14:58, one of the "false" accusations brought against him in the trial before the Sanhedrin is that he promised he would destroy the Temple built with hands, a characterization of the Jerusalem temple, and in three days build another not made with hands. Even though the testimony is offered as false, it is certain, given Jesus' own statement at 13:2, and the taunt of 15:29, which is not narratively disputed, that Jesus did speak dramatically against the Temple. Certainly, given the passion predictions of 8:31, 9:31, and 10:33–34, where Jesus included a reference to resurrection in the context of a three-day time period, Mark's readers could be expected to access the language of rebuilding the Temple in light of resurrection imagery. In other words, it would make perfect sense for a Markan reader to conclude with a specific meaning interpretation: Jesus' preaching intended the strategic goal of an apocalyptic Temple built as a house of prayer for all the nations (11:17) that would gather the elect from everywhere (13:27).

But this strategic goal could not be accomplished without the tactical overthrow and destruction of the present Temple; otherwise its nationalist strategic design and resulting exclusivistic tactical agenda would remain perpetual impediments to real kingdom transformation. This is the troubling, boundary-crossing message that Jesus preached, one that made even more sense in the Markan context of culture than it did in Jesus' own. For it was in Mark's setting at the height of the war that the Temple figured most prominently as an institutional symbol of zelotic-nationalistic exclusivism. Mark therefore presented Jesus as a messianic figure whose concerns were every bit as social and political as those of the messianic pretenders who were in control of the Temple as he wrote. Like them, Jesus entered Jerusalem bathed in royal, apocalyptic imagery. Like them, Jesus entered Jerusalem focussing his kingdom message and the effort it demanded on the Temple. Like them, Jesus foresaw that his apocalyptic vision mandated contemporary transformation. Unlike them, he believed this transformation would bring an end to the physical Temple and its institutional strategy.

MODE OF DISCOURSE

What is Mark's teaching objective in this narration? What does he want his text language to do? Even though I have made the argument that throughout

---

agrees with the general grammatical consensus that ναός refers to the sanctuary and ἱερόν to the outer dwellings as a whole (*Messiah and Temple*, 191–93).

38. David Seeley, "Jesus' Temple Act," *Catholic Biblical Quarterly* 55 (1993) 274.

Mark has presented a scenario whereby the disciples (and the readers through them) are called to follow Jesus in his tactical preaching ministry, in this case there is more on the evangelist's mind than mere literal following. It seems unlikely that it would be his intent that his readers follow Jesus' preaching as in the future forecasting of 11:1–6 (13:32–37) or the tree cursing of 11:12–14 (20–21). And yet, the symbolism involved with that cursing is certainly the place where our investigation should begin. I would argue that Mark intends his readers to understand that they, too, because of their tactical relationship with the extending power of God's eschatological kingdom, have the power to transform in ways that generate the same kinds of radical changes Jesus' own ministry realized. It is for this reason that Mark does not end his text at 11:19, but holds verses 20–25 in the climactic closing position.

11:20 maintains the bracket with 11:12–14 by reintroducing the cursed fig tree. The disciples all see that it has withered to the root. Peter's remembrance of Jesus' curse pushes him into conversation. It is at this point that Jesus appears to change both the tone and content of his thought. Suddenly, he is again on the track of creative miracles; and mountains, not trees, are the subject of their transformative activity. Mark uses the shift to speak dramatically and directly to his readers while Jesus is speaking in the narrative to his disciples. Jesus first tells them to have faith in God. The text reminds the reader of the programmatic preaching statement at 1:14–15. Though I have focussed thus far on the first half of the expected response to the realization that the kingdom of God is at hand, repentance, here it is clear that Mark turns his readers' attention to the second half, "belief in the gospel."

Believe, Jesus instructs, and anything is possible. Throughout the gospel, Mark makes a point of connecting his language of faith with that of Jesus' miraculous preaching manifestations. The noun "faith" ($\pi i\sigma\tau\iota\varsigma$) occurs rarely. But when it does, 2:5; 4:40; 5:34; 10:52, it does so in contexts of situation where Jesus' miracles are on effective display. A similar pattern holds for Mark's use of the verbal form "believe" ($\pi\iota\sigma\tau\epsilon\upsilon\omega$).[39] Indeed, Tolbert argues that in Mark's narrative, faith is so instrumental to Jesus' ability to perform miracles that in the latter portion of the text, when conflict with the authorities heightens, and faith as a literary concept all but disappears, Jesus' power to create miracles disappears with it.[40] It is faith, evidently, that enables preaching to power the kinds of apocalyptic interventions that signify the social, cultic, and political boundary transformations representative of the kingdom of God.

It is in this closing context of situation that the reader should finally assess the narration of the withering fig tree. The fig tree cursing symbolizes boundary-crossing, transformation. It is toward this symbolism that Mark directs the faith of his readers. In this case it would have the particular impact of suggesting that those readers who have faith in God will have the power to do what Jesus' fig tree cursing symbolized, to challenge the cultic, purity, social and political tra-

---

39. 1:15; 5:36; 9:23, 24, 42; 11:23, 24, 31; 13:21; 15:32. Once again, the bulk of the uses, particularly before Jesus' entry into Jerusalem in chapter 11, occur in miracle contexts of situation.

40. Cf. Tolbert, *Sowing the Gospel,* 183ff.

ditions as symbolized in the Temple, and transform them in a way that makes them more representative of God's kingdom intent. In the case of the Markan context of culture, no doubt this would have had a specific application toward the Gentile mission and the kinds of boundary-trespass this kind of ministry implied in the context of a Jewish/Roman war that instead fostered nationalistic tendencies of exclusion. Any community operating universally in such an exclusivistic environment could expect to attract condemnation. Suffering, in other words, was all but inevitable (13:9–13). But the call remained one of transformation, and with faith, it would occur, just as surely as would Jesus' vision of a temple not built with hands.

Telford's research suggests that such an interpretation could easily have been the access point of a Markan reader. Indeed, Telford argues that these verses which make up the fifth principal part, 11:20–25, were added by the evangelist or a later redactor.[41] While this may well be the case given the strange "fit" between these verses and the material that precedes them, it is, again, not my intent to deal with issues of redaction criticism, but to look at the text as we have it before us. And it is certain that as it stands, Mark's Gospel emphasizes a connection between the faith of the disciple (reader) and the power of that disciple (reader) to effect change in the life of his or her community. In this particular context of the cursed fig tree and the temple cleansing (11:17), the change could very well have to do with the institution of a Gentile mission in the Markan community, a mission not well received by the nationalistic forces who controlled the Temple and the traditions it represented at the time when Mark was writing.

The language of throwing a mountain into the sea fits this apocalyptic context

---

41. Telford, *Barren Temple,* 95–120. Cf. also C. E. B. Cranfield, *The Gospel According to Saint Mark, Cambridge Greek Testament Commentary* (Cambridge: Cambridge University Press, 1959). Sharyn Echols Dowd, *Prayer, Power, and the Problem of Suffering, Vol. 105, SBL Dissertation Series* (Atlanta: Scholars Press, 1986). Robert H. Gundry, *Mark: A Commentary on His Apology for the Cross* (Grand Rapids: William B. Eerdmans Publishing Co., 1993). William L. Lane, *The Gospel According to Mark* (Grand Rapids: William B. Eerdmans Publishing, Co., 1974). Jacques Schlosser, "Mc 11,25: Tradition et Rédaction," in *À Cause de L'Evangile: Mélanges offerts à dom Jacques Dupont,* François Refoulé, editor (Cerf: Publications de Saint-André, 1985) 277–301. Charles A. Wannamaker, "Mark 11:25 and the Gospel of Matthew," *Studia Biblica 1978: Papers on the Gospels, Sixth International Congress on Biblical Studies,* E. A. Livingstone, editor (Sheffield: JSOT Press, 1980) 329–37.

There is strong textual evidence for omitting v. 26, which is absent in early witnesses representing all text types (see Metzger's *Textual Commentary*). Verse 25 is more problematic since there is no external evidence for its exclusion. There is, however, good reason for its separation from 1–24. As many have pointed out, the connection with v. 24 is loose, the only connection being prayer. In 22–24, Jesus is talking about faith while verse 25 is about forgiveness. Matthew 21:18–22 follows this pericope only up to verse 24, while 25 is similar to Mt. 6:14 (though not as close as verse 26 is to Mt. 6:15). Only here in Mark (and in verse 26) does Mark use the phrase, "our father who is in heaven" (ὁ πατὴρ ὑμῶν ὁ ἐν τοῖς οὐρανοῖς), a distinctively Matthean phrase. Although establishing the precise relationship of verse 25 to the gospel of Mt. is difficult, redaction critics would argue that it is at least probable that verse 25 is an independent logion which should be separated from what precedes it. Whether the connection is made by Mark or not is difficult to say. Dowd (40–45), Wannamaker, and Schlosser see the connection between 24 & 25 as happening either prior to Mark or by Mark himself, though they understand 25 to be originally independent. Gundry (655) also argues that 25 is imported from a different setting.

of situation quite nicely. Telford points out that mountain-moving/uprooting was common in Jewish circles, particularly messianic ones.

> The function of this redaction is therefore to announce, we believe, that the "moving of mountains" expected in the last days was now taking place. Indeed, about to be removed was the mountain *par excellence,* the Temple Mount. The Temple, known to the Jewish people as "the mountain of the house" or "this mountain" was not to be elevated, as expected, but cast down![42]

In other words, in the messianic context of 11:1–19, especially 11:17, these concluding verses reflect the fact that Jesus' cursing of the fig tree is a pocket that represents the strategic reality of the future kingdom. Mark is telling his readers that Jesus' messianic-preaching actions will transform the Temple and the institutions it represents, turning them in the direction of a universality that was always prophetically intended. Those who follow Jesus, the disciples, Mark's discipleship community, must preach in the same transformative way with the same eschatological trust that their extension of the kingdom will further the ethnic transformation that Jesus' boundary-crossing initiated.

Now Mark is speaking directly to his readers. For it is in their time that the "war of apocalyptic myths" is taking place, that the nationalistic forces who have overtaken the temple are claiming that God is on their side and that the Temple, as a place of salvation for the Jews exclusively, will be sustained. Mark's message is directly opposed. He wants his community to preach (that is to say, transformatively enact — by the continuation and expansion of the Gentile mission in which they are already engaged) Jesus' alternative message of inclusion. He wants them to be assured that what Jesus preached decades ago is now coming to closure; the Temple will be destroyed because it has failed to live up to the universal vision intended for it. This is the message they must preach in a context that does not wish to hear it. They must preach universalism in a world determined to remain exclusivistic, believing, trusting, that the boundary transformation (the temple not built with hands) they preach will occur.

---

42. Telford, 119.

11

An Interventionist Meal

In the Gospel of Mark, the Last Supper is an interventionist meal. It expresses the conviction that God has invaded the past; it encourages the hope that God will interrupt the future. Its celebrants are an occupied people; their present is controlled by Rome. But as they look behind them in history, they cherish the memory of a divinely orchestrated liberation. Cutting through the boundary that separated the natural from the supernatural, the divine from the mortal, their God claimed their ancestors. On their behalf God routed Pharaoh's Egypt. And from the throng of slaves God's actions set free, God carved out a nation of believers and established a covenant relationship with them. God redeemed them.

In the future the celebrants envision another picture, this one of promise. This time the enemy is even greater. The battle has become apocalyptic. The strategic power of Satan has overwhelmed their world. Utilizing human forces like the kingdom of Rome and the leadership of Israel, this supernatural force has laid tactical claim to human history. The supper celebration anticipates that as God once intervened in Israel's past, so God will intrude upon the powers that represent Satan's strategic design in the present. This time when the liberation comes it will see no end. It will be God's consummate kingdom. This time God will redeem them forever.

In the middle of these two great moments, redemptive past and apocalyptic future, reclines the Jesus of Mark's Last Supper. It is of great significance that this messiah figure anticipates his climactic moment of suffering and resurrection in the festival meal of Passover. By drawing a connection between Jesus' final meal with his disciples and the Jewish Passover, Mark forces his readers to associate Jesus' transformative, boundary-breaking ministry with the revolutionary Exodus event of the past, and the apocalyptic transformation Israel looked for in the future.

[14:25] "Truly I [Jesus] tell you, I will never again drink from the fruit of the vine until that day when I drink it new in the kingdom of God."

FIELD OF DISCOURSE

Mark sets the narrative stage in the first principal part, 14:12–16. It is the first day of the Feast of Unleavened Bread, the day when the Passover lamb was being slaughtered.[1] His point: Jesus' last supper is a Passover meal.[2]

The Passover was first and foremost a commemoration of the Exodus intervention (cf. Exodus 12:14). The rite takes its name from the tactical maneuver God used to break the last vestiges of Egyptian resistance to God's strategic, liberative intent. While the avenging angel from heaven killed the first-born of all the Egyptians, he "passed over" the Israelites, whose homes had been marked with the blood of unblemished, slaughtered male lambs.[3]

Passover also represented the establishment of a covenant between God and Israel. Its seal was drawn as tightly for the people of the first century as it had been for their Exodus ancestors. God had promised Abraham that God would establish an everlasting covenant with him, and that his descendants would inherit a land of promise (Genesis 15:18). In order to fulfill that promise, God had to redeem, that is to say, liberate Abraham's offspring from their Egyptian captivity. The exodus, which the Passover remembers and rekindles, was understood "as that promised redemption and the beginning of the fulfillment of the promise of the inheritance of the land."[4] And so God initiated a covenant relationship between God and the people. The deal was drawn in the blood of sacrifice. Where it had once caused the Lord to pass over Israel's firstborns, at the foot of Mount Sinai it became the glue that, when sprinkled upon both the people and the holy mountain, bound God and Israel together (Exodus 24:8).

---

1. There are, to put it mildly, historical problems with Mark's timing. Bultmann argues that the reference is impossible in Jewish usage. He argues that while the Passover lamb was sacrificed on Nisan 14, the first day of the Feast of Unleavened Bread took place on Nisan 15. (Rudolf Bultmann, *The History of the Synoptic Tradition*, John Marsh, translator [New York and London: Harper and Row, 1963] 264.) For further debate on the issue of timing, cf. Barry D. Smith, *Jesus' Last Passover Meal* (Lewiston, Great Britain: Mellen Biblical Press, 1993); Hooker, *Mark,* 325 (Hooker argues that the difference in the way Jews and Gentiles reckoned their calendars may explain the problem. While the Jewish calendar switched at sunset from Nisan 14 to Nisan 15, in the Gentile calendar there would have been no calendar switch, thus allowing for the conflation Mark appears to show.); Nineham, 376. There is further argument that 14:12–16 was a later addition intentionally added to connect Jesus' meal to the Passover. Bultmann argues, for example, that the words were composed to give the meal a Passover connection it did not historically have (278). Wolfgang Schenk and Ludger Schenke follow Bultmann, while Rudolf Pesch argues that Mark's Passover context for the meal is historically accurate. Cf. Rudolf Pesch, *Das Abendmahl und Jesu Todesverständnis* (Freiburg: Herder, 1978). Schenk, *Der Passionsbericht nach Markus* (Berlin: Evangelische, 1974). Schenke, *Studien zur Passionsgeschichte des Markus* (Würzburg: Echter, 1971). For Smith's own conclusion, cf. 106–7. For references to others (Lohse, Léon-Dufour, Schenker, Schürmann, Marshall, Schweizer) on the probability of a historical Passover location for the Last Supper cf. B. D. Smith, 169–71.

2. See 12:14. Joachim Jeremias builds a strong case that Mark has crafted his narration of the Last Supper so that it fits the expectations of a Jerusalem Passover Meal. Cf. Jeremias, "πάσχα," *TDNT* 5.897 and *The Eucharistic Words of Jesus* (New York: Charles Scribner's Sons, 1966).

3. B. D. Smith demonstrates that the first-century celebration of the meal agrees with this biblical emphasis. He cites first-century sources Josephus (*Ant.* 3.248), Philo (*Spec. Laws* 1.146), *Jubilees* (49:2, 6, 15, 22).

4. B. D. Smith, 42.

It is not surprising, then, when Smith concludes that during the first century the Passover sacrifice did not have an expiatory significance. As its traditional origins directed, the meal commemorates the redemption of the people from socio-historical slavery rather than sin. Its blood symbolizes socio-political liberation on the one hand and the realization of a socio-historical covenant between God and Israel on the other. There seems to be general agreement among the sources he cites. The Mishnah, for instance, classifies the Passover as belonging to a category of sacred offerings that did not have expiatory value.[5] Josephus, too, categorizes the Passover as a memorial of the original sacrifices when God passed over the Israelites, but not as an offering of expiatory significance.[6] "*Jubilees* likewise does not view the paschal lamb as expiatory; rather, it is an acceptable offering before the Lord and a memorial well-pleasing before the Lord (*Jubilees* 49:9)."[7]

The first-century language of blood and sacrifice in the Passover is, however, drenched with meaning potential. Smith does acknowledge that R. Meir is quoted as teaching that the redemptive benefit of the blood of the original Passover lambs was the expiation of sin. In other words, "Forgiveness was obtained through the blood of the Passover lambs."[8] In a unique retelling of the exodus event in *Antiquities,* Josephus also implied that the Passover sacrifices expiated the sins of Israel.[9]

Despite these exceptions, however, Smith concludes that the general presumption in the first century was that the Passover sacrifices represented socio-historical liberation rather than expiation from sin. When the supper was celebrated it was this meaning that the participants usually had in mind.

The data pertaining to the interpretation of the first Passover sacrifices in post-Biblical Judaism can be summarized as follows. The blood of the Passover lambs together with the blood of circumcision was understood as effecting the redemption from Egypt.... Occasionally the blood of the Passover lambs was actually specified to have been expiatory (R. Meir).[10]

---

5. Cf. ibid., 43 (*m. Zebah* 5:6–8; cf. *Mek.* 12:46 [Pisha 15:76–82]).
6. Ibid. (*Ant.* 3.224–57, *Ant.* 2.313).
7. Ibid., 44.
8. Ibid., 45. Cf. *Exod. Rab.* 12:1 (15. 12).
9. Ibid., 46. Cf. *Ant.* 2.312.
10. Ibid., 46. It should be noted, however, that Smith, who builds his case by appealing to all of the synoptic accounts rather than only Mark, concludes that Jesus, like R. Meir, viewed death in the passover context as expiatory. "But when placed against a paschal background, Jesus' meaning can be further elucidated: Jesus was interpreting himself as the eschatological Passover lamb that would bring about redemption for eschatological Israel. Just as R. Meir saw the original sacrificial lambs as expiatory for the generation of the exodus, Jesus saw his own death as the corresponding eschatological expiation for sin. It was as an expiatory sacrifice for sin that Jesus saw his death as representative. (This is how Matthew understands Jesus' death, evidenced by the interpretive gloss connected with the word over the cup: for the forgiveness of sins)" (153). It should also be noted that Mark does not include such a gloss. Indeed, as I pointed out in the beginning phases of this work, the language of sin and sin forgiveness does not arise in Mark after 2:1–12.

It is, of course, possible then that some may have approached the meal thinking primarily of sin forgiveness. It is therefore possible that when Mark narrates Jesus' Last Passover his readers could have accessed the language as expiatory. However, given the principal manner in which the meal was accessed by first-century celebrants, such a reading would seem unlikely. In fact, Mark's narration intentionally directs his readers away from an access of the meaning potential that would lead to such a conclusion. Mark does not make the necessary move made in another traditional presentation of the meal. In the fourth gospel's narrative account Jesus' broken body (bread) and spilled blood (wine) represent the tactical maneuver of atonement. How else does one explain the fact that Jesus was crucified at the precise time on Nisan 14 when the Passover lambs were being slaughtered at the Temple (John 19:14)?[11] In John, Jesus' Supper is not a Passover meal (cf. 13:1–2; 18:28); he holds it well in advance of the prescribed time for the commemorative celebration. By the time the moment for the meal arrives, Jesus has himself been slaughtered on a cross at Golgotha. He becomes the sacrifice; he becomes the redemptive tactical tool. In John, the exodus is theologically re-tooled as an escape from the mythological-spiritual clutches of sin, not from the socio-political enslavement of a hostile, historico-political authority.

Hooker's debate over the differences in timing between the Markan and Johannine accounts leads her to the conclusion that John's timing is more historically accurate. Mark, she argues, has made a conscious effort to adjust the timing of the dinner in relationship to the Passover account. Her argument is persuasive.[12] But her point is not fully pressed. If, indeed, Mark has made a conscious adjustment in the timing of his presentation, one would think that he did so in an effort to highlight the theological agenda he has been pressing throughout his narration. This is certainly the case with John who consistently directed his readers to access Jesus as the Passover lamb (1:29, 36; 19:36). But

---

11. Cf. also 1 Cor. 5:7. B. D. Smith notes that there is some disagreement in the sources as to when the Passover lamb was to have been slain. No doubt, this was due to the fact that "there were so many passover victims that several hours were needed to process them" (28). What is clear is that they were slaughtered in the afternoon of Nisan 14. In fact, "The Mishna sets the earliest possible time for the valid sacrificing of a Passover offering at the sixth hour (*m. Pesah.* 5:3)" (ibid.). This is significant given the fact that in John's presentation Jesus is crucified not only on Nisan 14, but at the sixth hour (19:14).

12. Cf. Hooker, *A Commentary,* 333–34. Hooker points out several crucial problems with Mark's chronology. For example: (1) Key elements of the passover meal are not mentioned in Mark's account: the bitter herbs, the explanation of the ritual as an Exodus enactment, and most importantly, the passover lamb. (2) If Mark's dating is correct, then Jesus' arrest, trial and crucifixion all took place on Nisan 15, a holy day. This would be extremely unusual. Cf. also Schweizer, *Mark,* 295, who adds that in Mark's account there is no mention of women who would certainly have attended a passover meal. He also points out that Jesus' words of interpretation, though formally consistent with expectations, did not contain the content of the Passover *haggadah.* The fact that the Passover was an annual meal in contrast to the daily celebration of Jesus' last supper also suggested to Schweizer that Jesus had not been celebrating the Passover. While Hooker acknowledges Jeremias's claim that all of the exceptions can be explained, she contests that there are simply too many. Her conclusion: "It is much easier to understand, however, why Mark should have added details consistent with the meal being a Passover, if he in fact believed that this is what it was. . . . The weight of the evidence therefore seems to be in favour of the Johannine dating: in other words, it is likely that the Last Supper took place 'before the feast of the Passover' (John 13:1), and that the identification with the passover meal was made after the event" (333–34).

Mark's agenda cannot be sin atonement. If it were, and if Hooker is right that John's presentation was the more historical, Mark would only have needed to offer the account as historical tradition had circulated it. His adjustment actually served the opposite objective of leading a reader away from the representation of Jesus' death as an expiatory sacrifice.

Of course, Hooker could be wrong. It could well be that Mark's presentation is the more historically appropriate. This would mean that the Johannine account was adjusted so that it would emphasize the sacrificial nature of Jesus' atoning death.[13] In this case, the question would be, why did Mark not make the same move? Given that readers would more naturally access an account about the Last Supper as an eschatologically tinged commemoration of socio-political liberation from a socio-historical authority, any author with a theological agenda of atonement would need to make the kind of adjustments to the account that John did make and Mark did not. I am convinced that this is because Mark's portrait of the supper as a commemorative and anticipatory moment of liberation from hostile socio-historical authority fits the theological agenda he has been pressing all along. It fits because Jesus' interventionist supper is presented as the climactic moment of an interventionist preaching ministry that does precisely what the Passover meal commemorates God for doing. It commemorates divine resistance, which is to say, the divine trespass of oppressive boundaries established by repressive human authority. Jesus' body and blood are therefore broken and spilled as an inevitable result of his transformative preaching ministry. This is the language that preoccupies the evangelist throughout his Jesus story, not the language of sacrificial sin atonement. It therefore makes sense that, no matter how it actually happened, he would situate the Last Supper in the context of the socio-politically, liberative-redemptive Passover meal.

It is for this reason that the opening principal part, 14:12–16, like the opening to the triumphal entry and Temple cleansing texts, stresses a manifestation of Jesus' interventionist preaching ministry. As in 11:1–6, Jesus appears miraculously to know how a future quest by the disciples will pan out.[14]

The second principal part is 14:17–21.[15] Its primary concern is with the disciple who will betray Jesus to the ruling authorities. In an explicit echo of Psalm 41:9, Mark's Jesus predicts that one of his twelve, one who dips into the dish with him, will turn on him.[16]

---

13. Cf. Jeremias, "πάσχα," 900. "If the Last Supper is advanced 24 hours in John, this is perhaps due to the widespread comparison of Jesus with the paschal lamb, which led to a fixing of the death of Jesus at the same time as the slaying of the lambs during the afternoon of the 14th Nisan."

14. Cf. Hooker, *A Commentary*, 332. She points out that the similarity is striking at even the most fundamental level. "The similarity extends even to the vocabulary (eleven consecutive words in 14:3 are identical with those in 11:1f)." See also Vernon Robbins, "Last Meal: Preparation, Betrayal, and Absence (Mark 14:12–25)," in *The Passion in Mark: Studies on Mark 14–16*, Werner H. Kelber, editor (Philadelphia: Fortress Press, 1976) 23. Robbins offers a structural representation of the parallels between 11:1–6 and 14:12–16.

15. For discussion on the probability that verses 17–21 did not originally belong to the supper tradition, cf. Bultmann, *History of the Synoptic Tradition*, 264; B. D. Smith, 81–82; Jeremias, *Eucharistic Words*, 93; Nineham, 376.

16. Cf. Marcus, *Way of the Lord*, 172. "The very awkwardness of the belated phrase 'the one

Once again I must consider the tenor of discourse material out of turn. Because the issue of betrayal cannot be explored without an appeal to the presentation of Judas's character, it is necessary that I deal with it here. Judas's character has a relational role in the text. As Hooker points out, Mark is completely disinterested in his motivations. He is also insignificant in the case against Jesus. He therefore offers neither a dramatic character study nor a helpful indication as to why the rulers felt threatened by Jesus.[17]

What, then, is his narrative function? Judas's purpose is to remind the reader about the connection between Jesus' preaching ministry and the hostility of the leaders. Jesus' prediction jogs the readers' memory of Judas's encounter with the rulers at 14:10–11. A critical preliminary connection is drawn through the Markan narration. Once again, the evangelist has performed a framing of sorts. 14:1–2 and 14:10–11 present the similar information that the rulers wanted to put a stop to Jesus' preaching ministry. At 14:1–2, they have no mechanism with which to accomplish that goal. But at 14:10–11, Judas volunteers his dubious services. The material framed by these two pieces narrates the story of Jesus' anointing by an unnamed woman. While it is not my concern to deal with the intricacies of that text, it is helpful to note that it climaxes, at 14:9, with Jesus' statement that wherever the gospel is preached in the entire world, what she has done will be a remembrance of her. The key information in that verse is the reiteration of the message that I believe Mark has been making implicitly and explicitly throughout the course of his narrative; the gospel will be preached to the whole world. It is the trespass of this Jew/Gentile boundary, which Jesus' kingdom preaching represents, that Mark chooses to emphasize here through his structural emphasis on Judas's betrayal.

I believe Mark establishes this point in his deliberate use of the critical verb "to hand over, betray" (παραδίδωμι). After Mark introduces 14:17–21 with verse 17, he brackets the supper betrayal reference with "hand over, betray" at verses 18 and 21. The verb is also used in both verses 10 and 11, where Mark narrates the actual betrayal setup. But the verb has been used some 19 times in Mark's overall gospel presentation.[18] In the overwhelming majority of those cases it refers to a turning over that leads to suffering.[19] There is, then, a sense of literary purpose behind Mark's usage. There is also an explicit connection with the character Jesus. Again, in the overwhelming majority of cases, the verb defines how Jesus is turned over and made to suffer. There are only four exceptions, and the final three deal with a single characterization. On one occasion, 1:14, John the Baptist is handed over. The other three occasions occur together in chapter 13 (vv. 9, 11, 12). Here, Mark implies through Jesus' voice that Jesus'

---

eating with me' supports such an identification. Were the narrative not intent on echoing Psalm 41, a smoother sentence, such as 'one of you who are eating with me will betray me,' could have been employed."

17. "As to what Judas betrayed, there is no suggestion in Mark that he provided the priests with information about Jesus' teaching which might have given them a basis on which to bring charges: Judas does not appear at the trial as a witness" (Hooker, *A Commentary*, 330).

18. 1:14; 3:19; 4:29; 7:13; 9:31; 10:33; 13:9, 11, 12; 14:10, 11, 18, 21, 41, 42, 44; 15:1, 10, 15.

19. The exceptions being 4:29 and 7:13.

followers will be handed over to authorities and made to suffer precisely because they do as Jesus did, i.e., they preach. Indeed, the evangelist is even more specific. They will be handed over and made to suffer because theirs is an interventionist preaching; they cross the Jew/Gentile boundary and extend the gospel to all the world (13:10). I have already argued, most recently at the field of discourse discussions on the kingdom statements at 9:1 and 11:10, that Jesus, too, suffers because of his interventionist preaching ministry. The direct connection here at 14:17–21 (and 14:1–2, 10–11) between the betrayal (which is the event that leads to the ultimate form of his suffering) and the preaching of the gospel to all the world (14:9) reiterates and therefore confirms Mark's narrative suspicion that this interventionist preaching served as a primary motivation for the authorities' desire to entrap and destroy him.

This supposition seems to be confirmed by Mark's narration of Jesus' trial (14:55–64). As Hooker pointed out, it is significant that Judas is not needed as a witness. He does not serve his function by providing inflammatory testimony about Jesus. He serves it by providing an opportunity for the leaders to trap Jesus away from the festival crowds.[20] Indeed, the leaders already have what they need, or at least, what they desire; they have the words and deeds of Jesus' preaching ministry. This is why the first part of the trial focuses on an attempt to corroborate that Jesus truly preached in an interventionist manner that threatened the most sacred boundaries of institutional Judaism (14:58). Failing in an attempt to obtain valid evidence through that route, the chief priest solicited Jesus' own statements about his purpose. And surely enough, Jesus was honest enough to explain that he understood himself to be the representative of God's interventionist actions in human history. He was the messiah who presently represented the future kingdom. He would also soon be revealed as the Son of man who would usher in that kingdom in its consummate form. We have already seen how that kingdom, as Jesus preached it, represented the complete transformation of human institutional authority and power in both the present (e.g., 2:1–3:7; 7:1–23; 11:18; 11:27–12:44) and the eschatological future (12:1–12, esp. v. 9). It was for this reason that Jesus was perceived by the authorities to be a threat to their institutional control.

The use of "hand over, betray" also emphasizes God's control, even at a moment when it appears the strategic design of the ruling authorities will win out. It is interesting that Mark also pairs the verb "hand over, betray" with the suffering inevitability of the passion predictions. "The word *betray,* from the verb [hand over, betray] παραδίδωμι, echoes the word used in two of the passion predictions, where it suggests a 'handing-over' by God (9.31; 10.33; cf. 1.14; 14.41): even this supreme act of treachery by Judas can be used by God in working out his

---

20. Here I follow those scholars who argue that the controlling sentiment in 14:1–2 occurs through the use of the phrase ἐν δόλῳ (in deceit). This means that when Mark says the leaders, the scribes and chief priests, want to arrest Jesus μὴ ἐν τῇ ἑορτῇ (not during the festival), he means that they want to arrest him away from the "festival crowds." They are afraid that openly arresting Jesus, who has developed a strong popular following (cf. 12:12), would provoke a riotous uprising. Cf. Hooker, *A Commentary,* 326; Jeremias, *Eucharistic Words,* 71–73; B. D. Smith, 102.

purpose."[21] Here lies Markan irony. The ruling authorities have a tactical agenda whose success depends upon Judas's betrayal. Their tactical agenda is in response to Jesus' tactical activities. Because they have more earthly authority and power, the result of this tactical confrontation is Jesus' suffering and death. But their apparent tactical accomplishment will not achieve their strategic goal, which is to obliterate the satanic kingdom they believe Jesus' preaching represents (3:22). Certainly, when Judas appears before them in 14:10–11, it looks as though they are in control. The reader has been promised (9:2–8), however, that all their efforts will accomplish not their strategic end, but the kingdom vision that Jesus' preaching has established. By attempting through Judas to accomplish their institutional purpose they set in motion a chain of events which will ultimately lead to Jesus' resurrection, i.e., his vindication, thereby assuring that God's purpose, not theirs, will be realized. Indeed, Jesus, whose prophetic capability has been recently demonstrated (11:1–6; 14:12–16), and whose future word can therefore be trusted, has already prophesied this victorious outcome (8:31; 9:31; 10:34).

The third principal part, 14:22–25, introduces the reader to a great deal of meaning potential.[22] One cannot deny that there is an allusive connection to the Isaian Servant Songs which bears with it the strong implication that in his suffering Jesus, like the Servant, provides a salvific purpose and wins the eschatological victory. Therefore, it could certainly seem that Jesus' suffering is not "a *necessary stage on the way to* apocalyptic vindication; rather, in a certain sense Jesus' death already *is* an apocalyptic victory over the oppressive cosmic power of sin."[23] With this kind of vicarious understanding of suffering in mind, certainly Mark's community would have felt that it, too, like Jesus, was called

---

21. Hooker, *A Commentary,* 331.

22. It should be pointed out that there is serious debate about the unity of verses 22–25. Again, although it is my intent to analyze the material as it occurs in the final presentation, I do not want to dismiss recognition of the redactional concerns that surround the text. Consideration starts with 14:25, since, by both form and content, it seems to have been added on to the other verses. B. D. Smith points out that it is introduced by an ἀμήν (amen) formula. Schenke argues that this formal quality automatically suggests that the verse is of a different background than the verses which precede it. Then, there are the matters of content. The eschatological saying in 14:25 deals only with the cup, not with the cup and the bread that had figured so prominently as a symbolic unit in 14:22–24. Also Jesus says in 14:25 that he will drink wine anew in the kingdom; however, he has not been drinking it at all in 14:22–24. Finally, in 14:24 the cup is mentioned. Inside the cup is not wine but the blood of the covenant. In 14:25, however, the cup is explicitly not mentioned, only its content. And this time the content is wine.

The debate about the unity of the text centers primarily on these kinds of arguments. Pesch resists; he argues for the unity of the passage as historical narrative in which 14:25 acts as a dramatic and necessary eschatological conclusion to the supper incidents. Smith counters that the words of institution are from the liturgy of the early church. Bultmann, following Eichorn and Heitmuller, presses the more radical position that the entire text of 14:22–25 originated from a Hellenistic cult legend that was positioned with 14:12–16 to give it the narrative setting of a Passover meal. Evangelists like Mark laid them artificially in a narrative setting. In that sense, then, though 14:25 does help to illumine 14:22–24 in an eschatological manner, it was added on. Thus, though Smith disagrees with Schenke's position that the "amen" statements are necessarily secondary for Mark, he does agree to the composite nature of 14:22–25. Cf. B. D. Smith, 84–108 (also 151, where Smith argues that the liturgical origins of the bread and wine statements do not preclude the fact that they were spoken by Jesus at his last Passover meal); Bultmann, *History of the Synoptic Tradition,* 265.

23. Marcus, *Way of the Lord,* 195.

not to preach, but to suffer.[24] There are, however, even more direct connections to the Psalms of the Righteous Sufferer. This connection allows for an opposing theological access of the meaning potential of suffering that is decidedly non-vicarious.[25]

I would contend that in order to find out which one Mark and his readers would most likely have accessed as meaningful, we must read the final, and crucial principal part of the text, 14:22–25, and its Old Testament allusions, in light of the historical-contextual Passover setting that Mark intended to be the background for its reading. And, as we have seen, the sacrifice that sits at the center of this foundational ceremony bears a symbolism that is principally historico-political, not expiatory.

The attributes of Mark's meal presentation that would have most struck his readers are the interpretative statements about the bread and the wine. These same readers would have attempted to access these statements through the lens of the Passover tradition. No doubt, they would have picked up on the interventionist implications. The evangelist's use of the verbs "take" (λαμβάνω), "bless" (εὐλογέω), "break" (κλάω, κατακλάω — 6:41), and "distribute" (δίδωμι), in 14:22a, occur in a formulaic manner that intentionally directs the reader back to

---

24. Marcus argues (ibid., 153) that in chapter 14, particularly verses 21, 27, and 49, Mark depends on four key Old Testament texts: Zechariah 9–14 (14:27 is a direct formula quotation of Zechariah 13:7); Daniel 7; the Deutero-Isaian Servant Songs, especially Is. 53; and the Psalms of the Righteous Sufferer (cf. 14:21). (See Marcus, 189 for charting of the allusions to the Deutero-Isaian Servant Passages.) The intentional use of "hand over, betray" (παραδίδωμι) at 14:10, 11, 18, 21 and the statement in 14:24 that Jesus' blood is poured out for many suggest connections with Isaiah 53:6, 12. Mark uses the Servant imagery and gives it an apocalyptic transformation so that it fits Jesus' vindication through resurrection and the coming of the Son of man on the clouds of heaven. Marcus appeals to the atoning purpose of suffering in the Servant imagery to argue that this is also Mark's narrative agenda in this third principal part of the supper. Jesus' suffering, not his preaching ministry, therefore, brings about salvation. I would argue that if so serious an agenda had been on Mark's mind he would have made it more explicit. Even Marcus admits that the allusions "are not as pervasive as the allusions to the Psalms of the Righteous Sufferer" (194). Marcus must therefore build the vicarious nature of Jesus' suffering on non-pervasive allusions and the single preposition "on behalf of" (ὑπέρ) in 14:24. One wonders whether such a monumental theological motif should be allowed to rest on so dubious a foundation.

25. Ibid., 172. Marcus agrees that the narrative indication at 14:1–2 that the leaders are plotting deceitfully against Jesus should remind the careful reader of the Psalms. (See 174–75 for a table listing of the Markan allusions to the Psalms of the Righteous Sufferer. See also Psalms 10:7–8; 41:9.) In fact, Psalm 41:9 operates within the wider context of a meal betrayal. Equally important is the psalmist's conviction that he will be vindicated by God, for despite the treachery of betrayal, God remains in control. Marcus points out that there is an eschatological trajectory in the later use of the Psalms. In this case it appears that the emphasis is less on the vicarious nature of suffering than it is on the understanding that the righteous person suffers (and will be vindicated) because of his God-directed behavior. Quoting L. Ruppert, Marcus reflects that, "the basic picture of the Righteous Sufferer is of a person suffering *in spite of* his righteousness and calling for God to vindicate him by destroying his enemies *in this life*. In contrast, such apocalyptic sources as Wisd. Sol. 2:12–20; 5:1–7; 4 Ezra and 2 Apoc. Bar., as well as the New Testament, present the idea that the righteous one *must suffer on account of* his righteousness but that he will be *glorified at the eschaton*. The New Testament picture, then, reflects an apocalyptic transformation of the Righteous Sufferer motif" (177). This recognition certainly allows that a reader could access the meaning potential of Jesus' suffering as symbolized in the meal in such a way that the suffering occurs because of his "righteous" (that is to say, interventionist) kingdom behavior.

Jesus' feeding miracles with the five and four thousand (6:41; 8:6–7). In other words, Mark relays what Jesus does with the bread at the Passover in a way that rekindles two of his most flamboyant kingdom preaching moments. And no reader could miss the fact that the power of the kingdom successfully intervened through Jesus' miraculous preaching manifestation in both a Jewish and a Gentile context (6:42; 8:8: "they were satisfied" — ἐχορτάσθησαν). Through Jesus' preaching ministry, then, God provided for the physical needs of "all" his people. Along with the Passover foundation, this is the frame the evangelist evidently wanted in his readers' minds when they initiated their access of Jesus' Last "Feeding" with his twelve.

Of utmost significance is the fact that when Mark's Jesus compares the bread to his body he does not have Luke's language of sacrificial intent. Jesus does not say that his body is "given for you" (Luke 22:19). Indeed, Mark's understanding is very much in keeping with the introductory manner of the breaking of bread at a Jewish festival or ordinary meal. "In the NT, as in contemporary Judaism, breaking of bread at the beginning of a meal is not a cultic act...."[26] It is a preparatory one.

It does, however, have a symbolic function for Mark. Hooker advises that "Jesus' actions in breaking and distributing the bread are not just a dramatic illustration of his teaching; they are a symbolic representation of what is actually taking place, and the words explain the actions."[27] But what, exactly, is taking place? The answer lies in Mark's thematic presentation of "bread" (ἄρτος) throughout the narrative. He uses the term 19 times.[28] On almost every occasion it is used in relationship to Jesus' ministry as an interventionist, boundary-breaking kingdom event. The bulk of the uses (12 times, or 63%) occur in the feeding stories which demonstrate God's interventionist power working through Jesus to "satisfy" (χορτάζω) the physical needs of both Jewish and Gentile followers.[29] In the other instances a similar interventionist emphasis abounds. At 2:26, the term occurs in the context of Jesus crossing the Sabbath boundary, and claiming that his identity as Son of man allows, and, indeed, even mandates, such outrageous behavior. At 3:20, Mark narrates that he has performed so many preaching manifestations (miracles) that the admiring press of the crowd prevents him from taking nourishment ("bread"). At 7:2 and 5, "bread" figures prominently in activity and sayings regarding the trespass of institutional purity laws. The purity trespass signals the assault on an even more precious Israelite boundary. "The controversy about 'clean food' [7:1–23] reveals Mark's concern for preaching the Gospel to the whole world, including Gentiles...."[30] At 7:27, "bread" is the featured item in a boundary-shattering story that ends with Jesus allowing the "bread" of his interventionist preaching manifestation (bread which should be used only to satisfy — χορτάζω — Jewish hunger) to heal (satisfy?) the daughter of a Gentile woman.

---

26. Johannes Behm, κλάω..., *TDNT* 3:729.
27. Hooker, *A Commentary*, 341.
28. 2:26; 3:20; 6:8; 6:37, 38, 41, 44, 52; 7:2, 5, 27; 8:4, 5, 6, 14, 16, 17, 19; 14:22.
29. 6:37, 38, 41, 44, 52; 8:4, 5, 6, 14, 16, 17, 19.
30. Vernon Robbins, "Last Meal," 27.

Bread, it appears, is caught up in Mark's narration of an interventionist preaching that represents the future power of the kingdom in the present moment through the crossing of traditional boundaries, most notably those that serve to structure Israelite society: sabbath laws, piety/purity traditions, and Jew/Gentile separation. This is the "bread" imagery that Mark develops throughout the text and climaxes with its final presentation at 14:22.

Mark's interpretative presentation of the cup after the breaking of the bread also fits the contextual picture he has been narrating throughout the text. The evangelist has taken pains to identify "cup" (ποτήριον) with suffering in his Jesus story (10:38, 39; cf. 14:36). Jesus' boundary-crossing, preaching activities inevitably provoke resistance and therefore invite suffering. No wonder, then, that immediately after Jesus introduces the bread, which contextually represents that preaching, he moves to an even fuller discussion of the cup and its implications for his suffering. In Mark's world, one naturally follows the other.

Indeed, Mark has anticipated this interpretative move, and facilitated it, through Jesus' association of the *broken* bread with his body. As if the image of brokenness is not enough, Mark clarifies the suffering link by the way he uses "body" (σῶμα) in his narrative. He deploys it only four times. On three of those occasions it refers directly to Jesus' body; each of these occurrences takes place in the passion narrative (14:8, 22; 15:43). It is clear at both 14:8 and 15:43 that the term refers specifically to Jesus' corpse.[31] Jesus' pointed statement about the bread, then, is meant to raise in the readers' minds the specter of his suffering and death.

Again, though, the principal question is, is it a sacrificial death? The narrative indications encourage a negative response. We are reminded that for whatever reason, Mark does not include Luke's statement that his body is "given for you." We are also reminded that the interpretative statement about the bread occurs in a meal whose primary emphasis was the commemoration and eschatological expectation of a socio-historical liberation rather than a sin expiation. We also have evidence that "Elsewhere σῶμα [body] is practically never used in the vocabulary of sacrifice."[32] Finally, within Mark's overall context of situation, it appears certain that an explanation for the suffering, as directly linked to "bread," has already been given. Jesus suffers, his "body" is broken, in this contextual regard because of his transformative, boundary-shattering kingdom preaching. This is the image "bread" has served to raise in the readers' minds throughout the narrative; it would therefore not be surprising to expect that a first-century Markan reader would access this final bread statement this way. Not only would it fit Mark's overall narrative presentation; it would also be in line with the Passover frame into which Mark has located the supper and its bread saying.

14:23–24 introduces the cup. The evangelist now does what he did not feel it necessary to do for the bread; he offers a full interpretative statement. It is more than clear that this cup represents Jesus' blood of the covenant which is

---

31. The paralleling of "body" (σῶμα) at 15:43 with "corpse" (πτῶμα) at 15:45 makes the connection between the two certain.

32. Eduard Schweizer and Friedrich Baumgärtel, "σῶμα...," *TDNT* 7:1058.

being shed for many. On the surface the imagery seems clearly sacrificial and expiatory. However, before we pass judgment, we should remember the Passover setting and the overall Markan context of situation. The first thing we should note is that Matthew was insufficiently convinced that Mark's "cup" language was expiatory. At 26:28, Matthew noticeably adds that the cup was poured out for many *for the forgiveness of sins.* In order to make the theological assertion of sin expiation he must alter the Markan account. Perhaps he, too, recognized that Mark had another narrative agenda in mind, one he felt necessary to correct.

Mark's primary emphasis here is on the establishment of a new covenant through Jesus' activity. The question is, does that covenant establishment come through his preaching ministry or his sacrificial death? I have already been arguing that throughout the narrative the "saving" relationship that Jesus establishes between humans and God operates from his interventionist preaching ministry, a ministry to which he calls his disciples. But the connection of his cup (his suffering) with the sacrificial imagery of blood poured out for many leads one to the consideration of an alternative possibility. As Hooker suggests, the pouring of the blood reminds the reader of a sacrifice. "The blood of any sacrifice was poured out as an offering, and animals killed for human consumption must be drained of all blood before being eaten."[33] This was exactly the case with the slaughtered Passover lambs.

Mark's language, then, appears to be sacrificial. It suggests the imagery of a particular kind of sacrifice from the Exodus tradition of Israel, the sacrifice whose blood was used as a covenant seal between God and the newly formed people. At Exodus 24:8, God established a relationship between God and God's people. Half of the blood of the sacrifice was spread on the people, the other half symbolically on the mountain that represented God's presence. In this way the blood bound them together. As the scene played itself out through verses 8–10, it became clear that the blood of the covenant, as it is here in Mark's Last Supper account, was drawn out through the eating and drinking in the presence of the Lord. Jesus envisions a covenant between God and the people that is remarkably reminiscent of this Exodus imagery, with the signal exception that it is his blood that is now used as the apparent sacrificial offering.

Due to the recalcitrance of the people, this covenant did not hold. A new covenant was therefore prophetically envisioned. Or as Nineham puts it, "As the blood established the covenant of Moses, so the blood of Jesus established a new covenant (Jer 31:31–34) which had as its content perfect fellowship with God (Jer 31:33) founded upon God's forgiveness (Jer 31:34b) in his kingdom."[34] What is certain is that the covenant envisioned at Mark 14:24 was the covenant of Jeremiah 31:31–34. "Since Jeremiah (with Dt. Is.) was for Jesus the most familiar of all the prophets, we are undoubtedly to relate His saying concerning the new διαθήκη to Jeremiah 31:31ff., whose counterpart, the διαθήκη at Sinai after the Exodus, was constituted by blood."[35] What is not so certain is

---

33. Hooker, *A Commentary,* 342.
34. Nineham, 385.
35. Gottfried Quell and Johannes Behm, "διατίθημι, διαθήκη," *TDNT* 2.133.

that this new covenant had to be constituted by blood. In fact, Jeremiah does not mention in that prophetic text that blood would be the instrument of God's re-covenanting with the people. It is taken for granted that this has to be Mark's intent, principally because it appears to have been the intent of other representatives of the early church like Paul. The primary problem is that in Mark one would have to make this reading in defiance of the narrative presentation thus far. The implication that it is through Jesus' suffering and death, i.e., his sacrificial blood, that the covenant is established does not fit the presentation that Mark has been making up to 14:22 of his narrative.

I would suggest another approach to the material that falls within the register of the supper's language potential, and at the same time, fits Mark's overall context of situation. It is a given that Jesus believes that the cup represents a new covenant. The issue is, how is that new covenant achieved? I would argue that we take our cue from Mark himself. In his presentation this new covenant appears to be a correlate of the kingdom of God.[36] The new covenant, in other words, is a tactical representation of the strategic reality that will obtain in the kingdom. And Mark has offered in his presentation that this kingdom, in both its tactical and strategic realities, occurs not via sacrifice, but via the interventionist preaching of Jesus and those who follow him. In this sense, then, the new covenant is an ultimate form of boundary crossing. It is for this reason that Mark makes it clear to the reader that Jesus celebrates the meal with the δώδεκα (twelve), the ones whom he has told us before represent a new kind of believing community. They were to be the foundation of the community whose covenantal relationship with God had been re-established in the image that Jeremiah prophesied. They were to become the tactical pocket that represented the strategic consummation. It is for this reason that Xavier Léon-Dufour suggests that the significance of the supper imagery is not to be found in the transformation of the bread and cup, or even in the meaning assigned to them, but in the way in which the meal, particularly through the reference to a suffering (cup) which Jesus shares with them, establishes through them a new community of faith.

> The action over the elements is subordinate to this purpose. Through the gift which the Master symbolically makes of himself the group of twelve enters now (and will remain after the departure of Jesus) into a close contact with their host: they will be inseparable from him who is leaving them. The community thus established is a new community which nothing can destroy....[37]

Why, then, the emphasis on the blood? The answer comes from the cup imagery at 10:38, 39. There it is clear that Jesus and his disciples will share the same fate; this is what the cup and its suffering imagery symbolize. I would argue that the same representation obtains here in the Last Supper. Nineham's

---

36. Cf. Quell and Behm, 134; B. D. Smith, 155.
37. Xavier Léon-Dufour, *Sharing the Eucharistic Bread: The Witness of the New Testament*, Matthew J. O'Connell, translator (New York: Paulist Press, 1987) 196.

studies of the ancient world led him to the conclusion: "whoever drinks the cup of someone enters into a communion relationship with him (cf. e.g., the ideas lying behind Ps 14:4f. or 1 Cor 10:21)."[38] As Hooker points out, Mark waits until after the disciples drink from the cup before making his interpretative remarks. His concentration, therefore, seems to be on interpreting the act of sharing the wine, rather than on the wine itself.[39] They are full participants in Jesus' kingdom preaching ministry.

Mark has therefore achieved a balance between the symbolism of the bread/body and cup/blood that his extended discussion on the cup appears to deny. First, the blood represents Jesus' suffering and death, just as the bread represented his corpse. Second, in drinking and passing the cup, the disciples share in his suffering just as they shared in the breaking of his body when the bread was distributed among them. The symbolism, then, is not that of drinking the blood of sacrifice, which would have been reprehensible to a Passover-minded Jew,[40] but that of participation in Jesus' suffering which occurs as a result of his and their imitative interventionist attempts to establish the boundary-breaking conditions for a new covenantal relationship with God.

In fact, were Mark to suggest that the forgiveness of sins comes only here at Jesus' death, through Jesus' blood, he would be narratively inconsistent. Already, quite early in the story, at 2:1–12, in the last text where Mark employs the language of "sin" (ἁμαρτία), Jesus, as Son of man, demonstrates the interventionist power to save, that is, to forgive sins. The evangelist cannot be any clearer. When Jesus looks upon a paralyzed man and his friends and sees their faith, instead of demonstrating his kingdom power by healing the man, he demonstrates it by forgiving his sins. This is how he reestablishes the man's covenantal relationship with God. The language cannot be plainer; "your sins are forgiven" (2:5). The passive voice serves as a reminder that Jesus is not acting on his own, but as God's tactical representative. It is certainly God who forgives sins, but God has delegated this authority to Jesus as his messianic agent.[41]

This story opens the first controversy cycle in the gospel. In it the scribes, as representatives of the institutional leadership, balk at Jesus' grandiose self-presentation. The challenge they make is the correct one; indeed, only God can forgive sins (2:7). However, because they do not recognize Jesus as God's agent, they presume that his claim to this ability is an unauthorized supplanting of the divine prerogative. He has committed the ultimate cultic crime of blasphemy. We recall that it is this charge that is used in 14:64 finally to seal Jesus' fate.

---

38. Nineham, 382.

39. Hooker, *A Commentary,* 342.

40. Cf. ibid. "No Jew would have regarded the drinking of blood with anything but horror, for the blood represented the life of an animal and belonged to the Lord."

41. Cf. Joel Marcus, "Authority to Forgive Sins upon the Earth: The *SHEMA* in the Gospel of Mark," in *The Gospels and the Scriptures of Israel,* Craig A. Evans and W. Richard Stegner, editors (Sheffield: Sheffield Academic Press, 1994) 203. Marcus points out the Daniel 7 background of Mark 2:1–12. "First, the royal authority of the 'one like a son of man' is a *derived* one; he has it not by virtue of his own power but by royal grant from the true, heavenly king, the 'one that was ancient of days.' That Mark is aware of the subordinationism implicit in Daniel 7 and applies it to Jesus' relation to God is clear from 8:38, where we hear of the Son of Man 'com[ing] in the glory of *his Father.*'"

But at this early point in the narrative, Jesus responds by challenging the scribal leaders to recognize that in him God's future kingdom has dawned like a powerful pocket in present time.[42] He heals the paralyzed man in order to demonstrate that he wields God's interventionist, kingdom power. But in making this symbolic gesture he also reiterates that his is more than a mere healing power; it is a saving power. It is the power that ultimately realizes itself in the forgiveness of sins. He says, I heal this man "in order that you may know that the Son of man has the authority to forgive sins upon the earth."

We subsequently learned two critical things about this Son of man. He is also the one who will usher in the consummate kingdom. But, even more significantly in this case, because of the boundary-trespasses of his preaching ministry, such as this one where he violates the perceived boundary between the prerogatives of God and human, he will be made to suffer (3:6). In effect, then, according to Mark's narration, Jesus, already in chapter 2, suffers precisely because his tactical representation of God's strategic covenant design leads him to forgive sins. The suffering comes as a result of his forgiving sins. The suffering does not establish that forgiveness.

It is out of this context of situation analysis that Jesus' words at the supper should be read. As Léon-Dufour recognized, the critical verbal action in 14:24, "being shed" (τὸ ἐκχυννόμενον), is a present participle. That is to say, Jesus says that the cup is my blood of the covenant *now* being shed for many. He does not say, the blood that *will be* shed, presumably on the cross. Now the present participle can have a future sense, and this is quite certainly the way this particular participle has been read. I would argue, however, that in this case, in the absence of any contextual markers demanding the future reading, we should read it as Mark has offered it, in the present tense. For such a reading fits the context of situation Mark has been carefully establishing throughout the narrative. Jesus is already suffering, his blood is already being metaphorically spilled; indeed that process began as early as 2:1–12 when the scribal leaders began an angry internal discussion in their hearts that concluded in a determined external decision to discredit (3:22) and destroy Jesus (3:6; cf. also 11:18; 12:12). This was the only way they figured they could terminate his boundary-crossing, and, therefore, authority-threatening activities. The blood, then, is not literal in relationship to the wine, just as the bread is not literal in relationship to Jesus' body. Indeed, it can't be, as we have seen, for the Jewish twelve (δώδεκα) agreeably drink it. It is symbolic. It represents what Mark has been claiming all along, only this time in a climactic fashion; Jesus' interventionist, boundary-breaking, new-covenant-establishing, new-Israel-creating, kingdom preaching results in his suffering. Furthermore, if he does not stop, it will lead to his death.

Already Jesus' transformative preaching has negated the authority and power of the institutional rulers. He is the one who establishes relationship with God; the Temple and its priestly infrastructure is no longer necessary in the same

---

42. Ibid., 203. "The second reason for the importance of Daniel 7 as background to Mark 2 is that, despite the picture of enthronement beside God in heaven, the authority of the 'one like a son of man' is exercised not in heaven but *on earth.*"

way that it was. In fact, as we have seen, the temple has become so expendable that he can prophesy its destruction without fretting over the possibility that humans will subsequently be unable to establish relationship with God. For him, the relationship is not established cultically. He does not impose sacrificial rites designed to compete with the rites of the priests and the legal interpretations of the scribes. He establishes it through his preaching. In its teaching, healing and exorcistic manifestations this interventionist preaching brings the transformative power of the future kingdom into the present human reality. No wonder, then, that when Mark sparingly uses the σῴζω (saving) language he does so in these kingdom contexts. By bringing humans into the proximity of God and his kingdom Jesus effects a covenantal relationship for his new community of faith. If this message alone were not transformative, and therefore dangerous enough, Jesus augments it by implying through his words and actions that this new community will be composed of Gentiles as well as Jews. In this sense, then, the language in 14:24 coheres with the language of 14:9. Jesus' blood is being shed for "many," no doubt, the same many throughout the world to whom the Gospel story will be spread.

As he did in his passion predictions, Mark closes on a note of climactic hope. The final word is not that of suffering and death, but of resurrected vindication. Mark has taken over the imagery of the Passover and developed it eschatologically. Jesus uses his final comment about the wine to envision a future banquet of messianic proportions.[43] In the kingdom there is salvation, that is to say, there is relationship with God. Jesus anticipates it for himself and for those who follow him. Following his path will lead past suffering into glory. Mark wants his readers' final gaze in this Last Supper to focus on the ultimate realization of the kingdom, not the corpse and spilled blood that litter the road on the way to it. It is here that he places the final weight of his depiction of Jesus' last Passover with his disciples.

The literary taste left in our mouths is one of Markan irony. The ultimate attempt to stop Jesus' transformative kingdom preaching, the cross, as symbolized by the imagery of this supper, will lead not to his anticipated destruction, but to his prophesied vindication. The cross will lead to resurrection. Resurrection will lead to heavenly exaltation as the Son of man who will return to usher in the consummate kingdom that his preaching has realized as transformative, boundary-trespassing present pockets. Even at the end, Mark's Jesus reminds us of the transformative nature of Jesus' envisioned kingdom. The wine of the kingdom, which he symbolically associates with the wine he likens to his own blood, is "new" (καινόν). Mark uses the adjective only three other times in his entire narrative. At 1:27 his teaching is a new teaching. It is so judged because it is authoritative in a way that the teaching of the scribes has never been; it reflects the intrusive power of the kingdom of God. It is a teaching that crosses boundaries in the way it interprets cultic tradition, the Sabbath, the Temple, and Israel itself. It is a teaching that causes trouble for Jesus with the institutional leaders. At 2:21 and 22, the man who has just allowed himself and his disciples

---

43. Cf. Isaiah 25:6; 2 Baruch 29:5–8; Matthew 8:11; Luke 14:15; Revelation 19:19.

to be found eating with tax collectors and sinners, instead of ritually fasting, suggests that his new tactical presentation of the consummate kingdom is so unlike their traditional leadership that there can be no mixing of the two. The adjective spawns a sense of transformative difference for Mark, the kind of difference that also separates a human Passover feast in the present from the messianic feast in the kingdom on "that day."[44]

Only at this closing moment is it finally clear how we are to access the supper imagery. It is to be understood, as the Passover was ultimately to be anticipated, as an eschatological premonition of a banquet in the presence of God. That is to say, it represents the covenant relationship that Israel lost. It represents salvation. This is the reason that Jesus refers to it with the language of "that day," in this Passover context.[45] The imagery of the supper points, then, not only to the cross, but through the cross to the apocalyptic kingdom salvation that waits just beyond it.

MODE OF DISCOURSE

Mark's supper directive, then, is preach, and, no matter what the cost, preach transformatively. The transformations that occur, like the Gentile mission in which Mark's community is already engaged, will, like the supper imagery itself, represent the tactical realization of God's future kingdom like a pocket in present time. Just as certainly, the suffering that will inevitably come as a result of such preaching will not be the end product. God will guide them past the cross they share with Jesus (cup) and into the strategic conclusion that is relationship with God in the consummate kingdom.

---

44. This reading is consistent with the way Johannes Behm understands the use of καινός in the ancient world. Cf. Johannes Behm, "καινός...," *TDNT* 3:447–55. "Of the two most common words for 'new' since the classical period, namely νέος and καινός, the former signifies 'what was not there before,' 'what has only just arisen or appeared,' the latter 'what is new and distinctive' as compared with other things" (447). "καινός is what is new in nature, different from the usual, impressive, better than the old, superior in value or attraction..." (447).

45. John Navone, "The Last Day and the Last Supper in Mark's Gospel," *Theology* 91 (1988): 38–39. "The Last Day is that of a divine judgement. When God comes in judgement in such events as the Exodus, he overcomes evil and achieves a good for his people. Divine judgements or interventions are always liberation events that free his people *from* an evil *for* a good. The Last Day is the Last Judgement in which God finally overcomes the evils that afflict his people and achieves their ultimate blessedness (salvation) in a once-and-for-all event."

12

Mark's Main Mode

Preach!

In her excellent article, "The Reader in History: The Changing Shape of Literary Response," Jane P. Tompkins makes an important observation. Literary texts have meant different things to interpreters of different historical periods. The contrast she draws between contemporary interpreters and interpreters of the classical period is the most important for my own study. She argues that whether contemporary interpreters locate their emphasis in the text or in the reader's response to the text, their ultimate goal is to determine "meaning."[1] In the classical period, however, the goal was to determine a text's effect upon the audience. The difference is crucial. Whereas the modern interpreter wants to know what a text "means," the classical interpreter wants to know what a text "does." How does it impact its reading audience? What does it *do* to them? Language is power, and that power was harnessed in the form of a text for a purpose. It was the commentator's task to determine precisely what that function was.[2]

Mary Ann Tolbert recognized that Tompkins's observations were pivotal for the direction (or misdirection) of New Testament inquiry.

---

1. Jane P. Tompkins, "The Reader in History: The Changing Shape of Literary Response," in *Reader-Response Criticism: From Formalism to Post-Structuralism*, Jane P. Tompkins, editor (Baltimore and London: The Johns Hopkins University Press, 1980) 201. See especially 201–6 for her discussion on the classical period. Tompkins's primary contrast in contemporary interpretative methodology is between the more traditional "New Criticism" and reader-oriented criticism. New Criticism's interest is in the text; it is certain that there is where "meaning" resides. The New Critical endeavor considers "the poem itself as an object of specifically critical judgment" (201). As the name suggests, the theorists of reader-oriented criticism are united in their belief that meaning is instead to be located in the reader. Their similarity, however, remains striking. For, "although New Critics and reader-oriented critics do not locate meaning in the same place, both schools assume that to specify meaning is criticism's ultimate goal" (201).

2. Tompkins, 204. "The text as an object of study or contemplation has no importance in this critical perspective, for literature is thought of as existing primarily in order to produce results and not as an end in itself. A literary work is not so much an object, therefore, as a unit of force whose power is exerted upon the world in a particular direction."

Our contemporary obsession is with the *meaning* of a text, whether we choose to locate that meaning in the text itself or in the reader or somewhere in between. What it *means,* rather than what it *does,* is the concern of modern critics and exegetes, requiring them always to be involved in the task of interpretation.[3]

To stress meaning so unequivocally, however, is to access the text in a manner that was evidently foreign to its first interpreters. It is for this reason that I feel a sociolinguistic methodology can most effectively reconstruct the manner in which Mark's first readers accessed his narrative. Sociolinguistics maintains proper focus on a text's discourse mode. Field and tenor discussions do not begin and end the debate, as they often do in contemporary biblical interpretation; they clarify for the interpreter how a first-century reader approached the language in such a way that its "meaning" promulgated "behavior," both within the text (semantics) and without (discipleship). It has been my intent to ascertain exactly how that field and tenor information in the Markan kingdom language cultivated and encouraged response (mode) in the characters who inhabited the Markan context of situation and in the first-century readers who inhabited the evangelist's context of culture. And, as Tolbert points out, nowhere is it more important to recognize the functional intent — and, I would add, access of Mark's narrative language — than at the end of his gospel, 16:1–8, a text whose broader field contains the evangelist's final kingdom discourse.[4]

I have been arguing throughout this sociolinguistic evaluation that the evangelist presents Jesus as the tactical representative of God's strategic kingdom design and intent. But Mark does not make this presentation as a mere narrative point of information. He presents Jesus' representation of the supernatural for a purpose. As are his characters in the text, his readers are called to follow; that is to say, they are called to the same tactical representation of the strategic kingdom design. Jesus achieved this goal by preaching. Jesus' followers are to achieve it in the same way. Jesus' preaching, however, was not mere speech, but transformative, boundary-crossing activity that manifested itself in the form of miracle (healing), exorcism, and teaching. As dimwitted as the disciples often come across in Mark's narration, they nonetheless perform each of these preaching manifestations. They also preach the kingdom. They have the ability, in other words, to represent tactically what God is doing strategically. They wield kingdom power. They become a point of intersection in the process of the divine intervening in human affairs. Their following-ministry becomes a present

---

3. Tolbert, *Sowing the Gospel,* 289.

4. I am so persuaded by the evidence that has been amassed regarding the ending of Mark's narrative at 16:8 that I no longer feel pressed to offer argumentation on behalf of the point. Indeed, most recent commentaries follow suit. The conclusion reached by Myers, which is indicative of most recent New Testament scholarship, is appropriate. "This sudden ending to Mark has spawned much consternation. Indeed, many ... have hypothesized that the true ending was lost.... Such speculation can now be considered obsolete, along with the grammatico-literary objective that a book could not end in a *gar* clause" (399). For a summarization of the theories regarding the ending, cf. Reginald H. Fuller, *The Formation of the Resurrection Narratives* (New York: Macmillan, 1971) 64ff. For recent commentary discussion, cf. Hooker, *A Commentary,* 382–83 and 387–94.

pocket that utilizes the power and reality of the future kingdom to resist the boundaries that oppress people in their contemporary human situation.

Mark narrates this discipleship reality in order to compel his readers not only to emulate it, but to improve upon it. The narrative disciples ultimately fell short. But the readers are challenged to be like the interlopers who successfully demonstrate faith in brief but powerful cameos. The readers have the opportunity by virtue of the lessons taught in this story, the realization of vindication that comes at its end, and the charge given on the basis of that vindication to finish the "preaching" that Mark's Jesus and his disciples began.

We will see confirmed here at the end of the narrative what I have argued has been the case throughout: Mark's main mode of discourse is "Preach!" From the start this has been his narrative objective. He represents in the field and tenor of discourse a Jesus whose preaching ministry is the model for the ministry of those who follow him. Because it is a transformative preaching it inevitably results in his suffering and death (8:31; 9:31; 10:33–34). The same end can be predicted for those who follow him (13:9–13). But the suffering is not the expected action demanded by the narrative. It is a consequence, a result of it. The action (mode) that the language demands from the first kingdom statement to the last is preaching. For it is in the transformative, boundary-breaking preaching that the future kingdom of God becomes a present pocket for both Jesus and those who follow him.

> [15:43] Joseph of Arimathea, a respected member of the council, who was also himself eagerly awaiting the <u>kingdom</u> of God, went boldly to Pilate and requested the body of Jesus.

FIELD OF DISCOURSE: END INTERVENTION

The first principal part of this final kingdom discourse moves from 15:42 to 15:47. The evangelist identifies the time as early evening, the Jewish time of "preparation" (παρασκευή). In a nod to the fact that Gentiles have been invited — and are being invited to access the text — he explains that the day of preparation is the time just before the Sabbath.

Jesus, whose death has been related at 15:37, hangs as a corpse upon the cross. The narration is simple and direct. With apparent boldness, Joseph approaches Pilate and requests the body for burial.[5] Pilate marvels because the

---

5. Hooker points out that burials took place on the day of death whenever possible, on the following day at the latest. A death on a Friday (cf. dating discussion on 14:25 field of discourse) required immediate action since the sabbath followed, and one would not want to desecrate the sabbath with a burial. Hooker is right to point out, though, that, strictly speaking, Joseph's actions were too late. Were it evening, the sabbath had already begun (*A Commentary,* 380). There are also other disturbing details. Mark's chronology here, Hooker cautions, appears to conflict with the chronology of 14:12–16, where Friday was evidently the time of the Passover Feast. She seems correct in reasoning that "it makes little sense for Joseph to avoid desecration of the sabbath by burying Jesus on another holy day" (380). Her conclusion: "Once again, it seems that Mark's narrative supports the Johannine dating of the crucifixion (according to which Passover coincided with the Sabbath) rather than his own" (380).

petition has come so soon. Ordinarily, a crucifixion took much longer to reach its climax. The punishment was designed to draw death out, not accomplish it quickly. The theory was that the primary deterrent lay not in the expiration itself, but in the gruesome, protracted manner in which it was accomplished. Pilate therefore calls a centurion and inquires about Jesus' status. At the soldier's confirmation of death, Pilate releases the corpse to Joseph's charge. Joseph purchases a linen shroud, wraps the body in it, and places the body in a tomb hewn out of stone. The tomb was secured with the heaving of a great stone across its door. Jesus' body was buried. Mary Magdalene and Mary, the mother of Joses, were evidently watching the burial, for Mark tells us finally that they saw where (i.e., in which tomb) the body was laid.

The recognition of the women at the tomb reminds the readers of the presence of women in the death scene, and anticipates the presence of women at the empty tomb on the first day of the week. First, their witnessing of the burial place flashes us back to their witnessing of Jesus' death (15:33–39) from afar (15:40). Mark explains at 15:40–41 that three women, Mary Magdalene, Mary the mother of James the smaller and Joses, and Salome watched Jesus die. Mark also explains that these women were Jesus' disciples. When he identifies them he uses his own technical term for discipleship; when Jesus was preaching in Galilee they were following (ἠκολούθουν) him. They also "served" him, and were among a cadre of women who traveled with him on his journey to Jerusalem.

The second principal part, 16:1–4, opens with another narrative nod to the women's presence. The setting has shifted to the day after the sabbath, the first day of the week (16:1a; 16:2a). In other words, it is the third day. Any reader who has been paying attention, unlike the apparently clueless disciples and women (who apparently come to anoint a corpse, not greet a resurrection [16:1b]), recall Jesus' oft-repeated remark that he would die and on the third day be raised. With his staging, then, Mark has heightened the narrative expectation for the all-important interventionist moment of resurrection. The passive tense of the (passion prediction) recollections alerts the reader to the fact that the supernatural kingdom power of God would trespass the human boundaries of time, space, and death and overturn the human consequence of Jesus' boundary-breaking, preaching ministry. In so doing, God would also vindicate that ministry as the true tactical representation of the divine kingdom strategy. Jesus' preaching way, after all, was the right "messianic" way; which is to say, the way Mark's readers should follow.

Vindication, though, hinges on resurrection. And the only indication of this is the angelic testimony delivered to the women who come to the tomb and find it empty. Many commentators have pointed out that once again there is a shift in the actual naming of the women. There are differences in the citations found at 15:40, 15:47, and 16:1. The redaction-critical conclusion is that Mark is operating from a variety of sources, each of which has a different listing for the women.[6] Again, it is my intent to analyze the material as we have it before us.

---

6. Cf., for example, Hooker, *A Commentary,* 383. Adela Collins offers the interpretation that

And in this case it is clear that Mark is less concerned with the actual manner of identifying the women than he is with the function the women play in the narrative case he is building. It is their characterization that matters more than their individual identities. They are the vehicle the story relies upon for assuring the reader that not only was it Jesus' tomb that was empty (his followers did not go to a mistaken tomb where no one was buried, because the women saw him buried in this one), but that it was empty because God raised him from the dead. "Mark's purpose seems to be to establish this small group of women as witnesses of Jesus' death, burial and resurrection."[7]

The credibility of the voice that will proclaim Jesus' resurrection in 16:6 is established as early as the last two verses of this second principal part, 16:3–4. In the anguished deliberations of the women Mark sets the stage for constructing the speaker's interventionist identity. The reader has been forewarned that a stone lies across the door of the tomb. He/she is now told that it is an exceedingly large stone. In fact, it is much too large for three women to turn aside. Their journey, anointing spices in hand, therefore, makes no real sense. Since they saw Jesus buried, they already know the stone is exceedingly large, so any attempt to anoint Jesus without first attending to the removal of the stone is illogical.[8] Then, why do they go early in the morning without having first secured assistance?

Mark uses this piece of illogic to establish the certain closure of the tomb, the enormity of the stone's size, and the improbability of its movement in the reader's mind. It would, in other words, take a miracle for these women to accomplish their task. And this is precisely the line of reasoning Mark wants to evoke. At 16:4, then, when the women see that the stone has been removed, it is a miraculous rather than a rational explanation that Mark has carefully pre-established.

The language of intervention begins immediately at the opening verse of the

---

16:1–8 is a fictional creation of Mark's. He composed the story of the empty tomb in order to interpret the proclamation that Jesus had been raised from the dead. Cf. Adela Yarbro Collins, "The Empty Tomb in the Gospel According to Mark," in *Hermes and Athena: Biblical Exegesis and Philosophical Theology*, Eleonore Stump and Thomas P. Flint, editors (Notre Dame, IN: University of Notre Dame Press, 1993) 107–39, esp. 129.

7. Hooker, *A Commentary*, 383. We must be careful in pointing out, however, that this narrative vehicle probably does not represent "proof" in the technical sense. Birger Gerhardsson notes that according to Torah and tradition (esp. Deut 19), only male witnesses were acceptable in a formal legal proceeding. Cf. Birger Gerhardsson, "Mark and the Female Witnesses," *DUMU-E₂-DUB-BA-A: Studies in Honor of Ake W. Sjöberg*, Hermann Behrens, Darlene Loding, Martha T. Roth, editors (Philadelphia: Samuel Noah Kramer Fund, 11, 1989) 218. Adela Collins concurs. She argues that it is unlikely that the early church would have fabricated the story of the women at the empty tomb as "proof" of Jesus' resurrection. "Further, if the empty tomb story was invented to 'prove' the resurrection of Jesus, it is odd that the only witnesses to the emptiness of the tomb, at least in Matthew and Mark, are women. The status of women in the ancient world was such that a story fabricated as proof or apology would probably not be based on the testimony of women" (A. Collins, "The Empty Tomb," 114).

8. It seems clear from Mark's language in 16:3 (τίς ἀποκυλίσει ἡμῖν τὸν λίθον ἐκ τῆς θύρας τοῦ μνημείου; who will roll away the stone from the door of the tomb for us?), which parallels the language of 15:46 (προσεκύλισεν λίθον ἐπὶ τὴν θύραν τοῦ μνημείου, he rolled a stone across the door of the tomb), that Mark wants to connect what the women are doing with what Joseph the kingdom seeker did.

third principal part, 16:5–8. When the women enter the tomb in 16:5, they see a young man sitting on the right clothed in a white garment. They are amazed. Almost every element of the verse indicates the epiphany of an angel. Mark defines his characterization with the term "young man" (νεανίσκος), which, in sources like 2 Maccabees 3:26, 33, is an angelic descriptor. The designation of a seating on the right hand (δεξιός) reminds the reader of James's and John's request at 10:37, 40 to sit on Jesus' right hand in his glory, of Jesus' remark about the Lord sitting at the right hand of God at 12:36, and of Jesus' declaration at 14:62 that as Son of man he would sit at God's right. In Mark's usage, in other words, it is the language of heavenly glory. The young man's connection with this language contextually establishes him as a heavenly figure.[9]

The fact that he is dressed in a white garment reminds the reader of the same color vocabulary (λευκός) used at Jesus' transfiguration (9:3). In Jewish apocalypticism, as Daniel 7:9 makes clear, white was the color appropriate to God and the heavenly world.[10] Finally, Mark's description of the women's reaction, "they were amazed" (ἐξεθαμβήθησαν), assures us that Mark intended an interventionist access. The kind of amazement he describes was also displayed when people witnessed Jesus following his transfiguration (9:15). Robert Smith therefore draws the appropriate conclusion from the piling up of this interventionist terminology. "That the young man of 16:5 is an angel is clear enough from the context, the parallels, and from the way his garment is described (cf. Mark 9:3; Acts 1:10; 10:30; 2 Macc 3:26, 33; Dan 7:9)."[11]

The angel's divine pedigree gives validity to his claim in 16:6 that Jesus' tomb is empty because God has raised him from the dead. The ultimate kingdom intervention has taken place. The great boundary of death itself has been overcome.

But this good news comes to the women with a price. The indicative of resurrection precedes an imperative of human response. The women are to follow up God's interventionist action with a critical action of their own. They are to depart and tell the disciples and Peter that the risen Jesus goes before them to Galilee. It is there that they will now see him.

It is first of all, the language of restoration. Commentators routinely point out that here Mark's story allows the disciples who have fled and even denied Jesus to be reestablished in relationship with him. Nowhere is this recognition more poignant than in the separate naming of Peter by the angel. At 14:37, when it is clear that the slothful Peter is breaking down at Gethsemane, in a prelude to his tragic denial, Jesus calls him by his pre-apostolic name, Simon. Now, however, the angelic messenger refers to him once again as Peter, the new name Jesus awarded him at 3:16. As Myers notes, the community that has destructed in the two stages of discipleship flight and Peter's denial is now reconstructed in two parallel stages: tell the disciples; tell Peter.[12]

9. Cf. Walter Grundmann, "δεξιός," *TDNT* 2:37–40.
10. Cf. W. Michaelis, "λευκός, λευκαίνω," *TDNT* 4:241–51.
11. Robert H. Smith, "New and Old in Mark 16:1–8," *Concordia Theological Monthly* 43 (1972) 523.
12. Myers, 398.

It is, second, interventionist language that asks the characters, and through them the readers, to participate in God's interventionist activity by responding in a tactical manner that reflects Jesus' preaching intent. Tolbert points out that the imperative "go, depart" (ὑπάγετε) in 16:7, is the order most often given to those who have been healed. I agree with her assessment and wish to push it further. For indeed, the command is consistently connected not only to healings, but to all forms of interventionist activity. In fact, in almost all of the cases, the imperative demand occurs after Jesus has tactically contemplated or initiated an interventionist kingdom activity.[13] In other words, after Jesus acts, he sometimes asks his followers, as Mark, through him, asks his readers, to respond with interventionist activity of their own. In other cases, Jesus recognizes that his own interventionist activity has been based on their demonstration of faith in God's kingdom ability. They are, then, sent forth with the realization that it is faith that provides the atmosphere for this kind of transformative experience.[14] The most glaring examples occur at 1:44 (45) and 5:19 (20). In both those cases, after Jesus has healed, he tells the recipient of the kingdom benevolence to go and do a specific task. The narrative result is that each healed man *preaches* in such a way that others (from *everywhere,* 1:45; in the *Greek* Decapolis, 5:20), hearing their words, either flock to Jesus or glorify God.

It is, third, the language of vindication. The attempt to destroy Jesus (11:18; 12:12; 14:64) ends not with his defeat, but with his resurrection and presumable exaltation as Son of man. In the war of apocalyptic myths in which Mark is engaged, this word from the angel is as powerful a declaration to his suffering and persecuted readers as it should have been to his female text characters; the Jesus preaching path on which they walk is *the* path that represents God's strategic kingdom intent.

It is finally the language of closure. The narrative now cycles back to the place where Jesus' preaching ministry began. While some have conjectured that the verb "you will see" (ὄψεσθε) is an apocalyptic designation that refers to Jesus' parousia (cf. 14:62),[15] commentators are more and more convinced that Mark intends instead to remind the reader of the promise of the ministry's beginning. The promise, of course, is for the disciples. In Galilee, they were given the opportunity to follow Jesus, to fish as he fished, which is to say, to preach that the kingdom of God was at hand, and invite from others the appropriate response of following Jesus' kingdom way. Despite their shortcomings and failures, they are now given the opportunity once again. The reader is invited to return with them, to reflect upon Jesus' resurrection as a call to act as he acted, which is to say, to preach the coming of the kingdom. Galilee, where they will *see* the risen Jesus, then, is much more than a geographical designation. It represents the reality that now, the time of Mark's contemporary Jesus disciples, is the time to preach, despite the fact that Jesus' kind of preaching inevitably invites suffering and persecution. Or as Tolbert puts it, "Literal geography is not the point, for

---

13. Cf. 6:38 (miracle of feeding); 10:21 (teaching); 11:2 and 14:13 (miracle of foreknowledge).
14. Cf. 2:11 (5); 5:34; 7:29; 10:52.
15. Cf. Hooker, *A Commentary,* 386: Willi Marxsen, Ernst Lohmeyer. Cf. also Myers, 398, who points to Taylor and Fuller as adherents of the view that the verb implied the resurrection appearances.

Galilee represents the time of sowing [preaching], and the message of the empty tomb is that the time of sowing [preaching] still continues...."[16] The message the empty tomb wants to relay through the three women is, "Go Preach!"

The women, however, are too afraid to honor their part of the deal. The language of fear in the final verse of the Gospel is palpable. They flee the tomb. They are consumed by fear and trembling. They say nothing about this to anyone. For they are afraid. A careful reader might suspect that the Galilee scenario could still come to pass since Jesus had already forewarned the disciples in 14:28 that he would return to them in Galilee. But the dullness of the male disciples throughout the narrative is as palpable as the fear of the female disciples here at the narrative's close. Apparently the reader can expect little hope that the vindicating and challenging message of the angel will come to its desired end. And thus Mark's powerful interventionist story appears at first sight to end on a tragic note of herculean proportions.

Given what we now know about the functional intent of the classical literary writer and commentator, an appropriate question comes to mind. What does Mark intend this kind of ending to *do?* What is the effect he wants to make upon the audience he believes will access it?

TENOR OF DISCOURSE: WHO WILL FINISH THE STORY?

Mark sets the reader up to expect story closure from one of the text characterizations. One of them, through its words or actions, will teach the reader how he or she should respond to the calamity that has befallen Jesus. After all, Jesus, whose character normally establishes direction for the reader as well as for the other characters in the text, is now dead. Some other characterization must assume the burden of leadership both within the narrative and without. In its actions, as it once was with the actions of Jesus, the readers will discover what Mark wants them to do.

The first candidate for consideration is Joseph of Arimathea, a fellow seeker of the kingdom. Matthew explains that he was a rich man who was also a Jesus disciple.[17] Unlike the twelve who have scattered, this disciple goes to Pilate and requests Jesus' corpse. When Pilate orders it remanded to him, he wraps the body in a linen shroud and places it in his own unused tomb. As Mary Magdalene and the other Mary watch while sitting opposite the sepulcher, Joseph seals the tomb with a great stone.

Luke explains that Joseph was a member of the Sanhedrin council that condemned Jesus to death. Joseph, however, being a good and righteous man, had not consented to either the purpose of the council or the decision that followed. In Luke's account, too, Joseph asks Pilate for the body and lays it in a tomb where no one else had ever been laid. Once again the women, though unnamed

---

16. Tolbert, *Sowing the Gospel,* 298.
17. Matthew 27:57–61.

in this account, are there with Joseph, close enough not only to see where Jesus is laid, but to see how.

Common to both synoptic accounts is the fact that Joseph is a heroic figure who sees kingdom qualities in Jesus. His character is presented in such a way that the reader can positively identify with him and his purpose. They can also expect some behavioral guidance from the heroic example he sets.

This is not the case in Mark. The first synoptist did not offer Joseph as a heroic figure in whose actions his readers could find direction for the mode of their own discipleship behavior. Mark simply says that he was waiting for the kingdom of God. Given the evangelist's focus on the kingdom, this identification in itself might suggest a characterization worthy of emulation. But this designation does not distinguish Joseph from any pious Jew of the period. Even the scribes and priestly leadership that led the call in council chambers for Jesus' death expected the coming of the kingdom. Indeed, in both Jesus' and Mark's cultural contexts, an apocalyptic war of myths existed precisely because there were competing kinds of kingdom expectations.

In fact, the more one considers Mark's portrait, the more it appears that, far from being a disciple of Jesus, Joseph was probably one of the traditional leaders who sought an end to his interventionist preaching ministry. "Since *all* of the council had earlier condemned Jesus to death (14:55, 64), Joseph must be among Jesus' former opponents who rejected his claim to be 'the Son of the Blessed' (14:61–62)."[18]

Raymond Brown builds a persuasive case. His historical research reveals that the Romans often allowed family members or others to bury a person who had been executed. The only difficulty came in the situation of a person convicted on charges of treason or sedition. In this case the Romans did not want the criminal to receive an honorable burial, fearing that he might be regarded as a hero who should be imitated. The purpose of the horrific punishment of crucifixion, after all, was to deter similar kinds of offenses. Part of the deterrent lay in the dishonor the body suffered as it was allowed to decompose on the cross. Many times it hung there until birds and rodents had picked apart and devoured the softer, fleshier parts. The message was a brutal but evocative one. No doubt it was also effective. It was therefore highly unlikely that the body of a person charged with such a crime would be handed over to persons thought to be his disciples and/or followers. Jesus, tagged with the charge "King of the Jews," would no doubt have fallen into this category. "Therefore, the possibility that the prefect Pilate would give the body of a crucified would-be king to his followers for honorable burial is low."[19]

Jewish law took a rather different approach to the burial of the executed. Deuteronomy 21:22–23 is clear. A body hung on a tree should not remain all night for it is accursed by God and defiles the land.[20] It is no wonder then that

---

18. Tolbert, *Sowing the Gospel*, 293.

19. Raymond E. Brown, "The Burial of Jesus (Mark 15:42–47)," *Catholic Biblical Quarterly* 50 (1988): 235–36. Cf. 234–36 for fuller discussion on Roman attitudes toward burial.

20. R. E. Brown points out that in Philo and the *Temple Scroll* 64:10–13 this text is used in relationship to crucifixion (236).

Josephus argues that the Jews were careful to remove even crucified bodies from their crosses and have them buried by sunset.[21]

When all of these details are considered together, as they are presented in Mark's narrative, it seems clear that Mark understood Joseph to be a member of the council who was observing Jewish law and piety when he requested Jesus' corpse. To allow the body to remain on its grisly perch through the night, particularly since the next day was the Sabbath, was unthinkable. Joseph, the Sanhedrin member, therefore thought to approach Pilate. Certainly this was a bold move. One would not want, in the case of someone crucified on charges of sedition, to appear sympathetic either to him or his cause. The Romans, as Brown's research demonstrates, were as inhospitable to followers of a seditious person as they were to their crucified leader.[22] "What would save Joseph would be his status as a member of the Sanhedrin that had handed Jesus over to Pilate."[23]

Given Joseph's status as a Sanhedrin member, Pilate would not expect an honorable burial, and would therefore have been more likely to release Jesus' body to him. Indeed, Brown demonstrates that the burial was not an honorable one. The tomb is not described as "new," as in Matthew and Luke. There was no washing of the body. And there was no anointment with spices as was the custom in such "honored" cases.[24] It is precisely this lack of honor that evidently motivated the women to go to the tomb with spices on the first day of the week.

Unlike Matthew and Luke, Mark's narration does not suggest that the women who watched the burial did so in close physical proximity to Joseph. The women, whom Mark has described as disciples, evidently do not feel comfortable in the company of Joseph even as he is burying their Lord. He, obviously, is not a disciple. "Lack of cooperation between a Sanhedrist responsible for the death of Jesus, whose only wish is to get the criminal corpse buried, and women followers of Jesus is quite intelligible."[25]

Clearly, then, the direction the reader seeks at this jarring end of the narrative cannot come from Joseph. He has not been presented as a characterization with whom the reader can identify, much less follow. But even here, Mark has a powerful interventionist message that keeps the reader focused on Jesus' transformative preaching ministry. There is a rather delicious irony. Jesus' preaching ministry has been dedicated to the trespass of cultic, purity, and socio-political boundaries. That is why the ruling authorities want him destroyed. They are the guardians of the traditions that Jesus' interventionist ministry challenges. In fact, it is because of that piety that Joseph is motivated to prevent Jesus' corpse from suffering the ultimate degradation of public decomposition and perhaps scavenging. While he certainly doesn't give Jesus an honorable burial, he does prevent the ultimate dishonor. The reader can almost hear the evangelist

21. Ibid., 236 for citations. *War* 4.5.2; 3.8.5.
22. Ibid., 241.
23. Ibid.
24. Ibid., 242.
25. Ibid., 244.

chuckling in the background as he finishes Joseph's scene. Joseph, the representative of the boundary-traditionalist, because of his commitment to those boundaries, must assume the challenge of requesting the release and burial of the great boundary-breaker. Joseph's commitment to the very boundaries that Jesus challenged compels him to entomb Jesus. His actions therefore set the stage for the empty tomb and the accompanying angelic message that serve to interpret the resurrection as a sign of God's vindication for Jesus' boundary-breaking, preaching ministry.

This leads us, of course, to the other primary characterization in the narrative, the women. (I am presuming that the angel, though a characterization, as a completely supernatural figure, is to be obeyed rather than emulated.) As I have already pointed out, Mark's following (ἀκολουθέω) language (15:41) identifies the women as Jesus disciples. Other language also implies that they were disciples, perhaps even financial patrons of Jesus' ministry. Mark narrates that they were serving (διηκόνουν) Jesus. Even though Mark uses the term to describe the service Peter's mother-in-law provided for Jesus and his disciples after Jesus healed her, the evangelist obviously intends much more than mere housekeeping. This is the same verb he uses to describe the angels' ministering to Jesus at 1:13. It is also the language Jesus uses at 10:45 when he says that the Son of man comes to serve (διακονῆσαι).

Apparently, then, these women disciples who have served Jesus throughout his preaching ministry come one final time to serve him by honoring his corpse with the anointment of spices. It is in this sad recognition of his death that I believe Mark makes the connection with his reading audience. The women are experiencing the sadness and grief of separation. Even at the first moment of visualizing the emptiness of the tomb there is horror rather than joy. What the scene defines first of all is the absence the disciples, through the characterization of these women, feel. There is a distance separating them and Jesus. Even though the women watch his death, they do so from afar. Afraid of the Sanhedrin member, Joseph of Arimathea, they fear even to approach the burial of their teacher. And now, having evidently forgotten his promise of resurrection after three days, they come to find an empty tomb. The character traits of separation pile up until the feeling of loss is almost unbearable.

It is only in the relationship with the supernatural, the angel, that some semblance of relationship with Jesus can be maintained. It is not the kind of relationship the disciples previously had with Jesus. It is trust in the angel's version of events that provides the connection the women have lost with their leader. Jesus has risen; Jesus goes before his disciples to Galilee where the preaching ministry started, where it can start over again if the disciples heed the message. The symbolism is clear. The relationship with Jesus will be reestablished with Jesus in Galilee. But it will not be as it was before, obviously. For now the relationship will be with the resurrected Lord. But there is no hint that the kind of ministry has been altered. It is, in fact, the mention of Galilee that takes the reader back to Jesus' programmatic kingdom statement in 1:14, 15. Galilee represents the kick-off and drawing out of the preaching ministry. Going back represents a rekindling of that very ministry. But this time it will happen in Jesus' absence.

I cannot help but think that it is in this interaction between the characterization of the women and the message of the angel that Mark wants to bring home his message to his readers. For they, like the women, experience the tragic separation from their Lord. And, like the women, because they are followers of the Lord, they experience fear. In their case it is the imminent danger of suffering and persecution. Mark's counsel for a return to Galilee, then, applies as appropriately to them as it does to the women. But it remains a representative counsel. With the language of a Galilee return to meet the risen Lord, Mark challenges them, I think, to return to the place where Jesus' boundary-shattering ministry started, where Jesus made his kingdom proclamation and called disciples to follow. There is where their discipleship begins. With that same call. Now that they know what the kingdom ministry is, interventionist, boundary-breaking, preaching, they are in a better position to execute it. On this "return" to Galilee, on this second time around, they, like the women and the other disciles in the story, will be ready to understand for the first time what Jesus' call to "fish" in light of his proclamation of the kingdom really means for them. So equipped, they will be finally ready to finish the preaching ministry that Jesus began. In using his ending to point back to Jesus' beginning, Mark is telling his readers what Jesus felt he was told by God: "Go Preach!"

The only problem is the ending. At 16:8 Mark declares that the women were too afraid to tell the disciples about the angel's message. In Jesus' case the future kingdom became a present pocket because of and through Jesus' interventionist preaching. Mark's narration indicates that the disciples' preaching has the same interventionist effect. But this transformative effect will not occur unless the disciples, in relationship with the risen Lord, maintain this kingdom preaching. How, then, will the kingdom intervention be maintained since the women are too afraid to pass along the angel's message? How will the strategic design of the future kingdom find tactical expression in the contemporary human moment? It can't. That is, not unless the readers finish the story the women were afraid to finish. It can't unless the reader is willing to take the representative journey back to Galilee and hear Jesus' call to go preach the coming of the kingdom. This is what Mark's writing has ultimately been all about. He has shown Jesus' kingdom preaching and the transformative effect it can have. He has shown that the disciples have the power to emulate that transformative preaching. And he has demonstrated the promise of this transformative preaching that comes from the historical transformation that Jesus' ministry accomplishes (the crashing of cultic, purity, social, and most of all the religio-political Jew/Gentile boundaries) and the eschatological kingdom that it envisions. Though called to finish this kingdom preaching ministry the disciples are too afraid to accomplish the mission. In the starkness of their failure Mark challenges the reader to step in and finish what they and Jesus started. He challenges them to represent tactically, in their present pockets of resistance, the strategic intent and design of God's future kingdom. He challenges them to Go Preach!

THE MAIN MODE:
FINISH THE PREACHING STORY

I am well aware, of course, that my interpretation of Mark's intent is a minority one. The common interpretation, operating from the premise that Mark intends to mean something rather than do something with his project, is that the primary focus in the gospel is on the Passion Narrative and the cross. No doubt the oft-repeated remark that Mark's Gospel is a Passion Narrative with an extended introduction still lies somewhere in the background of this traditional understanding. Everything that happens prior to Mark 14–16 can therefore be considered to be a prelude to the interventionist activity of the cross. Mark intends to "mean" that Jesus suffers vicariously as the ultimate sacrifice for human sin. As the successful sacrifice he therefore re-establishes the broken relationship that exists between humans and God. The language of 10:45 and 14:24 make this clear.

Of course, to arrive at this kind of clarity one must read the entire Gospel in light of those two verses instead of reading those two verses in light of the Gospel's overall context, or even the kingdom context of situation. The latter approach, which I have attempted in this work, demonstrates that the language of both verses is better suited to the understanding that Mark draws throughout the narrative; it is the intervention of the kingdom of God into human time and space that draws humans into proximity with the divine. This intervention takes place through Jesus' preaching ministry and is destined to be fulfilled in the preaching ministry of those who follow him from Galilee onward.

But if the common consensus is correct, and Tompkins's assessment is also correct (that this ancient writer intended his writing to *do* something), then the end result is that Mark calls his readers to suffer as Jesus suffered. This, of course, fits the contextual situation we have reconstructed for Mark, but only in a descriptive sense. Mark's readers evidently are experiencing persecution. One questions, however, whether it is a suffering they seek as a voluntary means to vicariously establish a relationship between humans and God. Marcus, for example, depending on the allusions in the Passion Narrative to Deutero-Isaiah's suffering servant, argues that Jesus' salvific purpose, which also includes the Gentiles, is accomplished precisely in his sacrificial suffering. Because of the discipleship image of following, the community, too, is called to suffer, although here Marcus begins to hedge his bets. "We should emphasize, however, that if indeed the idea of the vicarious suffering of the community is present in Mark, that suffering is only efficacious because of its linkage with the sufferings of Jesus, because it is a suffering 'for his sake and the gospel's' (see again 8:34–35)."[26] He seems unsure that the idea of the community's vicarious suffering is present. If it is, it is certainly not so for the community in the way that it was for Jesus. Their call to suffering, in other words, is just that, a call to experience pain and suffering. The only motivation appears to be that one must experience it because Jesus experienced it. There is, however, none of the

---

26. Marcus, *The Way of the Lord,* 195.

transformative power available that was demonstrated in Jesus' suffering. It is, then, by all accounts a suffering for the imitative cosmetology of suffering's sake alone.

Of course, that is true only if it is Mark's intent to call his readers to suffer. My sociolinguistic investigation, operating from the premise that the text should be read as a narrative whole, without preference for one part (the Passion Narrative) over the other (the "extended" introduction), indicates that it was in Jesus' preaching that the power of God's kingdom intervened in the contemporary human circumstance. Mark's call then is that those who read his text do what Jesus' own disciples were called to do, that is, follow him in the kingdom preaching ministry. This is why, at the end, he calls his disciples, and his readers through them, to return to Galilee, not to the cross.

The Galilee ministry overturned traditional boundaries, boundaries responsible for religious, social and political organization of society in both Jesus' and Mark's time. Because of its "trespassing," transformative nature, it inevitably invited suffering and persecution. And though Mark portrays a wide variety of trespassed boundaries to make his point, clearly, in his own contextual context, the most problematic of the transformative behaviors would have been the one that challenged the traditional separation between Jew and Gentile. It was the crossing of this socio-political boundary that Jesus' own preaching ministry initiated and Mark's community, in a precarious context of Jewish and Gentile conflict, followed. This is the kind of preaching, a preaching to all the world, that invited the suffering that Mark saw as an inevitable consequence of following Jesus (13:9–13).

Indeed, when one considers Mark's narrative flow as it transpires up to the moment of the cross and beyond to the declaration of the angel in 16:6–7, it appears that the cross, though an instance of momentous signification and function, is a part of Mark's message, rather than that message's sole intent. In fact, the cross, though a powerful dramatic moment in the narrative, is not the same kind of apocalyptic moment as the baptism, the transfiguration, and the empty tomb/resurrection. Indeed, the cross is a manifestly human activity. It is indeed a part of God's strategic plan, but so has been all of Jesus' preaching ministry. It is, like many other moments in Jesus' preaching ministry, an interventionist moment where the power of the kingdom breaks through into the human context. This is demonstrated most particularly right after Jesus' death when the temple veil tears in two from top to bottom (15:38). Compared to Matthew's variation of the post-death account (Matthew 27:51–53), where the earth shakes, rocks split, tombs open, and the dead are resurrected and walk about Jerusalem, Mark's version is hardly impressive. Certainly it is an interventionist moment like so many moments in Jesus' ministry. It is different because Jesus suffers and dies; it is not different because the apocalyptic quotient is increased. It is increased at the baptism because of the supernatural voice from heaven. Similarly, there is a supernatural voice from heaven heard at the transfiguration. These two places easily qualify as apocalyptic crescendos in the narration. In both cases, what is uppermost on the evangelists' mind is the relationship of Jesus with God; that is to say, Jesus' exalted status. The suggestion woven into the narrative from these scenes appears to be one of vindication. No matter how provocative Jesus' boundary-breaking becomes, no matter how vulnerable he appears, even on the cross, it is to be understood that he is the one who stands and walks with God. His way should be followed because it is God's way, the way that represents God's strategic kingdom design. The only other place where such powerful apocalyptic imagery is on display comes immediately *after* the cross. After the scene where it appears Jesus has lost, the reader is given one final time a divine voice. This time there is even an accompanying divine presence. In fact, it is the only supernatural/divine characterization in Mark's entire tenor of discourse. No doubt this is a climactic and instructive apocalyptic moment. What was implied in the previous apocalyptic crescendo moments is now made explicit; Jesus has risen above the attempts to disqualify his kingdom preaching. Jesus has been vindicated. Jesus' way is the way that leads to relationship with God. Jesus' way is the way that saves. Jesus' preaching way is therefore the way that the disciples of Mark's community must follow. Any other proffered way comes from false prophets and counterfeit messiahs.

It was Jesus' kind of preaching that re-established the relationship between God and humans. When the kingdom drew near, God's presence drew near. When the power of the kingdom intervened, the power of God's strategic kingdom (i.e., salvation) design drew near. In Jesus' pocket moments, humans were re-drawn into relationship with God. This was the power and the value of his preaching. It is why this same preaching ministry was established as the call for his disciples to follow. For in their preaching, too, God's transformative and salvific power, in pocket moments of resistance, overturned illness and demonic possession. Humans became a point of intersection between the supernatural and the natural. Humans became conduits of the kingdom power. Their method, and their call, to establish this conduit was not suffering, but preaching. It is no wonder, then, that at the end of the Gospel the angel would direct the women, and through them the Markan readers, back to Galilee where the kingdom preaching began.

Notwithstanding Mark's presentation of the disciples wielding kingdom power in their preaching activities, a damaging question can still be anticipated: how can human beings construct the kingdom? They cannot. This, indeed, is why I approach Mark's preaching mandate from the perspective of strategy and tactics. Mark demands a tactical activity that processes the intervention of divine power into the human realm, not the establishment of a spatial, strategic goal. Indeed, this conclusion fits the understanding that many scholars hold regarding the definition of the kingdom.

Tolbert looks at a parallel between the Aramaic word *malkuth* and the Greek term *basileia* (βασιλεία). She argues that the Aramaic carries a stronger verbal sense, meaning the rule of God, whereas the Greek carries a stronger spatial sense, meaning the domain of God's rule. She then concludes that because of the way Mark presents Jesus' conduct the term kingdom should be understood from Greek rather than Aramaic parameters. Appealing particularly to the parable of the Sower, which she thinks is central to Mark's presentation, she writes,

For Mark, the kingdom of God is God's ground which produces of itself and in transforming abundance. It is not so much God's reign that is at issue but the land over which God legitimately rules, a land that has at least in part been usurped by evil powers.[27]

God's kingdom is, then, a *space* which humans are invited to inhabit.

But not according to Marcus. He argues that the prophetic writings, particularly those of Deutero-Isaiah, form the background for the synoptic sayings about entering the kingdom. And in Deutero-Isaiah Yahweh's kingdom is understood in terms of an extension of God's kingly power. This gives us a totally different picture of what the kingdom is. He writes,

> Read with this background in mind, the Synoptic sayings about entering the βασιλεία conceive of the βασιλεία not as a *place* but as God's eschatological extension of his kingly power into a lost world, and human beings are invited to *enter into* — that is, participate in — the divine extension of power.[28]

In Rabbinic usage, too, the kingdom language relates to God's active sovereignty, a reign that endures forever. After Mount Sinai God's sovereignty was manifested on earth in Israel and the Israelites' experience this kingdom, God's sovereignty, by obeying the Law. As George Ladd writes,

> The daily repetition of the Shema with the reading of Deuteronomy 6:4–10 was regarded as a repeated taking upon oneself of the yoke of the sovereignty of God. When a Gentile became a Jewish proselyte and adopted the law, he thereby took upon himself the sovereignty of heaven.[29]

In Jewish apocalyptic literature, kingdom remains defined as God's rule. Pointing to Qumran as an example, Ladd points out that the kingdom as God's divine sovereignty exists in this age when humans submit themselves to the divine rule. God initiates it; humans implement it tactically by responding to it. This is what Ladd means of Qumran when he writes, "The initiative in bringing God's Kingdom to earth rests with men."[30] This refers to the present age, of course. Eschatologically, God's action alone will establish the kingdom at the end of the age.

This description fits the language of strategy and tactics I have been employing throughout this investigation. The kingdom is itself God's strategic interjection of divine power and rule into the human realm. The tactical response of humans is to participate in that rule by absorbing that power and using it to

---

27. Tolbert, *Sowing the Gospel,* 172.
28. Marcus, *The Way of the Lord,* 33.
29. George E. Ladd, *Jesus and the Kingdom: The Eschatology of Biblical Realism* (New York: Harper and Row, 1964) 127.
30. Ibid., 128.

further interject and establish God's rule in human history as pockets of resistance. Seen against this background, Jesus' preaching would necessarily speak of the kingdom as God's rule. And the call for disciples to preach the kingdom as Jesus preached it would likewise imply their participation in the implementation of a divine power rather that the establishment of a divine space.

If indeed God's strategic kingdom is realized as a tactical act in the present that will be consummated at the close of the age, then the appropriate human preaching action is not the creation of and drawing into a place or realm of salvation. It is the acting out, that is to say, the preaching of the transformative power of God's own salvific power. In the language of contemporary colloquial Christianity one might even argue that it is not so much about *being saved* as it is about *saving* in tangible, that is to say, boundary-breaking ways.

What is this kingdom rule that the disciples represent in their tactical activities, then? I think the answer comes from the way Mark has structured his narrative about Jesus' kingdom preaching as boundary-crossing. Like Jesus, the disciples, and the Markan readers through them, are called to wield the kingdom power in ways that have a tangible socio-political impact. That is to say, their preaching must be transformative and boundary-crossing. In that boundary-crossing is the strategic kingdom design of God tactically represented.

I come to this conclusion by following Mark's own procedural process. Once again I resort to a simple mathematical equation to illustrate my point. If A=B, and A=C, then B=C. In Mark's narrative context of situation, "A" represents Jesus' preaching. That preaching manifests itself as miracle (healing), exorcism, and teaching pockets of resistance. "B" represents the boundary crossings and trespasses that these preaching manifestations establish. Preaching thereby equals boundary trespass in Mark's representative narration. But preaching "A" also equals "C" the manifestation of the kingdom of God as a present pocket. If, therefore, preaching equals socio-political, boundary-crossing activity, and preaching also equals the tactical manifestation of the kingdom of God, then it should follow that the socio-political, boundary-crossing activity of Jesus equals the tactical representation of God's future kingdom.

Here lies the path upon which the disciples are called to walk. When called to preach, they are, in essence, being called to breach social, cultic, economic and political boundaries, and in so doing wield the power of the future kingdom in such a way that it is realized as a present, transformative pocket. This realization has particular importance for the contemporary twentieth-century Markan reader. For while this reader, living in a non-mythological age, may feel that an imitation of Jesus' (and the disciples') miracles, exorcisms, and supernaturally authoritative teaching is impossible, he or she can know that it is possible to imitate what those mythological activities represent. Even though one cannot heal, exorcise, or teach with heavenly authority, one can breach the boundaries that separate humans from God and from each other. In this representative way the contemporary Markan reader can become a participant in the kingdom preaching ministry with the characterized Markan disciples and the first-century Markan readers.

I have maintained throughout that I believe that the key boundary in this regard is the one that cultically, socially, and politically divides Jew from Gentile. This is the boundary Mark encourages his community (which has evidently already begun a Gentile mission) to continue. This is how they can specifically finish the Jesus kingdom preaching story. This is how they can, in their own time and place, tactically re-present the future kingdom in the present moment. Thus, I believe Mark's narrative presentation of boundary in cultic, purity, economic, social, and political forms stands in for (that is to say, represents) the one critical boundary that Mark knows is crucial in the lives of his reading audience. Their trespass of this boundary provokes the same kind of hostility that Jesus' trespass of Mark's narrated boundaries triggered in his Gospel account. And yet he calls his readers to follow Jesus' model despite this inevitable consequence (13:9–13). As did Jesus, so must they preach transformatively. This path is the path that tactically represents God's strategic kingdom design. The kingdom explodes as a pocket of resistance in this activity of transformative, boundary-crossing.

Mark's call to preach the gospel to all the world is therefore a boundary-breaking demand to resist the dividing wall that separates people as they stand separated from God. But to engage in such an activity in the context in which Mark and his community found themselves was to guarantee the kind of suffering that comes from persecution. The cross, then, in Mark's narrative acts as a signpost. Its presence demonstrates that the disciple is on the right, that is to say, the provocatively transformative, path of dragging the future into the present. Transformation creates conflict. The conflict then, symbolized in the narrative as the cross, demonstrates the "correctness" of one's tactical discipleship behavior. The cross, then, is not for Mark a sign of redemption from sin; it is a sign that the boundary-crossing preaching activity that is imitative of Jesus' own preaching is indeed re-presenting in the present the transformative power of God's future.

And yet, the goal of a tactical manifestation of the strategic kingdom intent of salvation (relationship with God) in the human present, was worth the obstacle that stood before it. In fact, Mark was narrating Jesus' boundary-breaking way as the only way to accomplish this goal. The heavenly power itself made the case in the apocalyptic glimpses of Jesus' glory at the baptism and transfiguration, and at the vindication of his preaching ministry in the words of the angel at the empty tomb.

In demanding a return to Galilee, this is the preaching message that the angel and Mark leave with his reading community. The narrative characters are afraid to finish this preaching story; the readers must, regardless of the consequences. As Hooker puts it, "It is typical of Mark's gospel that the message should be in the form 'Go and you will see him,' for it demands a response."[31] Tolbert is even more direct. "If the women frustrate the hopes of the authorial audience for individuals to prove faithful to the courageous example of Jesus and follow his way by going out and sowing the word abroad [preaching], is there anyone

---

31. Hooker, *A Commentary*, 393.

else available to fulfill that task?...Of course there is: the audience itself."[32] If the women won't take the charge then the audience must. They become the recipients of the angel's charge. Mark's narrative has been written to provoke them to do what the women and the disciples apparently fail to do, that is, to go to Galilee to meet Jesus. In other words, to Go Preach!

> The problem posed by the epilogue in strong rhetorical terms through the unfulfilled expectations raised by the named women is, If these followers will not go and tell, who will? In the end, Mark's Gospel purposely leaves each reader or hearer with the urgent and disturbing question: What type of earth am I? Will I go and tell?[33]

That is to say, Will I break boundaries? Will I foment present pockets of the future kingdom? Will I — go preach?

---

32. Tolbert, *Sowing the Gospel,* 297.
33. Ibid., 298–99.

Part IV

The Meaning of Mark's Kingdom Message for Today's Black Church

13

A Correspondence of Relationships

Mark and Today's Black Church

I must admit that upon graduation from seminary in 1981 I did not believe that there was much correspondence between Mark's world and the world of the black church I was about to enter. The historical-critical method had convinced me that the first-century realities of the biblical evangelists were completely foreign to the twentieth-century circumstances of contemporary black Christians. The surroundings, people, and the terms used to describe them are different. So, in most cases, were their agrarian-based concerns and the mythological manner in which they dealt with them. Therefore, when I studied the text, my primary goal was to determine what it meant in and for Mark's intended first-century audience. This was text interpretation. The ancillary procedure of homiletical hermeneutics was an acceptable follow-up. The good interpreter recognized, however, that this process remained secondary; it was infested with *eisegetical* influence. That is to say, any attempt to establish correspondence between the two settings is a personal rather than a scientific-historical endeavor and should be regarded skeptically. In this historically "uncontrolled" phase of the interpretative process, the researcher's own presuppositions and the concerns of his or her faith community determined what kinds of meaning conclusions were drawn. I was convinced that a good researcher isolated and avoided such influence the way a good biochemist quarantined a deadly contagion. The historical-critically driven pastor or teacher taught the text as it was understood in the first century, and then, as best as he or she could, given the difficulty of the differences in social and historical location, demonstrated how lessons learned long ago might have some bearing on the lives of people lived today.

My work in sociolinguistics has convinced me, however, that the contrary lesson I learned as a pastor in a black church community is more appropriate to the task of biblical interpretation. Correspondence exists. Indeed, it exists at the most fundamental levels. The text *came* alive in the first century for the same reason that it *comes* alive in the contemporary black Christian community. It *was not* for Mark, and *is not* for the black church, a historical presentation of the "facts" about Jesus. Mark never intended to write a Life of Jesus. He intended instead to *interpret* the traditions about Jesus in such a way that they would come alive in the specific communal context he was addressing. He interpreted the material from his own personal understanding about who Jesus was and what Jesus' life meant, and integrated those thoughts with the concerns, feelings and fears of his faith community. Or, as Rowland and Corner point out in their discussion of Clodovis Boff's *Correspondence of Relationships* model, "the primary intention of the biblical writers was to awaken a commitment of faith from their readers, not simply to inform them of events that had taken place."[1] It is the same motive that drives the interpreter who operates out of and for the black church.

Boff's model offers a critical interpretative distinction. He resists the trend followed in much of contemporary Latin American liberation theology. In this case, the historical Jesus and his political context are assumed to have a one-to-one correlation with the contemporary Christian community and its political context.

$$\frac{\text{Jesus}}{\text{His Political Context}} = \frac{\text{Christian Community}}{\text{Its Political Context}}$$

This mistaken model implies a correspondence of terms. Events and people of the first century are thought to correspond directly (notice the equal sign) with events and persons of the twentieth century. For example, the United States is Rome. The perception of many Latin American peasants that their economies and destinies are controlled by the interests of the United States could therefore be directly likened to the colonization and domination of Palestine by Rome. Just as Rome parceled out its rule to local dictators like Herod the Great, so the United States farmed out its oppressive control to the likes of the Nicaraguan dictator Anastasio Somoza Debayle. Thus, when Jesus spoke words of liberation and freedom in his oppressive Palestinian context, those words had direct bearing upon the corresponding oppressive Latin American context.

> The argument is that a community with experience of persecution, exile and torture is justified in representing the biblical story in terms of its own environment precisely because of a historical correspondence between its own life and that of the Jesus movement in its early days.[2]

Boff justifiably criticized the correspondence of terms approach for its naive disregard of the social and historical chasm that separates the first and twentieth centuries. Nevertheless, as he and other liberation theologians also recognized, correspondence does exist. Mark meaningfully adapted, that is to say, interpreted the traditions about Jesus according to the contextual concerns of his

---

1. Christopher Rowland and Mark Corner, *Liberating Exegesis: The Challenge of Liberation Theology to Biblical Studies* (Louisville: Westminster/John Knox, 1989) 60.
   2. Ibid., 56.

first-century audience and Palestinian circumstance. In doing so, he was following the interpretative lead of his professional and religious forebears. As Rowland and Corner note, Gerhard von Rad had already demonstrated that "the Old Testament was constituted by way of a constant renewal of old traditions in view of new situations."[3] Von Rad's point was that the prophetic writings of the Hebrew Bible demonstrated the principle of adapting earlier traditional divine messages and sacred traditions to new situations. As an example he pointed to the application of Balaam's prophecy to the Greeks in Numbers 24:24. The use of messianic prophecy from Amos in Acts 15:16–17 is a helpful New Testament example.[4] "The point about renewing old traditions in view of new situations applies as much to Christian as to Jewish sacred writings."[5] Rowland and Corner present this correspondence of relationships model with the following formula:

$$\frac{\text{Scripture}}{\text{Its Context}} = \frac{\text{Ourselves}}{\text{Our Context}}$$

The interpretative situation of scripture and its context is *like* the interpretative situation that surrounds and activates our twentieth-century exegetical process. In other words, interpreters operating out of the black Christian experience in the United States can and should meaningfully adapt Mark's interpretative process to the twentieth-century circumstances of African-America. In doing so they would be following Mark's own interpretative lead. Contemporary black interpreters who try to bring Mark's kingdom text alive by focussing their interpretations on unique twentieth-century, African-American concerns are, then, in correspondence with Mark's own agenda and effort. They are extending what Mark himself — and a long line of biblical prophets and writers before him — considered a vital part of the (tradition/text) interpretative process.

Rowland and Corner argue, therefore, that when the theology of liberation applies the Exodus tradition to the situation of the oppressed seeking freedom from persecution in poor countries of the world today, it is operating as the biblical authors themselves operated. There is a correspondence of interpretative procedure that both allows and encourages such a contemporary move. It is exactly in this way that the Markan text about Jesus comes alive in a black Christian context, just as Mark's own story about Jesus brought the prophetic traditions of classical Israel alive in a new, interventionist way in the first century. The Africans who appropriated the Exodus story as their own in the slave spirituals and sermons operated intuitively with this interpretative strategy. So, too, do the African-Americans who grapple with Mark's message of the kingdom today. In their hands the first-century interventionist message proclaims a kingdom imperative that meets the precise and unique needs of the twentieth-century black circumstance.

If Mark's kingdom message is to impact today's African-American church and community it cannot be exegeted as a dead text whose indicative meaning

---

3. Ibid., 61.
4. Ibid., 62.
5. Ibid.

and imperative impact died when the pages of the first century turned to a close. Certainly, it is appropriate and necessary to begin with a reconstruction of that period and to continue by determining how Mark's message would have been understood within its time and socio-political frame. That process, however, is only the means to an end, not the end itself.

As I have argued in an earlier work, any and every historical reconstruction, no matter how methodologically controlled, is influenced by the contemporary-contextual position and perspective of the researcher.[6] Indeed, every methodology presents its own unique contemporary-contextual biases. The very attempt to determine what a text meant in its own environment necessarily makes a researcher an accomplice to the practice Mark and his colleagues accepted as an interpretative commonplace. The act of analyzing a text or tradition is always either in large part or small, consciously or unconsciously, a "renewal of the old traditions in light of new situations."

Still, even though the process is driven by contemporary-contextual concerns, careful attention to sociolinguistic detail can help establish the range of meaning potential for a targeted text. Texts do not mean anything an interpreter wants them to mean. And yet, there is a vast amount of potential that can be sociolinguistically accessed. The purpose of accessing that potential is to bring it alive within the life of a new communal situation.

I am not suggesting that contemporary believing communities write their own kingdom script. I am arguing instead that they access the potentiality of Mark's kingdom language in such a way that it speaks with particular insight, meaning and direction for their unique situation. This would negate the reality that has developed in contemporary biblical exploration. The historical and literary models of biblical criticism operate from particular principles that do not value the perspectives of the oppressed and disempowered in our society. The exegetical enterprise remains a middle- and upper-class, European dominated undertaking. It is not surprising, then, that where the kingdom language is concerned, spiritual, a-political, status-quo serving, other-worldly conclusions dominate the discussion. Such conclusions are not only driven by middle-class, European presuppositions, they service the kind of church and society that fosters the continued dominance of their interpretations and way of life. Furthermore, the declaration that only interpretations that operate from such principles and motives are "historically" and "scientifically" accurate prejudge investigations from an oppressed perspective as historically inaccurate and personally or communally biased. Sociolinguistic inquiry indicates just the opposite can in fact be the case. Even though the conclusions drawn may be quite different from those appropriated through historical or literary means of inquiry, they may well be just as accurate, if not more accurate, understandings of the meaning potential of the kingdom texts. The difference would be that the shift in social location allows for and fosters a new access point and therefore a different meaning conclusion.

It is my intent in these closing sections to bring this sociolinguistic principle

---

6. Cf. Brian K. Blount, *Cultural Interpretation: Reorienting New Testament Criticism* (Minneapolis: Fortress Press, 1995).

to life from the perspective of African-America, particularly its urban component. Having looked at Mark's kingdom language and its relationship to its contexts of culture and situation, I now want to explore the African-American, twentieth-century contexts of situation and culture. In the correspondence of relationships that develops between Mark's world and my own there can be, I believe, a kingdom word come alive for the social, historical, and political moment of today's black church.

MARY ANN TOLBERT AND THE POETICS OF LOCATION

I anticipate resistance. Scholarship, like a court of law, is loath to accept new directions of inquiry unless a precedent that helps bridge the divide between the old and the new can be cited. It is for this reason that I am particularly grateful for the work of Mary Ann Tolbert in Volume Two of *Reading from This Place: Social Location and Biblical Interpretation in Global Perspective*. Tolbert's fine article, "When Resistance Becomes Repression: Mark 13:9–27 and the Poetics of Location," is helpful for two reasons. First, even though she does not use the language "correspondence of relationships," it is clear that she recognizes the procedural similarity between the way ancient and contemporary communities bring texts to life. In other words, she realizes that the manner in which twentieth-century interpreters access the language potential of a text corresponds to the way language was interpreted in the first century. Twentieth-century conclusions shift because the access point has shifted. The interpretative process is the same; the intent in the first and twentieth centuries is to give the traditional text contemporary life.[7] In fact, it is precisely because she is afraid that contemporary repressive communities will bring the text to life in oppressive ways that her work is ultimately directed toward what she calls an ethics of interpretation. Second, she uses as her test case an apocalyptic text from Mark 13, the chapter that most scholars use as the foundation for reconstructing Mark's social location. Her look at this interventionist text in light of both Mark's first-century and her own twentieth-century context is analogous to my own effort to relate Mark's contextualized kingdom language to the contemporary African-American circumstance.

Tolbert begins her analysis by considering what I have called the context of situation of Mark 13. Her conclusions agree with my own; Mark's readers, because they are expected to identify with the feelings of persecution exhibited by and expected of Jesus' followers, were most likely experiencing persecution. Mark 13:9–13 indicates that kings, governors, and councils are arrayed

---

7. Cf., for example, Mary Ann Tolbert, "When Resistance Becomes Repression: Mark 13:9–27 and the Poetics of Location," in *Reading from This Place, Volume 2: Social Location and Biblical Interpretation in Global Perspective*, Fernando F. Segovia and Mary Ann Tolbert, editors (Minneapolis: Fortress Press, 1995) 332. "Since a politics of location insists on the complexity, multiplicity, and contextuality of each person's 'identity,' a poetics of location needs to recognize the legitimacy of self-consciously adopting different perspectives on a text at different times. Thus, such a poetics quite obviously eschews claims for universal readings in favor of local readings that are careful to indicate their context and limits."

politically and religiously against Jesus and his message (cf. also 12:1–12). Mark, Tolbert concludes, should therefore be understood as a polemic against traditional social, religious and political power. And, given that Mark expected his readers to identify with Jesus' narrative position and the evangelist's own literary polemic, it seems clear that "the intended audience was very likely composed of those from marginal groups in antiquity who were excluded from access to social, economic, political, and religious power. . . . "[8]

This conclusion is, of course, quite harmonious with my own. Tolbert goes on to describe the probable Markan historical-contextual situation as that of a "colonized people under the thumb of an imperial power."[9] As do I, however, she finds that Mark's invective is directed most intensely against the Palestinian leadership rather than the powers in Rome. Mark's community, then, if Tolbert's reading of the context of situation is accurate, has found itself at odds with the leadership in Palestine during the time of the Roman-Jewish war. The community interprets its circumstance through the story of Jesus, whose ministry, according to Mark's retelling, put him at odds with those same powers decades before. "Clearly, the enemies they face are the present political and religious leaders, who hate them and wish to persecute them for their beliefs. Mark 13:9–27 serves primarily as an encouragement to the faithful to *resist* all the terrors thrown at them by the colonial powers."[10]

In my terminology, that is to say, Mark presents the tensive symbol of the kingdom as a pocket of resistance whose rule is inaugurated and fostered by Jesus and can be manipulated and extended by those who would follow him. It is precisely when I argue for human participation in the manipulation of the kingdom that I am, of course, pushing beyond the conclusions that Tolbert draws. Still, the similarities up to this point are noteworthy. Tolbert concludes that when one reads Mark 13:9–27 from such a (historical) contextual reconstruction, its meaning potentiality is accessed as a literature of resistance against colonial powers. Her conclusions not only validate my own sociolinguistic reading of Mark's kingdom language, they also demonstrate quite clearly that the evangelist expected his first-century readers to interpret his language through the lens of their shared cultural context.

Tolbert understands, though, that other interpretative contexts exist. She also recognizes the validity of an access to the meaning potential of Mark 13:9–27 from those "other" contextual perspectives. The contemporary-contextual case where readers operate from a context of power and privilege would be particularly interesting. In fact, this is precisely the dilemma Tolbert wants to confront. She herself is a contemporary-contextual interpreter of two contrasting worlds. On the one hand she is a woman operating in a male-dominated world and profession, and she therefore shares the perspective of the oppressed when she comes to the text. But another part of her comes from the first-world, Euro-American context of privileged scholarship, a middle- to upper-class life

---

8. Ibid., 335.
9. Ibid., 336.
10. Ibid.

of opportunity and possession that seeks conservative foundation rather than revolutionary foment from the biblical text — even, and perhaps especially, an apocalyptic one like Mark 13:9–27.

She is right to observe that now the kings, governors and councils, the local powers, are mostly Christian. The text then has to be re-read from a new perspective, one where the enemies are not those who are presently in control, but those who want to be in control, that is, who want to take power away from controlling Christians. "Mark 13:9–27 and other texts like it are often read in the ruling communities of the colonizers as *proleptic texts,* predicting what will happen to Christians, if they lose their dominance in local or world affairs."[11] The shift in the contemporary context therefore demands a radical shift in reading and interpreting the same apocalyptic, biblical material.

Because the two interpreting communities operate from such dramatically different contextual positions, the conclusions they reach are diametrically opposed to one another. How, then, Tolbert asks, do we adjudicate between them? Having rejected the possibility of church courts deliberating over such opposing interpretative conclusions, she appeals to the direction initiated by Johann Philip Gabler. His inaugural address in 1787 at Altdorf, Germany, argued for a separation of biblical and dogmatic theology. Dogmatic theology operated from what I call contemporary-contextual presuppositions and biases of the interpreter and his or her community. Gabler believed it should be separated out and saved for the final, hermeneutical stage of the interpretative process. At the head of the process stood biblical theology. As Tolbert points out, this biblical theology was only "true" if it was true to the religion expressed in the biblical texts themselves. Later biblical scholarship built upon Gabler's work by establishing a historical-critical method that would equate "true" with "historically original." In other words, the closer an interpreter got to the actual historical reconstruction of the context of a biblical text and the original meaning the text had in that context the more accurate his or her interpretation was bound to be. The search for what the text "meant" in the first century was on.

There are three critical problems with such an approach. First, as I have already pointed out, this process kills the living value of a text. The only meaning is the meaning it held in the first century, and since the first century is radically different from the twentieth, the text can at best have only tangential importance for contemporary Christians. Second, as Tolbert points out, present understanding may reveal that the original situation in which the text came to life was itself repressive. For example, the original situation of the first century was clearly patriarchal. Contemporary women forced to interpret the text out of this historical-contextual perspective would, instead of finding a dead letter, nonetheless encounter a living word with the power and the inclination to kill.

In the case of apocalyptic, it is clear that the language and the symbolism expects and encourages the utter destruction of the world and everyone in it who does not belong to the elect. Appropriately, Tolbert wonders whether such a violent, vengeful perspective, even if it is the contextual perspective of the

---

11. Ibid., 338.

first-century readers who first accessed Mark's text, remains the best way to bring God's Word alive today. Tolbert is right to warn that valuing the historical period over the contemporary one — simply because Jesus and Paul lived in those periods — threatens the ability of the text to reveal the living word of God anew in and for contemporary historical circumstances. ". . . [u]sing historical originality as the main criterion for evaluating biblical interpretations is, in the second place, inadequate for a poetics of location because it legitimizes only one location for reading the Bible: the scholarly development of an ancient situation."[12]

Third, the historical approach does not understand that history is always selectively established. Sociolinguistics demonstrates that any historical-contextual reconstruction will be influenced as much by the researcher's contemporary-contextual variables as by the data analysis. This is because all data analysis takes place through contemporary-contextual lenses. This is what we mean when we say that language is social. To use it, to access it is a social endeavor; our social make-up is always involved whether we are creating language or interpreting it.

How, then, should we determine meaning when radically opposed communities interpret the texts out of their own unique contexts? Tolbert advances an ethics of interpretation. It starts from the recognition of the power for both good and evil that biblical interpretation has in the lives of believers and non-believers today. It is therefore necessary that one draw on the best of moral discourse, philosophical thought, science and history in developing a set of criteria for evaluating biblical interpretations in each situation, "recognizing that these criteria may be different in different locations."[13] She then offers her own mediating principle. It operates from the affirmation of a Creator God of love whose primary mandate is that no human creation of God should be treated as less than human. Biblical interpretations that run counter to such a principle, whether historically defensible or not, should be challenged. In the end, "The Bible's 'truth' for today must be evaluated on the basis of its ethical impact, its blessing or its curse, on God's creation as a whole."[14]

Tolbert's conclusion is an intriguing one; I am tempted to follow it precisely because I agree with the principle on which she fixes her interpretative line. My problem is that no matter how universally appealing her principle appears, there have been and remain Christians and non-Christians who, while holding to it or similar principles thematically, operate in the practical arena in ways directly contradictory to it. In the African-American experience particularly, we have seen Euro-Americans proclaim lofty principles, such as the belief that all are created equal, while simultaneously acting in overtly and covertly discriminatory ways. The African-American problem with the "moral principle" position is not unique, of course. I only raise it because it is my intent to value that perspective in this work. Furthermore, it is not only the case that moral principles can themselves, like the biblical text, be interpreted in wildly

---

12. Ibid., 345.
13. Ibid., 346.
14. Ibid.

different and highly contextualized ways; it is also true that different communities may hold radically different and in many cases opposing moral principles. The shift in principle, then, will dictate a shift in biblical interpretation. This would be particularly problematic if one community's principles were inimical to another community's well-being. The biblical interpreter, then, ends up with a two-layered problem. Not only must he or she adjudicate between the contextual interpretations of the biblical material, he or she must also adjudicate between the different moral principles used to create and/or validate those interpretations.

My own experience in African-American congregations suggests that the process would be deemed complicated, impractical, and, in the end, unacceptable. Even when it was appropriated only orally during slavery, the biblical text, and not human moral principle, remains the interpretative and ethical foundation for the majority of black Christians.[15] I would dare say that, given the perception that the persons empowered to establish and enforce "moral" principles on a broad societal basis are rarely themselves African-American. Most African-Americans are *concerned* about placing their well-being, and perhaps their lives, in such hands. Such principles have too often been established and/or interpreted in ways that have been damaging for the interests and lives of black people in the United States.

A supra-human norm has therefore always been preferable where African-Americans, and I would dare say most oppressed minority communities, are concerned. African-American Christians have tended to locate that norm in the biblical stories. They have tended to appropriate that norm by bringing the biblical stories to life in the light of their contemporary contextual situations. The black church, in other words, has always made historical-contextual text interpretation a contemporary-contextual endeavor. That is to say, the biblical text has always been viewed through the hermeneutic of the black experience. Indeed, the human context has been so important to the black interpretative effort that black Christians have even challenged the historically contingent language of the biblical text whenever that language connected more with human than what blacks considered divine sentiment.

The discovery of the biblical understanding of universal human equality provided not only theological grounds for opposing racism but also a means of evaluating the authority of the Bible itself. Accordingly, the black churches have never hesitated to disavow any interpretation of Scripture that would attempt to legitimate racism, slavery, or any other form of human bondage. One can conclude that there have been no sacred

---

15. Cf. Stephen Breck Reid, "The Theology of the Book of Daniel and the Political Theory of W. E. B. Du Bois," in *The Recovery of Black Presence: An Interdisciplinary Exploration*, Randall C. Bailey and Jacquelyn Grant, editors (Nashville: Abingdon Press, 1995) 38. "Traditionally, Black church interpretation represents intratextual theology: it builds from a scriptural foundation as opposed to a philosophical position."

scriptures for blacks apart from the hermeneutical principle immortalized in the black Christian tradition.[16]

And yet it remains clear that the starting point for the black Christian community is the biblical story. The hermeneutical principle develops from that story; only then does it become the standard against which the language used to tell that story is measured. In other words, the biblical story is the ground upon which human principle, and even biblical language, stands.

My task, then, is to bring the texts of the biblical story, particularly Mark's kingdom story, to life in a way that recognizes the need to make contextual distinctions between the biblical period and our own. In this way it would be clear that the biblical period and its human contextual biases and concerns, like those which accept slavery as a historical given, should not be privileged over the human and moral concerns of the twentieth century. This would be the case particularly where the radical shift in context has allowed the contemporary human to view God's word from a perspective that is less patriarchal, violent, etc. It would also, however, allow for a foundation that is not based in human moral principle, which itself can be highly contextualized and situationally driven.

The need, then, is for a foundation that exists outside the realm of human moral and philosophical thought and control, an objective source whose meaning potentiality, while vast, remains constant, and therefore, challenging as well as affirming. The biblical text played and continues to play this role in African-American Christianity. It has provided an external, objective source against which even the most highly regarded human values and principles could be evaluated, and, if need be, transformed. As we will soon see, it was precisely in this way, for example, that biblical symbols, particularly the kingdom of God, inspired civil rights leaders like Martin Luther King, Jr., to challenge American segregationist law that was supposedly grounded in the freedom principles of the U.S. Constitution and Declaration of Independence.[17] Another external, the coming kingdom of God, heightened the value of the foundational biblical text by adding the senses of primacy and urgency to the need to comprehend and follow its mandates.

My own approach to the interpretative quandary, then, would be a continued attempt to reconstruct the Markan contexts of culture and situation. This operation would take place with the assumption that any such endeavor is itself driven by my own contemporary-contextual concerns. But this is a positive recognition rather than a begrudging admission. It is precisely because this process is driven

---

16. Peter J. Paris, "The Bible and the Black Churches," in *The Bible and Social Reform*, Ernest R. Sandeen, editor (Philadelphia and Chico, CA: Fortress Press and Scholars Press, 1982) 135.

17. Cf., for example, Forrest E. Harris, Sr., *Ministry for Social Crisis: Theology and Praxis in the Black Church Tradition* (Macon, GA: Mercer University Press, 1993) 39–40. "Martin Luther King, Jr., used the biblical symbol of the reign of God more effectively than any other church leader of recent times. The focus of King's liberation praxis was the vision of the reign of God or the beloved community as the ultimate norm and goal for civil rights, economic justice, and world peace."

by contemporary-contextual concerns that Mark's world and the text he fashions from it can come alive as a renewal of the old traditions in the light of the new, African-American situation. The goal, then, would not be to determine what the text meant in the first century as a rule against which we could then judge African-American (or any other) interpretations in the twentieth century. We would instead be attempting to give the contemporary interpreter some insight into the potentiality of the language meaning. That is to say, it would be the researcher's quest to determine how much the language could mean and could do in its first-century context. Such a determination could then act as a range in which and through which contemporary, particularly contemporary African-American, interpretative efforts could operate.

Consider the case of the repressive community accessing Mark 13:9–27. Tolbert was right to consider how contemporary communities of privilege can and do interpret the material repressively. But she also pointed out that in order to do so these communities had to adjust the language to fit their situations. They did not interpret or renew the language in such a way that it corresponded to the circumstance of Mark's own context of situation and culture. Therefore, instead of the text being interpreted as a challenge to contemporary Christians who are now kings, council members, and governors, her interpretative flexibility allowed what many contemporary Christian communities also allow, that the text interpretation operate outside the potential range established by the Markan language. Human principle takes over exactly at this point. Christians make an ethical decision that the text can be and must be adjusted to fit their situation as kings. This maneuver, even though it may seem so on the surface, is not like the interpretative moves established by the biblical writers who renewed traditions and texts in novel situations. Here the novel situation has forced a change in the text's historical-contextual range of meaning. The text has not come alive; it has been recreated.

The fundamental principle of sociolinguistic interpretation is that all of the macro functions of language must be engaged simultaneously in the interpretative process, just as they are simultaneously engaged in the language creation process. This means that the interpreter must consider the textual, ideational, and interpersonal components when analyzing the material. I would argue that the repressive approach to Mark 13:9–27 has considered only the interpersonal functions of the text language. The control that resides in the complementary textual and ideational components has been lost. I would argue that in order to bring the text alive in a way that not only agrees with the most laudable of contemporary human principles, but that may also challenge and protest what we often *consider* laudable human principle, we must locate the interpretative foundation in the text, not in human principle. This is not to say that the text is a fundamentalist word that must be obeyed in a literalistic fashion. The historical-contextual reconstruction through a contemporary-contextual lens assumes the historical contingency of the text and the contextual limitations of the authors. At the same time, however, it enables the interpreter to engage that author's message and meaning, and then build principle from it, rather than the other way around. It is, in other words, in the dialectical interchange between the historical-contextual reconstruction (which values the textual, ideational, and historical-interpersonal variables) and the contemporary-contextual perspective and principles of the interpreter and his or her community that text-language meaning is best accessed. Each interpersonal component, the historical-contextual and the contemporary-contextual, thus acts as a check against the other. There is in this sense a balance of interpretative power.

In the language of the kingdom which I have been exploring, this means that it is possible to interpret Mark's message in such a way that the indicative language of intervention can be accessed and understood within Mark's own historical frame. And while this indicative continues to have value, the manner in which Mark applied it as an ethical imperative can be seen as historically contingent. Tolbert is right to suggest that the apocalyptic imperative that Mark declares is contrary to many of the moral and ethical sensibilities of contemporary moral thought and faith. There is no question that when Mark speaks of violence against all but the elect that he has followed the vengeful apocalyptic line of interventionist interpretation. And yet, the indicative statement about God's past and expected intervention into the human circumstance need not be locked into his single mode of imperative application when it is renewed in a novel, African-American contextual circumstance.

In other words, start with Mark's apocalyptic indicative of intervention. Realize, however, that we don't need to accept all of the imperatives he derives from it. Indeed, the imperatives are the most contextually driven and historically contingent parts of his kingdom language. Realizing this, renew the interventionist indicative in the contemporary historical and moral circumstance in which we live. In this way the interventionist indicative can challenge and compel us with ethical imperatives that relate specifically to the African-American sociolinguistic situation.

TOWARD A WORKING MODEL:
STEPHEN BRECK REID, DANIEL, AND DU BOIS

Stephen Breck Reid's article, "The Theology of the Book of Daniel and the Political Theory of W. E. B. Du Bois," offers an intriguing example of interpretative renewal. Reid takes a fascinating look at the work of Du Bois in light of Daniel's apocalyptic message. His work suggests a correspondence on three critical levels. First, Daniel and Du Bois, though separated by many centuries, developed their messages in a similar interpretative context of oppression and colonization. Second, both Daniel and Du Bois followed the interpretative strategy of renewing old traditions in light of new situations. Just as Daniel fashioned an apocalyptic understanding that related to the specific situation of his people's Seleucid occupation, so Du Bois developed a perspective that fostered hope in the political life of African-Americans preoccupied by the forces of racial segregation and discrimination. Third, life in their respective contexts fostered a corresponding preunderstanding of intervention. This multi-leveled correspondence in context, interpretative strategy, and preunderstanding suggests right from the outset of analysis that the tradition/text interpretative messages these two men proclaimed to their struggling peoples would be strikingly similar.

Reid begins with what I would call a historical-contextual reconstruction of Daniel's location through his own African-American lens. "A competent reader attempts to reconstruct the social world of the Second Temple period (especially the Hellenistic part)."[18] The problem, he warns, is that this period, at least from the perspective of the Jews, was one of oppressive colonization. It was "colonial in the sense that it was part of the political world of the Ptolemies, the Seleucids, and eventually the Romans."[19] Anyone attempting to reconstruct this world from a contrasting position of repression and power would therefore have difficulty accessing it. "...[T]hose of us who have never traveled self-consciously into the colonial world will struggle to grasp the book of Daniel."[20]

His position is clear: because he operates from the minority position of the oppressed in the United States (as an African-American), he can and will reconstruct Daniel's context through his own contemporary-contextual lens. Because that lens refracts reality in the same way that Daniel's did, it appears that his kind of reconstruction, and the interpretative meaning that develops from it, should bear more weight than the meaning that originates from a reconstruction that occurs in and from a position of privilege. Whether Reid's claim is finally correct or not, I think he is right to suggest that a correspondence between the contexts of the interpreter and the interpreted text improves the probability that the text will be renewed rather than recreated.

Reid's reconstruction operates carefully from a textual, ideational, and historically oriented interpersonal look at the binary world of the colonized and the role of oppositional literature that apocalyptic plays within it. In a reality of competing perspectives, that of the oppressed and that of the oppressor, the dualistic character of apocalyptic fits quite neatly. God chooses sides. Historical-apocalyptic writers like Daniel and Mark believe that God has and will imminently and ultimately intervene in such a circumstance to bring historical restoration and socio-political salvation to those presently existing on the underside of history.

In the meantime, however, the believing community is forced to live in two worlds. As Reid explains, it cannot afford the luxury of a cultural monism; it has to engage the oppressor's culture and survive within it at the same time that it tries to maintain and pass on its own. The community, in this sense, is more universal than the dominant society that controls it. The community in power need not learn the ways of the oppressed community; the latter lacks sufficient power to punish non-compliance with its values and beliefs. The oppressed community must, however, at least publicly, demonstrate an awareness of, and quite often an allegiance to the values proffered by the dominant societal group. It is a context that African slaves and later African-Americans, like

---

18. Reid, 39.
19. Ibid., 38.
20. Ibid., 39.

Daniel and his compatriots, know all too well. White people in the contemporary United States need not learn the values, beliefs, mores and culture of African-Americans. Black people have learned, however, often at the price of individual and/or communal peril, that they must know the principles, values and norms of Euro-America as well as they know their own. It is the reality that Du Bois called a "double-consciousness."

Ironically, of course, because God sides with the oppressed in the apocalyptic frame, real power, in both its present pocket and future consummate senses, ultimately lies with them. It is this knowledge that allows the oppressed person to endure, that is, to resist the indignities and horrors perpetuated by the ruling powers. In fact, the very alliance of the oppressed with the values of God, which necessarily in this dualistic frame are values that oppose and resist the values of the oppressing community, makes the oppressed believer an exceptional person. Daniel and his compatriots were exceptional in precisely this manner. "The Jews exhibit exceptional knowledge rooted in religious experience and piety.... The exceptional ethics connect with a salvation eschatology where God breaks the progress of Gentile rule."[21] In other words, God's present pocket interventions (for example, Daniel's miraculous escape from harm in the lion's den and Shadrach, Meshach, and Abednego's protection from the flames of the fiery furnace) occur precisely because members of the oppressed community maintain this exceptional faith and the ethics that derive from it. Divine intervention, as pocket moments of kingdom power, is thereby directly linked with human faith and the exceptional activity based in that faith.

Reid now turns to W. E. B. Du Bois's agenda for a black political theology. To be sure, Reid forces the comparison for us. He admits that he does not know whether Du Bois ever made an interpretative evaluation of Daniel when developing his own thought. Reid therefore artificially creates a kind of Du Bois interpretation of Daniel. Still, even though the interpretation is manufactured, we can learn from it. We can see precisely how a link can be established between a contemporary interpreter and the apocalyptic message and mandate of a biblical writer.

Du Bois operates from the understanding that black persons live in a binary culture within the United States. Double-consciousness occurs as a result. Blacks are forced to live in two worlds. While this forces blacks to be more culturally universal than whites, it also has the stigmatizing effect of creating a situation where blacks are always looking at themselves through the eyes of others, "...of measuring one's soul by the tape of a world that looks on in amused contempt and pity."[22]

Du Bois developed a cultural criticism in the light of this binary existence that laid the groundwork for social change. His program contained the five elements of economic cooperation, art and literature revival, political action, education, and organization.[23] Key to the success of the program was the ac-

---

21. Ibid., 41–42.
22. In ibid., 44.
23. Ibid.

tivity of a group of African-Americans whom he called the "talented tenth." This talented tenth would be composed of the most highly educated and socio-economically established black Americans who would lay the foundation for a cultural transformation that would ultimately bring a positive change for all African-Americans. Reid points out that Du Bois's strategy was built on more than elitism; it was also grounded in a realistic appraisal of the lack of financial resources to bring economic, political and educational achievement to all blacks simultaneously.

The book of Daniel depicts the rulers as unwise and therefore in need of guidance by Daniel and the other Jewish elite. Likewise the talented tenth are to function as educators of the white community as well as their own African-American kin. These exceptional persons in both the Daniel narrative and the African-American circumstance are to act as the catalysts for socio-political transformation precisely because of their exceptional resources, knowledge and faith. In both cases, they are the ones called upon to initiate the pockets of resistance that tactically energize the power of the kingdom in the human circumstance.

The book of Daniel, Reid advises, is an exceptionalist document. Divine intervention in the human present occurs as a result of the exceptional qualities and activities displayed by the faithful among its narrative characters. The message that Reid lifts out of his manufactured Du Bois interpretation is that the African-American community must energize its own exceptional forces if it is to initiate kingdom pockets in the present moment. Such a conclusion is apparently what prompted Reid to open his work with the provocative words, "The call of the Gospel requires that we implement the reign of God."[24] Daniel and his compatriots implemented it through their exceptional piety and activity; African-Americans, one should conclude, will do so in the same way.

Now, there is no doubt that there is a *great* danger in following Du Bois's interpretative lead. Reid is aware of it; he cautions us about the "elitism" inherent in such a position. In many ways, though, it no longer matters whether one's egalitarian sensibilities are offended by Du Bois's challenge to create a talented tenth. We have come to a point in African-American life in which, whether we think it appropriate or not, a divide exists. William Julius Wilson's works are provocative reminders that a great class chasm has opened up in the life of African-America. Upper- and middle-class blacks are achieving economic, educational, and political success rates that move them further and further away from the economic, educational and political plight of what Wilson calls the black underclass. Indeed, he points out that one of the primary problems in inner-city black communities is that upper- and middle-class blacks have left the inner city for more comfortable living environs. Their "exceptional" abilities and presence once provided stabilizing ethical direction and positive role modeling of educational and economic opportunity. The migration from the cities has opened up vacuums of leadership and hope that have helped create the chaos

24. In ibid., 37.

of catastrophic black on black crime, epidemic drop-out rates, family-shattering teen-age pregnancy, and on and on.[25]

If Wilson is correct and the Du Bois interpretation of Daniel that Reid manufactures is brought to bear, then the interventionist conclusion must be a call for the "talented" upper- and middle-class black community to act as transformative pockets that resist the destructive trend that threatens to consume the black underclass. The "exceptional" status they enjoy, if the Daniel story is to be a guide, is not a celebratory privilege, but a transformative responsibility. As it was for Daniel and his compatriots, it must be used as a tool to teach the white community about its oppressive structures and practices, while simultaneously energizing the black community to resist and overcome them. It is in such a way that the tactical explosion of God's kingdom will break into the human historical moment in which we live like a pocket of transformative resistance.

Though Reid doesn't go this far, it would seem, then, that "talented" blacks have a mission in the inner cities. In this case, perhaps their very presence, certainly their transformative socio-political action, represents tactical kingdom pockets. Here Daniel's words, through Du Bois's manufactured lens, create not only an indicative word of interventionist hope for the oppressed, that their circumstance can and will be transformed, but also an interventionist imperative that the "talented" become one of the mechanisms of that transformation. It is, in other words, their challenge to become pockets that resist the underclass trend of the inner cities, and thereby represent the reign of God breaking into the human urban reality.

This formula only works, of course, if contemporary African-American believers share not only Daniel's context of culture but also the preunderstanding that the text maintains in the midst of that culture. The preunderstanding is decidedly interventionist. God has intervened on behalf of the people in the past; God will intervene ultimately to establish the kingdom in the future. Chapters 7–12 highlight this strategic reality. In the present, though, as the hero stories of chapters 1–6 indicate, the kingdom is tactically realized through the exceptional efforts of exceptional believers. Their effort is directly linked to their interventionist faith.

If one's preunderstanding is that human history cannot be changed by supernatural intervention and/or human activity, then the response to a cultural context like Daniel's might well be either an otherworldly speculation that leads to a this-worldly accommodation or a privatized spirituality that resists any form of

---

25. William Julius Wilson, *The Truly Disadvantaged: The Inner City, the Underclass, and Public Policy* (Chicago and London: University of Chicago Press, 1987) 7–8. Wilson opens with the thesis that even though racism existed in a more overt form in the 1940s, 1950s and 1960s, inner-city black urban communities experienced less social dislocation. He attributes this circumstance to the fact that all classes of blacks were at the time confined by segregationist housing policies to living in the same urban areas. When discriminatory policies eased and housing opportunities opened up enough that middle-class blacks could escape the inner cities, the underclass, he argued, was left isolated. The result is that even though racism, at least in its most overt forms, has been challenged on several fronts, the plight of inner-city blacks has steadily deteriorated. "In the earlier years, the black middle and working classes were confined by restrictive covenants to communities also inhabited by the lower class; their very presence provided stability to inner-city neighborhoods and reinforced and perpetuated mainstream patterns of norms and behavior" (7).

socio-politically energized faith. While the latter occurred in the existentialist thought of Rudolf Bultmann, the so-called "Negro" church of the first half of the twentieth century represents the former.[26] The preunderstanding of the historical apocalypse like Daniel, however, is interventionist. God will intervene strategically; humans can and must represent that intervention tactically. If Daniel's work, and the work of other historical apocalyptic writers like Mark, have a message for the contemporary African-American community, then it lies here, with a call to intervention. It is the demand that those African-Americans who have been blessed to be members of the educationally, financially, and politically talented use their exceptional identity and status to broker transformation for that part of their community that still suffers the extreme pathos of living in a binary world.

---

26. Cf. E. Franklin Frazier, *The Negro Church in America* (New York: Schocken Books, 1974).

14

Corresponding Contexts of Culture

Mark and the Black Church

Black Americans have outlived their usefulness. Their raison d'etre to this society has ceased to be a compelling issue. Once an economic asset, they are now considered an economic drag. The wood is all hewn, the water all drawn, the cotton all picked, and the rails reach from coast to coast. The ditches are all dug, the dishes all put away, and only a few shoes remain to be shined.[1]

I am not going to prove that the African-American context of culture bears a one-to-one correlation with the cultural context in which Mark wrote. I'm not even going to try. The apocalyptic context in which Mark wrote, the particular kind of interventionist preunderstanding that was encoded in his and other historical-apocalyptic, mythological stories is quite foreign to the twentieth-century, scientific frame in which African-Americans now live. And yet, one finds, once one investigates Mark's socio-cultural circumstance, an intriguing correspondence of relationships between the situations in which the principals, Mark's first-century readers and African-American twentieth-century readers, found and find themselves. This contextual correspondence is important because, as I've already argued, it is this context that forms the foundation for the interpretative access of Mark's text. It is the context of colonial oppression.

I spent the first section of this work presenting the data which indicates that Mark wrote to an occupied people whose religious and political destiny lay in foreign, Roman hands. Indeed, it was this sense of colonial occupation that fueled the revolutionary apocalyptic stories that competed with Mark's interventionist Jesus presentation. Mark interpreted the traditions he received about Jesus in the light of this grievous cultural circumstance. I believe it all but certain that his first readers accessed it through the lens of that same circumstance.

---

1. As quoted in William Pannell, *The Coming Race Wars? A Cry for Reconciliation* (Grand Rapids: Zondervan Publishing House, 1993) 49. Quote from Samuel F. Yette, *The Choice: The Issue of Black Survival in America* (Silver Spring, MD: Cottage Books, 1988).

As Tolbert argued in the article I discussed in chapter 13, Jesus' story illumined through such a contextual light was a different story than it would have been under the reading lamp of power and privilege.

The manner in which contemporary communities interpret texts and traditions is, I have argued, similar to the interpretative strategies of Mark and his first readers. If we are trying to bring the text alive, if we are trying to make what will otherwise be a dead letter, a living word, then we still read out of and for our cultural locations. This is certainly the orientation that African-American Christians have always had in regard to the biblical stories. If, then, the context of culture from which we read the Markan materials corresponds to the context in which Mark wrote, we might expect that the living word in the text would breath in a hauntingly similar way.

> The appeal of the biblical story upon the African American religious sensibility is that the Bible was written almost totally within a context of oppression in which images of community and non-community had revolutionary implications for black people's freedom.[2]

Corresponding interpretative locations do not, of course, guarantee corresponding text interpretative conclusions, but they do enable a vantage point on the text that is much more akin to the vantage point of the original readers than a reading from a radically different, or even opposite contextual station. I sense a correspondence between the African-American church and the first-century Markan community precisely because, as the quote which opens this chapter demonstrates, one community was and the other one is occupied and oppressed.

The statistical and documentary evidence of the oppressed and colonial status of African-Americans is staggering. To be sure, it is not the same kind of colonization experienced by Mark's Palestinian readers, but it is colonization nonetheless. In a Princeton Theological Seminary master's thesis, Bruce T. Grady argues that contemporary African-America exists under the duress of a "psychological occupation" that amounts to what Pansye Atkinson calls "internal colonialism." Building from arguments by Atkinson, cultural historian Harold Cruse and Brazilian educator Paulo Freire, Grady argues rather convincingly that colonialism is not controlled solely by territorial criteria. That is to say, it need not be the case for colonialism to exist that a people's land must be invaded and held by an outside force, as was the case in Mark's Roman-dominated Palestine. The essence of colonialism exists instead where a people's institutions are dominated and controlled by interests foreign to the well being of those people themselves. In this case, two peoples can occupy the same territorial space, call that same territorial space home, and yet exist as occupier and occupied, depending on the particular power dynamics between them.

> Internal colonialism occurs when the colonized are part of the same state. From these two terms, one can deduce the meaning of "psycholog-

---

2. Forrest E. Harris, Sr., *Ministry for Social Crisis: Theology and Praxis in the Black Church Tradition* (Macon, GA: Mercer University Press, 1993) 34.

ical occupation." This condition describes the state in which the psyche of a people is mostly controlled by an oppressor who makes necessary distinctions between the oppressor's interests and those of the victim.[3]

Such is the situation that exists in the case of African and European Americans in the United States.

Certainly this is the contextual nemesis that civil rights leaders like Martin Luther King, Jr., spent their lives fighting. King's words render a stirring definition of the reality Grady and his sources call psychological occupation.

> Being a Negro in America means trying to smile when you want to cry. It means trying to hold on to physical life amid psychological death. It means the pain of watching your children grow up with clouds of inferiority in their mental skies. It means having your legs cut off, and then being condemned for being a cripple. It means seeing your mother and father spiritually murdered by the slings and arrows of daily exploitation, and then being hated for being an orphan. Being a Negro in America means listening to suburban politicians talk eloquently against open housing while arguing in the same breath that they are not racists. It means being harried by day and haunted by night by a nagging sense of nobodyness....[4]

To be sure, for the majority of African-Americans, this is not a reality that ended with the transient successes of the Civil Rights movement. Contemporary conditions remain pervasively oppressive. This is why Theodore Walker, Jr., can write that "Our social location in the 1990s, and through the generations of the great African diaspora, is appropriately described in the language of enslavement and oppression."[5] Cornel West is more specific. He describes a three-fold crisis in African America that demonstrates the pervasiveness of the internal colonialism that haunts it. He speaks of the economic crisis that takes the form of unprecedented levels of unemployment, cutbacks of industrial workers, and career ceilings for professionals. There is, second, a political crisis which has developed from the intensifying perception that African-Americans are less important to the increasingly conservative views of a Democratic Party that was once its primary political ally. Finally, there is a spiritual crisis that manifests itself as a distrust among blacks themselves, leading to horrendous rates of

---

3. Bruce T. Grady, "Contemporary Attempts to Improve Education for African Americans within Public Schools and a Proposal from the Black Church Perspective," Princeton Theological Seminary Master's Thesis, Peter J. Paris, Thesis Advisor, 1996. Cf. Pansye Atkinson, *Brown vs. Topeka: An African American's View of Desegregation and Miseducation* (Chicago: African American Images, 1993) and Paulo Freire, *The Politics of Education: Culture, Power and Liberation* (South Hadley, MA: Bergin & Garvey Publishers, Inc., 1985).

4. Martin Luther King, Jr., *Where Do We Go from Here: Chaos or Community?* (New York and London: Harper and Row, 1967) 119–20.

5. Theodore Walker, Jr., *Empower the People: Social Ethics for the African-American Church* (Maryknoll, NY: Orbis Books, 1991) 11.

suicides and homicides.[6] No wonder, then, that many researchers and writers believe that the position of African-Americans in the United States is a precarious one best described by the language of oppressive colonialism. A look at individual areas of social and political concern makes the case an even more alarming one.

I begin with the issue of racism and its societal partner, segregation. The first thing we need is a clear definition of the demon we're dealing with. West's essay, "Toward a Socialist Theory of Racism," is helpful because it makes the necessary separation between racism and capitalism; the latter does not engender the former. West explains quite convincingly that racism pre-dated capitalism. He points to the work of François Bernier, a French physician in 1684, as the foundation for classifying human bodies according to "race," which was, as it remains, primarily determined by skin color. The first racial division of humankind, West continues, was found in the work of the eighteenth-century naturalist, Carolus Linnaeus. His 1735 *Natural System* was, like Bernier's work, racist precisely because it degraded and devalued non-Europeans.[7] The foundational premise of racism, then, is that of European superiority. By itself it is a value judgment, a prejudice. Institutionalized by the force and structure of societal institutions which are primarily overseen by Europeans and European Americans, so that non-Europeans are systematically denied opportunities routinely available to those of European heritage, it becomes racism.

West posits a three-step line of analysis which helps locate and examine racism in contemporary society. At the first level a researcher should inquire into the modes of European domination. That is to say, one should evaluate the ideological discourses which give racism its grisly logic. There are three primary discourses. The first is the false Judeo-Christian one which operates from the biblical account of Ham, who was allegedly cursed with black skin for disrespecting his father's privacy and authority. The second is the pseudo-scientific logic that celebrates Greek culture, heritage and image, while denigrating the images and cultural heritage associated with blacks. The third is the psychosexual racism which simultaneously endows non-European men and women with extraordinary sexual prowess, dirt and bodily smell. These forms of pseudo-religious, scientific, and psychological logic enable and indeed encourage the belief that those of European heritage are the superior breed of humankind.

At the second level of inquiry the researcher should analyze the societal mechanisms that sustain white supremacist discourse. Here statistics of crime, welfare, and issues of fear and terror are narrated against a backdrop that reminds citizens of European background that such communal ills are endemic to the lifestyles and genetic make-up of those of non-European heritage.

Finally, at the third level, the researcher can begin to look at the actual types of European exploitation. Here one can look at racist practices like housing seg-

---

6. Cornel West, *Prophetic Fragments: Illuminations of the Crisis in American Religion & Culture* (Grand Rapids: William B. Eerdmans, 1988) 35.

7. Ibid., 100.

regation to see how they develop from, and subsequently enhance, a systemic view of European superiority and non-European inferiority.[8]

Michael Eric Dyson instructs that the contemporary liberal understanding of racism falters precisely because it does not deal with the institutional quality that West so clearly perceived. Liberal theorists, Dyson argues, attempted to explain racism in terms of the white European immigrant experience. Focusing on the more general category of ethnicity, which includes such broad variables as religion, language, and nationality, these theorists were unable to explain the continuing difficulty of black people in the American cultural circumstance. This is because the problems of integration and cultural assimilation cannot be explained in terms of ethnicity. Race, particularly as it relates to skin color, remains a primary problem, especially in light of the enduring societal preunderstanding that celebrates the superiority of European peoples and their heritage.

> Much of the time, [liberal race theory] cannot explain why blacks have failed to "assimilate" because it has not acknowledged the unique structural character of racism or historical content of racial oppression — slavery, Jim Crow laws, structural unemployment, gentrification of black living space, deeply ingrained institutional racism.[9]

The end result is that racism feeds on itself. It is cannibalistic. The explanation for the problems that blacks experience in societal assimilation can be found in black people themselves, in some inherent defect within their culture, heritage, and genetic code.[10] They should, therefore, be treated differently, which is to say, as if they are inferior.

It is this institutionalized form of racism that accounts for the feeling of psychological occupation experienced by so many African-Americans across so many different generations. Racism, the structural, societally institutionalized form about which West and Dyson speak, has endured through the centuries. Like the cockroach who witnessed the extinction of the dinosaur era and lived to scurry unscathed through the dark corridors of the human epoch, structural racism refuses to be stamped out. Even as humankind has allegedly made the celebrated move into the post-industrial, post-modern era, it has taken pains to pack racism in its bags of progress and haul it along.

Indeed, racism has endured for so long and widened to such a scope in its affliction of African America, that George Kelsey can be forgiven for defining it as a faith.

> Racism is a faith. It is a form of idolatry.... In its early modern beginnings, racism was a justificatory device. It did not emerge as a faith. It arose as an ideological justification for the constellations of political and economic power which were expressed in colonialism and slavery. But

---

8. Ibid., 102–4.

9. Michael Eric Dyson, *Reflecting Black: African-American Cultural Criticism* (Minneapolis and London: University of Minnesota Press, 1993) 137.

10. Ibid.

gradually the idea of the superior race was heightened and deepened in meaning and value so that it pointed beyond the historical structures of relation, in which it emerged, to human existence itself.[11]

Racism has many effects. "The social problems of urban life in the United States are, in large measure, the problems of racial inequality. The rates of crime, drug addiction, out-of-wedlock births, female-headed families, and welfare dependency have risen dramatically in the last several years, and they reflect a noticeably uneven distribution by race.[12] The fact that these social problems are graphically presented without the context of structural racism, enables racism once again to feed off of its own effects. The problem is thought to lie within black people themselves. The perception is exacerbated as politicians, more in pursuit of the power of elective office than the real transformation of systemic societal ills, bait the electoral public with images of non-Europeans, particularly African-Americans, whose sole purpose is the achievement of easy gain at the expense of Euro-America's hard labor and security. No wonder Bernard C. Watson can write in his article for *The State of Black America 1995* that,

> Demagogues, bigots, and political chameleons of both major political parties fan the flames of divisiveness by using code words like "crime in the streets," "welfare mothers," and "quotas." Much of White America has come to equate affirmative action and civil rights with preferential treatment for African-Americans, and has come to believe that "unqualified minorities" are taking jobs, promotions, or seats in college classrooms from "qualified white males."[13]

Perhaps the most visible effect of institutionalized racism in the United States remains the segregated pattern of American housing. Despite the many achievements of the Civil Rights movements of the 1960s and 1970s, America remains a divided country where living patterns are concerned. In his *State of Black America* article, Julius L. Chambers notes that "Twenty-two years after passage of the Fair Housing Act of 1968, housing in the United States continues to be characterized by a high degree of racism and segregation."[14] He points out further that since 1950 the average level of residential segregation between blacks and whites had declined by only seven percent. Does racism play a role? Apparently so. As late as 1987, the Department of Housing and Urban Development estimated that more than two million instances of housing discrimination were occurring every year.[15]

---

11. Quoted in King, 69.
12. Wilson, 20.
13. Bernard C. Watson, "The Demographic Revolution: Diversity in 21st Century America," in *The State of Black America, 1995,* Billy J. Tidwell and Paulette J. Robinson, editors (New York: National Urban League, Inc., 1995) 199.
14. Julius L. Chambers, "Black Americans and the Courts: Has the Clock Been Turned Back Permanently?," in Tidwell and Robinson, editors, 249.
15. Ibid.

Even as African-Americans make progress educationally and economically, the barriers remain in place.

> [T]he creation of predominantly black suburbs for the black middle class will also mean that residential segregation will continue to be a major part of the fabric of American life. In spite of the fair housing laws, most African Americans still cannot live where they want to, even when they can afford it. Instead, the assigned "place" is still a prominent feature of black life in the United States.[16]

Furthermore, since schools are normally populated via housing patterns, the racism that leads to residential segregation cultivates the existence of school segregation that has for decades been the cause of tremendous societal debate and disturbance. Once again, racism finds a way to feed upon and thereby extend itself.

The sense of psychological occupation caused by institutional racism is exacerbated in contemporary American society by the rise of an aggressive and hostile neo-conservatism which targets non-European Americans, and even the poor among its own European ranks, as a deleterious and undesirable drain on the American drive to economic and social excellence. Dyson is one among many authors who have linked the rise of this "new breed of racism" to the legacy of the Reagan presidency. Though covert in form, the new style of racism is just as unyielding and devastating in its effects. And, significantly, since it operates through contemporary political "populism," it is openly accepted by the middle- and upper-class public as a progressive political agenda rather than the reactionary, though subtle, discrimination that it is.

> The weaknesses of populism consist of the worst of the xenophobic and jingoistic tradition of a European settler society: racism, sexism, homophobic, inward and backward-looking, preoccupied with preserving old ways of life, defensive, provincial, and, at times, conspiratorial. This seamy side of populism is grounded in the cultural conservatism of a deeply isolationist people, a conservatism and isolationism reinforced by geographical autonomy, economic prosperity, and cultural insularity. Yet it is this side of populism which looms large in the eyes of Afro-Americans.[17]

Whether in black (Dyson considers it a "cruelly ironic twist" that a forceful number of African-American thinkers and political figures have joined its ranks) or white face, this new breed of racism has generated public policy and law that have "had a devastating impact on black America."

---

16. C. Eric Lincoln and Lawrence H. Mamiya, *The Black Church in the African American Experience* (Durham, NC and London: Duke University Press, 1990) 159. Cf. also Pannell, 35–36 which cites a 1988 *Atlanta Journal-Constitution* report that detailed the extensive discrimination in the banking loan policies and real-estate activities that maintained segregated housing communities.

17. West, 30–31.

The Reagan administration's laissez-faire attitude toward the enforcement of laws and governmental policies that protect minorities and its outright attack on the hard-won rights of America's poor and dispossessed helped set the tone for an almost unmitigated viciousness toward these groups.[18]

One such place where this viciousness can be seen is in the courts of the U.S. legal system. The courts, particularly the U.S. Supreme Court, have traditionally been the ally of the dispossessed in American society. The famous *Brown v. Board of Education, Topeka, Kansas* (1954) is the classic example of the court weighing in with a controversial but just decision that was supported by neither the U.S. Congress nor the majority of the voting American public at the time. Indeed, it was this fierce dependence on the belief that the federal courts would interpret law according to the spirit of equality and justice as proclaimed in the U.S. Constitution that encouraged civil rights leaders in their struggles against American legislation that had become "increasingly the medium of institutionalized racism and of routinized, systemic violence against black people."[19] In his book, *Conjuring Culture: Biblical Formations of Black America,* Theophus H. Smith points out how black Americans employed the legal process as an instrument for not only manumission and emancipation, but also civil rights. It was, effectively, an act of "conjure." Black people used a societal tool (law) whose primary purpose is negative, that is, to restrain and to enforce bondage, and transfigured it into a counter-cultural, transformative force.[20]

In the America of the post-Reagan revolution, however, the law has once again become a tool that enforces codes of discrimination. The "conjure tool" has itself been transformed. Attorney Julius L. Chambers documents a litany of Supreme Court decisions that have made it more difficult for African-Americans to protest or transform discriminatory situations.[21] His conclusion:

> The recent decisions by the Court suggest that: it no longer favors employment discrimination claims; it will require stringent standards for establishing liability of an employer; it will limit the relief available; and it will discourage private attorneys who seek to represent victims of discrimination.[22]

Chambers was not alone in his assessment. The compilation of decisions prompted former Justice Thurgood Marshall to suggest that "the Supreme Court is no longer a friend to civil rights."[23]

The contemporary recipient of the mantle passed on through the Reagan discipleship corps is the species of conservatism that has developed at the knee of

---

18. Dyson, 238–39.
19. Theophus H. Smith, *Conjuring Culture: Biblical Formations of Black America* (New York and Oxford: Oxford University Press, 1994) 95.
20. See ibid., 9.
21. Cf. Chambers, 242–46 for an annotated listing and evaluation of cases.
22. Ibid., 246.
23. Ibid.

the current speaker of the U.S. House of Representatives, Newt Gingrich. As Andrés Tapia accurately reflects,

> Especially worrisome to many blacks is what they perceive as a hostile political and social climate against minorities, including Newt Gingrich's Contract with America. "When Gingrich talks about *normal Americans,* most black folk know he means *white Americans,*" says Bill Pannell, professor of evangelism at Fuller Theological Seminary and author of *The Coming Race Wars?* "The attack on welfare mothers, affirmative action, and other hard-fought-for social programs instills in many a sense that these are perilous times to be black in the U.S.A."[24]

Interestingly enough, at a time when he was fighting an older, more overt form of racism, Martin Luther King, Jr., was prescient enough to recognize that the new breed had already put down its clandestine roots. And though he directed his ire primarily at the white liberal who sustained the racist effects of American society by his or her preference for efficiency over fairness, his words paint a very clear picture of the contemporary neo-conservative circumstance.

> Over the last few years many Negroes have felt that their most troublesome adversary was not the obvious bigot of the Ku Klux Klan or the John Birch Society, but the white liberal who is more devoted to "order" than to justice, who prefers tranquility to equality.[25]

The reason the Contract with America works is that it promises a life of tranquility for middle- and upper-class America at the expense and neglect of those who subsist in the economic ranks beneath them. It is self-service mutated by obsession into the kind of hostile neglect whose effects are so destructive it demands a soothing rationale. In this case, the balm comes in the form of an ingrained belief that those who will be hurt by the harshness of such a contract have brought it upon themselves. This, too, King foresaw. "The danger will be that the problems will be attributed to innate Negro weaknesses and used to justify further neglect and to rationalize continued oppression."[26]

The cannibal continues to feed upon itself, ironically burgeoning rather than diminishing, fueling from its own existence the rationale and the power to breed itself in ever more novel forms. We should be convinced, as King was when he witnessed the form racism took in his time, that we have not seen the last of its metamorphoses. And yet, as William Julius Wilson cautions, we should also refuse to accept racism as the single cause for the problems that plague the African-American context of culture. Other forces just as critical are at play. The most significant of these is socio-economic. Wilson points out

---

24. Andrés Tapia, "Soul Searching: How Is the Black Church Responding to the Urban Crisis," *Christianity Today* 40 (1996) 26.
25. King, 88.
26. Ibid., 109.

that contemporary explanations of social dislocations among the urban, black underclass

> should emphasize the dynamic interplay between ghetto-specific cultural characteristics and social and economic opportunities. This would necessitate taking into account the effects not only of changes in American economic organization but also of demographic changes and changes in the laws and policies of the government as well. In this connection, the relationships between joblessness and family structure, joblessness and other social dislocations (crime, teenage pregnancy, welfare dependency, etc.), and joblessness and social orientation among different age-groups would receive special attention.[27]

Indeed, King had already seen that the fundamental problem in the life of black Americans was the inability to access equal economic opportunity. "At the root of the difficulty in Negro life today is pervasive and persistent economic want. To grow from within, the Negro family — and especially the Negro man — needs only fair opportunity for jobs, education, housing and access to culture."[28] Jobs, though, particularly for blacks living in urban areas where some sixty percent of the country's poor African-Americans live,[29] are difficult to find. Wilson points to two structural economic changes that have occurred recently. Both have severely impacted the financial position of urban African-Americans. The first is the shift from goods-producing to service-producing industries. The second consists of the polarization of the labor market into low-wage and high-wage sectors, the innovations in technology, and the relocation of manufacturing jobs out of the cities.[30]

The impact of these structural changes is either under- or unemployment. The underemployed are those who work the service jobs which increasingly do not pay enough to support a family. Even with both parents employed, these families fall within the category of the so-called "working poor." A June 1996 report by the Annie E. Casey Foundation, a Baltimore-based charitable organization that focuses on disadvantaged children, found that one-third of all America's poor children, or about 5.6 million, are members of such "working poor," two-parent families.[31] Still, though the service jobs such parents work are the lowest paying, mostly minimum wage, they are increasingly the only employment opportunities left for urban African-Americans. In her 1995 contribution to the Urban League's *State of Black America,* Marian Wright Edelman pointed out that 1989's federal minimum wage of $3.35 an hour had not been raised to compensate for inflation since 1981.

27. Wilson, 18.
28. King, 108.
29. Cf. Pannell, 32–33.
30. Wilson, 142.
31. Associated Press Wire Reports, 3-Jun-1996 EDT. REF5150.

This wage stagnation has had a dramatic impact on a family's ability to provide for itself. Full-time, year-round work at the minimum wage now [1989] yields annual earnings that are less than 70 percent of what is needed to lift a family of three out of poverty ($9,690) and less than 60 percent of what is needed to lift a family of four out of poverty ($11,650).[32]

The impact on African-Americans: In 1986 more than 600,000 young black families, "nearly one-half (46 percent) of all young black families in America," were poor.[33]

While time has marched forward since Edelman's remarks, the plight of African-Americans has not. On August 20, 1996, Bill Clinton signed legislation that raised the minimum wage to $5.15, the first increase since its elevation to $4.25 in April 1991. The increase was incremental. On October 1, 1996, it moved to $4.75; it reached its current high on September 1, 1997. While the 90 cents increase earned workers an additional $1,800 annual income, it was not enough to significantly alter the grim report Edelman had chronicled in 1989. A single wage earner working 40 hours per week, 52 weeks a year at the present minimum wage ($5.15) would earn $10,712. The poverty threshold for a family of two is $10,360. For a family of four it is $15,600. A U.S. News Online report calculated that even with the additional support of food stamps and earned-income tax credits such a worker would barely clear the four person family poverty threshold by realizing a $16,000 annual income.[34] The impact on African-Americans: According to the figures of the U.S. Census Bureau, in 1996, 2.1 million, or 26.4 percent of ALL African-American families were poor.[35]

The primary weapon against poverty is employment. But black unemployment rates remain dangerously elevated. As of 1996, while the overall rate was 5.9 percent for persons over 16 years of age, among blacks it was almost double that at 11.6 percent. The figures for African-American males rose even higher to 14.2 percent, almost three times the 5.1 percent unemployment among their white counterparts.[36] The numbers are particularly devastating for the youngest

32. Marian Wright Edelman, "Black Children in America," in Tidwell and Robinson, 73.
33. Ibid., 74.
34. U.S. News Online, "Raise the Minimum Wage?" 4/29/96. Internet Address: http://www.usnews.com/usnews/ISSUE/WAGE.HTM.
35. U.S. Bureau of the Census, "Selected Economic Characteristics of Persons and Families, by Sex and Race: March 1996." Internet Release Date: June 26, 1997. Internet Address: http://www.census.gov/population/socdemo/race/black/tabs96/tab02-96.txt. Also see Claudette Bennett, "The Black Population in the United States: March 1996 (Update)," U.S. Bureau of the Census Current Population Reports. Internet Address: http://www.census.gov/prod/2/pop/p20/p20-498.pdf. For information on poverty thresholds see, "Federal Poverty Guidelines," Federal Register Highlights, March 4, 1996. Internet Address: http://mass.iog.wayne.edu/FR/fr960304.htm and "Poverty Thresholds: 1996," U.S. Bureau of the Census. Internet Address: http://www.census.gov/hhes/poverty/poverty96/pu96thrs.html.
36. U.S. Bureau of the Census, "Selected Economic Characteristics of Persons and Families, by Sex and Race: March 1996." Internet Release Date: June 26, 1997. Internet Address: http://www.census.gov/population/socdemo/race/black/tabs96/tab02-96.txt.

African-American males. In 1996, 36.9 percent of 16–19-year-olds were unemployed. And the 19.2 percent figure for 20–24-year-olds is more than triple the national unemployment figure.[37] Many black males are simply not educationally qualified for the high technology jobs that are opening. And with the movement of industry out of the urban areas, when jobs which they often can perform and have historically performed do open, they are out of geographical range.[38]

The employment picture for African-American females, though better, is still a great cause for societal concern. Their 9.2 percent figure is more than double the 3.9 percent unemployment of white females.[39] And when jobs are secured, institutional discrimination persists. Even though black women in two-income families are responsible for 50 percent of the family income, black women in the mid-1980s earned only 78 percent of black men's weekly wages, and only 53 percent of white men's weekly income. In 1996, while the median income of black women 18 years and older with high school and college degrees was $11,011 and $24,030 respectively, comparable median incomes for black male high school and college graduates was $16,580 and $30,170 respectively. Where white males are concerned the gap broadens almost as appreciably as it had a decade earlier. The median income of a white male high school graduate, $22,319 almost equals the earning power of the black female college graduate! The $38,489 median income of the white male college graduate means that a black female earns at only 62 percent of his societal standard.[40] And despite the fact that their share of the family economic load is greater than that of white women (50% as compared to 35%), black women

> do considerably less well than white women: they have considerably less total income and wealth, even when their labor earnings are similar; their unemployment rates are two-and-a-half times that of their white counterparts; and they must work longer hours in order to achieve earnings parity with white women. Finally, the gains of African-American women have been limited to certain sectors of the economy. Research indicates that 80 percent of professional black women work for either the government (federal, state, or local) or the nonprofit sector. Even the most skilled of African-American women have been locked out of the private, for-profit sector.[41]

The consequences of this employment picture are devastating for African-American children. Dyson records that in 1993 fully one-third of all black

---

37. Bureau of Labor Statistics, "Civilian labor force 16–19 yrs. Black Male." Also "Civilian labor force 20–24 yrs. Black Male." Both tables found at Internet Address: http://146.142.4.24/cgi-bin/surveymost?1f.

38. Ibid., 41–45, and Hugh B. Price, "Black America, 1994: An Overview," in Tidwell and Robinson, 1.

39. Bureau of Labor Statistics, 41–45.

40. U.S. Bureau of the Census, "Income by Educational Attainment for Persons 18 Years Old and Over, by Age, Sex, Race, and Hispanic Origin: March 1996." Internet Address: http://www.census.gov/prod/2/pop/p20/p20-493.pdf.

41. Lynn Burbridge, "Toward Economic Self-Sufficiency: Independence Without Poverty," in Tidwell and Robinson, 120.

Americans lived below the poverty line. "For black children under six, the poverty rate is a record high 51.1 percent."[42] The effect is devastating.

> Although many factors put children at risk, nothing predicts bad outcomes for a kid more powerfully than growing up poor. Study after disheartening study confirm the links between living in poverty and suffering a host of lousy developmental, educational, and adult outcomes. Poor children are more likely to be sick and underweight as toddlers; they are less likely to be ready for kindergarten; they are more likely to fall behind as grade-schoolers; they face a much higher prospect of dropping out of high school; they are more likely to become teen parents; they face far greater odds of being either a victim or a perpetrator of crime; and they are far less likely to be economically successful as adults.[43]

No wonder there is difficulty in raising the educational achievement levels of many urban African-Americans. Not only must these children deal with the institutional racism that expresses itself in segregated schools with significantly smaller per-pupil expenditures and fewer educational resources than their white and more affluent African-American peers, but they must do so out of a context of subsistence living. "When these African-American children enter school, they will be unprepared for success."[44]

The problems these economic statistics cause are manifold. Chief among them is the havoc wreaked upon the black family. Wilson notes the public sentiment that the primary nemesis of the black family has been and is the welfare state. He points out, however, that there is little evidence to support such an argument. While it does have a modest effect on separation and divorce, particularly among white women, its total effect on the proportion of all female householders is small.[45] "By contrast, the evidence for the influence of joblessness on family structure is much more conclusive."[46] Further research demonstrates that while the rise in rates of separation and divorce among whites was connected mainly to the increased economic independence of white women, the decline in intact African-American marriages was associated most significantly with the declining economic status of black men.[47]

This economic condition has led to a reality where too many African-American families are led by women. Lynn Burbridge reports that since 1940 black female-headed households have increased by 140 percent. In 1989 almost 44 percent of black families were headed by a woman with no husband present.[48]

---

42. Dyson, 238.

43. The Annie E. Casey Foundation, "1996 KIDS COUNT Overview," p. 1. Internet Address: http://www.aecf.org/kc1996/overview.htm.

44. Shirley M. McBay, "The Condition of African-American Education: Changes and Challenges," in Tidwell and Robinson, 32.

45. Wilson, 145.

46. Ibid. See also Burbridge, 120: "Statistical studies have consistently found a relationship between male joblessness or low wages on marital dissolutions or nonmarriage."

47. Wilson, 145.

48. Burbridge, 123. Cf. also Wilson, 21.

In 1996 that number increased to 46.8 percent.[49] The difficulty here lies not with the family leadership skills of African-American women, which have been proven factors in the survival of the race during and beyond the history of en-slavement and segregation. The difficulty lies in the fact that families led by black women will in all probability be poor. "Even if a female householder is employed full time, her earnings are usually substantially less than that of a male worker and are not likely to be supplemented with income from a second full-time employed member of the household."[50] Wilson notes further that of all American families in 1983, of the almost four million that reported incomes of less than $5,000, 57 percent were headed by women. The 1996 accounting that 45.1 percent of black female-headed households is poor, while tragic, is no longer surprising.[51] And yet, it is still a frightening social narrative. Almost half of all black families are headed by a single woman (46.8%). And almost half of those families is poor.

The condition of the African-American male is, if it is imaginable, even worse. Even a summary accounting of the statistics makes it clear that pundits who refer to the African-American male as an "endangered species" are no longer speaking only in hyperbole. It is now quite conceivable that the light which this part of the species contributes to the brightening of the human condition is in danger of being extinguished forever. Already, black males are expected to live ten fewer years than their white counterparts. As of 1985 the life expectancy of the white male was almost 75 years; for the black male it was 65. Between the ages of 15 and 34 the primary cause of death for these black males was homicide. One out of every 21 African-American males will be murdered, most at the hands of another African-American male. Quoting Earl Hutchinson, the author of *The Mugging of Black America,* W. Franklyn Richardson writes in his 1994 *State of Black America* article that "A staggering 44,428 black males were murdered between 1980 and 1985 — nearly equal the total number of Americans killed during the entire Vietnam conflict."[52]

The external threat to the life of the black male is almost equalled by a horrendous internal threat that no doubt is fueled by the tensions of living poor, jobless, and uneducated in the land of American prosperity. Between the ages of 18 and 29, the leading cause of death for the black male is suicide. Overall, suicide now ranks as the third leading cause of death for black male teenagers and young adults. Adding to this gruesome scenario are the prison statistics for African-American males. It appears that their rate of unemployment is exceeded only by their rate of imprisonment. While all African-Americans make up only 12 percent of the American population, they make up 48 percent of

49. U.S. Bureau of the Census, "Selected Social Characteristics of the Population, by Sex, Region, and Race: March 1996." Internet Release Date, June 26, 1997. Internet Address: http://www.census.gov/population/socdemo/race/black/tabs96/tab01.96.txt.

50. Wilson, 27.

51. U.S. Bureau of the Census, "Selected Characteristics of the Population Below the Poverty Level in 1995, by Region and Race." Internet Release Date: June 26, 1997. Internet Address: http://www.census.gov/population/socdemo/race/black/tabs96/tab15-96.txt.

52. W. Franklyn Richardson, "Mission to Mandate: Self-Development through the Black Church," in Billy J. Tidwell, editor, *The State of Black America 1994,* 114.

the nation's prison population, with black males accounting for 89 percent of that figure.[53] These and other statistics like them offer a chilling picture of what life in the future, if allowed to proceed on its present course, will be like for African-American males. "According to [Jawanza] Kunjufu, by the year 2000, 70 percent of all African-American males between the ages of 17 and 44 will be in gangs, jail, unemployed, murdered (one out of 20 black boys born in the U.S. today will be killed by his twenty-first birthday), on drugs, or have AIDS."[54]

Wilson records some of the same statistics. His report is helpful because it also initiates an explanation. Looking at the city of Chicago, he notes that the homicide rates varied significantly according to the economic status of a community, "with the highest rates of violent crime associated with the communities of the underclass."[55] He uses the largest public housing project in the city, Robert Taylor Homes, as a graphic illustration. A complex of twenty-eight sixteen-story buildings, it sits on ninety-two acres of land. Though its official 1980 population was 20,000, it was estimated that an additional 5,000 to 7,000 occupied the grounds as unofficial residents. The median family income for its black households was $5,470, and 93 percent of the families were headed by a single parent. Robert Taylor Homes comprised only 0.5 percent of Chicago's 3 million population. And yet, it accounted for 11 percent of the city's homicides, 9 percent of its rapes, and 10 percent of its aggravated assaults.[56] Though other factors were certainly involved, the powerlessness of the economic situation was no doubt a primary factor of such widespread violence.

Pannell, for one, is convinced that "powerlessness is the source of violence among any people."[57] I would agree. Violence brings with it an aura, false though it may be, of control for those who are denied expressions of power through other, more communally sanctioned means. In the moment that a black male strikes out he is attempting to manipulate his environment, an environment that other forces wield against him. There is the mistaken sense that in lashing out violently such control has been achieved, that respect has been attained.

The real power brokers in society see such violence as meaningless and unprovoked, refusing to recognize institutional motivations like racism or poverty. The result is that once again racism becomes an operational force feeding upon itself. European Americans, convinced that there is no other cause for such behavior, attribute the violence to the genetic make-up of the African-American male. They can thereby celebrate the unusual ones who have progressed beyond their "natural" destructive tendencies. Simultaneously, they can reject any public effort of social transformation as an expensive, guaranteed-to-fail waste of government effort and taxpayer resource, since the difficulty lies in the people rather than the conditions impressed upon them.

Given the prevalent racism and the horrific economic plight facing most ur-

---

53. Statistics compiled from Dyson, 90, 184.
54. Tapia, 27. Kunjufu is the author of *Countering the Conspiracy to Destroy Black Boys* (Chicago: African American Images, 1995).
55. Wilson, 25.
56. Ibid.
57. Pannell, 87.

ban African-Americans, one can see why many adopt a view that transformative intervention is impossible. Those outside will not undertake it; those inside, lacking the necessary skills and levels of education, cannot. Education would be one avenue for change. It would create a community skilled in the abilities required in the contemporary job market, assuming, of course, institutionalized racism would allow equal opportunity for equally trained applicants. It does not. Edelman notes that, "a black college graduate faces about the same odds of unemployment as a white high school graduate who never attended college."[58] If employment is secured, racism has no less an effect. In her report, Shirley McBay adds that African-American men, regardless of high school or college education, continue to earn only about 75 percent of what white men earn.[59] Economic constraints hamper progressive possibilities well before the achievement of a college education. Levels of poverty encourage educational failure. Edelman observes further that regardless of race, youths from poor families are three to four times more likely to drop out of school than those from affluent families.[60] Given the already reported poverty levels of African-Americans, one is no longer surprised at the disturbing drop-out rates they experience.[61]

When these economic statistics are combined with the continued prevalence of racism, there can be no doubt that the plight of African-Americans is a difficult one indeed. Federal programs like Head Start, which Edelman and others contend have demonstrated their worth, have never been funded in a way that would help all of the children who need its services.[62] Programs that provide loans and other financial incentives to furthering an education are being cut rather than strengthened. There is no doubt that without them it is impossible for many African-Americans to generate hope of a college education. "A major determinant of college enrollment and graduation of African Americans is the availability of financial aid. Given the median family income of African Americans [$25,970 in 1995], it is not surprising that these families require substantial financial assistance to enable their children to attend college."[63] The cumulative result of such cuts and lack of economic and political interventions is the growing feeling of powerlessness that contributes to the violence and hopelessness that progressively debilitates the urban African-American community.

Given such statistical circumstances, one wonders what apocalyptic message Mark might have said to the community plagued by them. "Go Suffer!" hardly seems to be an appropriate living word, as, I think, it hardly would have seemed

---

58. Edelman, 72.

59. McBay, 33–34. According to 1996 Census reports the figures remain constant. Male African-American high school graduates earn 74 percent of their white male counterparts. Male African-American college graduates earn only about 78 percent of their white counterparts. (U.S. Bureau of the Census, "Selected Social Characteristics of the Population, by Sex, Region, and Race: March 1996." Internet Address: http://www.census.gov/population/socdemo/race/black/tabs96/tab01-96.txt.

60. Edelman, 81.

61. For statistics on the drop-out rates of African-Americans and their connections to income levels, cf. McBay and Edelman.

62. Edelman, 81.

63. McBay, 37. 1995 figure comes from U.S. Bureau of the Census, "The Black Population in the U.S.: March 1996." Internet Address: http://www.census.gov/Press-Release/cb97-105.html.

appropriate, or necessary, to the communal circumstance of his first-century reading audience. Indeed, both communities already suffered extensively. And, clearly, at least in the case of the black community, suffering need not, and, more often than not, does not have redemptive value. "Black Christian eschatology focuses on praxis against suffering, not reflection upon it; personal and collective resistance to suffering, not a distancing from it. And ultimately, with the aid of divine intervention, suffering is overcome."[64]

Suffering in the black community compounds the despair that already exists. Suffering adds to the debilitating spiritual ethos that helps shatter hopes for economic and racial intervention. Suffering is a prison camp one escapes, not a spiritual enclave one covets. Only a people who do not suffer, who live in the relative security that protects them from suffering, can access suffering into one's life as a desirable presence that should be romanced. From the middle- and upper-middle class Euro- and even in many cases African-American contexts of culture, suffering is reasonably understood as a kind of call that emulates the cross-bearing act of Jesus in a redemptive manner.

Given my sociolinguistic look at Mark's Gospel from the perspective of the kingdom symbol, I would argue that, though suffering is inevitable due to Jesus' transformative activity, it is not the *goal* of Jesus' kingdom ministry, nor the calling of those who would follow him. Instead, the cross is the inevitable result of the transformative behavior that Mark's Jesus story demands. The cross occurs when people preach with an interventionist agenda. Who better to receive such a cross call than a people who live in circumstances of suffering? Who better to call than a people who without intervention are doomed? Who better to call than the contemporary African-American community?

Mark's kingdom message makes sense here precisely because it was crafted for the suffering community that will continue suffering unless there is a substantial and sustained pocket moment of intervention. Mark's message is that we can be the bearers of that transformative kingdom power. We can represent the strategic kingdom in the present moment. We can be present pockets of future resistance. In such a context, the message that I believe made the most sociolinguistic sense in Mark's first-century reading audience makes the most sense in the twentieth and twenty-first century African-American audience. The message is: Go Preach!

---

64. West, 165.

15

Toward a Corresponding Preunderstanding

Intervention

To be sure, the litany of current sociological detail I included in the preceding chapter is unusual for an exegetical work. After all, biblical exegesis is about the biblical period and should, if it is to remain "true" biblical theology, segregate itself from the unsavory character of contemporary contextual concern. The reader of a biblical work is allegedly interested in what the biblical text says and how its saying it related to the contextual circumstance of the first-century audience to which it was written. My entire effort has been waged in the interest of demonstrating that such "purity" of investigation does not exist, and would not be desirable if it did. Such an effort would produce a dead text which had little if any meaning for the lives of people searching it in their present context. In order for the text to live it must have power and meaning to address prevailing issues and concerns. The old traditions and texts, in other words, must be renewed. A sociolinguistic investigation of the biblical material both describes and encourages such a process. It describes, through the lens of the contemporary interpreter's reading perspective, how the first-century biblical authors and readers accessed the traditions and text through their own contextual lenses. And it encourages that contemporary interpreter to renew the first-century meaning access with a specific twentieth-century emphasis. The emphasis that most concerns me is that of the African-American church.

I emphasize first and foremost that if Mark's kingdom message is to impact the world that the African-American church serves, then that message must reflect that church's contextual origins. Biblical and theological thought that comes from the African-American church should access the kingdom symbol through the "colonial" culture in which the majority of African-Americans still find themselves. Otherwise, it is not only a dead letter, it is a homicidal one that draws those who hear it into the grave with it. It disappoints and disinterests; it spiritualizes and stupefies. It talks about the power of God without empowering God's struggling people to act transformatively.

Forrest Harris points to a duality in the life of the African-American church. Two interrelated but also competing traditions exist within the same body. The survival tradition leans toward self-affirmation, internal spiritual freedom, and social accommodation. The liberation tradition proclaims self-help and self-reliance, and demands interior and exterior freedom, moral resistance, and the social conflict necessary to acquire them.[1] The church is its healthiest when there is an ongoing dialogue between these, when the two poles serve to complement, extend, and critique one another. I am convinced, however, that unless biblical interpretation develops out of an intimate awareness of the context in which its community lives, particularly if that community is an oppressive one, the liberative components of the meaning potential will be overlooked, if not dismissed. The result, particularly where the kingdom of God language is concerned, is an other-worldly looking church that waits passively for God to intervene and change the great injustices that plague its communal members. The belief that humans can tactically participate in that transformation is lost. Perhaps this is why Harris warns that the difficulty the African-American church often experiences in the doing of social ministry is "the failure to ground theological reflection in contextual thinking."[2]

A church that does not operate biblically from its own context is not a church that operates in an objective, historical manner; it is a church that adopts the contextual perspective of some other interpretative community as though that community were the sole gatekeeper to "accurate" biblical exegesis. When the African-American church interprets the biblical material from the Euro-American, middle- to upper-middle-class, historical-critical perspective, it not only becomes passive and other-worldly in its kingdom understanding; it becomes a white church with a black facade, regurgitating the biblical text instead of interpreting it.

> [A]ll theological thought arises out of contextual experiences in which people struggle to know the meaning of their humanity. Failure to perceive that the black church's theological thought arises out of the contextual experiences of the black community, and not vice versa, results in distortions of church's ecclesial life.[3]

Harris is convinced that when the African-American church has properly grounded its biblical interpretation in its contexts of culture and situation, it will understand itself and its membership to be about the business of trespassing oppressive social boundaries.

> Praxis, as understood in the context of the black Christian tradition, suggests that black church ecclesiology be grounded in concepts of the reign of God, that is, relationality and community. This concept challenges black

---

1. Forrest E. Harris, Sr., *Ministry for Social Crisis: Theology and Praxis in the Black Church Tradition* (Macon, GA: Mercer University Press, 1993) 22.
2. Ibid., 57.
3. Ibid.

Christians to be agents of social justice and human liberation. . . . The black church reality participates in the vision of the reign of God.[4]

In my language this means that the African-American church would no longer understand itself to be waiting for God to intervene with the kingdom, but would sense its calling to intervene tactically as pockets of resistance that deploy God's future transformative power in the present moment.

But there is no guarantee that interpreting out of the oppressive context in which African-Americans find themselves will lead to a meaning access of the kingdom language that is liberation oriented. Indeed, as I have already mentioned, much has been made of the so-called "Negro Church" of the pre-Civil rights, segregation-era United States. Interpreting the biblical text out of this egregious set of circumstances, the Negro Church operated with an interpretative agenda that saw the transformative reality of the kingdom as an otherworldly phenomenon. Its power would usher in with the future, supernatural intervention of God and God's messiah. However, in this world the Negro Church counseled its members to wait patiently and passively; spiritual transformation and personal redemption were promoted instead. Its orientation was, in Harris's terminology, survivalist.

In my book, *Cultural Interpretation: Reorienting New Testament Criticism,* I argued that the preunderstanding of the Negro Church determined its response to its cultural context.[5] The preunderstanding of the church was that social evil was a fated given that could not be changed by human effort. Only the in-breaking of God's consummate kingdom would bring about the transformation of justice that the Negro parishioner and pastor sought. The only hope for change was otherworldly. Given the dual realization that humans could not usher in that consummate kingdom, and that no other force could transform the social evils of this world, the faithful had but one avenue of action. While waiting for the Lord to act, they would have to do what they could; they would have to survive. They would focus their transformative efforts on the private, spiritual lives of their followers. Here the church could make a difference. Here, in the personal arena, was therefore where the church made its stand and expended its resources. The Negro Church's tacit accommodation to the segregationist United States of the pre-Civil Rights era was, then, directly related to the preunderstanding it maintained within its context of culture. As such, it was preunderstanding that was in direct opposition to the interventionist preunderstanding characterized by the Jesus of Mark's Gospel.

The contemporary African-American context of culture, as the preceding chapter documents, is an oppressive one. Transformation is required. But churches will only engage in transformative actions if they operate from the preunderstanding that energized the "black church" of the Civil Rights era. Contextual interpretation is not enough. We must not only counsel an interpretative process that emulates Mark's interpretative strategy; we must encourage

---

4. Ibid., 58.
5. Blount, *Cultural Interpretation,* 78–79.

an emulation of his interventionist preunderstanding. We must encourage the African-American church to "be like Mark." Correspondence must occur not only at the contextual level, but also at the level of preunderstanding. Not only must the African-American church read its traditions and texts in the light of its colonial context of culture; it must do so with the preunderstanding that humans can, through their preaching activity, tactically usher in the kingdom of God. It is only with such a preunderstanding that the African-American church will feel compelled and enabled to sow future pockets of present resistance.

Mark's preunderstanding was that the world can be transformed. It had been transformed, in the Exodus event. It will be transformed, in the coming of the Son of man on the clouds of heaven. It is being transformed in the kingdom preaching ministry of Jesus. The fact *that* God intervened and *that* God will intervene is what drives the narrative. It is also what drives Mark's discipleship call to Go Preach!, despite the fact that such transformative activity will likely cost the disciples their lives. Why? First, it's worth the cost. Their preaching is the only way to participate in God's strategic transformation that has already begun in their activity. Kingdom preaching is the only way to participate tactically in what God is doing strategically. Given their context of culture, the goal of transformation is worth the price many of the kingdom preachers will have to pay to achieve it. Second, there will be vindication. The suffering, the cross, is not the end. The one who participates in kingdom preaching can be assured that this way is truly God's way. The apocalyptic moments of Jesus' baptism, transfiguration, and resurrection prove it.

The question now is, does the contemporary African-American church, whose context of culture corresponds to Mark's in so many ways, share Mark's preunderstanding? My answer would be no. To be sure, it is not the accommodationist preunderstanding that resulted from the Negro church's belief that social evil was a fated given that could not be transformed in the present. It is more sophisticated. It is the intentional preunderstanding John Shea advocates. The African-American church, though it does not share the cultural context of mainstream Euro-American churches, has nevertheless adopted their intentional preunderstanding. The focus is no longer on the fact *that* God did intervene, will intervene, and somehow, therefore, does intervene, but instead on *the reason why* God should intervene. The emphasis is on moral implications that arise from the realization that God would be angry with the cultural context of contemporary African-Americans. Given this divine disfavor, humans should likewise be chagrined. Humans should therefore act. The sense of urgency that comes with the interventionist perspective is lost. The sense of a future bearing down upon and thereby firing up the pace of transformative behavior in the present is lost. The belief that what God will do in the future is now being done in the present, through the preaching activity of those who follow Jesus, is lost. Indeed, in the intentional perspective, that future is far off, at the end of history, if, even, it is really the future at all. By contrast, in the interventionist perspective it is an imminent reality that demands urgent action in the contemporary human circumstance. Having lost the tangible belief that God will intervene in a strategic way, humans no longer feel the same pressure to represent that strategic activity tactically. The result is that too many African-American churches now proclaim the *why* of salvation; too few preach the *that* of the kingdom.

Historically, however, this has not been the case. Both the Christian belief of the slaves and that of the Civil Rights-era black church operated from an interventionist preunderstanding.[6] The more recent phenomenon of the Civil Rights era black church is instructive. As Peter Paris notes, its cultural context has been its window on the biblical text. And it has tended to peer through that window with an interventionist preunderstanding. "[T]he black churches have always had a profound concern for the bitter and painful realities of black existence in America as well as an abiding hope in a bright and radiant future (eschaton) free from any form of racial injustice."[7] Its belief *that* God has, will, and does intervene is the spark that has ignited its generations of socio-political activism.

> When we African-Americans conceive of ourselves across generations sufficient to include this churchly heritage, we cannot fail to think in terms of radical and revolutionary struggle. To be sure, Gayraud S. Wilmore's classic work *Black Religion and Black Radicalism: An Interpretation of the Religious History of Afro-American People* teaches us that, throughout our history, African-American churches and religions have been a relentless source of "radical thrusts" for liberation. Moreover, we cannot fail to remember that the civil rights movement and the black power movement were virtually born in our churches. The history of African-American churches must be told in the language of radical and revolutionary struggle for religious and secular liberty.[8]

When Cornel West speaks about the black church, he defines it as

> a shorthand rubric that refers to black Christian communities of various denominations that came into being when African-American slaves decided, often at the risk of life and limb, to "make Jesus their choice" and to share with one another their common Christian sense of purpose and Christian understanding of their circumstances.[9]

6. Ibid., 55–71, 78–79 for discussion about the preunderstanding in the Negro Spirituals and slave sermons.

7. Peter J. Paris, *The Social Teaching of the Black Churches* (Philadelphia: Fortress Press, 1985) 2.

8. Theodore Walker, Jr., *Empower the People: Social Ethics for the African-American Church* (Maryknoll, NY: Orbis Books, 1991) 9. Cf. also Harris, 36–37. Harris also notes that "the black Christian story is a shared experience of survival and the quest for liberation" (36). But it is clear that in the hermeneutics of the black church of the Civil Rights and post-Civil Rights era an interventionist preunderstanding has resulted in a preference for an emphasis on liberation. Harris delineates five basic convictions of the black Christian hermeneutic: (1) The God of the Bible liberates and acts historically in real events of oppression. (This is an essentially interventionist understanding.) (2) God has been active in the history of African-Americans' struggle for freedom. (3) God calls and invites the oppressed to participate in the inner and outer realities of divine freedom and justice. (4) The black church is called to embody and respond to God's freedom. (5) God's liberating Word of freedom moves through concrete praxis (37). Clearly, the last two points emphasize the role of the disciple in participating tactically in God's strategic act of intervention.

9. West, 4.

To be sure, there is a consensus of culturally conditioned belief that seems to apply to every church tradition within the African-American experience. Peter Paris has referred to it as the "black Christian tradition."[10] It is this tradition whose commonality both distinguishes them from other American Christian entities and gives a sense of linkage and identity with other churches that have endured the oppressive cultural context that plagues African-Americans. This "tradition" is so significantly shared by churches of disparate geographical and temporal locales that observers can legitimately speak of these individual entities as though they were members of a single church.

In their work, *Soul Theology: The Heart of American Black Culture,* Henry Mitchell and Nicholas C. Cooper-Lewter point out that the commonality exists because all churches in the African-American experience have tended to operate biblically and theologically out of that experience. Unlike traditional Western forms of Christendom which have tended to begin from a corpus of doctrinal assumptions and then reason deductively from them, African-American Christians have tended to reason inductively. That is to say, they have operated primarily from experience. Experience became the criterion of meaning, even when that meaning was biblical. In other words, biblical images and the meaning garnered from them were refracted through the cultural condition of enslavement and oppression. It was only then that they became meaningful in the lives of American Christians of African descent.

Their experience led them in a particular symbolic direction. Imprisoned within a culture that treated them as unequal and inferior, African-American Christians grabbed hold of the biblical emphasis on God's universal role as divine parent. This means, of course, that God is not the parent of some elements of the human race, but that God is parent to all human beings, regardless of racial identity. "The black churches have always discerned this doctrine to be the bedrock of the biblical perspective on humanity, and they have given prominence to biblical passages that make it unequivocally clear."[11]

They have also given prominence to the key implication that develops out of this primary principle. If, indeed, God is the divine parent of all, then all races must be of the same family. This kinship denies the basic premise of racism, that the different races are of different origin, and, that, therefore, some are inferior. The linkage to the same divine parent gives all races an equal standing before God that demands an equal standing before each other. This indicative understanding must, if God's kingdom reality is to have a tactical expression in the human arena, become the imperative calling of the African-American church.

Because this socio-political imperative is based upon a theological principle, spirituality and politics necessarily mix in this tradition. The spiritual reality of

---

10. Cf. Peter J. Paris, "The Bible and the Black Churches," in *The Bible and Social Reform,* Ernest R. Sandeen, editor (Philadelphia and Chico, CA: Fortress Press and Scholars Press, 1982) 134, and *The Social Teaching of the Black Churches* (Philadelphia: Fortress Press, 1985) 10. Also Henry H. Mitchell and Nicholas C. Cooper-Lewter, *Soul Theology: The Heart of American Black Culture* (San Francisco: Harper and Row, 1986) 3–13, chapters 8 and 10. These authors use the terminology "core belief," but in the end, I believe, refer to the same kind of common tradition that links black churches together.

11. Paris, "The Bible and the Black Churches," 135.

God's divine parentage demands a historical realization of racial equality that, given the circumstances of African-American life, cannot come about unless African-American Christians involve themselves in socio-political activism.

> Finally, it is politically significant that the black Christian tradition justifies all action that is in opposition to racism insofar as its quality is commensurate with its goal, that is, affirming and establishing the equality of all persons under God. In other words, means and ends must be integrally related.[12]

Given the historico-political institutionalization of racism in America, the means must necessarily be socio-political. In the black church tradition, then, the spiritual and the political are completely intertwined. The African-American church represents the strategic reality of the kingdom of God in the way that it operates socio-politically to break down the boundaries that institutionalize racism and its communal effects.

It is a socio-political representation that began with slavery. In a sense, African-American Christianity is the very embodiment of its most prominent socio-political activity. It not only broke boundaries, it was itself the very representation of boundary trespass. It existed because African traditions broke through and overwhelmed the traditional outlines of European-American Christianity. The synthetic result was a Christian tradition unlike anything that existed before.

> The African-American Christianity that developed was neither a dark version of the Christianity preached by slaveholders nor a continuation of African religion disguised as Christianity. The story of the emergence of African-American Christianity is a story of an emergent African-American culture as well as of residual African cultures, a story of innovation as well as of tradition, a story of change as well as of continuity.[13]

Because of initial slave resistance to the Christian tradition and the fear among slaveholders that baptism would mandate manumission, the earliest slaves, like those recently transplanted, held on to their African traditions and beliefs.[14] It was not until the period of the Great Awakening, beginning in the 1740s, that the slaves were evangelized; by this time the new faith met a people entrenched in their own spiritual heritage and traditions. The result was

---

12. Paris, *The Social Teaching of the Black Churches,* 16.

13. Charles Joyner, " 'Believer I Know': The Emergence of African-American Christianity," in *African-American Christianity,* Paul E. Johnson, editor (Berkeley: University of California Press, 1994) 19.

14. Cf. Paris, "The Public Role of the Black Churches," 43; Lincoln and Mamiya, 200; Albert J. Raboteau, "African-Americans, Exodus, and the American Israel," in Johnson, 2–4.

synthesis rather than takeover.[15] And it was an uneasy synthesis at that. The express purpose of the slave owners was to inculcate in their slaves a feeling that Christian fellowship meant obedience to the socio-political situation of slavery.[16] Ironically, then, it was the slave owner who solidified this integral connection between Christian tradition and political circumstance for the African-American. The idea was to encourage the slave to believe that a spiritual life committed to Jesus was at the same time a socio-political life committed to American enslavement. The spiritual commitment mandated the human socio-political reality and the slave's acquiescence to it. This socio-political/spiritual connection reinforced the understanding that had already come from the African tradition that the two realms were inseparable.[17] It is no wonder, then, that as African-American Christianity developed, its followers shattered the boundary Euro-American Christianity had erected between the spiritual and socio-political realms of life.

What African-American Christianity never did accept was the belief that some humans are intrinsically superior to others, and are, therefore, given the privilege of enslaving or oppressing them. Operating from the core belief that would become the centerpiece of the "black religious tradition," the slaves broke down the principal spiritual/political boundary established by the slave owners, the one which separated the two races into separate categories of human being. The synthesizing slave, accessing biblical symbolism like the kingdom of God through the cultural context of oppression, understood the same biblical stories and traditions in a way wholly different from what their masters were teaching them. Having been encouraged at the outset by both their own African heritage and the teachings of their masters to fuse the spiritual and the political, they maintained the connection at precisely the point where their masters wanted them to entertain separation. They understood the biblical stories and symbols of freedom as indicative signs and imperative encouragement of socio-political as well as spiritual liberation. "One of the ironies of American history is that the slaves, indoctrinated in this alien religion of the masters, nevertheless discovered its true meaning — its liberative, redemptive essence — over against this emasculation."[18]

This trend continued in the African-American Christian tradition that developed after slavery. From reconstruction through Jim Crow and segregation, the African-American Christian tradition continued to ignore the boundary that Euro-American Christianity wanted to maintain between the secular and the

---

15. Cf. Harris, 12. "In creating a synthesis between their African religious heritage and the distortions of Western interpretations of Christian faith, slaves sought to achieve inner and outer liberation. As the first expression of this liberative praxis in freedom, slaves formed the plantation's 'invisible church.' . . ."

16. Cf. Raboteau; Joyner, 20–25.

17. Cf. Lincoln and Mamiya, 199–200. "First, prior to and during the rise of the Atlantic slave trade, the traditional worldviews, cosmologies, and societies of the Africans themselves were permeated by religion, with no division between sacred and secular, especially between religion and politics. Under the sacred canopy of traditional African religions, kings and queens and chiefs were not only political leaders but religious ones as well."

18. Peter C. Hodgson, *Revisioning the Church: Ecclesial Freedom in the New Paradigm* (Philadelphia: Fortress Press, 1988) 71.

spiritual realms of life. Again, context was key. African-Americans found themselves in a context where the church was the only stable and independent institution in their lives. It was also the most economically firm, and was, therefore, the one source of socio-political as well as spiritual security. By necessity of the cultural context, then, the boundary between the two realms was once again shattered.

Given the circumstances of this "Negro Church" period, it was the spiritual institution, the church, that had the freedom, the resources, and the mandate to impact the social, political and economic arenas of African-American life. "[B]lacks made their churches agencies for teaching the race how to respond to racial hostility in creative and constructive ways."[19] Certainly these "ways" had a theological foundation. The church, as Paris notes, embodies the core belief that God is the parent of all humans. All humans are therefore intrinsically related. But this theological foundation had socio-political ramifications for the church in the African-American experience. The church became the place, the one place in society, where this theology was concretely realized. It was the one place that transformed the spiritual into the social, communal, and political. It did so in a variety of ways.

Individually, it enabled African-Americans to assume positions of authority, thereby enabling a sense of self-respect, and an ability to develop leadership skills in the public arena that would otherwise have been denied. These skills benefited not only the organizational structures of the churches, however. Black leaders used them to impact the larger political landscape that was so oppressive to African-Americans. "Black clergy, particularly those who were employed full-time by the larger churches in the community, were expected to speak out about the pressing issues of the day, especially about the problems of racial discrimination."[20]

But its most critical impact was communal. The church became a social agency for African-Americans. Through its own secular endeavors and the efforts of mutual aid societies created in connection with its own ministry, and often under its watchful eye, it became during this period of segregation a virtual nation within a nation.[21] This "spiritual" institution by necessity took upon itself the political and social survival of its people. Lincoln and Mamiya describe the process as one of partial differentiation. "The notion of partial differentiation emphasizes the continuous interaction and interrelationships between churches and areas like politics, economics, education, and culture."[22] In the Negro churches, the lines between the spiritual and the socio-political were consciously

---

19. Paris, *The Social Teaching of the Black Churches,* 7.
20. Lincoln and Mamiya, 207.
21. Lincoln and Mamiya point out that a symbiotic relationship existed between the churches and the mutual aid societies. Sometimes churches grew out of the societies, at other times societies grew from the churches. As examples they point to the two earliest recorded mutual aid societies, the African Union Society of Newport, Rhode Island in 1780 and the Free African Society of Philadelphia in 1787. Both gave rise to urban churches (116). Cf. also Emmett D. Carson, *A Hand Up: Black Philanthropy and Self-Help in America* (Washington, DC: Joint Center for Political and Economic Studies, 1993) 7–10.
22. Lincoln and Mamiya, 123.

blurred. If the church acted only in the spiritual arena, African-Americans would have been left without a voice and resource in the socio-political one.

Unfortunately, this "partial differentiation" did not occur without cost. Harris, pointing to the work of Gayraud Wilmore, remembers that the identity of the church as an agent for social change and liberation shattered under the weight of the great demand for social services.[23] The multitudes of blacks migrating from the south between the turn of the century and the Great Depression taxed all of the church's resources. It was for this reason that the Negro Church was castigated by E. Franklin Frazier and others. Black Pentecostalism developed as a force during this period. Exhausted by social demands, this growing wing of the church emphasized a full concentration on the church as a spiritual agent for personal redemption. Even the components of the Negro Church not dominated by Pentecostalism turned away from its role as a liberative voice. Weighed down by the social needs of its growing membership, it separated itself from the larger world. Using its aid resources and its spiritual forum it sheltered African-Americans from the conditions of racism. It therefore allowed the forces that perpetuated racism the ability to operate without the hindrance of the church's prophetic voice. Preoccupied with satisfying its people's social services needs, it lost both the motivation and the power to engage the circumstances that caused them. The Negro Church was a church locked into a survival mode.[24]

The lean back toward liberation came in the era of Civil Rights that launched what C. Eric Lincoln has called the black church after Frazier.[25] The period, which saw the demise of the Negro Church in the explosive birth of black consciousness, opened with two impressive tactical salvos against racism and the segregationist system it fostered. In both cases the church was intimately involved. The first was the Supreme Court decision in *Brown v. the Board of Education, Topeka, Kansas* in 1954. The Reverend Oliver Leon Brown of the St. Mark's A.M.E. church in Topeka, with the assistance of the NAACP Legal Defense Fund, sued the Board of Education on behalf of his daughter Linda Brown and all other black children in the public schools.[26] As a result, the high court struck down a key premise in the plank of the Jim Crow state. It concluded that separate educational facilities for blacks and whites were inherently unequal to blacks and therefore were against the provisions of the U.S. Constitution. The second was the 1955 Montgomery Bus Boycott spearheaded by the Reverend Martin Luther King, Jr., and executed with the backing and power of the black churches. These two tactical events helped shape the mindset of the church of African-America and the African-Americans who populated it. The move from survival to liberation mode was underway. As Lincoln and Mamiya note,

> the radical change in consciousness among black people...yielded new
> perceptions of self and society....The birth of a new consciousness
> was difficult and painful, but it was authentically liberating as African

---

23. Harris, 17–18.
24. Ibid.
25. Cf. C. Eric Lincoln, *The Black Church Since Frazier* (New York: Schocken Books, 1974).
26. Cf. Lincoln and Mamiya, 211.

Americans gained in self-respect and self-confidence in this strange new confrontation of a world they had never had the opportunity to plumb before.[27]

In many ways King became a symbol of the movement that began in the decade of the 1950s. It is critical to note that he, like many of the other leaders of the Civil Rights movement, was firmly grounded in the black church tradition. He operated from it. His vision, and the tactics he used to implement it, were first and foremost based in its theological premise of divine parentage and universal kinship.[28] And, like the leaders of this black church tradition before and after him, King saw no impregnable boundary between the sacred and secular arenas of life. For him the spiritual had implications for the political, and political circumstances mandated particular kinds of actions from spiritual devotees of Christ. It was because of this connection, fostered within the black church tradition, that he was able to use his God language in a way that challenged Americans to live up to their political visions in the social arena. Operating from his church base he hammered home a liberationist Christian message that drew heavily upon the secular notions of freedom and equality to which all Americans had allegedly pledged themselves. "In short, King appealed to the very documents that are central to American civil life — the Constitution, the Declaration of Independence — and pointed out their basis for a moral understanding and interpretation of concepts like equality, justice, and freedom."[29]

Most significantly, he incorporated this synthesis of spiritual and sociopolitical imagery into his language about the kingdom. "Martin Luther King, Jr., used the biblical symbol of the reign of God more effectively than any church leader of recent times. The focus of King's liberation praxis was the vision of the reign of God or the beloved community as the ultimate norm and goal for civil rights, economic justice, and world peace."[30] For King, the kingdom was a strategic reality that could and should be tactically implemented in the human arena. It was not only the imminent future arrival of God's justice that mandated urgent action for justice in the here and now; it was also the present transformative reality that opened up when humans who anticipated the kingdom's arrival worked as though they could facilitate it in present, tactical ways. This is why Harris could conclude that, for King, such a kingdom community "arises out of a context of active participation in society on behalf of the values of God's reign."[31]

Even more exciting is the realization that for King and other leaders of this "black church," the tactical activities on the ground represented, as they did for Mark's Jesus, the kingdom activities God was deploying strategically. As Jesus' preaching manifestations were representations of God's mythical battle with the forces of Satan, so the liberative actions of the "black church" were

27. Ibid., 166.
28. Cf. West, 7; Dyson, 229–30.
29. Dyson, 231.
30. Harris, 39–40.
31. Ibid., 40.

understood to be representations of the battle God was waging against evil on a more ultimate level. Human civil rights leaders and followers, then, were actually participating in God's kingdom movement, ushering in on the tactical level the victory that God had already ordained on the strategic one. It is for this reason that J. Louis Martyn remembers a black Baptist deacon in a 1963 Birmingham church describing their civil rights work as the work of God. "One of the old deacons interrupts the speaker," Martyn recalls, "politely but firmly calling out, 'We're not doing this! *God* is doing this!!' "[32] Martyn's memory illustrates that African-Americans at every level of the church, not just the leadership, understood intuitively that they were engaged in a battle that represented God's own movements. Their action was therefore essential. Their victory assured.

> The deacon is simply saying that the *real* struggle in Birmingham is a struggle in God's apocalyptic war; that the *full* contours of this struggle can be seen only in the bi-focal vision concentrated on what *God* is doing in the world. However this or that individual battle may go, the ultimate outcome of God's war is not in question.[33]

The state and mindset of the church, however, is in question. Particularly today, given the oppressive context of culture in which the majority of African-Americans find themselves, there is a need for the church to remobilize its tactical efforts on behalf of the kingdom of God. The question is, what version of the church do we have before us? As my comments about the experience of church in African-America since the period of slavery implies, I believe that West's definition of the black church is too broad. I believe it despite the apparent "core-commonality" that has existed in the black church tradition throughout. Though the church populated by African-Americans has had a form whose spiritual traits fit the general quality that West's quote acknowledges, socio-politically, it has been a much more complex phenomenon. Clearly, the black church has been the preeminent social, economic and political force in African-American life. But the way it has manipulated that force has been quite different depending on the preunderstanding its leaders and members have had at any given time.

I would argue that there have been at least four primary manifestations of the entity that West describes as the "black church": the slave church, the Negro Church, the black church, and, now, the African-American church.[34] The first

---

32. J. Louis Martyn, "From Paul to Flannery O'Connor with the Power of Grace," *Katallagete* 7 (1981): 13.

33. Ibid.

34. I should note that these are admittedly general categories. In assigning them I am looking at the broad characteristics of the church at particular periods in American history. On a more detailed and complex level I would agree that not every church during these "periods" fit the characterization I am arguing. Peter Paris, for instance, looking at the detailed discussion of African-American churches, found four principle categories (pastoral, prophetic, political, and nationalist) which could be in evidence at any of the periods I am suggesting. (Cf. Paris, "The Public Role of the Black Churches," esp., 47–56, and "The Bible and the Black Churches," esp., 136–52.) I do not mean to argue such contrary manifestations did not exist. For example, a nest of prophetic churches could have existed during the more generally accommodationist

three we have already discussed. Their contexts of culture and preunderstanding are a matter of historical record. The final one is currently under construction. And because it is, we have the opportunity to influence its direction in terms of its lean toward the liberation or survival mode about which Harris speaks so appropriately. To be sure, the two modes must remain in tension. Inevitably, however, the church shifts in one or the other direction, as the Negro version did toward survival, as the slave and "black" manifestations did toward liberation. The post-Civil Rights cultural context remains one of colonial oppression for African-Americans. Indeed, in his remarkable work, William Julius Wilson records how the social conditions actually worsened during the twenty-year period following the movement. The statistical survey of chapter 14 makes this point quite graphically. The primary concern for the contemporary church, then, is one of preunderstanding. It is the preunderstanding of the contemporary African-American church that will determine its slant. I believe that a perspective on the church that operates through the language in the Gospel of Mark mandates an interventionist preunderstanding that both anticipates and actualizes the kingdom of God. The end result will not only be a liberationist lean, but a liberationist priority. Survival is accomplished in this scenario not through otherworldly premonitions of a future world where redemption is spiritual and justice will be transplanted from above; it is accomplished through the liberative activity of preaching disciples who, having sensed the imminence of God's future kingdom, work themselves to bring pocket glimpses of it into the present.

Beyond the "black church's" era of civil rights, then, lies the need for a tactical plan of African-American church activity that approximates and represents in the present the strategic reality of God's past and future interventions. This means going beyond the social services status of the Negro Church. I mention it again because contemporary African-American churches are preoccupied with individual ministries of clothing, food, shelter, local business formation, etc. It is not my argument that these are expendable and unnecessary. Given the far-flung influence of racism and economic injustice, and their consequences of hunger, homelessness and societal dis-ease, African-American churches must certainly expend vital efforts toward relieving these symptoms of a sick society. But here lies the crucial point. These situations represent the symptoms, not the illness itself. A single-minded concentration on such symptoms will address need in very localized and temporary ways, but it will fail to address the systemic societal afflictions that perpetuate those symptoms. As was the case with the Negro Church and its focus on mutual aid and social service, such efforts will certainly assuage the feelings and conditions of particular families and individuals, for the specific period of time in which they qualify for the assistance, but they will not challenge the socio-political conditions that allow such wounds to fester. Only a tactical plan aimed at the socio-political causes of such symp-

---

"Negro church" period. I mean to suggest instead what appeared to be the primary overall thrust of Christianity in an African-American guise during such periods when the church's overall orientation went in the general direction of a particular manifestation.

tomatic situations can do that. Only a united African-American church operating in a coordinated fashion that is committed to manifesting kingdom preaching in tangible socio-political ways can do that.

One might well point out that in Mark's narrative presentation Jesus' preaching manifestations assisted *individuals* who were hungry, homeless, or oppressed. Certainly programs of clothing, food, shelter, etc., imitate this kind of preaching. I would argue, however, that in Mark's presentation, Jesus' actions, even when on an individual level, were always orchestrated with an overall mythological objective of eliminating the power of Satan in the human arena. Jesus' individual acts were attacks on this power base, and were understood to be part of a plan that was representative of God's own strategic war with the powers of evil. In that sense, Jesus' acts were never individual; they were always linked together in the programming of a single tactical objective, the overthrow of the forces who represented Satan's dominion on earth. It was the assumption in Jesus' tactical kingdom engagements, as it was in God's strategic activity, that when this larger conflagration was won, the individual injustices would, cut off from their lines of communication and resupply, wither away. It is this orientation toward socio-political activity that I believe Mark's kingdom message demands today. That is to say, there needs to be a clearer understanding of what the church believes God is doing in the world. Only when the church understands what it believes God is doing strategically can it mount representative tactical maneuvers. Certainly God is doing more than feeding, providing shelter, or even opening local businesses on previously abandoned property. God is challenging the very structures of power that institutionalize and systematize oppression and injustice. Human tacticians who want to represent that divine strategy on earth must likewise be systemically oriented.

If Mark's narration is to be a guide, if the interventionist preunderstanding that he expressed is currently maintained, then the message must be that God is engaged with the powers of racial oppression and economic injustice that manifest themselves in various ways in the African-American circumstance. The discipleship response to this strategic reality is the tactical implementation of God's kingdom battle plan. It may include individual mission projects and programs, but it must never end there. Such projects would be helpful only if and when they were connected to a larger, organized, structured plan of attack. I would argue that in most mission programs of today's African-American church such connected activity on a large scale is unusual. Churches, or perhaps denominations, stake out a turf, sometimes within the confines of a single small neighborhood, and replicate programs and mission to deal with the symptoms of oppression, injustice, and racism, but do not orchestrate a joint tactical plan to strike these evils themselves. The result is good conscience within the confines of individual churches, but the perpetuation of the injury our churches only manage to massage, but never really heal. Given the cultural context of African-Americans at the end of the twentieth century and the beginning of the twenty-first, more is required. A tactical plan that operates as systemically as the systemic economic, racial, and political forces that oppress African-Americans is required. A church that seeks to create in the here and now what it believes

God did in the Exodus and will do in the coming of the Son of man on the clouds of heaven is required.

> Unless local black churches are equipped with praxis models for in-depth, social and theological analysis, ministry ends up being a reactionary, occasional, and isolated response to social crisis without the power or the imagination for sustained liberation praxis. This praxis model is necessary if there is to be social change.[35]

This model resides in Mark's symbolic representation of the kingdom of God and the interventionist preunderstanding he attached to it.

---

35. Harris, 7.

16

A Corresponding Mode

Go Preach!

Another distinctive feature of black theological social ethical reflection is that we do not fail to employ our preaching voice. In most scholarly social ethical reflection, the voice of the preacher is rarely heard; but in this work, not only do we refer to the words and deeds of our preachers, we also make use of the preaching genre in presenting some aspects of our social ethical reflection. This is consistent with the fact that black theological social ethical reflection is nourished by black churchly traditions, and it is consistent with our effort to speak in a voice that is most welcome among our church people.[1]

Black theological social ethical reflection is also consistent with Mark's primary mode of discourse. Mark's language, I have been arguing, was designed to *do* something in the lives of his readers. It was designed to move them toward interventionist kingdom preaching. It *is* designed to do the same thing in any corresponding context of culture, such as the contemporary African-American context, where transformation depends on boundary-breaking activity. Mark's point is that this hope for boundary-trespass is initiated in the present by those who foresee and anticipate God's consummate act of transformation in the future. In this way, through their boundary-breaking preaching activity, the future reality of the kingdom will take shape as a pocket force of resistance in the present. The consummate overhaul of the present oppressive reality will not occur until God's strategic design executes its final invasion of the human arena. But, according to Mark's narrative plan, that outcome has already occurred mythologically. His narrative is designed to involve his readers in re-presenting that mythological reality on the human landscape. It is designed to provoke them into doing now, in the form of pocket moments of boundary-breaking resistance, what God has already done mythologically, and, therefore, will certainly do historically.

---

1. Walker, 13.

If the corresponding context of culture is the colonial circumstance, and the corresponding preunderstanding is intervention, the corresponding mode of discourse activity that can address and alter, that is to say transform, that circumstance, is preaching. In the Gospel of Mark, the kingdom of God is the boundary-breaking preaching of Jesus and the disciples who follow him. It is this activity that ushers in and represents the force and reality of the future kingdom in present, pocket moments of socio-political metamorphosis. Contemporary African-American disciples of Jesus will find, as they approach their current colonial context through the interventionist perspective of Mark's kingdom language, that it is such disruptive "preaching" activity that represents the kingdom of God today.

Indeed, given the correspondence that I believe exists between the Markan circumstance and that of the contemporary African-American, there is also a corresponding set of ways in which African-American preaching might manifest itself. Exorcism, teaching, and miraculous healing are still applicable categories, even if in Mark's understanding they were mythologically based. The power of evil remains real, even if we conceptualize it differently in the scientific/technological age of the twentieth and approaching twenty-first centuries. Only the manner in which we understand it historically has altered, so as to fit the mindset of our new historical era. But the fact remains, there appears still to be an overwhelming power of evil that represents itself tactically in socio-political oppressions and injustices. If Mark's language holds in the present circumstance, then certainly God (however God is conceived, mythologically, existentially, etc.) is engaged in a strategic battle with this force. God's victory, according to Mark, is assured. In fact, it has already happened on the mythological level. It will happen on the historical level once God ushers the supernatural kingdom into the human arena. Until that moment, the job of Jesus-followers is to represent that victory in present tactical engagements. The tactical weapon of choice is the preached word and deed. The particular manifestations of that weaponry are, as they were described in Mark's narration, exorcism, teaching, and miraculous healing. The same manifestations accomplished mythologically by Jesus and his first-century disciples, I would argue, can be implemented historically by his twentieth-century disciples.

I begin where I think much of Mark's thinking began, with the racial animus that represents a human separation from the will of God. This vertical alienation is so radical that it lives itself out as ethnic division, hatred, and prejudice. It is the problem Mark addressed in counseling a Gentile mission in a land torn by Jewish/Gentile strife. The African-American context of the twentieth century has been marred by a corresponding ethnic division, the color line that W. E. B. Du Bois called a veil between black and white, that has erupted at significant moments in American history and threatens a major moment of conflagration still. How does one build a universal church in a world where people of different ethnic and racial origins distrust one another deeply, and then build that distrust into their institutions, laws, and faiths? Mark's answer was that one follows the risky preaching path of Jesus, whose powerful moments of kingdom transformation were directed at Gentiles as well as Jews. Was this way the correct way? Certainly the answer mattered for a Markan community already engaged in following Jesus' lead with a Gentile mission of their own, and suffering persecution because of it. Mark's narration of Jesus' baptism, transfiguration, and, most importantly, resurrection indicate that it was the correct way. Despite the suffering it brought, it was God's way; it was the way God vindicated as truly representative of the divine kingdom strategy. The only way one could represent the future kingdom whose admission policies were universal in respect to ethnic and racial identity was to break down, to trespass the ethnic/racial boundaries that separated humans in the historical arena. This is what interventionist kingdom preaching was all about.

It is what interventionist kingdom preaching in the African-American cultural context *is* all about. For Mark it began with the church. The believing community of Jesus-followers was the place where, in imitation of Jesus' own narrated Gentile excursions, the boundaries between Jew and Gentile were to be broken down. The worshipping community was the pocket reality that resisted the racial animus that separated Jew and Gentile; in this regard it represented the strategic reality of the future kingdom of God in the present moment. The implications for the contemporary African-American church are clear. If, indeed, racial animosity also threatens to tear apart our contemporary society, the church has a leadership role to play. It can embody in its corporate being the reality of the kingdom that exemplifies God's strategic design of universality. In so doing it not only represents the future kingdom in the present moment, it acts as a transformative burr in the side of the divided and racist larger American society, rather than as an accommodating mirror of its divisions and prejudice.

To make such a call, however, as Mark clearly understood, invites criticism, and even persecution. In a world where the races are battling for turf and control, neither side pursues real relationship with the other, and both sides vilify members of their own camps who break ranks and make such attempts unilaterally. Fear is palpable. Even within church camps there is the dread that power will be lost, identity will be thrust aside, that the smaller will be swallowed up, or that the voices of the minority will be so impassioned that the majority will lose its nerve and its way. The result is a continuation of the comfortable status quo, a church that exemplifies the worst of the American racial condition. If segregation has been jolted elsewhere on the U.S. landscape, it has not felt even a quiver of concern in the sanctuaries of American churches. When Americans gather together to worship it is still, by common consent, with other Americans who are their racial and ethnic kin.

In the Gospel of Mark the kingdom of God is surely not like this. Mark's image of a universal church, pursued by his own community's Gentile mission and his narration of Jesus' Gentile activities, represented for him what God was doing on the mythological level in the divine battle with the forces of Satan. Mark's word to his persecuted community of believers was that they were called to maintain their representation of that strategic reality in their tactical mission activities. The implications of such a message for the contemporary African-American church are clear. If the kingdom is a universal reality, then it is the mandate of those who represent it tactically in the contemporary human circumstance to work for that universality in the here and now. Perhaps this is what Robert E. Jones means when he writes,

> I believe that the greatest challenge facing the local church in urban metropolitan areas is the summons to move beyond racial, cultural, and socioeconomic division toward being multicultural, multiracial congregations. I believe this is an educational, pastoral, and theological challenge, a challenge called for by the gospel. After all, the gospel focuses on the building of a visible presence of the kingdom of God.[2]

But certainly this is not the case in contemporary American society. Whether we believe the kingdom of God will be multiracial and multiethnic or not, we anticipate it currently in our Christian communities as a segregated reality. If a non-Christian were to believe that our current communities represent the future reality of the kingdom, that reality would be a distasteful one indeed. It would be a future marred by the same ecclesial apartheid tendencies of the present. Whatever we are doing in our segregated churches, it is certainly not what Mark believed the community of believers should be doing, which is to say, representing the supernatural reality of God in the human frame. What our churches currently represent is division and exclusion, the very forces the universal kingdom must operate against. Like the scribes who came down from Jerusalem and charged that Jesus was in league with Satan, only to find Mark leveling this very accusation against them, we find our "righteous" selves representing the very evil we thought we were allied with God against. "It is significant to note that less than 10 percent of all black churches have taken part in any kind of interracial cooperation with white churches. Racial segregation in American society is most clearly seen in religion."[3]

Certainly, though, this church separatism has not been the goal of the black church. From its inception it has always maintained a vision of universality. Even during the formative period of institutional black church denominations, when church leaders broke away from their white counterparts in order to find free and equal expression of worship, there remained a hope for a church reality that imaged the kingdom vision of universality. "But the most important reason for desiring a continuing association with the white churches lay in the moral and social implications of that ideal societal vision that has always inspired the black churches, namely, the vision of a society in which race would have no significance."[4] So strong was this impulse that during the Civil Rights movement Martin Luther King, Jr., hoped even to incorporate it in the tactical design

---

2. Robert E. Jones, "Learning to Face Diversity in Urban Churches," in *Urban Church Education*, Donald B. Rogers, editor (Birmingham: Religious Education Press, 1989) 84.

3. Lincoln and Mamiya, 157.

4. Paris, *The Social Teaching of the Black Churches,* 46. Paris points out further that in its earliest stages black churches separated themselves from white churches not because of a hatred for whites, but because it was the only way white Christians would allow them freedom of worship and freedom in worship. "Just as Martin Luther, John Wesley, and others had no desire to form new churches, so also the founders of the black church independence movement would have chosen otherwise had viable options been available to them. Some evidence of the desire of

of his freedom organizations. He saw both theological and practical benefit in encouraging organizations which sought equality for African-Americans to emulate within their make-up the universal vision they hoped their efforts would ultimately achieve.

> Every time a Negro in the slums of Chicago or on the plantations of Mississippi sees Negroes and whites honestly working together for a common goal, he sees new grounds for hope. This is why I always have in the past and will in the future insist that my staff in SCLC be interracial. By insisting on racial openness in our organizations, we are setting a pattern for the racially integrated society toward which we work.[5]

Unfortunately, in the middle of the twentieth century King was far ahead of both white and African-American churches at the century's close. Where the structures of his secular organization were designed to represent the vision of the future kingdom in the present, our contemporary churches represent the very reality that kingdom is battling against.

This common trend does not mean, of course, that there are no such efforts at representing the universal vision of the kingdom in the present moment. Lincoln and Mamiya discuss one clear example of a ministry designed to trespass the racial boundaries that divide American churches. Partners in Ecumenism (PIE) was organized as an entity within the National Council of Churches. Its stated mission is "the fostering of partnerships between black and white churches at the local as well as the national level, specifically for the reason of pursuing social, political, and economic changes in the life circumstances of residents of the nation's central cities."[6] In the Gospel of Mark the kingdom of God is *like* this.

To be sure, though, even organizations so ideally intentioned recognize the power of the boundaries they hope to transgress. Lincoln and Mamiya state that one of PIE's primary goals has been to challenge the white church to be more responsive to black concerns. PIE apparently recognizes the power of sin, a mythological evil perhaps, but one that has exuded a very tangible human manifestation of racism. Racism prompts white churches to ignore or dismiss the concerns of African-American Christians. Racism prompts misuse of power by white Christians and paralyzing fear from African-American Christians. Attempts to represent the universality of the kingdom cannot dismiss the fact that such efforts draw their sponsors into a battle not unlike the mythological battle that Mark believed God was waging with Satan. Humans are drawn into the reality of this supernatural conflict as they attempt to tactically execute God's divine agenda in human history. Those who attempt such representative acts must recognize that the opposing mythological force also has its tactical representatives. Just as Mark understood Satan was represented in first-century Palestine

---

white churches for racial justice would have constituted the grounds for such an alternative" (41). Cf. also 108–9.

5. King, 94.

6. Lincoln and Mamiya, 193.

by the leaders of the people, so contemporary Christians must acknowledge that sin has many historical forms. One of the most heinous is racism. One of its most tragic operatives has been the Christian church. Its power goes beyond the racist act that plagues any single African-American Christian. Its power base is metaphysical. It must therefore be attacked by persons convinced that they represent a reality of even greater metaphysical power. In Mark's language, this reality is the kingdom of God.

It is a reality whose tactical expression should not be expected any time soon. For as Lincoln and Mamiya point out, black and white Christians appear resolved that the church will emulate current societal ideology rather than future kingdom strategy.

> But the hopes among some black and white Christians that the Black Church will eventually merge itself into mainline Christianity seem increasingly unrealistic as these racial communions seem more and more resigned to the realities of religious separation in a society where secular separation remains the ideological norm.[7]

But then African-American merger, and hence disappearance, into the larger white communion is also not representative of a universal strategy. The creation of a multi-colored white church is not universalism; it is "co-optism." The disintegration of the African-American church in the interests of religious integration does not build the whole church, it simply increases the global number of commonly identified Christians by destroying one very viable and potent part of the church.

> One fervently hopes that as the black churches enter the ecclesial mainstream they will bring with them their distinctive qualities, helping to transform the whole, enabling their paradigm of what it means to be a church to become productive for all people. A *truly integrated* Christian church in North America would be something radically different from anything we now know.[8]

It will be radically different and radically universal because it incorporates the best from all traditions instead of divesting one to build the other. And while I can certainly applaud Hodgson's comment, I must point out that even as he attempts to speak in a way that will establish this universal vision, he demonstrates the problematic tendency to assume that something needs correcting in African-American Christianity before there can be the establishment of more universal communion. Black churches need not enter the ecclesial mainstream; they already exist with contemporary white churches in the ecclesial mainstream. Just as there are non-mainstream white churches, there are also non-mainstream African-American churches. But to suggest that all African-American churches

---

7. Ibid., 394.
8. Hodgson, 72.

are moving toward the mainstream is to suggest that on the whole there are deviations within its larger sense of church that are being and need to be cleansed away. Such an orientation, no matter how well-meaning, puts African-American churches at a disadvantage, and creates a sense of suspicion on the part of African-American Christians. The implication is that something within their communion must change and adapt, must move toward "correct" witness. Only when white churches recognize that African-American witness, no matter how unique, is as "mainstream" as any white church or denomination, can white Christians truly affirm and accept African-American Christian traditions as equal to their own. Without such an understanding, there can be no move toward the universalism Mark's kingdom vision pictured, because the move is always weighted toward white Christianity, not just quantitatively, which is, in the U.S. context, inevitable, but also qualitatively.

Once again, I suggest that the contemporary church, African-American and Euro-American, begin with an understanding of God's strategic kingdom design as regards this question of universalism. What is the future reality of the kingdom in this regard? I find it difficult to believe that the majority of Christendom would argue for a segregated consummate kingdom. The kingdom strategic design, at least if Mark's language is to be a guide, is universalist. Given this reality, the next step is to determine how we can tactically bring that reality about by trespassing racial boundaries in the present. It is this call to tactical action that brings me to the vision of non-segregated churches in the here and now. To be sure, though, the reality of sin and its manifestation of racism makes this vision a difficult one to enact. The model of inclusion cannot take place with white churches taking over African-American ones for this very reason. African-Americans will always be at a disadvantage. It also does not work with white churches evangelizing individual African-Americans two or three at a time. This results in tokenism, not universalism. I believe it begins with African-American and white communities of believers operating on the tactical level of mission before attempting the tactical realization of corporate union. In this way, African-American and white Christians can feel the tactical movement of the kingdom through joint efforts that allow them to feel an equal representation of God's power operating in the contemporary human circumstance. Only after such working together can there begin to be hope of joining together, after Christians of different backgrounds recognize and appreciate through such tactical activity the distinct theological premises that prompt similar kinds of tactical kingdom activity. In other words, a move must be made to push beyond a desire simply to integrate the church; we must progress toward the hope that we can use the church as a tool to tactically realize pocket moments of the future kingdom. We then allow those pocket moments to begin a process of coagulation whose gravitational pull eventually drags us closer and closer to a church that not only works together, but exists together. Universal reality will follow the lead of universal activity, for it is only in such joint tactical activity that different Christians come to know and trust each other as oriented toward the same future goal in the present moment.

This religious universalism has dramatic implications for secular society.

African-Americans, too, must begin to concentrate primarily on the strategic design of God's kingdom as they attempt to enact that kingdom through tactical boundary-breaking preaching activities. This means that the universalism called for in the constitution of church must be enacted in the programs of social welfare and reform. I am convinced that William Julius Wilson is on to something when he argues that the thrust toward transforming the socio-political and socio-economic structures of our society should be more universal in its orientation.[9] That is to say, even when African-Americans make the argument, the argument should be made on behalf of *all* the economically and politically oppressed rather than only economically and politically oppressed African-Americans. Wilson's reasons are political; America has tired of dealing with the difficulties of its minorities, whether dealing with those difficulties is just or not. The widespread perception that minorities are being given special consideration has virtually destroyed the possibility of enlarging or even sustaining programs like Affirmative Action and welfare as we now know it. The practical solution to this problem is not to abandon poor and politically oppressed African-Americans, but to include them within the general category of the impoverished and oppressed in the United States. The goal, then, would be to program solutions for the entire population of the underclass. Given that African-Americans are disproportionally represented in the urban underclass, this universalist approach would therefore disproportionately assist African-Americans, but the fact that it is universally based would be much more defensible to tax-paying middle- and upper-middle-class Americans.

I believe that Wilson's pragmatic approach also has an interventionist kingdom foundation. If, indeed, the kingdom is universal in its orientation, then any tactical implementation of it must also be universal in its scope. This means, of course, that where communities of Jesus-followers are concerned, the emphasis should be on the breaking of boundaries that oppress all socially, economically, and politically oppressed persons, regardless of race or ethnicity. Certainly this is the implication behind Mark's presentation of a kingdom symbol whose primary tactician did not appear bound by geographical or ethnic boundaries. A church with a universalist orientation toward the poor and oppressed represents the kingdom imagery in a purer way than one dedicated singularly to the needs of its own ethnic and racial kin.

A final challenge that we face as a result of our great dilemma is to be ever mindful of enlarging the whole society, and giving it a new sense of values as we seek to solve our particular problem. As we work to get rid of the economic strangulation that we face as a result of poverty, we must not overlook the fact that millions of Puerto Ricans, Mexican Americans, Indians and Appalachian whites are also poverty-stricken. Any serious war against poverty must of necessity include them.[10]

---

9. Cf. Wilson, esp., chapters 5–7.
10. King, 132.

Perhaps the lesson here is that the African-American kingdom tactician must, as Jesus suggested in Mark 8, surrender self-interest and self-consideration. Self-denial will mandate policy actions that are not oriented simply to assist middle- and upper-middle-class African-Americans. Purged of the need to whine about our own discomforts we must break down the barriers of self-interest and self-concern, and, instead of marching in protest, preach, which is to say, find systemic social and political ways to work together through the combined forces (as opposed to individual ministries) of our churches and secular agencies for transforming the economic injustices of our society that destroy those who are too impoverished to fight for themselves.

Devise strategies to fit the times. Coalitions must be formed around issues, rather than racial groups. Poverty, injustice, poor education, and inadequate health care affect citizens and immigrants, blacks and whites. Successful confrontation and action will be far more likely if strategies of cooperation and inclusion are adopted.[11]

Here, however, is where I also believe the interventionist orientation takes us beyond Wilson's argument. Wilson believes that racism is in this case secondary to economics. I believe that they must be dealt with together, for they are equal representations of the mythological power of sin against which the powers of the consummate kingdom are arrayed. Our tactical representation of the kingdom must therefore demonstrate an equal awareness and defiance. To assume that a careful and successful economic program would necessarily transform the lives of impoverished African-Americans without an accessory consideration of the racism that compounds and reinforces the existence of an underclass is to misunderstand or ignore the metaphysical force of sin whose power is realized in many different ways. All of its key manifestations must be attacked if any maneuvers against it are to be successful. This means that an attack against the way economic injustice is structured in American life, as Wilson suggests, is a necessary but ultimately insufficient means to trespass the boundaries that harness the freedoms of many of the poor he seeks to assist. To represent the strategic activity of a kingdom at war with sin, human tacticians must operate as globally, as universally as the kingdom itself. Racism and its effects, whether this is acceptable to mainstream white America or not, must be attacked as a tactical representation of sin with the same vigor that is applied to the oppressive economic structures that perpetuate systemic poverty in the U.S. Even if it seems ethnically oriented only toward African-Americans and other racial minorities, in reality, such a tactical orientation fully represents a universal kingdom strategy. For the elimination of racism ultimately brings both African-Americans and white Americans more closely in line with the representative image of the kingdom in the human circumstance. While African-Americans would enjoy the freedom that such boundary-breaking activity would bring, white Americans

---

11. Bernard C. Watson, "The Demographic Revolution: Diversity in 21st Century America," in Tidwell and Robinson, 222.

would themselves be freed from the power of sin which has so often captivated and enslaved even those who feel themselves politically free. The elimination of racism, then, is a universal endeavor; it enables white Americans as well as African-Americans to represent the future kingdom in their present acts of religious and secular community.

The difficulty here lies not just in the grand sweep of such a universal vision, it also lies in the fact that our contemporary churches and their leaders have lost the interventionist orientation that provokes energy and action toward such a vision, no matter how utopian it appears. When there is no real belief that such a vision exists, even on the plane of the consummate kingdom, there are no human tacticians willing to exert the energies and take the risks necessary to represent it historically. The result is a church of segregated spiritual communion and socio-political witness that speaks so eloquently of salvation but has so very little to offer in the way of socio-political transformation. No wonder William Pannell can exclaim,

> So far no one [and no church] has come forward who is willing or able to lead the country into its promising future — which is another way of saying that so far no one has come forward who is willing to transcend race and class to give all Americans a promising future.[12]

The person or church who does come forward will, I believe, come forward preaching. And, as I have suggested, I believe this preaching can manifest itself in ways that correspond to the preaching activity of Jesus and the disciples who followed him in Mark's narrative. In the evangelist's account, the preaching manifestation of exorcism was a decidedly mythological activity. Jesus' power over demonic forces represented God's ultimate power over the strategic design that Satan had orchestrated for the human arena. God had already achieved the decisive victory in the mythological realm; Jesus' victorious encounters with demonic forces fed from that triumph and allowed it a tactical preview on the historical stage. Some examples, and I emphasize that I have the space to offer only a limited number, of the contemporary manifestation of preaching as exorcism follow.

To be sure, the satanic realm and the demonic legions who march from it, have lost a great deal of their credibility and luster in the contemporary world. As author Walter Wink has written, "Demons...are the drunk uncle of the twentieth century: we keep them out of sight. Modern psychiatry had explained them all away as primitive approximations of mental illnesses now more exactly named, if not, arguably, better treated by modern drugs and therapies."[13] And yet, there appears still to be a pattern of evil that represents itself tactically in human affairs. Sin manifests itself in myriads of negative, *historical* ways; the power of God's kingdom must do no less. I have already discussed the manifestation of racism that represents human alienation from God; it lives itself out as

---

12. Pannell, 69.
13. Walter Wink, *Unmasking the Powers* (Philadelphia: Fortress Press, 1986) 41.

systemic, historical prejudice. The kingdom tactician must find a way to represent God's strategic battle plan, and, if Mark's vision is correct, to exorcise the demonic ability racism has to drive wedges between humans of different racial and ethnic origin. One of the most fundamental modes of such "exorcism" activity would be the universalist mission and membership agenda of contemporary churches that I have already mentioned. The church's most potent voice against racism would be its "preached" life of universalism. The church will not be able to create in the world what it does not live in its own existence. To preview the universalism of the kingdom in the way it tactically structures its own life and mission would be the most likely way in which the church could become a present pocket that utilizes future kingdom power to "exorcise" the demonic force of racism. What God has already accomplished, the defeat of sin's satanic power of racial prejudice, can be realized in and thereby cultivated through the preached life of the communities that live and work in the name of God's most accomplished tactician.

Tactical operations against the demonic force of the drug world is another area where the contemporary church can represent God's strategic kingdom activity in its current preaching word and deed. Once again we are faced with what appears on the surface to be a case of non-correspondence. The contemporary drug culture is a result of our world's hyper-scientific, technological foundation. Contraband products can be produced a world away, packaged, shipped and sold illegally in local African-American neighborhoods at huge profits due to laboratory skills and distribution techniques that have been mass produced at the lay level. Many of the most volatile and dangerous talents of economics and science are no longer the dominion only of the educated and professionalized elite. Common criminals now make use of sophisticated science to mass produce a culture of psychological and physical addiction. It is the very picture of demonic possession, and it is choking the life out of inner-city African-American communities. Mark's image of the Gerasene demoniac bruising himself beyond repair in the hostile confines of a cemetery corresponds quite graphically to whole neighborhoods and entire classes of human beings (e.g., the African-American male) shooting and snorting their lives into oblivion.

As one of my students recently wrote in a paper, "the twentieth century remains largely in the grip of systemic evil that defies adequate explanation by psychological, political and socio-economic interpretations. Time and again sweet reason comes up short in the face of crises that, while ebbing and flowing in prominence, collectively make us feel that we are helpless to resist 'the submerging [of] our age into night.' "[14] His remarks were occasioned by his reflections on a Camden, New Jersey woman who told him, while pointing out three crack houses on her block, "It's like we're possessed."

In the Gospel of Mark, people and communities so possessed were set free by the preaching manifestation of exorcism. Again, these were not simply indi-

---

14. Mark C. Harper, "Recovering the Witness of Exorcism: Reflections on Collective Possession and the Temple Action in Mark," For New Testament 350, Princeton Theological Seminary, October 25, 1993, 2.

vidual acts which occasioned only the independence of a single person or group; they were tactical acts which represented God's global attack against the entire front of evil. Similar acts of preaching must be engaged in today. It is not enough to move against individual drug pushers or even individual crack houses; churches must find a way to represent God's systemic attack against the evil which perpetuates these individual acts. Churches must, in other words, find a way to make a systemic attack against an evil that is systemically attacking the people they serve. In his article, "African Americans in the Urban Milieu: Conditions, Trends, and Development Needs," Lenneal J. Henderson points to one such tactical "preaching" manifestation:

> In Oakland, CA, Safe Streets Now! is an innovative, low-cost, and effective program that empowers neighborhood residents with a safe, fast, and efficient step-by-step program to eliminate drug houses in their neighborhoods and to prevent them from reforming. Its primary purpose is to provide citizens with direct action tools to eliminate neighborhood nuisances house by house, street by street, and neighborhood by neighborhood. Under the guidance of a community organizer, neighbors take control of drug trafficking by pursuing legal action against property owners who rent to drug dealers. Since 1989, Safe Streets Now! has trained over 3,500 citizens to close over 250 drug houses.[15]

In the Gospel of Mark, the kingdom of God is *like* this.

Sexism is another contemporary force whose scope and magnitude give it an almost demonic presence in African-American society. Once again, the church, instead of leading the way in offering models of preaching activity which can "exorcise" this evil from our midst, reflects the very societal impulses it has been charged to transform. Lincoln and Mamiya report that of the nation's seven historic denominations, fewer than five percent of the clergy are female.[16] Jawanza Kunjufu demonstrates the magnitude of imbalance when he notes that the contemporary African-American church is 75 percent female. "How can a church have a membership of 75 percent females, and yet have females constitute only 5 percent of the church leadership?"[17] It can only do so by denying women the same opportunities of church leadership offered to men, and by helping to perpetuate the attitude among many of the church's laity that women cannot adequately represent God's Word in their preached words and deeds.

In Mark's presentation nothing can be further from the strategic representation of the kingdom reality. Certainly Mark demonstrates that women serve as disciples of Jesus, that they follow him, listen to his teachings, and in many cases act as his benefactor. But Mark makes his point even more precisely in his narration of the Syrophoenician Woman account (7:24–30). The impact here

---

15. Lenneal J. Henderson, "African Americans in the Urban Milieu: Conditions, Trends, and Development Needs," in Tidwell and Robinson, 111.

16. Lincoln and Mamiya, 127.

17. Jawanza Kunjufu, *Adam! Where Are You? Why Most Black Men Don't Go to Church* (Chicago: African American Images, 1994) 20.

comes as much from the fact that she is female as that she is Gentile. In her story it is not only the disciples who learn about faith, but it is also Jesus who marvels at and appears to learn from her caustic reply to his own determination not to assist her because of her Gentile status. Her response to Jesus opens Mark's narrative field in such a way that it becomes clear that God's gift of healing that comes in the package of Jesus' person and kingdom preaching activity is universal in its design and scope. Her words and actions *preach* a powerful message in Mark's gospel, a message that is critical for his readership. She, then, is the kind of preacher many — indeed, if the statistics are correct, most — contemporary African-American churches do not allow women to be.

This realization is doubly damning given the fact that women represent the lifeblood of African-American congregations. The problem lies not only with male leaders who deny women opportunities of service and preaching ministry. Male leaders of African-American churches who do not encourage, recruit, and assist capable women in the leadership roles of the churches represent a picture of the church where women can serve, and indeed must serve as members in order for the church to survive, but cannot lead. It is a sketch which must be at odds with the strategic image of the universal, consummate kingdom. Once again it appears that those who seek to do battle with the enemies of the kingdom, i.e., African-American male Christian leadership, find themselves inhabitants of the wrong camp.

How to preach the word in such a circumstance? It begins with a coordinated effort at the denominational levels that sweeps down into the laity, an effort designed to open African-American Christian communities to the vast potential of leadership capability in its talented pool of African-American women. Because many African-American male leaders have implied through their biblical teachings that women are incapable of preaching God's Word through their preached words and deeds, these same leaders must take it upon themselves to teach the biblical message sociolinguistically. That is to say, they must recognize and teach their congregants to recognize that the biblical materials often present a patriarchal attitude toward women. Women are treated as secondary (if treated at all!) in many biblical narratives. The biblical writers in these cases were very much mirroring the attitudes of the society around them as they offered God's Word through their very human lenses. African-American church leaders must teach this historical reality to their laity and then be careful to teach that while the gospel message remains valid for the contemporary circumstance, the first-century packaging in which it was cast must in many cases be recast in contemporary terms of universalism and equality.

On the next level, African-American churches must begin a strong recruitment process which engages young women who demonstrate interest in and ability for church leadership. This recruitment must go beyond the stages of verbal interest and encouragement, but must be realized in concrete practices of financial support and networking with seminaries and schools of theology. A concerted, systematic effort must be put into place that on the one hand teaches the church about the value of female preaching leadership, and on the other hand, finds, encourages, and provides opportunities for female preachers. By engaging in such an effort the African-American church will be taking a first step at manifesting its preaching by exorcising the demon of sexism that continues to possess and strangle it. Instead of mirroring the sexism of its surrounding human environment, it can begin the process of becoming a pocket that resists, and ultimately transforms it.

Similar examples of the preaching manifestation of teaching can be offered. And when I talk about teaching as a manifestation of kingdom preaching, I mean much more than lecturing and note taking. I mean what Paulo Freire calls "conscientization," which is, "making oppressed people aware of their potential to determine their own destiny."[18] It is teaching of this type that not only illumines and educates, but also plants the seeds of transformation. "Conscientization is a process of bringing oppressed people to self-awareness of their internal and external powers to act, to reason and interpret their social context, and to be self-determining in the realization of their potential for shaping the world in freedom, justice, and love."[19]

In considering this manifestation of preaching, I choose an example of contemporary concern which is of specific interest to me: economic development. An economic depression debilitates urban African-American communities. The church has a major role to play in transforming this predicament to one of economic hope and opportunity. The "poor in spirit" are charged with trespassing the boundaries that keep the physically destitute locked in their cycles of deprivation.

> The poor are blessed, according to the gospel, not because of their poverty but because God's kingdom is near, the kingdom that means the end of exploitation and poverty and other forms of dehumanization.... Just as Jesus' solidarity with sin was not to idealize it but to redeem from it, so our spiritual solidarity with material poverty is not to idealize it but to liberate from it. One cannot really be with the poor unless one is struggling and protesting against poverty.[20]

In other words, one must preach. Unfortunately, the black church suffers a historical deficiency in this area. Lincoln and Mamiya point to Peter Paris's observation that "Although many black economic enterprises had their beginnings in the black churches, and although the churches themselves constituted major economic institutions, they never gave high institutional priority to black economic development."[21] Paris's historical remark was backed up by Lincoln and Mamiya's contemporary statistical data. The results of their survey led them to the conclusion that,

> While a few elite black churches and pastors have been engaged in important projects that could help the economic development of their local

---

18. Harris, 41.
19. Ibid.
20. Hodgson, 78.
21. Cf. Lincoln and Mamiya, 262. From Paris, *The Social Teaching of the Black Churches,* 70.

areas, the majority of pastors and churches lacked adequate knowledge about financial investments and about the economic development of their own institutions and that of the surrounding community.[22]

Clearly, here is a place, given the plight of the African-American context of culture, where the church can become a kingdom pocket of resistance. Here is where its teaching must move beyond the confines of the scriptures and civil rights and into the economic agenda of economic self-help and financial strategy and planning. The church has the resources with which to make a difference; it needs only the training necessary to put those resources to a systematic developmental and therefore transformative use.

According to James Joseph, a 1986 Gallup Poll showed that 75 percent of all philanthropic dollars in the black community was funneled through religious institutions.[23] Since that polling the figures have tilted even more heavily in the direction of church dominance. "Emmett D. Carson, author of *A Hand Up: Black Philanthropy and Self Help in America,* writes that '90 percent of all black giving is channeled through the church' ($2 billion in offerings, according to the studies of black church historian C. Eric Lincoln)."[24] Kunjufu notes that when real estate and other assets are considered, the black church as a whole is worth approximately $50 billion.[25] W. R. Richardson, in an article for *The State of Black America, 1995,* writes that "The black church has at its beckoning call the economic strength of some small countries when pooled and resourced properly. It is a dynamic force."[26] He adds, "The collective buying power of the black community has been estimated at $400 billion, more than the gross national product of Canada."[27] He points to a 1993 random survey conducted by the New York Entertainment Committee of the National Baptist Church as a selective example of the church's economic resource. In the New York area the survey found that some 600 churches deposited $152 million annually in 21 banks, and that they had over $40 million in loans. Each Monday morning, the survey suggests, those churches deposited over $3 million in New York banks.[28] No wonder that many believe the church should use its power to secure credit to invest in and build communities rather than new church edifices. Richardson goes on to suggest that the church, if it were to pool its efforts, already can "facilitate policy changes and eliminate discrimination in lending and hiring practices."[29] The church has the power, the voice, and the economic leverage to make a difference if it uses its ability to teach its own and related memberships how to coordinate economic programs and projects with specific tactical programs of economic development in mind. "The church finds itself in a situation

---

22. Lincoln and Mamiya, 262.
23. James A. Joseph, *Remaking America: How the Benevolent Traditions of Many Cultures Are Transforming Our National Life* (San Francisco: Jossey-Bass Publishers, 1995) 83.
24. Tapia, 28.
25. Kunjufu, 13.
26. Richardson, 117.
27. Ibid., 124.
28. Ibid., 117.
29. Ibid.

where it is the best continuing, organized entity in the black community for the acquisition and redevelopment of land, the building of business enterprise and the employment of people."[30]

Operating as single and separate institutions African-American churches can continue to boast of social mission projects; operating jointly in coordinated efforts these same churches can begin to transform whole communities with new jobs, new businesses, new financial institutions, new access to loans and capital, and a new economic perspective of transformative hope. But vision is necessary, as is the teaching that can make the visionaries economic tacticians. Churches can begin to provide the opportunities for such teaching by securing professionals who can teach finance and economic empowerment to the laity and the ordained leadership, and then by working toward the kind of trust among different churches of different denominational affiliation in the same urban areas to coordinate efforts and pool economic resources toward the common goal of economic transformation.

Lincoln and Mamiya point to the Opportunities Industrialization Centers (OIC) as an example of just such economic effort on the part of the African-American church. Under the leadership of the Reverend Leon Sullivan of the Zion Baptist Church in Philadelphia, OIC developed in 1964 as a community-based employment training facility. Its objective was to train African-Americans with the kinds of skills necessary to compete in the technical employment market. Another piece of the developmental strategy of OIC was the 10–36 plan initiated in 1962 in Sullivan's church. "The plan called for church members to contribute $10 for thirty-six months to support the Philadelphia Community Investment Cooperative."[31] The group of 227 original subscribers grew to over 5,000 from some 400 participating black churches. $200 of every $360 dollars was invested in a for-profit organization which built the first and largest black-owned shopping complex in the United States. It was also tasked with building an apartment building, a garment manufacturing plant and a chain of convenience stores. The non-profit trust portion of the funding was used to sponsor programs like housing for the disadvantaged, remedial education, and other human services activities. OIC eventually became a nationwide phenomenon operating in 70 U.S. cities. Within five years it was handling government contracts worth $18 million. At its height in 1980 OIC operated in 160 cities and had trained and placed close to 700,000 people in jobs. Though there are certainly other ways in which churches can pool efforts and operate with and without the assistance of federal grants and funding, OIC represents one powerful example of the African-American church working not simply to do individual social ministry, but to use its resources to teach an entire community how to transform itself and the world around it. In the Gospel of Mark, the kingdom of God is *like* this.

It is *like* Baltimoreans United in Leadership Development (BUILD). A

---

30. Lloyd Gite, "The New Agenda of the Black Church: Economic Development for Black America," *Black Enterprise* 24 (1993): 54–56.

31. Lincoln and Mamiya, 263.

church-based community group of more than 40 different religious organizations, BUILD is an example of a systemic effort of societal transformation. In its effort to represent the work of God in the world, it has moved its concern beyond the walls of the sanctuary in which its various members gather for worship and taken that concern into the lives of the oppressed who subsist in its inner city. BUILD's agenda operates from four different prongs. Under the topic "Work," it has pushed for a social compact that would deny government subsidies to businesses or projects that do not pay employees a wage above poverty levels. It also has inserted itself into the debate about the city's unemployment rate, and has demanded target rates of reduction. From its work agenda sprouted the Baltimore Commonwealth, a public-private partnership offering education and career assistance to city youth.

Under the topic "Safety," BUILD has pushed for more trained police officers in the city's police districts. Under the topic "Youth," BUILD has involved itself in debates about per-pupil spending allocations in the school system. It has also encouraged the use of funds from city attractions for neighborhood libraries, recreation centers, and other projects devoted to children. Its agenda calls for the creation of a $10 million Child First Authority that would develop education and recreation programs.

Finally, under the topic "Housing," BUILD has pushed for better housing for low- and moderate-income workers. Out of its agenda sprang the Nehemiah project, a program designed to build such houses in one of the city's most devastated centers. Working with other community-based groups, BUILD was able in 1990 to secure $2.2 million in pledges that leveraged millions more in federal, state, and city funds.

BUILD's efforts in these four areas is not limited to the individual achievements I have listed here. They provide only the foundation of an organization of interventionist-oriented groups and churches devoted to the vision of a transformed community. And to make certain that the politicians who manage the city are aware of their concerns, the members of BUILD maintain an ongoing program of political awareness that challenges persons running for elective office to speak to the communal issues and concerns they have established. This is the kind of transformative vision that breaks down the barriers of urban oppression. It is a coordinated, systematic, tactical assault on the boundaries that limit human potential. It is, for that reason, *like* the kingdom of God in the Gospel of Mark.[32]

> History has taught that "we cannot live by prayer and fasting alone"; we need economic empowerment.... Community investment not only helps members of local congregations learn about poverty and wealth, examine their understanding of stewardship, and put capital at the service of

---

32. Material on BUILD compiled from the following sources: Ann LoLordo, "Nehemiah Project Donors Celebrate Successful Start of New Homes for Poor in West Baltimore," *Baltimore Morning Sun,* Friday, June 26, 1992. Wiley A. Hall, "BUILD Wants to Take Candidates to Next Step," *Baltimore Evening Sun,* Thursday, June 8, 1995. Editorial, "BUILD's Agenda for the City," *Baltimore Evening Sun,* Tuesday, August 1, 1995.

the gospel," but it also serves as a way of mobilizing African Americans' consciousness and promoting the black church as a viable part of the African-American community.[33]

There is finally the manifestation of miracle. Traditionally miracles are defined by the breaking of some physical law of nature, such as the overcoming of a biological disability with a word, or the interruption of nature with an authoritative command. In this case, it is more an interruption of historical, social and political expectation. Contemporary miracles need not have the explosiveness of a storm quelled or an illness removed to make transformative waves. The miraculous transformation of a community can be just as enthralling, perhaps even more so. In this case there is a stronger sense of correspondence between what God is doing strategically, triumphing over the power of sin and its various manifestations of evil, and what humans can do tactically.

The statistical data on the African-American context of culture demonstrates that radical change, one could say miraculous change, is necessary in many areas of black life. The family has been devastated by economic and racial pressures. The odds are long, the expectations low. Here is an opportunity for the church to represent socially what Jesus did individually, effect a human cure that represents God's divine healing. There are, of course, many areas within the category of the black family that could be addressed, including drop-out rates, teen pregnancy, female-headed households, unemployment, poverty levels, and crime rates. I choose for consideration here what I believe is one of the most severe problems within the community, the plight of the African-American male. His predicament was documented in chapter 14. His prospects are dim. His prognosis for survival bleak. Here the church can take upon itself the preaching manifestation Mark's narrative called the miraculous. For indeed, it will take a great power, a great tactical force, united with other committed and similarly directed forces, to turn the fortune of this endangered species. One church cannot achieve results alone, no matter how nobly it approaches its social ministries programming. It will take what African-American churches are traditionally hesitant to give, a coordinated, systematic effort that requires trust among congregations and a sharing of economic resources and a pooling of political clout to make a difference. In 1967 Martin Luther King, Jr., argued that

> While not ignoring the fact that the ultimate way to diminish our problems of crime, family disorganization, illegitimacy and so forth will have to be found through a government program to help the frustrated Negro male find his true masculinity by placing him on his own two economic feet, we must do all within our power to approach these goals ourselves.[34]

In the latter 1990s, having seen the cutbacks in government funding to help the dispossessed and the racial backlash against African-Americans in general

---

33. Richardson, 119–20.
34. King, 125.

and African-American males in particular, we now know that we must do most, if not all, of the work to approach these goals ourselves. Where do we start? I believe we begin with the economic resources and political influence of African-American churches throughout the country, and with the universal cooperative effort of black and white churches working resourcefully together.

Recently I heard the Reverend Samuel Proctor remark that a strategy should be devised to make use of closed military bases for the use of training African-American males. I had long thought that schools dedicated solely to the purpose of educating African-American males in a science and math knowledge and skills base that would make them competitive future prospects for jobs and colleges were necessary. However, until hearing Dr. Proctor I had not overcome the problem of how to establish such enterprises in the absence of the physical facilities needed to accommodate them. Proctor has a promising idea, I think. Continued use of such facilities would be more preferable than the idling of abandoned bases which can still serve a positive public use. An emphasis on military discipline and comportment could serve as a means around which to structure a learning environment that could separate at-risk African-American males from the local environments that so often lead them into trouble or disillusionment. The physical training combined with first-rate educational opportunity could begin to offer a possibility for transformation that is currently unavailable to many young African-American males.

Given the data amassed by Lincoln, Mamiya and others, it is clear that the African-American church operating systemically has the resources to bring such a vision to reality. In cooperation with state and federal funding sources, and a cooperative white church, the possibilities could be even brighter. Using such schools as an alternative to detention or jail for many young offenders would also offer an opportunity out of the cycle of violence and destruction that captures so many. A nation already spending a fortune to incarcerate these young men with no hope of obtaining a return on its investment would, I would think, be attracted by an opportunity to create citizens with high levels of motivation and skill. Still, given the complexity of the problem and the lack of interventionist vision on the part of Christians gathered religiously in the sanctuaries, it would take a miracle. One only wonders whether the church that follows the Jesus of Mark's narrative considers the realm of the miracle a part of its kingdom preaching call.

These examples serve only as illustrations of the kinds of preaching manifestations the African-American church, provoked by an interventionist perspective and agenda, could utilize in an effort to transform the socio-political condition of its constituents. Mark's Gospel provides both an inspiration and a model for activity. The evangelist envisioned a Jesus who saw the kingdom coming and understood the gravity of that realization. His narrative task was to pass on that grave sense of urgency and the provocation to act in boundary-breaking ways. Mark's sociolinguistic task has been to *do* the same thing in the minds, spirits, and lives of his readers, those who first read his words in the charged Palestinian context of the first century, and those who now read those same words in the corresponding African-American contexts of the urban twentieth and twenty-first centuries. The charge is: Go Preach!

> This is the challenge. If we will dare to meet it honestly, historians in future years will have to say there lived a great people — a black people — who bore their burdens of oppression in the heat of many days and who, through tenacity and creative commitment, injected new meaning into the veins of American [and, I would add, Christian] life.[35]

---

35. Ibid., 134.

Bibliography

Abrahams, I. *Studies in Pharisaism and the Gospels.* New York: KTAV Publishing House, Inc., 1917.

Anderson, H. *The Gospel of Mark.* London: Oliphants, 1976.

Atkinson, Pansye. *Brown vs. Topeka: An African American's View of Desegregation and Miseducation.* Chicago: African American Images, 1993.

Balz, Horst and Günther Wanke. "φοβέω, φοβέομαι, φόβος, δέος." *TDNT* 9:189–220.

Bauckham, Richard. "Jesus' Demonstration in the Temple." In *Law And Religion: Essays on the Place of the Law in Israel and Early Christianity,* Barnabas Lindars, editor. Cambridge: James Clarke & Co, 1988.

Bauer, Walter, William F. Arndt, and F. Wilbur Gingrich. *A Greek-English Lexicon of the New Testament and Other Early Christian Literature.* Second edition. Chicago: The University of Chicago Press, 1979.

Beasley-Murray, G. R. *Jesus and the Kingdom of God.* Grand Rapids: William B. Eerdmans, 1986.

Behm, Johannes. "ἐκχέω, ἐκχύν(ν)ω." *TDNT* 2:467–69.

———. "κλάω...." *TDNT* 3:726–43.

———. "καινός...." *TDNT* 3:447–55.

———. "ἄρτος." *TDNT* 1:477–78.

Best, Ernest. *Following Jesus: Discipleship in the Gospel of Mark.* Sheffield: JSOT Press, 1981.

Beyer, Hermann. "διακονέω, διακονία, διάκονος." *TDNT* 2:81–93.

———. "εὐλογέω...." *TDNT* 2:754–65.

Blount, Brian K. *Cultural Interpretation: Reorienting New Testament Criticism.* Minneapolis: Augsburg/Fortress Press, 1995.

———. "Preaching the Kingdom: Mark's Apocalyptic Call for Prophetic Engagement." *Princeton Seminary Bulletin* Supplementary Issue, no. 3 (1994): 171–98.

———. "The Social World of Bandits." In *The Good Samaritan (Luke 10:25–37): An American Bible Society Interactive CD-ROM for Windows.* New York: American Bible Society, 1996.

Boers, Hendrikus. "Apocalyptic Eschatology in I Corinthians 15." *Interpretation* 21 (1967): 50–64.

———. "Reflections on the Gospel of Mark: A Structural Investigation." *SBL Seminar Papers* 26 (1987): 255–67.

———. *Who Was Jesus? The Historical Jesus and the Synoptic Gospels.* San Francisco: Harper & Row Publishers, 1989.

Boomershine, Thomas E. "Epistemology at the Turn of the Ages in Paul, Jesus and Mark: Rhetoric and Dialectic in Apocalyptic and the New Testament." In *Apocalyptic and the New Testament,* Joel Marcus and Marion L. Soards, editors, 147–67. Sheffield: JSOT Press, 1989.

———. "Biblical Story Telling in the City." In *Urban Church Education,* Donald B. Rogers, editor, 143–51. Birmingham: Religious Education Press, 1989.

Borg, Marcus J. *Jesus, A New Vision: Spirit, Culture, and the Life of Discipleship.* San Francisco: Harper & Row Publishers, 1987.

Bornkamm, G. "μυστήριον, μυέω." *TDNT* 4:802–29.

Braun, Herbert. "ποιέω...." *TDNT* 6:485–64.

Brown, Raymond E. "The Burial of Jesus (Mark 15:42–47)." *Catholic Biblical Quarterly* 50 (1988): 233–45.

Brown, Schuyler. "The Secret of the Kingdom of God (Mark 4:11)." *Journal of Biblical Literature* 92 (1973): 60–74.

"BUILD's Agenda for the City." Editorial, *Baltimore Evening Sun,* August 1, 1995.

Buchanan, George Wesley. "An Additional Note to 'Mark 11.15–19: Brigands in the Temple'" *Hebrew Union College Annual* 31 (1960): 103–5.

———. "Mark 11.15–19: Brigands in the Temple." *Hebrew Union College Annual* 30 (1959): 169–77.

———. "Symbolic Money-Changers in the Temple?" *NTS* 37 (1991): 280–90.

Büchsel, Friedrich. "δίδωμι, δῶρον...παραδίδωμι...." *TDNT* 2:166–74.

Bultmann, Rudolf. *The History of the Synoptic Tradition,* translator John Marsh. New York and London: Harper and Row, 1963.

———. *Jesus and the Word,* translator Louise Pettibone Smith. New York: Charles Scribner's Sons, 1934.

———. *Jesus Christ and Mythology.* New York: Charles Scribner's Sons, 1958.

———. "ἀφίημι, ἄφεσις,..." *TDNT* 1:509–12.

Burbridge, Lynn. "Toward Economic Self-Sufficiency: Independence Without Poverty." In *The State of Black America, 1995,* Billy J. Tidwell and Paulette J. Robinson, editors, 117–32. New York: The National Urban League, 1995.

Carson, Clayborne. "Martin Luther King, Jr., and the African-American Social Gospel." In *African-American Christianity,* Paul E. Johnson, editor, 159–77. Berkeley: University of California Press, 1994.

Carson, Emmett D. *A Hand Up: Black Philanthropy and Self-Help in America.* Washington, DC: Joint Center for Political and Economic Studies, 1993.

Casey, Maurice. "The Original Aramaic Form of Jesus' Interpretation of the Cup." *Journal of Theological Studies* 41 (1990): 1–12.

Catchpole, David R. "The 'Triumphal' Entry." In *Jesus and the Politics of His Day,* Ernst Bammel and C. F. D. Moule, editors, 319–34. Cambridge: Cambridge University Press, 1984.

Chambers, Julius L. "Black Americans and the Courts: Has the Clock Been Turned Back Permanently?" In *The State of Black America 1995,* Billy J. Tidwell and Paulette J. Robinson, editors, 241–54. New York: National Urban League, Inc., 1995.

Chapman, Mark. "The Kingdom of God and Ethics: From Ritschl to Liberation Theology." In *The Kingdom of God and Human Society,* Robin Barbour, editor, 140–63. Edinburgh: T & T Clark, 1993.

———. "Walter Rauschenbusch and the Coming of God's Kingdom." In *The Kingdom of God and Human Society,* Robin Barbour, editor, 173–90. Edinburgh: T & T Clark, 1993.

Charlesworth, James H., editor. *The Old Testament Pseudepigrapha,* Volume I: *Apocalyptic Literature and Testaments.* Garden City, NY: Doubleday & Company, 1983.

Chilton, Bruce and J. I. H. McDonald. *Jesus and the Ethics of the Kingdom.* Grand Rapids: William B. Eerdmans Publishing, 1987.

Collins, Adela Yarbro. *The Beginning of the Gospel: Probings of Mark in Context.* Minneapolis: Fortress Press, 1992.

————. "The Empty Tomb in the Gospel According to Mark." In *Hermes and Athena: Biblical Exegesis and Philosophical Theology,* Eleonore Stump and Thomas P. Flint, editors, 107–39. Notre Dame, IN.: University of Notre Dame Press, 1993.

————. "Response to Kretzmann." In *Hermes and Athena: Biblical Exegesis and Philosophical Theology,* Eleonore Stump and Thomas P. Flint, editors, 151–55. Notre Dame, IN.: University of Notre Dame Press, 1993.

Collins, John J. *The Apocalyptic Imagination: An Introduction to the Jewish Matrix of Christianity.* New York: Crossroad, 1984.

————. "The Jewish Apocalypses." *Semeia* 14 (1979): 21–59.

————. "The Kingdom of God in the Apocrypha and Pseudepigrapha." In *The Kingdom of God in 20th-Century Interpretation,* Wendell Willis, editor, 81–95. Peabody, MA: Hendrickson Publishers, 1987.

————. "Towards the Morphology of a Genre." *Semeia* 14 (1979): 1–20.

Comay, Jean. *The Temple of Judaism.* New York: Holt, Rinehart, and Winston, 1975.

Cook, John G. *The Structure and Persuasive Power of Mark: A Linguistic Approach. SBL Semeia Studies.* Atlanta: Scholars Press, 1995.

Cotterell, Peter. "Sociolinguistics and Biblical Interpretation." *Vox Evangelica* 16 (1986): 61–76.

Cranfield, C. E. B. *The Gospel According to Saint Mark. Cambridge Greek Testament Commentary.* Cambridge: Cambridge University Press, 1959.

Davies, J. G. (John Gordon). *Christians, Politics and Violent Revolution.* London: SCM Press, 1976.

De Q. Robin, A. "The Cursing of the Fig Tree in Mark XI. A Hypothesis." *NTS* 8 (1962): 276–81.

Derret, J. Duncan. "Moving Mountains and Uprooting Trees (Mk 11:22; Mt 17:20, 21:21; Lk 17:6)." *Bibbia e Oriente* 30 (1988): 231–44.

Dewey, Joanna. "Point of View and the Disciples in Mark." *Society of Biblical Literature Seminar Papers* 21 (1982): 97–106.

Dodd, C. H. *The Parables of the Kingdom.* New York: Charles Scribner's Sons, 1961.

Donahue, John. *Are You the Christ?: The Trial Narrative in the Gospel of Mark.* Missoula, MT: Society of Biblical Literature, 1973.

Donaldson, Terence L. "Rural Bandits, City Mobs and the Zealots." *Journal for the Study of Judaism in the Persian, Hellenistic and Roman Period* 21 (1990): 19–40.

Douglas, Mary T. *Purity and Danger: An Analysis of the Concepts of Pollution and Taboo.* London: Routledge and Kegan Paul, 1966.

Dowd, Sharyn Echols. *Prayer, Power, and the Problem of Suffering, Vol. 105, SBL Dissertation Series.* Atlanta: Scholars Press, 1986.

Dyson, Michael Eric. *Reflecting Black: African-American Cultural Criticism.* Minneapolis and London: University of Minnesota Press, 1993.

Edelman, Marian Wright. "Black Children in America." In *The State of Black America 1995,* Billy J. Tidwell and Paulette J. Robinson, editors, 71–83. New York: National Urban League, Inc., 1995.

Elmore, W. Emory. "Linguistic Approaches to the Kingdom: Amos Wilder and Norman Perrin." In *The Kingdom of God in 20th-Century Interpretation,* Wendell Willis, editor, 53–65. Peabody, MA: Hendrickson Publishers, 1987.

Enslin, Morton S. "A New Apocalyptic." *Religion in Life* 44 (1975): 105–10.

Epp, Eldon Jay. "Mediating Approaches to the Kingdom: Werner Georg Kümmel and George Eldon Ladd." In *The Kingdom of God in 20th-Century Interpretation,* Wendell Willis, editor, 35–52. Peabody, MA: Hendrickson Publishers, 1987.

Evans, Craig A. "Jesus' Action in the Temple: Cleansing or Portent of Destruction?" *Catholic Biblical Quarterly* 51 (1989): 237–70.

———. "Predictions of the Destruction of the Herodian Temple in the Pseudepigrapha, Qumran Scrolls, and Related Texts." *Journal for the Study of the Pseudepigrapha* 10 (1992): 89–147.

Fasold, Ralph. *The Sociolinguistics of Language.* Cambridge, MA: Basil Blackwell, 1990.

Foerster, Werner. "ὄρος." *TDNT* 5:475–87.

Foerster, Werner and Knut Schäferdiek. "σατανᾶς." *TDNT* 7:151–65.

Frazier, E. Franklin. *The Negro Church in America.* New York: Schocken Books, 1974.

Fredriksen, Paula. "Jesus and the Temple, Mark and the War," David J. Lull, editor. *Society of Biblical Literature 1990 Seminar Papers* 29 (1990): 293–310.

Freire, Paulo. *The Politics of Education: Culture, Power and Liberation.* South Hadley, MA: Bergin & Garvey Publishers, Inc., 1985.

Friedrich, Gerhard. "κῆρυξ...κηρύσσω." *TDNT* 3:683–717.

———. "εὐαγγελίζομαι, εὐαγγέλιον...." *TDNT* 2:707–37.

Fuellenbach, John. *The Kingdom of God: The Message of Jesus Today.* Maryknoll, NY: Orbis Books, 1995.

Fuller, Reginald H. *The Formation of the Resurrection Narratives.* New York: Macmillan, 1971.

Gager, John G. *Kingdom and Community: The Social World of Early Christianity.* Englewood Cliffs, NJ: Prentice-Hall, Inc., 1975.

Gerhardsson, Birger. "Mark and the Female Witnesses." In *DUMU-E₂-DUB-BA-A: Studies in Honor of Ake W. Sjöberg,* Hermann Gehrens, Darlene Loding, Martha T. Roth, editors, 217–26. Philadelphia: Samuel Noah Kramer Fund, 11, 1989.

Giblin, Charles Homer. "The Beginning of the Ongoing Gospel (MK 1, 2–16, 8)." In *The Four Gospels 1992: Festschrift Frans Neirynck, Volume II,* C. M. Tuckett, G. Van Belle, J. Verheyden, F. Van Segbroeck, editors, 975–85. Leuven: Leuven University Press, 1992.

Gite, Lloyd. "The New Agenda of the Black Church: Economic Development for Black America." *Black Enterprise* 24, no. 5 (1993): 54–59.

Goodman, Martin. "The First Jewish Revolt: Social Conflict and the Problem of Debt." *Journal of Religious Studies* 33 (1982): 417–27.

Grady, Bruce T. *Contemporary Attempts to Improve Education for African Americans within Public Schools and a Proposal from the Black Church Perspective.* Master's Thesis: Princeton Theological Seminary. Thesis Adviser Peter J. Paris. 1996.

Greenway, Roger S. and Timothy M. Monsma. *Cities: Missions' New Frontier.* Grand Rapids: Baker Book House, 1989.

Greeven, Heinrich. "εὐσχήμων." *TDNT* 2:770–72.

Grundmann, Walter. "δεξιός." *TDNT* 2:37–40.

———. "δεῖ, δέον ἐστί." *TDNT* 2:21–25.

———. "ἰσχύω, ἰσχυρός...." *TDNT* 3:397–402.

Gundry, Robert H. *Mark: A Commentary on His Apology for the Cross.* Grand Rapids: William B. Eerdmans Publishing Co., 1993.

Gutiérrez, Gustavo. *The God of Life,* translator Matthew J. O'Connell. Maryknoll, NY: Orbis Books, 1991.

Hale, Janice E. "The Transmission of Faith to Young African American Children." In *The Recovery of Black Presence: An Interdisciplinary Exploration,* Randall C. Bailey and Jacquelyn Grant, editors. Nashville: Abingdon, 1995.

Hall, Wiley A. "BUILD Wants to Take Candidates to Next Step." *Baltimore Evening Sun,* June 8, 1995.

Halliday, M. A. K. and Ruqaiya Hasan. *Language, Context, and Text: Aspects of Language in a Social Semiotic Perspective.* Oxford: Oxford University Press, 1990.

Hamilton, Charles V. "On Parity and Political Empowerment." In *The State of Black America 1995,* Billy J. Tidwell and Paulette J. Robinson, editors, 257–66. New York: National Urban League, Inc., 1995.

Handy, Robert T., editor. *The Social Gospel in America 1870–1920: Gladden, Ely, Rauschenbusch.* New York: Oxford University Press, 1966.

Hare, Bruce R. "Black Youth at Risk." In *The State of Black America 1995,* Billy J. Tidwell and Paulette J. Robinson, editors, 85–97. New York: National Urban League, Inc., 1995.

Harkness, Georgia. *Understanding the Kingdom of God.* Nashville: Abingdon, 1974.

Harper, Mark C. "Recovering the Witness of Exorcism: Reflections on Collective Possession and the Temple Action in Mark." For New Testament 350, Princeton Theological Seminary, October 25, 1993.

Harris, Sr., Forrest E. *Ministry for Social Crisis: Theology and Praxis in the Black Church Tradition.* Macon, GA: Mercer University Press, 1993.

Hauck, Friedrich. "παραβολή." *TDNT* 5:744–61.

———. "θερίζω, θερισμός." *TDNT* 3:132–33.

Heil, J. P. "Mark 14, 1–52: Narrative Structure and Reader-Response." *Biblica* 71 (1990): 305–32.

Henderson, Lenneal J. "African Americans in the Urban Milieu: Conditions, Trends, and Development Needs." In *The State of Black America 1995,* Billy J. Tidwell and Paulette J. Robinson, editors, 101–32. New York: National Urban League, Inc., 1995.

Hendrickx, Hermann. *The Miracle Stories: Studies in the Synoptic Gospels.* San Francisco: Harper and Row, 1987.

Hiers, Jr., Richard H. "Pivotal Reactions to the Eschatological Interpretations: Rudolf Bultmann and C. H. Dodd." In *The Kingdom of God in 20th-Century Interpretation,* Wendell Willis, editor, 15–33. Peabody, MA: Hendrickson Publishers, 1987.

———. "Not the Season for Figs." *Journal of Biblical Literature* 87 (1968): 394–400.

Hobsbawm, E. J. *Bandits.* New York: Dell, 1969.

———. *Primitive Rebels.* New York: Norton, 1965.

Hodgson, Peter C. *Revisioning the Church: Ecclesial Freedom in the New Paradigm.* Philadelphia: Fortress Press, 1988.

Hooker, Morna D. *A Commentary on the Gospel According to St. Mark.* London: A & C Black, 1991.

———. *Jesus and the Servant: The Influence of the Servant Concept of Deutero-Isaiah in the New Testament.* London: SPCK, 1959.

———. "Trial and Tribulation in Mark 13." *Bulletin of the John Rylands University Library of Manchester* 65, no. 1 (1982): 78–99.

Horbury, William. "Christ as Brigand in Anti-Christian Polemic." In *Jesus and the Politics of His Day,* Ernst Bammel and C. F. D. Moule, editors, 183–96. Cambridge: Cambridge University Press, 1984.

Horsley, Richard A. "Ancient Jewish Banditry and the Revolt Against Rome, AD 66–70." *Catholic Biblical Quarterly* 43 (1981): 409–32.

———. "Bandits, Messiahs and Longshoremen: Popular Unrest in Galilee Around the Time of Jesus." In *Social World of Formative Christianity and Judaism,* J. Neusner, editor, 50–68. Philadelphia: Fortress Press, 1988.

———. "High Priest and Politics in Roman Palestine." *Journal for the Study of Judaism* 17 (1986): 23–55

———. *Jesus and the Spiral of Violence: Popular Jewish Resistance in Roman Palestine.* 1st ed. Minneapolis: Fortress Press, 1993.

———. "Josephus and the Bandits." *Journal for the Study of Judaism* 10 (1979): 37–63.

————. *Sociology and the Jesus Movement.* New York: Crossroad, 1989.

————. "The Zealots: Their Origin, Relationships and Importance in the Jewish Revolt." *Novum Testamentum* 28 (1986): 159–92.

Horsley, Richard A. and John S. Hanson. *Bandits, Prophets, and Messiahs: Popular Movements in the Time of Jesus.* New York: Winston Press, 1985.

Hultgren, Arland J. *Jesus and His Adversaries: The Form and Function of the Conflict Stories in the Synoptic Tradition.* Minneapolis: Augsburg Publishing House, 1979.

Hurston, Zora Neale. "Sometimes in the Mind." In *The Book of Negro Folklore,* Langston Hughes and Arna Bontemps, editors, 93–102. New York: Dodd, Mead and Company, 1958.

Jennings, Theodore, and Hendrikus Boers. *Text and Logos: The Humanistic Interpretation of the New Testament.* Homage series. Atlanta, GA: Scholars Press, 1990.

Jeremias, Joachim. *The Eucharistic Words of Jesus.* New York: Charles Scribner's Sons, 1966.

————. *Jesus' Promise to the Nations.* London: SCM Press, 1958.

————. "πάσχα." *TDNT* 5:896–984.

————. "γραμματεύς." *TDNT* 1:740–42.

Jones, Robert E. "Learning to Face Diversity in Urban Churches." In *Urban Church Education,* Donald B. Rogers, editor, 84–101. Birmingham: Religious Education Press, 1989.

Joseph, James A. *Remaking America: How the Benevolent Traditions of Many Cultures Are Transforming Our National Life.* San Francisco: Jossey-Bass Publishers, 1995.

Joyner, Charles. " 'Believer I Know': The Emergence of African-American Christianity." In *African-American Christianity,* Paul E. Johnson, editor, 18–46. Berkeley: University of California Press, 1994.

Juel, Donald. *The Messiah and the Temple: A Study of Jesus' Trial before the Sanhedrin in the Gospel of Mark.* New Haven: Yale University, Ph.D. Dissertation, 1973.

Käsemann, Ernst. "The Beginnings of Christian Theology." In *New Testament Questions of Today,* 82–107. Philadelphia: Fortress Press, 1969.

————. "On the Subject of Primitive Christian Apocalyptic." In *New Testament Questions of Today,* 108–37. Philadelphia: Fortress Press, 1969.

Kaylor, R. David. *Jesus the Prophet: His Vision of the Kingdom on Earth.* Louisville: Westminster/John Knox Press, 1994.

Kee, Howard Clark. *Community of the New Age: Studies in Mark's Gospel.* Philadelphia: Westminster Press, 1977.

————. "The Function of Scriptural Quotations and Allusions in Mark 11–16." In *Jesus und Paulus: Festschrift für Werner Georg Kümmel zum 70. Geburtstag,* E. Earle Ellis and Erich Grässer, editors, 165–88. Göttingen: Vandenhoeck & Ruprecht, 1975.

————. "The Social Setting of Mark: An Apocalyptic Community." *SBL Seminar Papers* (1984): 245–55.

————. "The Transfiguration in Mark: Epiphany or Apocalyptic Vision?" In *Understanding the Sacred Text: Essays in Honor of Morton S. Enslin on the Hebrew Bible and Christian Beginnings,* John Reumann, editor, 135–52. Valley Forge: Judson Press, 1972.

Keegan, Terence J. "The Parable of the Sower and Mark's Jewish Leaders." *Catholic Biblical Quarterly* 56 (1994): 501–18.

Kelber, Werner. *The Kingdom in Mark: A New Place and a New Time.* Philadelphia: Fortress Press, 1974.

Kertelege, Karl. "Das Abendmahl Jesu im Markusevangelium." In *Begegnung mit dem Wort: Festschrift für Heinrich Zimmermann,* Josef Zmijewski, editor, 67–80. Bonn: Peter Hanstein Verlag GmbH, 1980.

King, Jr., Martin Luther. *Where Do We Go from Here: Chaos or Community?* New York and London: Harper and Row, 1967.

Kittel, Gerhard. "ἀκολουθέω...." *TDNT* 1:210–16.

———. "ἀκούω...." *TDNT* 1:216–25.

Kotter, Wendy J. "For It Was Not the Season for Figs." *Catholic Biblical Quarterly* 48 (1986): 62–66.

Krause, Deborah. "Narrated Prophecy in Mark 11.12–21: The Divine Authorization of Judgment." In *The Gospels and the Scriptures of Israel,* Craig Evans and W. Richard Stegner, editors, 235–48. Sheffield: Sheffield Academic Press, 1994.

Kretzmann, Norman. "Resurrection Resurrected: Comments on the Paper of Adela Yarbro Collins." In *Hermes and Athena: Biblical Exegesis and Philosophical Theology,* Eleonore Stump and Thomas P. Flint, editors, 141–50. Notre Dame, IN: University of Notre Dame Press, 1993.

Kümmel, Werner Georg. *Promise and Fulfillment: The Eschatological Message of Jesus.* London: SCM Press, 1957.

Kunjufu, Jawanza. *Adam! Where Are You? Why Most Black Men Don't Go to Church.* Chicago: African American Images, 1994.

Ladd, George E. *Jesus and the Kingdom: The Eschatology of Biblical Realism.* New York: Harper and Row, 1964.

Lambrecht, Jan. *Once More Astonished: The Parables of Jesus.* New York: Crossroad, 1983.

Lane, William L. *The Gospel According to Mark.* New International Commentary on the New Testament. Grand Rapids: William B. Eerdmans Publishing, Co., 1974.

Laws, Sophie. "Can Apocalyptic Be Relevant?" In *What About the New Testament?: Essays in Honour of Christopher Evans,* Morna Hooker, editor, 89–102. London: SCM Press, 1975.

Léon-Dufour, Xavier. *Sharing the Eucharistic Bread: The Witness of the New Testament,* translator Matthew J. O'Connell. New York: Paulist Press, 1987.

Lincoln, C. Eric. *The Black Church Since Frazier.* New York: Schocken Books, 1974.

Lincoln, C. Eric and Lawrence H. Mamiya. *The Black Church in the African American Experience.* Durham, NC and London: Duke University Press, 1990.

Linthicum, Robert C. *City of God, City of Satan: A Biblical Theology of the Urban Church.* Grand Rapids: Zondervan Publishing House, 1991.

Lohse, Eduard. *The New Testament Environment.* Nashville: Abingdon Press, 1976.

LoLordo, Ann. "Nehemiah Project Donors Celebrate Successful Start of New Homes for Poor in West Baltimore." *Baltimore Morning Sun,* June 26, 1992.

Loury, Glenn C. "Beyond Civil Rights." In *The State of Black America 1995,* Billy J. Tidwell and Paulette J. Robinson, editors, 277–87. New York: National Urban League, Inc., 1995.

Louw, Johannes P. and Eugene A. Nida, editors. *Greek-English Lexicon of the New Testament Based on Semantic Domains.* Second edition, Volume 1. New York: United Bible Societies, 1988, 1989.

Lundström, Gösta. *The Kingdom of God in the Teaching of Jesus: A History of Interpretation from the Last Decade of the Nineteenth Century to the Present Day,* translator Joan Bulman. Richmond: John Knox Press, 1963.

Lupton, Robert D. *Theirs Is the Kingdom: Celebrating the Gospel in Urban America.* Barbara R. Thompson, editor. San Francisco: Harper & Row Publishers, 1989.

McBay, Shirley M. "The Condition of African-American Education: Changes and Challenges." In *The State of Black America 1995,* Billy J. Tidwell and Paulette J. Robinson, editors, 31–45. New York: National Urban League, Inc., 1995.

Malbon, Elizabeth Struthers. "Disciples/Crowds/Whoever: Markan Characters and Readers." *Novum Testamentum* 28 (1986): 104–30.

———. "The Jewish Leaders in the Gospel of Mark: A Literary Study of Marcan Characterization." *Journal of Biblical Literature* 108, no. 2 (1989): 259–81.

———. *Narrative Space and Mythic Meaning in Mark.* San Francisco: Harper and Row, 1986.

Malina, Bruce J. "Reading Theory Perspective: Reading Luke-Acts," Jerome H. Neyrey, editor. In *The Social World of Luke-Acts,* 3–23. Peabody, MA: Hendrickson Publishers, 1991.

———. "The Social Sciences and Biblical Interpretation." *Interpretation* 36 (1982): 229–42.

Marcus, Joel. "Authority to Forgive Sins upon the Earth: The *SHEMA* in the Gospel of Mark." In *The Gospels and the Scriptures of Israel,* Craig A. Evans and W. Richard Stegner, editors, 196–211. Sheffield: Sheffield Academic Press, 1994.

———. "The Jewish War and the *Sitz im Leben* of Mark." *Journal of Biblical Literature* 111, no. 3 (1992): 441–62.

———. "Mark 4:10–12 and Marcan Epistemology." *Journal of Biblical Literature* 103 (1984): 557–74.

———. *The Mystery of the Kingdom of God.* Atlanta: Scholar's Press, 1986.

———. *The Way of the Lord: Christological Exegesis of the Old Testament in the Gospel of Mark.* Louisville: Westminster/John Knox Press, 1992.

Martyn, J. Louis. "From Paul to Flannery O'Connor with the Power of Grace." *Katallagete* 7, no. 4 (1981): 10–17.

Marxsen, Willi. *Mark the Evangelist: Studies on the Redaction History of the Gospel.* James Boyce, Donald Juel, William Poehlmann, Roy A. Harrisville, translators. Nashville: Abingdon Press, 1969.

Mendels, Doron. *The Rise and Fall of Jewish Nationalism.* New York: Doubleday, 1992.

Merkel, Helmut. "The Opposition between Jesus and Judaism." In *Jesus and the Politics of His Day,* Ernst Bammel and C. F. D. Moule, editors, 129–44. Cambridge, MA: Cambridge University Press, 1984.

Metzger, Bruce. *A Textual Commentary on the Greek New Testament.* Stuttgart: United Bible Societies, 1971.

Michael, Chris. "Glimpses of the Kingdom of God in the Urban Church." In *Urban Church Education,* Donald B. Rogers, editor, 41–49. Birmingham: Religious Education Presss, 1989.

Michaelis, W. "ὁδός...." *TDNT* 5:42–114.

———. "πάσχω...." *TDNT* 5:904–39.

———. "λευκός, λευκαίνω." *TDNT* 4:241–51.

———. "λύχνος, λυχνία." *TDNT* 4:324–27.

Mitchell, Henry H. and Nicholas C. Cooper-Lewter. *Soul Theology: The Heart of American Black Culture.* San Francisco: Harper and Row, 1986.

Moloney, Francis J. "The Eucharist as Jesus' Presence to the Broken." *Pacifica* 2 (1989): 151–74.

Moxnex, Halvor. *The Economy of the Kingdom: Social Conflict and Economic Relations in Luke's Gospel.* Philadelphia: Fortress Press, 1988.

Myers, Ched. *Binding the Strong Man: A Political Reading of Mark's Story of Jesus.* Maryknoll, NY: Orbis Books, 1988.

Navone, John. "The Last Day and the Last Supper in Mark's Gospel." *Theology* 91 (1988): 38–43.

Neusner, Jacob. "Money-Changers in the Temple: The Mishnah's Explanation." *NTS* 35 (1989): 287–90.

Neyrey, Jerome. "The Idea of Purity in Mark's Gospel." *Semeia* 35 (1986): 91–128.

Nickelsburg, George W. "Social Aspects of Palestinian Jewish Apocalypticism." In *Apocalypticism in the Mediterranean World and the Near East,* David Hellholm, editor, 641–54. Tübingen: J. C. B. Mohr, 1983.

Nineham, D. E. *The Gospel of Saint Mark.* New York: Pelican Books, 1979 (first published in 1963).

Oakman, Douglas E. "Cursing Fig Trees and Robbers' Dens: Pronouncement Stories Within Social-Systemic Perspective. Mark 11:12–25 and Parallels." *Semeia* 64 (1994): 253–72.

Oepke, Albrecht. "βάπτω, βαπτίζω, βαπτισμός, βάπτισμα...." *TDNT* 1:529–45.

Quell, Gottfried, et al. "ἁμαρτάνω, ἁμάρτημα, ἁμαρτία." *TDNT* 1:267–317.

Pannell, William. *The Coming Race Wars? A Cry for Reconciliation.* Grand Rapids: Zondervan Publishing House, 1993.

Paris, Peter J. "The Bible and the Black Churches." In *The Bible and Social Reform,* Ernest R. Sandeen, editor. Philadelphia and Chico, CA: Fortress Press and Scholars Press, 1982.

———. "The Public Role of the Black Churches." In *The Church's Public Role: Retrospect and Prospect,* Dieter T. Hessel, editor. Grand Rapids: William B. Eerdmans, 1993.

———. *The Social Teaching of the Black Churches.* Philadelphia: Fortress Press, 1985.

———. *The Spirituality of African Peoples: The Search for a Common Moral Discourse.* Minneapolis: Fortress Press, 1995.

Patrick, Dale. "The Kingdom of God in the Old Testament." In *The Kingdom of God in 20th-Century Interpretation,* Wendell Willis, editor, 67–79. Peabody, MA: Hendrickson Publishers, 1987.

Perrin, Norman. *Jesus and the Language of the Kingdom.* Philadelphia: Fortress Press, 1976.

Pesch, Rudolf. *Das Abendmahl und Jesu Todesverständnis.* Freiburg: Herder, 1978.

Petersen, Norman. "When Is the End Not the End? Literary Reflections on the Ending of Mark's Narrative." *Interpretation* 34 (1980): 151–66.

Price, Hugh B. "Black America, 1994: An Overview." In *The State of Black America 1995,* Billy J. Tidwell and Paulette J. Robinson, editors, 1–5. New York: National Urban League, Inc., 1995.

Procksh O., and F. Büchsel. "λύω...ἐπιλύω...." *TDNT* 4:328–56.

Quell, Gottfried and Johannes Behm. "διατίθημι, διαθήκη." *TDNT* 2:104–35.

Raboteau, Albert J. "African-Americans, Exodus, and the American Israel." In *African-American Christianity: Essays in History,* Paul E. Johnson, editor, 1–17. Berkeley: University of California Press, 1994.

Rappaport, U. "Jewish-Pagan Relations and the Revolt against Rome in 66–70 C.E." *Jewish Cathedra* 1 (1981): 81–95.

Rauschenbusch, Walter. *Christianity and the Social Crisis.* Louisville: Westminster/John Knox Press, 1991.

———. *Christianizing the Social Order.* New York: The Macmillan Company, 1914.

———. *The Righteousness of the Kingdom,* Max L. Stackhouse, editor. Nashville: Abingdon Press, 1968.

———. *A Theology for the Social Gospel.* Nashville: Abingdon Press, 1978.

Reid, Stephen Breck. "The Theology of the Book of Daniel and the Political Theory of W. E. B. Du Bois." In *The Recovery of Black Presence: An Interdisciplinary Exploration,* Randall C. Bailey and Jacquelyn Grant, editors, 37–49. Nashville: Abingdon Press, 1995.

Rengstorf, K. H. "ληστής." *TDNT* 4:257–63.

———. "μανθάνω, καταμανθάνω, μαθητής...." *TDNT* 4:390–461.

———. "ἀποστέλλω...ἀπόστολος." *TDNT* 1:398–447.

———. "διδάσκω, διδάσκαλος...." *TDNT* 2:135–66.

Rhoads, David. *Israel in Revolution, 6–74 C.E.: A Political History Based on the Writings of Josephus.* Philadelphia: Fortress Press, 1976.

———. "Social Criticism: Crossing Boundaries." In *Mark and Method: New Approaches in Biblical Studies,* editors Janice Capel Anderson and Stephen D. Moore, 135–61. Minneapolis: Fortress Press, 1992.

Rhoads, David and Donald Michie. *Mark as Story: An Introduction to the Narrative of a Gospel.* Philadelphia: Fortress Press, 1982.

Richardson, W. Franklyn. "Mission to Mandate: Self-Development Through the Black Church." In *The State of Black America 1994,* Billy J. Tidwell, editor, 113–25. New York: National Urban League, Inc., 1994.

Ritschl, Albrecht. *The Christian Doctrine of Justification and Reconciliation,* translators H. R. Mackintosh and A. B. Macaulay. Clifton, NJ: Reference Book Publishers, Inc., 1966.

Robbins, Vernon. "Last Meal: Preparation, Betrayal, and Absence (Mark 14:12–25)." In *The Passion in Mark: Studies on Mark 14–16,* Werner H. Kelber, editor. Philadelphia: Fortress Press, 1976.

Rogers, Donald B., editor. *Urban Church Education.* Birmingham: Religious Education Press, 1989.

Rohrbaugh, Richard L. "The Social Location of the Marcan Audience." *Biblical Theology Bulletin* 23 (1993): 114–27.

Rowland, Christopher and Mark Corner. *Liberating Exegesis: The Challenge of Liberation Theology to Biblical Studies.* Louisville: Westminster/John Knox, 1989.

Salyer, Gregory. "Rhetoric, Purity, and Play: Aspects of Mark 7:1–23." *Semeia* 64 (1993): 139–69.

Sanders, E. P. "The Genre of Palestinian Jewish Apocalypses." In *Apocalypticism in the Mediterranean World and the Near East,* David Hellholm, editor, 447–59. Tübingen: J. C. B. Mohr, 1983.

———. *Jesus and Judaism.* Philadelphia: Fortress Press, 1985.

———. *Judaism: Practice and Belief 63 BCE–66 CE.* London: SCM Press, 1992.

Schlosser, Jacques. "Mc 11,25: Tradition et Rédaction." In *À Cause de L'Evangile: Mélanges offerts à dom Jacques Dupont.* François Refoulé, editor, 277–301. Cerf: Publications de Saint-André, 1985.

Schneider, Johannes. "σταυρός...." *TDNT* 7:572–85.

Schnellbächer, Ernst L. "The Temple as Focus of Mark's Theology." *Horizons in Biblical Theology* 5 (1983): 95–112.

Schrenk, Gottlob."εὐδοκέω, εὐδοκία." *TDNT* 2:738–50.

———. "λέγω, λόγος...." *TDNT* 4:69–193.

Schürer, Emil. *The History of the Jewish People in the Age of Jesus Christ,* G. Vermes and M. Black, editors. New English edition, 4 volumes. Edinburgh: T & T Clark, 1979.

Schüssler Fiorenza, Elisabeth. "The Phenomenon of Early Christian Apocalyptic. Some Reflections on Method." In *Apocalypticism in the Mediterranean World and the Near East,* David Hellholm, editor, 295–316. Tübingen: J. C. B. Mohr, 1989.

Schweitzer, Albert. *The Quest of the Historical Jesus: A Critical Study of Its Progress from Reimarus to Wrede*. New York: Macmillan Publishing Company, 1968.

Schweizer, Eduard. *The Good News According to Mark*. translator Donald H. Madvig. Atlanta: John Knox Press, 1970.

Schweizer, Eduard and Friedrich Baumgärtel. "σῶμα. . . ." *TDNT* 7:1024–94.

Seccombe, David P. "Take Up Your Cross." In *God Who Is Rich in Mercy: Essays Presented to Dr. D. B. Knox,* Peter T. O'Brien and David G. Petersen, editors, 139–51. Grand Rapids: Baker House Books, 1986.

Seeley, David. "Jesus' Temple Act." *Catholic Biblical Quarterly* 55 (1993): 263–83.

Seesemann, Heinrich. "ὀπίσω, ὄπισθεν." *TDNT* 5:289–92.

Segundo, Juan Luis. *The Historical Jesus of the Synoptics,* translator John Drury. Maryknoll, NY: Orbis Books, 1985.

Shea, John. *Stories of God: An Unauthorized Biography*. Chicago: The Thomas More Press, 1978.

Smallwood, E. M. *The Jews Under Roman Rule from Pompey to Diocletian*. Leiden: E. J. Brill, 1976.

Smith, Barry D. *Jesus' Last Passover Meal*. Lewiston/Queenston/Lampeter, Great Britain: Mellen Biblical Press, 1993.

Smith, Charles W. F. "Fishers of Men." *Harvard Theological Review* 52 (1959): 187–203.

Smith, Robert H. "New and Old in Mark 16:1–8." *Concordia Theological Monthly* 43 (1972): 518–27.

Smith, Theophus H. *Conjuring Culture: Biblical Formations of Black America*. New York and Oxford: Oxford University Press, 1994.

Smith, Wallace Charles. *The Church in the Life of the Black Family*. Valley Forge, PA: Judson Press, 1985.

Snyder, Howard A. *Models of the Kingdom*. Nashville: Abingdon Press, 1990.

Sturm, Richard E. "Defining the Word 'Apocalyptic': A Problem in Biblical Criticism." In *Apocalyptic and the New Testament,* Joel Marcus and Marion L. Soards, editors, 17–48. Sheffield: JSOT Press, 1989.

Swartley, William M. "The Structural Function of the Term 'Way' (Hodos) in Mark's Gospel." In *The New Way of Jesus: Essays Presented to Howard Charles,* William Klassen, editor, 73–86. Newton, KS: Faith and Life Press, 1980.

Tannehill, Robert C. "The Disciples in Mark: The Function of a Narrative Role." *The Journal of Religion* 57 (1977): 386–405.

Tapia, Andrés. "Soul Searching: How Is the Black Church Responding to the Urban Crisis." *Christianity Today* 40, no. 3 (1996): 26–30.

Telford, William R. *The Barren Temple and the Withered Tree: A Redaction-Critical Analysis of the Cursing of the Fig Tree in Mark's Gospel and Its Relation to the Cleansing of the Temple Tradition*. Sheffield: JSOT Press, 1980.

———. "More Fruit from the Withered Tree: Temple and Fig-Tree in Mark from a Graeco-Roman Perspective." In *Templum Amicitiae: Essays on the Second Temple Presented to Ernst Bammel,* William Horbury, editor. Sheffield: JSOT Press, 1991.

Theissen, Gerd. *The Gospels in Context: Social and Political History in the Synoptic Tradition,* translator Linda M. Maloney. Minneapolis: Fortress Press, 1991.

Tidwell, Billy J., editor. *The State of Black America 1994*. New York: National Urban League, Inc., 1994.

Tidwell, Billy J. and Paulette J. Robinson, eds. *The State of Black America 1995*. New York: National Urban League, Inc., 1995.

Tolbert, Mary Ann. *Sowing the Gospel: Mark's World in Literary-Historical Perspective*. Minneapolis: Fortress Press, 1989.

————. "When Resistance Becomes Repression: Mark 13:9–27 and the Poetics of Location." In *Reading from This Place,* Volume 2: *Social Location and Biblical Interpretation in Global Perspective,* Fernando F. Segovia and Mary Ann Tolbert, editors, 331–46. Minneapolis: Fortress Press, 1995.

Tompkins, Jane P. "The Reader in History: The Changing Shape of Literary Response." In *Reader-Response Criticism: From Formalism to Post-Structuralism,* Jane P. Tompkins, editor, 201–32. Baltimore and London: The Johns Hopkins University Press, 1980.

Tuckett, Christopher M. "Mark's Concerns in the Parable Chapter (Mark 4:1–34)." *Biblica* 69 (1988): 1–26.

Viviano, B. T. "The Kingdom of God in the Qumran Literature." In *The Kingdom of God in 20th-Century Interpretation,* Wendell Willis, editor, 97–107. Peabody, MA: Hendrickson Publishers, 1987.

Vorster, William S. "The Function of Metaphorical and Apocalyptic Language about the Unobservable in the Teaching of Jesus." In *Text and Logos: The Humanistic Interpretation of the New Testament,* Theodore W. Jennings, Jr., editor, 33–51. Atlanta: Scholars Press, 1990.

Walker, Jr., Theodore. *Empower the People: Social Ethics for the African-American Church.* Maryknoll, NY: Orbis Books, 1991.

Wannamaker, Charles A. "Mark 11:25 and the Gospel of Matthew." *Studia Biblica 1978: Papers on the Gospels, Sixth International Congress on Biblical Studies.* E. A. Livingstone, editor, 329–37. Sheffield: JSOT Press, 1980.

Watson, Bernard C. "The Demographic Revolution: Diversity in 21st Century America." In *The State of Black America 1995,* Billy J. Tidwell and Paulette J. Robinson, editors, 199–224. New York: National Urban League, Inc., 1995.

Weeden, Theodore J., Sr. *Mark: Traditions in Conflict.* Philadelphia: Fortress Press, 1971.

Weiss, Johannes. *Jesus' Proclamation of the Kingdom of God,* translators and Richard Hyde Hiers and David Larrimore Holland, editors. Philadelphia: Fortress Press, 1971.

West, Cornel. *Prophetic Fragments: Illuminations of the Crisis in American Religion & Culture.* Grand Rapids: William B. Eerdmans, 1988.

Wheelwright, Philip. *Metaphor and Reality.* Bloomington, IN: Indiana University Press, 1962.

Willis, Wendell. "The Discovery of the Eschatological Kingdom: Johannes Weiss and Albert Schweitzer." In *The Kingdom of God in 20th-Century Interpretation,* Wendell Willis, editor, 1–14. Peabody, MA: Hendrickson Publishers, 1987.

Willis, Wendell, editor. *The Kingdom of God in 20th-Century Interpretation.* Peabody, MA: Hendrickson Publishers, 1987.

Wilson, William Julius. *The Truly Disadvantaged: The Inner City, the Underclass, and Public Policy.* Chicago and London: University of Chicago Press, 1987.

Wink, Walter. *Unmasking the Powers.* Philadelphia: Fortress Press, 1986.

Wright, Jr., Nathan. *Let's Work Together.* New York: Hawthorn Books, 1968.

Wright, N. T. *The New Testament and the People of God.* Minneapolis: Fortress Press, 1992.

Wuellner, William H. *The Meaning of "Fishers of Men."* Philadelphia: Westminster Press, 1967.

Yette, Samuel F. *The Choice: The Issue of Black Survival in America.* Silver Spring, MD: Cottage Books, 1988.

General Index

Scripture Index

OLD TESTAMENT

APOCRYPHA AND PSEUDEPIGRAPHA

NEW TESTAMENT